PIRACY AT SEA

EDITED BY ERIC ELLEN Q.P.M.

Published in March 1989
ICC Publishing SA
38, Cours Albert 1er
75008-Paris France
Tel. (1)45.62.34.56
Telex 650 770 Incomerc

Cover designed by Stephen Wells
Printed by Redverse Ltd., England

Publication No. 455

ISBN No. 92-842 1078 X

It is emphasised that the opinions expressed are those of the authors of the papers included, and do not necessarily represent the views of their parent organisations or the ICC International Maritime Bureau.

Contents

Preface vii
James Broadus, Director Marine Policy Center, Woods Hole Oceanographic Institution

Introduction ix
Eric Ellen, Director ICC International Maritime Bureau

Part 1: The Reality of Piracy

Chapter 1 Contemporary Piracy 3
I R Hyslop

Chapter 2 An Historical Perspective on the Incidence of Piracy 41
M J Peterson

Chapter 3 The United States and Post-War Piracy 61
Samuel P Menefee

Part 2: An Aspect of Piracy The Boat People

Chapter 4 The Gulf of Thailand 83
Pascal Boulanger

Chapter 5 Two Personal Insights into the South China Sea 97
Maurice Vitty & Francis Wiyono

Chapter 6 Anti-Piracy in South-East Asia: US and International Efforts and Programmes 101
Harry C Blaney III

Chapter 7 Refugees on the High Seas: A Dangerous Passage 107
Joachim Henkel

Chapter 8 The Situation of Refugees in the Territorial Waters of Thailand 113
Bhirabongse Kasemsri

THE BOAT PEOPLE: CONFERENCE DISCUSSION 120

Part 3: The Law of Piracy

Chapter 9 Piracy – Past, Present and Future 131
P W Birnie

Chapter 10 The Law of Piracy – Does It Meet Present and Potential Challenges? 159
Burdick H Brittin

Chapter 11 The Law of Piracy 168
Thomas A Clingan Jr

Chapter 12 The UNCTAD Perspective on Piracy 173
Naomichi H Terazaki

Chapter 13 The *Achille Lauro* and Similar Incidents as Piracy – Two Arguments 179
Samuel P Menefee

Chapter 14 Piracy, Law and Marine Insurance 181
Jonathan Ignarski

THE LAW OF PIRACY: CONFERENCE DISCUSSION 188

Part 4: The Control of Piracy

Chapter 15 Rethinking Piracy Control in a Modern Maritime Context 201
Rear Admiral Bruce Harlow

Chapter 16 The MARAD View of Maritime Piracy 206
Frank Pentti

Chapter 17 Aspects of International Action to Combat Piracy at Sea 213
Jaap A Walkate

Chapter 18 Piracy Control in Nigeria's Territorial Seas 219

Chapter 19 Thefts and Robberies On Board Ships in the Singapore Strait 224
Sharon Tan

THE CONTROL OF PIRACY: CONFERENCE DISCUSSION 212

Conclusion: The Way Forward 234
Eric Ellen

Appendices

1. The IMB Chronology of Pirate Attacks on Merchant Vessels 1981-1987 241
2. Analysis of the IMB Chronology 273
3. Piracy Statistics – Thailand 282
4. Piracy Statistics – Regional Overview 283
5. Summary of Arrests, Prosecutions, Convictions and Sentences in Thailand for Piratical Offences Against Boat People 286
6. Gulf of Thailand – Anti-Piracy Activities and Selected Maritime Claims 290
7. Chronology of Piracy Incidents Affecting Vietnamese Refugees – January-October 1987 291
8. UNHCR Guidelines for Disembarkation of Refugees 296
9. Rescue at Sea 304
10. The Orderly Departure Programme 1979-1988 306
11. Indo-Chinese Refugees in Camps 307
12. Some Instances of Possible Yacht Piracy Involving US Vessels and Nationals 308
13. Proposed Yachtjacking Countermeasures (Coast Guard Operations Center) 311
14. Convention on the High Seas, Geneva 29 April 1958 (Articles 1-23) 312
15. UN Convention on the Law of the Sea 1982 (Articles 100-107 & 110-111) 315
16. Recommendations for Security: MARAD 318
17. Recommendations for Security: BIMCO 319
18. Recommendations for Security: International Shipping Federation 320
19. Recommendations for Security: Swedish Shipowners Association 321
20. Recommendations for Security: ICC IMB 323
21. IMO Resolution – Measures to Prevent Piracy and Armed Robbery Against Ships 325
22. A "Piracy and Maritime Violence Incident Report" 326
23. Seven Initiatives for the Future 328

Notes on Contributors 329

PREFACE

James M Broadus
Director, Marine Policy Center, Woods Hole Oceanographic Institution

In addressing the modern problem of piracy at sea, this volume is intended to provide a distinctive and, we believe, useful combination of vigorous scholarship and practical orientation. The Marine Policy Center, which organised the 1985 Conference on Modern Piracy and co-hosted the ICC International Maritime Bureau's 1987 update workshop on Piracy at Sea, is the multi-disciplinary social science and policy research unit of the Woods Hole Oceanographic Institution. Since its establishment in 1971, the Marine Policy Center has been a principal source of independent, authoritative assessment of issues associated with uses of the world's oceans. Emphasis is placed on the economics of ocean space, such as the costs and inhibitions still imposed by the recurring problem of piracy. A resident staff and Research Fellows at the Marine Policy Centre stress academic scholarship in their studies, and the Centre also welcomes the problem oriented, practical perspective achieved through this collaboration with the IMB.

Special thanks are due Mr Burdick Brittin for his encouragement and leadership in initiating this examination of modern piracy, and to Marine Policy Research Follow Dean Cycon who coordinated the 1985 international conference in Woods Hole. Important organisational support was provided by Ellen Gately and Pugrid Desilvestre of the Marine Policy Center, and by Kuo Shiao-Lin and Chun Fan-Lau of the IMB. Helpful comments and discussion were provided by Dr Allyn Vine, Scientist Emeritus at Woods Hole, Dr Arthur Gaines of the Marine Policy Center, and Commander Lawson Brigham of the US Coast Guard and Guest Investigator at the Marine Policy Center.

INTRODUCTION BY THE EDITOR

Old fashioned piracy still casts its shadow of fear and misery over today's seafarers. Some observers claim piracy is an inevitable reflection of social and political upheaval in the regions it affects—this, however, is not true. Concerted action by national governments and international organisations could effectively control the maritime muggers that cynically prey on ships, yachts and the hapless boat people.

Whilst I therefore have pleasure in introducing the substantive. authoritative and practical chapters that make up this volume, it is with great sadness that I remember the individual tragedies and financial disasters that are its subject.

Why is it that governments still permit these horrific attacks to take place in the closing years of the twentieth century? Why does one European shipowners' association have to advise its members to develop a barricaded "fortress" within a ship's accommodation, and how long will it be before action is taken to ensure that ships are safe?

Action is needed now to stamp out the attacks and make the world's sea routes safe from these ruthless thieves and thugs.

Eric Ellen, QPM.
Director of the ICC International Maritime Bureau.

Part 1. The Reality of Piracy

CHAPTER 1

CONTEMPORARY PIRACY

I R Hyslop

Introduction

By the beginning of 1983 armed attacks on merchant vessels had increased to the extent that concern was being expressed both by shipping interests and by governments. This concern was reflected by the two submissions to the UN International Maritime Organization (IMO) and the resulting "Resolution to prevent Acts of Piracy and Armed Robbery against Ships" in November 1983 which are mentioned below at page 29.

Before this resolution was made, in May 1983, the IMO had called upon the International Chamber of Commerce's International Maritime Bureau (IMB) to report on the current situation concerning armed attacks. This request was repeated in 1984 and 1985. These three requests resulted in formal papers prepared by the IMB and submitted to the IMO.

As mentioned in the preface to this book, an international meeting on modern piracy was held at Woods Hole Oceanographic Institution, Massachusetts in April 1985 and supplemented by a follow-up meeting in December 1987. This book depends, largely, on the papers, and ideas, generated by these meetings. These papers and ideas are specially enriched by the authoritative contributions made to them by representatives of official organisations involved in the fight against piracy.

The purpose of this introductory paper to the book is to consolidate the information which the IMB collated for its three reports to the IMO, to update it in view of what has happened since our last report was published in 1985, and to combine it with additional insights acquired in our capacity as a focal point for maritime problems. This chapter then attempts to place this material in the context of the diverse and scholarly papers which follow, and which are arranged in four parts as described in the following paragraphs.

Part 1, of which this chapter forms a part, provides an overview of piracy from different aspects—contemporary, historical and from the particular point of view of the United States. Chapter 2 includes a, chronologically and geographically, wide ranging study of the development of piracy with emphasis on the balance between private and state action. Chapter 3 explores piracy as it has affected US vessels in a number of ways, one of the most important of which is attacks on small boats in the Caribbean.

Part 2 is devoted to the plight of the boat people—refugees attempting to make their way from Vietnam across the South China Sea to other south-east Asian countries. It begins with a broad general analysis of the position, in Chapter 4; continues, in Chapter 5, with two special insights from people involved in humanitarian work; and concludes with three official statements from the United Nations, and the governments of the United States and Thailand, in Chapters 6, 7 and 8.

Part 3 addresses the complex subject of the law of piracy. Chapter 9 examines the historical basis of piracy in international law and the confusion of attempts to reconcile this with municipal law. Chapter 10 assesses possible changes in international law to deal with modern piracy. Chapter 11 further clarifies the distinction between municipal and international law. Chapter 12, written from the UN Commission on Trade and Development (UNCTAD) perspective, adopts an interesting approach by suggesting a possible equation between piracy and fraud. A thread running through Chapters 9-12 is the practical need for cooperation—whether bilateral, regional or international. Finally, Chapter 13 places the attacks on the *Achille Lauro* and *City of Poros* in a legal context; and Chapter 14 offers the specialist view of the professional insurer.

Part 4 is concerned with the control of piracy. In Chapter 15 maritime crime is categorised and a number of clear initiatives for dealing with it formulated. Chapter 16, which presents the view of the US Maritime Administration (MARAD), places piracy worldwide in the context of trade and assesses the potential for international action. Chapter 17 contains an overview of current activities at the international level. Chapters 18 and 19 consist of official insights from two of the most seriously affected governments—Nigeria and Singapore.

Many points made in the papers are developed further in the Woods Hole conference discussions on the boat people, piracy law and piracy control which appear at the end of the corresponding parts of this book. These discussions culminated in seven initiatives for piracy control, which are stated at Appendix 23. In a restricted sense these initiatives, which are further developed in the Editor's Conlusions, can be described as the results of the Woods Hole conference, and of this book.

A further "dynamic" product of the meetings is the draft "Piracy and Maritime Violence Incident Report" at Appendix 22. The requirement for information is emphasised later in this chapter and in several other papers in this book. The IMB believes that the Report at Appendix 22 goes some way to meet this requirement and invites comments on it. No recommendation is made as to who might receive the Forms, and analyse and disseminate the information contained in them. However this is a task which the IMB would consider undertaking, if it was asked, in conjunction with the work already being done by the IMO and the International Criminal Police Organisation (Interpol).

An important part of our work in preparing this book has, of course, been processing the raw information of piracy—the reports of attacks. The results of this processing appear at Appendix 1—The IMB Chronology of Pirate Attacks 1981-1987. The 733 entries in the Chronology have been researched from the IMO, shipowners, P & I (Protection and Indemnity) Clubs, the press, and academic sources. It is necessary at this stage to make six remarks about the Chronology.

One, it is far from complete, because very many piratical attacks are not reported. It is difficult to estimate the number of attacks not reported, but it is likely to be at least half, and it may in some cases be as high as ninety per cent. There are a number of reasons for this under-reporting. Masters fear a reflection on their discipline and watchkeeping, or fear delays in port while an attack is investigated, or fear an increased risk of further attack by drawing attention to themselves. Owners fear a possible loss of commercial intelligence or credibility. They may also be afraid of causing diplomatic offence to the country with which they are trading, or of being perceived by local officials as "complainers". Additionally, insurance costs may rise and there may be difficulties, and demands for high risk payments, from crew unions. States themselves may also wish to keep attacks secret for commercial or national security reasons. This said, the names of some vessels repeat themselves throughout the Chronology—suggesting that some owners and governments are more conscientious about reporting incidents than others. As will be seen on page 9, the interest which the government of the Federal Republic took in piracy in the mid-1980s ensured that almost every attack on a West German vessel became known.

Two, as evident from the abundance of question marks in the Chronology, some reports are more complete than others. Where less than complete information about an attack has been received from a credible source, the details which are known have been included.

Three, the Chronology may in a sense be too complete. In the absence of clear evidence to the contrary, if a master or an owner has reported an incident of piracy, but declined to elaborate on it, it has been accepted as such. However it is likely that some of the incidents included were simple thefts, or even accidental losses, rather than "piracy". An attempt is made in Appendix 2 to distinguish these incidents from confirmed piratical attacks. This leads into the grey area of definitions which, as stated below, is crucial to any study of piracy.

Four, the Chronology is mainly concerned with attacks on merchant vessels, including certain attacks which could arguably be defined as terrorist. Nevertheless, pirate attacks on yachts in the Caribbean are included where they are known. In addition, one or two attacks on land by notorious pirates, as well as one or two attacks on river craft, are included. The Chronology does not deal with attacks on the boat people in the South China Sea, which are analysed extensively in Part 2 of this book (and, for 1987, listed at Appendix 7). There are other major gaps in the coverage—notably attacks on boats other than cargo vessels in south-east Asia, which are however analysed at page 15 below. Attacks on yachts outside the Caribbean, and particularly in the Gulf of Aden and the Red Sea, are also generally omitted.

Five, the Chronology starts in 1981. This is regrettable in some respects, but it is necessary for practical reasons of length and because it roughly coincides with the period examined by the IMB on behalf of the IMO. (This chapter, insofar as it purports to be a study of contemporary piracy, also generally restricts itself to incidents occurring since 1981).

Six, the reports for the most recent years may be particularly incomplete, because of late responses to the IMO and other sources.

The Chronology is followed by an Analysis at Appendix 2. This is an attempt to highlight the most important features of its 733 chronologically arranged entries and present them in a more digestible and readily understood form, and in particular, as stated above, to isolate "real" piracy.

Piracy is basically aggravated theft. Although there are significant exceptions, it is generally straightforward and involves comparatively small amounts. This is one factor that ensures that it remains fairly tightly regionalised. The only clear common factors shared by piracy around the world are poverty and temptation provoked by a glimpse of a better way of life on board a ship from a richer part of the world, together with inadequate law enforcement. There is currently no evidence of any international organisation behind this type of crime, or of any other international dimension—although, as will be seen below, Interpol is currently examining this possibility.

This means that any meaningful analysis of piracy must be made on a regional basis. In this chapter attacks on merchant vessels (or "mainstream" piracy) are examined as they occur, firstly, in West Africa, secondly, in the Malacca Straits area, thirdly, together with certain other types of piracy, in south-east Asia excluding the Malacca Straits area and, finally, in the rest of the world. This is followed by an examination of the subject of control, from the shipboard, national and international viewpoints. There then follows consideration of two special varieties of piracy—attacks on small boats in the Caribbean, and, most serious of all in its human consequences, attacks on the boat people.

The importance of definitions in any approach to the subject of piracy is highlighted by the fact that most of the papers in this book begin by making one. The following analysis, on which the definitional approach of this chapter, and of the Chronology, is based, is provided by Mr Burdick H Brittin.

By usage and perception the word "piracy" has a variety of meanings based on who is using the word and for what purpose it is meant. In a thumbnail description there are four categories or definitions of piracy.

One, the international law of piracy is set forth in the 1958 Law of the Sea Convention and reiterated in the 1982 Law of the Sea Convention (see Appendices 14 and 15). It governs such acts as they take place beyond the limits of national jurisdiction at sea and is prescribed by the definition of piracy in Article 101 of the 1982 Convention. It is that body of law that the international community, through governments, looks to in meeting the challenge of piracy.

Two, the domestic law of the coastal state determines and governs piracy or piratical acts within its internal waters and territorial sea. It is based on the sovereignty of the coastal state over these waters. What constitutes piracy within this area can be, and frequently is, different from piracy on the high seas, based on the legislation of the individual coastal states.

Three, as is seen from Chapter 14 below, the community of marine insurers establishes and changes its rules on what constitutes piracy from the standpoint of good business. Their definitions can vary from international law and domestic legislation, as well as from each other. Their system works well except when a claim goes to court and throws it into relief against international and domestic law, as happened in the case of the *Andreas Lemos*, described on page 186.

Four, the perception of the general public or press is that any act of violence anywhere on the oceans is piracy. It is a popular word coming down through the centuries; it certainly does not conform to the more constrained limits of piracy as noted above. Thus the word "piracy" in the popular sense has a broader impact than the actuality of a variety of violent acts, or their threats, that occur on the world's seas.

This chapter and the Chronology, which aim simply to state what is going on, will incline towards Mr Brittin's fourth category. This is a similar robust approach to that taken in the historical analysis in Chapter 2, and can be amplified as follows.

Most importantly, any provision requiring piratical acts to take place outside territorial waters is ignored. Any other approach would be fatal to the documentary nature of this chapter, and the Chronology, because there is no doubt that the majority of piratical attacks (especially since the agreements concerning territorial waters within the area of the Malacca Straits) do occur *inside* national jurisdictions. Additionally, technical questions on the point whether more than one ship has to be involved are ignored.

Piracy for the present purposes is loosely defined as any violent attack (more conveniently, "depredation") on a vessel, or any attack which has the *potential* for violence. This qualification is intended to include the case when intruders, possibly armed, take something unobserved but would have met resistance, had it been offered, with force. As stated above, many events which may not meet this definition have been given the benefit of the doubt for the purposes of the Chronology.

It is tempting to add a further qualification such as "for private ends" or "for gain", so as to exclude events more commonly understood as terrorism. In any case, it is intended to exclude state action, or insurgency, amounting to acts of war.

A further possible refinement would be to *in*clude fund raising ventures undertaken for "political" purposes—analogous to bank raids made on land by, for example, the Irish Republican Army—but to *ex*clude attacks made for a *direct* political purpose, and which have no financial (or other personal) motive. Regard is however taken of the views expressed in Chapters 10 and 13 that qualifications of this type present in the current law do not afford the protection that the public are entitled to expect.

The above analysis probably will not stand, and is not intended to stand, close study. For example, the requirement above that intruders *would* have met resistance with force is no doubt too subjective. It is intended as a working definition.

West Africa

Piracy in West African waters in general, and in Nigerian waters in particular, is examined in Chapter 18. As far as the timescale of the IMB Chronology at Appendix 1 is concerned, West African piracy has to be considered in two parts—from 1981 to 1985 and from 1985 to 1987.

West African piracy peaked, along with maritime fraud, during the years of the "cement armada" following 1970, when the value and volume of imports increased dramatically. Ships, particularly European roll-on roll-off and container vessels, had on occasion to wait for weeks or months for a berth in inadequate harbours. They were attacked both in port and at anchor—sometimes as far as 20 miles offshore.

There were over 90 reported piratical attacks in West Africa in 1981, around 50 in 1982, 40 in 1983, 22 in 1984, and 46 in 1985. Over 50 of these attacks were serious, though not always successful, armed attacks on cargoes. It is not possible to resist the temptation to single out one incident at this stage—the attack on the laundry of the (appropriately named) mv *Amazona* by a group of lady pirates in October 1983.

At the start of the 1980s around half of the reported attacks took place in Nigerian waters or harbours. Others took place in Sierra Leone, and the remainder were fairly evenly distributed among a number of West African coastal states. After 1982 the proportion of attacks occurring in Nigerian jurisdiction reduced greatly, and by 1984 and 1985 had declined to around two and three attacks a year. The reasons for this are dealt with below and in Chapter 18.

Vessels at anchor were typically attacked at night and by gangs of up to 30 men—the average was around 15—using several small boats with outboard engines. These boats were sometimes disguised as fishing vessels, and the nets used as camouflage in case of customs or police intervention. Sometimes the boats ferried the loot to a mother ship in the distance. Attacks in port were often made by as many as 100 men who either discharged the cargo on the quay or transferred it to fishing boats moored alongside the ship.

Pirates stayed on board for several hours—sometimes days—breaking into containers stowed on deck. Break bulk cargo was usually ignored—it was more difficult to attack because hold and hatch covers were generally well secured. If the opportunity presented itself the pirates would also commit rape.

In at least 20% of the cases in the IMB Chronology the pirates were armed with firearms, or with knives and bows and arrows. Sometimes the arrows were dipped in poison or excreta. Crews were often threatened, and occasionally injured. The only four incidents in the IMB Chronology which resulted in fatalities concerned mv *Baltic* and the vessel at Agbowa in 1985, mentioned below, a fishing vessel (the *Portoseuta*) in 1981 and a yacht in 1984. In the case of both the *Baltic* and the yacht the deceased were pirates rather than victims.

The pirates were well organised—for example they gained information not only by corruption, as mentioned below, but also by monitoring radio traffic. They also jammed the emergency radio channels, frequently with popular music. However, even when a vessel's distress call got through, it was not often answered.

With the attack on mv *Vanelius* at Freetown, Sierra Leone in May 1985 lawlessness degenerated almost into farce. The vessel was "protected" while leaving port by two Sierra Leone soldiers on board. This did not deter 20 pirates from approaching her in a boat, and firing and throwing stones at her. The troops returned the fire until they ran out of ammunition. There was then nothing to stop the pirates from boarding and taking what they wished—household appliances and frozen chickens—from containers.

For reasons already stated, by no means all attacks were reported to the port authorities. Nevertheless, the Federal German police liaised very closely with shipowners over the peak years, and there is no doubt that almost every attack on a West German vessel was reported—this explains the fact that over 80 of the reported incidents in 1981-1985 in Appendix 1 were on vessels registered in the Federal Republic.

In many incidents there were indications that the pirates had prior knowledge about the content and location of the containers they selected. Pay for port staff in West Africa was low—inadequate to meet the cost of living in the area. The police, port authorities, and local consignees and agents were known sometimes to cooperate with thieves, or to take things themselves. But it must be emphasised that the Federal German police, in their investigations, found no evidence of systematic collusion of this type.

Although attacks on West German vessels continued up to 1986, the pattern of West African piracy was by that time beginning to change. In 1986 and 1987 the IMB confirmed only three significant piratical attacks on cargoes. In 1987 the special piracy desk at the Bundeskriminalamt was put in suspense.

Pirates now usually restrict their attention to what they can most easily lay their hands on—ship's equipment, particularly mooring ropes, and crew's personal effects. The attacks are typically by small groups of around half a dozen pirates. A scenario of "petty" (in comparative terms) piracy, similar to the opportunist attacks in the Malacca Straits area, mentioned below, has therefore developed.

This change in pattern has been fairly dramatic and largely reflects the decline in trade to the region and the decongestion of the ports. Although the proportion of attacks in Nigerian waters has risen again to around fifty per cent of all West African attacks in the IMB Chronology (around 18 out of 34) for the period 1985-1987, it would be quite incorrect to ignore the significance of the Nigerian enforcement effort, which is examined below and in Chapter 18.

It would also be incorrect to infer that all the problems have been solved. In February 1988 pirates boarded a vessel at Abidjan during the night, threatened the crew and took stores and personal property. They returned the following night and did the same thing again. In the same month a gang of ten pirates forced the storeroom on a vessel at Bonny, but fled when the crew sounded the alarm and switched searchlights on. In general, it is too early to assess the effect of the fall in the price of oil and the consequent increased poverty in the region. Further, it is not known what effect a future upturn in the West African economies would have.

An insight into conditions at West African ports in 1982 can be obtained from this account of the odyssey of mv *Nedlloyd Steenkerk*.

The *Nedlloyd Steenkerk* arrived at Apapa on 17 August 1982. Five miles from the coast she was fired on by pirates and two members of her crew were wounded. The pirates forced containers and holds and stole cargo. In spite of many calls by VHF, no help came from land. She berthed at Apapa the following day. The master called a doctor to treat his wounded men, and hired local guards with bows and arrows.

The vessel continued to Cotonou, Benin where the master again took the precaution of hiring local guards; but this did not prevent further major cargo thefts. This scenario re-created itself at the next port of call, Lome in Togo. Again, at Dakar in Senegal mv *Nedlloyd Steenkerk* was attacked by pirates while she was waiting at anchor for a pilot. Three mooring ropes were stolen, and there were further cargo thefts. No help from the police was forthcoming.

At Banjul, Gambia, there were serious cargo thefts, facilitated by the presence on board of watchmen and police who were in collusion with the thieves. Crew members were threatened when they tried to interfere. At Freetown, Sierra Leone the crew was again threatened in spite of the presence on board of watchmen and policemen. The situation became so dangerous that the vessel left, abandoning part of her cargo on the quay.

Finally, at Monrovia, Liberia the captain was advised to anchor 20 miles from the coast to avoid attacks, but there were still large scale thefts when he eventually berthed.

The *Nedlloyd Steenkerk* may have been unlucky, but it is difficult to believe that her experience was unique, and this reinforces the belief that many incidents went unreported. There follows a sample of piratical attacks during the "West African peak".

At 05.15 on 1 December 1982 mv *Baltic* was attacked by pirates armed with guns. All the crew, except the cook, locked themselves in the engine room. The cook was forced at gunpoint to show the raiders where the money and valuables were kept. Another vessel, mv *Pacific Marchioness*, circled the *Baltic* while this was happening, shining searchlights. The pirates fired upon this vessel. At 06.25 a patrol boat arrived and attacked the pirate vessel, killing one of the pirates and causing at least four others to drown.

Over a period of two days, from 27 to 28 July 1983, mv *La Minera* was attacked by around 100 pirates at Conakry, Guinea. Two heavy hydraulic jacks were stolen and numerous containers were broken into and their contents stolen. The Chief Officer and one oiler were attacked on deck. The authorities did not intervene.

At 15.20 on 28 December 1984 mv *Nedlloyd Westerhamm* had almost completed discharging at Freetown, Sierra Leone when an unknown number of pirates boarded from the seaward side of the vessel. In spite of the presence on board of five armed guards, nine port security watchmen and two gangway watchmen, the pirates forced open three containers which had been stored on deck. They stole a quantity of textiles and 40 cases of cigarettes. Fortunately no one was hurt. It is believed that this attack could not have succeeded without the collusion of the port security watchmen and guards.

This is an extract from the master's report of a piratical attack in Lagos roads on a vessel with a cargo of stockfish on 5 July 1981:

> At 0255 the First Officer on bridge watch caught sight in the glare of the search light by which he, after orders, was regularly searching the horizon, that a big canoe equipped with an outboard motor and with about eight or ten native black people on board was trying to go alongside the vessel on her starboard side.
>
> The crew was alerted at once by the general alarm, and they came to the bridge very fast. The engine crew was ordered to make the engine ready immediately.
>
> At 0300, before the engine was ready, three or four robbers succeeded in coming on board the vessel, armed with knives and bottles which were used as missiles. Shortly after the engine was ready. By means of various manoeuvres with the engine, and the rudder, several attempts were made to disengage the canoe, but it failed, and several more robbers swarmed on board armed with crowbars, wire cutters and knives and they shouted threatening "We do not kill you, if you do not stop us."
>
> The engine was stopped and the crew was advised not to try preventing the robbers in robbing the cargo.
>
> In a short while the robbers succeed in cutting the Yale lock of the midships access hatch to the cargo hold, and then started to remove bales of stockfish from the tweendeck, the bales then being thrown down into the canoe to their helpers.
>
> At 0310, in vain it was tried to get into contact by VHF with East Mole Signal Station with emergency call. At last it succeeded and they were told, that the ship was being attacked by armed robbers. East Mole Signal Station regret, that they could do nothing regarding calling in patrol boats as the phone connection was out of order.
>
> Some of the other anchorlayers closest to the vessel who did hear the call by VHF of help, fired some parachute distress signal rockets, but no patrol boat did come out on the road.
>
> At 0330 the robbers had heavy loaded their canoe with a lot of bales of stockfish,

nothing else, and they disappeared.

At 0340 the anchor was weighed, and the ship went at sea by slow speed.

The Malacca Straits Area

The area around the Malacca Straits attracts the heaviest concentration of merchant shipping in the world, which generally has to slow down in order to pass through narrow channels. The Straits have traditionally been plagued by pirates, and remain in the 1980s the world "growth point" for piracy against merchant vessels.

Piracy has enjoyed a lingering cultural and historical acceptability in the area since at least the sixteenth century when impoverished local inhabitants first reacted to the control of their economies by foreigners. In less elaborate terms, some villages even today claim that they have to rob to live.

Most attacks take place around the Horsburgh Lighthouse, 25 miles east of Singapore, or in the Phillip Channel, ten miles east of Singapore. Eastbound traffic is directed into the Phillip Channel, which is only a mile wide at its narrowest point and links the Indian Ocean with the north and west Pacific Ocean, by the Singapore Strait separation scheme.

Figures for these attacks will be found in Chapter 19 and in the IMB Chronology at Appendix 1. The figures in Chapter 19 are based on reports to the Singapore authorities, and there are therefore certain limited discrepancies between the two sets of statistics. Total annual attacks in the area, reported in the IMB Chronology, range generally from around 15 to over 30—although the figures for 1982 and 1983 were higher (64 and 52 respectively). Perhaps more significant is the fact that in 1987 52% (29 out of 56) reported worldwide attacks on merchant vessels were in the area. The equivalent combined figure for the other six years reviewed by the Chronology is 32% (216 out of 677 attacks).

In spite of the compact area of the Malacca Straits, and its advanced communication systems, it is clear that not all attacks are reported. There is reason to think there is really at least one attack each week. But this, together with the remarks in the preceding paragraphs, should be kept in proportion—over 200 vessels transit the Malacca Strait each day (a slightly lower survey figure for one month in 1984 will be found on page 225).

It will be seen from the analysis in Chapter 19 that piracy in this region has never been particularly sophisticated—most attacks are equated with "petty thefts and housebreakings". In particular, piracy has not taken the form of coordinated attacks by large gangs on container cargoes which were, at least until recently, prevalent around West Africa.

The pirates tend to operate in small groups—two to five is the average. Typically, they approach at night in fast boats—although occasionally they stow away when the vessel is in port. Sometimes pirates approach vessels posing as ship's chandlers, who are patronised by masters on the move wishing to save port charges.

The pirates interest themselves in cash and disposable items, and often make straight for the ship's safe or the crew's cabins. If they cannot open the safe, they may take it with its contents intact. Usually they remain on board for a very short time—again in contrast to some attacks in West Africa which lasted two or three days.

No type of ship is immune, but the pirates favour laden tankers and similar vessels with low freeboards which make them easy to board, for example with grappling irons, even when travelling at twelve knots or more.

In around 29% (70 out of 245) of attacks in the IMB Chronology, the pirates were either totally unseen (and therefore obviously no one was hurt or threatened) or the IMB has no detailed information about the nature of the attack. This places the attacks in the "unconfirmed" category as defined in Appendix 2—that is to say there is no evidence that they were "real" piracy.

There is a further distinctive category in which cabins have been quietly entered, and their occupants—most often the master—have been threatened and tied up. The pirates have then taken what they wanted and left, before anyone else on the vessel realised what was happening.

The pirates usually arm themselves with knives, sometimes with cutlasses or sickles. However, on only comparatively few occasions (10% of attacks, compared with a worldwide average of 17%) have they been observed to carry firearms.

There is no doubt that many pirates are prepared to use their weapons if necessary. As stated above, members of crews are frequently tied up or threatened—either because they get in the way or because the pirates want to know where the safe or the safe keys are. No fatalities appear in the IMB Chronology, and as in piratical attacks on commercial vessels elsewhere in the world, it is rare for a crew member actually to be injured. However, as elsewhere, this is because few are so unwise as to resist.

An exception to this was the chief engineer of mv *Slutsk* who successfully fought off a pirate, but then had to go to hospital with knife wounds. This case was also remarkable in that a Soviet vessel was selected for attack. The, alleged, characteristic Soviet method of dealing with piracy is explored on page 23.

An insight into the tactics used from the point of view of one pirate was obtained from a resident of the Rhio Archipelago, on the southern side of the strait, quoted in *AsiaWeek* in May 1988: "These shipowners are very rich. While they're passing through the straits we ask them for a donation. It's like a toll. We don't carry guns and we never injure anyone. We just accept whatever money they give us. If they have no money, we leave."

Apart from the potential violence, there are considerable navigational dangers when masters are distracted from negotiating a difficult stretch of water. There may also be a danger of oil spillage if something goes seriously wrong. Both these dangers are highlighted in the IMO Resolution at Appendix 21.

There is some evidence, in addition to the statement of the gentleman quoted above, that many pirates come from the Indonesian islands on the southern side of the strait, adjacent to the eastbound separation zone. For example, the five pirates mentioned on page 27, who attacked an Indonesian oil tanker in August 1983, were arrested at a base on Batam Island in the Rhio Archipelago.

Allegations of involvement in piracy by certain Indonesian customs officials are mentioned on page 17.

The following six examples are intended to give a flavour of what it is like to be attacked by pirates in the Malacca Strait area.

At 22.35 on 23 August 1981 mv *Corsicana* was attacked by three men armed with knives whilst she was transiting the Phillip Channel at over twelve knots. In spite of being threatened by the pirates, the first officer continued to navigate the vessel. The pirates left after six minutes, taking with them at least £4,000.

At 23.20 on 7 July 1983 mv *Stena Oceanica* was transiting the Phillip Channel when the Chief Engineer noticed that the master's quarters had been ransacked. He then came across the radio officer who had been attacked and tied up by three men with knives when he left his cabin to investigate a noise. The pirates appear to have boarded as the vessel was entering the Channel at 13 knots. They took the safe which contained, among other things, medical supplies and £294 cash. The master and the radio officer also lost their watches.

During the night of 29 January 1985 mv *Falcon Countess* was underway in the Strait of Malacca when she was boarded at the stern by six pirates using bamboo poles with hooks. Members of the crew were held at knife point and the master was tied up. The pirates took $19,500 from the safe before escaping in a speed boat.

At 05.15 on the morning of 24 April 1987 in the Phillip Channel the master of mv *Evelyn Maersk* woke to find four men standing over him with 50 cm knives and shouting at him to keep quiet. His visitors tied his hands, forced him to indicate the location of the safe and hand over the key. They then opened and emptied the safe, ransacked the cabin and tore off his wristwatch and gold neckchain. The master was then ordered to lie on the berth while his hands and feet were tied with plastic rope. Nothing had been seen from the bridge, and the only sign the pirates left was a series of black footprints. This happened when the vessel was going at full speed with a sharpened lookout aft.

At 02.15 on 3 May 1987 mv *Lydia* had just passed the Horsburgh Light. A seaman who had been ordered to shine a light around the vessel noticed a boat port aftside. The master sounded the whistle, used the public address system to alert the crew, and reported the attack on VHF. This caused the pirates who had boarded from the boat to leave hurriedly. Although they were only on board a few minutes they had time to ransack the master's cabin and take a complete steel safe with cash and valuables inside, as well as jewellery, perfume and radio equipment. They were therefore very fast and very expert.

Finally, there follows the master's report of a piratical attack in the Malacca Straits area on 12 November 1982.

> During our recent transit of the Singapore Straits, at approximately 0300 ship's time, this vessel was boarded by a group of armed men. The second officer was forcibly restrained in his cabin by these men and robbed of cash and personal effects.
>
> Having experienced a similar robbery on another vessel last year, it is my practice, on transiting the Singapore Straits in the hours of darkness, to fully illuminate the after end of the ship with floodlights, and instruct the lookouts posted on both bridgewings to maintain an efficient lookout both behind the vessel as well as forward. This was being carried out at the time. In addition, at frequent intervals, I also checked aft.
>
> In checking the facts, it is felt that the boarding occurred in the vicinity of Buffalo Rock. As there had been a recent stranding in this area, and much activity was in evidence trying to refloat it, it is felt that the lookout's attention must have been diverted to watching the spectacle at the time of the boarding.
>
> On the following day, this morning, at about the same time and in the same position, another vessel was boarded and robbed. Again, only one cabin was affected.
>
> Having informed the local water police, at the time of the incident, giving them all details, they informed me that they were unable (or unwilling) to act, as the occurrence had happened in international waters.

South-East Asia

Attacks on vessels passing through the Malacca Strait present a fairly consistent picture. But when the picture is enlarged to take in the entire south-east Asian region, it becomes much more diverse. As stated above, the IMB Chronology, and this Chapter, generally restrict themselves to attacks on merchant vessels (and yachts in the Caribbean). However the different strands of piracy in the greater south east Asia area, and their continuing importance as this book is published in 1989 require that the area be given separate treatment here, and that some consideration be made of attacks other than those on commercial vessels. (However, for the purposes of the analysis in Appendix 2, south-east Asia, excluding the Malacca Straits area, is grouped with the "rest of the world").

There are over 50 attacks on merchant vessels in south-east Asia, away from the Malacca Straits, mentioned in the Chronology. These took place in, among other places, Thai waters and Java. The following two paragraphs indicate a current and developing problem around Manila, and in the Bangka Strait, 500 km south of Singapore.

In December 1987 one vessel, the *Cristal*, was believed sea-jacked by armed men at Manila. In January 1988 a second vessel, the *Patrick GS* was seized by pirates in Manila. Five of the six crewmembers, including the master, were forced overboard—three are still missing. The authorities found the vessel emptied of her cargo of 3,000 barrels of bunker oil and 53,000 litres of fuel. They later also found the cargo in a barge moored in Manila's south harbour.

At 05.30 one April morning in 1988 four men, armed with parangs and a gun,boarded mv *Klang Reefer* as she was transiting the Bangka Strait. In a technique reminiscent of many attacks in the Malacca Strait to the north, they went unseen to the master's cabin and held him up. The following month this scenario re-created itself on another vessel in the same location.

However there are also many attacks on smaller vessels in south-east Asia—notably on the motor launches which "commute" between islands in the southern Philippines, and on private boats in this area. There may be as many as a hundred attacks of this type each year. Three cases are presented by way of example in the following paragraphs.

In September 1981 mv *Nuria 767*, a 135 ton launch, was attacked by four men. This gang is believed to have consisted of two members of the crew and two stowaways. They robbed the crew and passengers before herding them up and opening fire. Eleven were shot dead, there were 20 survivors and 24 were reported missing. The pirates transferred to two passing fishing boats with $380,000 in cash and $126,500 in goods.

On 11 August 1984 there was another vicious attack on a small boat when 33 people were killed and three teenage girls abducted by pirates as they sailed from Malaysia to the southern Philippines, near the south-western island of Tawi-Tawi. The 15 survivors were picked up along the coast of Sabah.

In April 1986 there was an attack on a private boat, fortunately without loss of life. The French owned luxury yacht *Odyssee* was approached by twelve pirates in high speed launches off the south coast of Mindanao. The pirates set the crew of four adrift, unharmed, in a rubber raft after stealing $71,000 in cash and belongings. This event provoked a thorough investigation by the Coast Guard and Navy around the Philippine islands—amidst alleged sightings and rumours that the *Odyssee* had reached the well known pirate and rebel base areas on the Zamboanga Peninsula.

Fishing vessels throughout the region are vulnerable. Indonesian fishermen have now begun, with some success, to protect themselves with government issued high powered guns, against murderous attacks, intimidation and blackmail. Thai fishermen have been accused of attacking, and in some cases throwing overboard, Malay and Bangladeshi fishermen—several hundred have disappeared in recent years. The Bangladeshis have introduced special maritime patrols to resist this activity, and Malay fishermen have been known to carry money and cigarettes to offer to the Thais in return for their safety. Thai fishermen are themselves the victims of violent attacks—sometimes by Kampuchean, or other, pirates, and sometimes by Vietnamese government forces.

South-east Asian pirates appear to come from all the affected states. Many are illegal migrants between these states. Some of the pirates belong to "straightforward" criminal gangs, and are motivated, like pirates elsewhere, by poverty and unemployment. But there are also

Moslem rebels—known as *ambuk pare* ("Jump, buddy"), from an order which they frequently issue to victims. There is also a clear involvement by the separatist Moro National Liberation Front.

It follows that some attacks, like those on the Philippines ferry in August 1981 and on the *Sidharta* in April 1983 (and on the *Achille Lauro*) were arguably examples of military action, or terrorism, rather than piracy. However attention is drawn in this connection to the definitional arguments concerning "fund raising" on page 7.

This "political" dimension also helps to ensure that no one is short of arms, or equipment (most pirates prefer powerful Japanese engines). By contrast, Indonesian, Malaysian and Philippines law enforcement agencies, who will always be handicapped by the difficult geography of the islands, are generally undermanned and under equipped. The Thai authorities found themselves similarly at a disadvantage around 1984 against a notorious pirate gang which, operating in groups of 20 and using specially designed speedboats, attacked passenger and merchant vessels in the Gulf of Thailand.

Shipowners have alleged that Indonesian customs officials, disappointed when entry permits between Singapore and Indonesia were abolished in 1985 and with them a system of "incentives" to avoid very long delays, are behind some attacks on merchant vessels in the area, including the Malacca Strait. Indonesian officials have also been accused of attacking and harassing Malay fishermen. However there is no real evidence of this and it is (perhaps not surprisingly) denied by the Indonesian authorities.

It may be inferred that many people have died as a result of piracy in south east Asia, away from the Malacca Strait area. Around a dozen cases may be extracted from the IMB Chronology, but it must be remembered that this primarily lists attacks on *merchant* vessels, and will therefore greatly underestimate the toll in human life. It must be further emphasised that no account is taken here of attacks on the Vietnamese boat people, which are dealt with in detail in Part 2. In conclusion, it is recalled that in the case of mv *Semporna* in October 1981, it was the pirates who were killed by the police.

In order to complete this section, an incident of "river" piracy, two incidents of "territorial" piracy and one incident of "dubious" piracy are mentioned in the following paragraphs.

In February 1988 a 59 year old British woman holidaymaker and a Thai crewman were shot dead, and two other British women were wounded, when pirates ambushed a convoy of tourist boats on a river in northern Thailand. The owner of the boat saw the pirates and tried to make a run for it. The effect of this decision was, regrettably, to cause the pirates to open fire indiscriminately. It is accepted that this attack, together with the attack on the *Samual Antonio* mentioned on page 19, can only be classified as piracy by the use of a fairly broad definition.

There are two land based, "peripheral" acts of piracy included in the

IMB Chronology. Firstly, a Swiss businessman was kidnapped while picnicking with a female companion on a Philippines beach in 1986. This is included because the offenders were notorious local pirates. Secondly, there was a ruthless attack from the sea on the Sabah village of Lahad Datu, Malaysia in 1985, which resulted in quick and severe government reprisals—although whether these reprisals were taken against the correct people may be questionable. It is also questionable whether this was an act of piracy in any sense, rather than political terrorism.

Finally, on 26 July 1987 mv *Thai Wong* was boarded by 20 masked pirates, armed with rifles and pistols, in the Gulf of Thailand. The leader of the gang spoke in English, but his men spoke in Thai. They used a blue speedboat, which resembled an official boat. The crew were handcuffed and pushed into cabins. Also handcuffed, the master was told to follow navigational directions for about twenty hours, before being locked in his cabin. The vessel's cargo value $751,000, together with radar, radio and rescue equipment value $10,000, was then transferred at sea to another vessel. The reality of this attack may be less dramatic than it appears. The crew of the *Thai Wong* never made a formal statement to their insurers or P & I Club and, as far as is known, no claim for the loss was ever made to any insurers. Much of the cargo was later identified being hawked around the local islands. The truth is unclear, but there are indications of collusion.

The Rest of the World

This section considers attacks on merchant vessels in parts of the world other than West Africa and south-east Asia including the Malacca Straits. In the period reviewed by the IMB Chronology at Appendix 1 (1981-1987) there were around 130 reported attacks in this category. This total is (fairly) evenly distributed over the years. The most outstanding feature of this "residual" geographic category is its disparate nature—from the point of view of both type of attack and location. It is therefore useful neither to make generalisations about these attacks, nor to try to extract a pattern from them.

Around 30 of the attacks occurred in South American waters—notably around Colombia, Guyana and Nicaragua. Between 1981 and 1985 there were, at least, an additional 30 reported attacks at Santos, Brazil—some observers estimate that in one two year period alone there were as many as one hundred attacks. At least half of the reported attacks were confirmed as serious thefts, or attempted thefts, of cargo. There is no clear reason why Santos should have been affected in this way. The report of a master whose ship was attacked there is cited below.

There were a number of attacks around the Indian sub-continent, and Sri Lanka. Attacks in this region peaked in 1986 at eleven—on a par with reported attacks in that year around Nigeria—out of a worldwide total of 83. Three of these attacks were "related" incidents at Colombo, and another was alleged in the bizarre story told by the crew of mv *Pahlawan*. Other attacks in that year were at Madras, Chittagong and Mangalore.

In 1981-1987 there were around 25 reported incidents in the Caribbean. Most of these—at least 13— were attacks on yachts. However, there were, for example, attacks on merchant vessels at Jamaica in 1984 and 1985.

There were only three confirmed reports of "real" piracy (as defined in Appendix 2), as opposed to reports of what may in reality be simple thefts, at "first world" ports. The crew of the USNS *Truckee* at Naples in February 1983 chased two pirates off—one into the water and the other into a waiting boat. In June 1983 the crew of a vessel at Olympia, USA were attacked, and cash was stolen from them. In May 1985 a crewmember of a Greek vessel at Rouen was attacked and robbed in his cabin.

There were of course other attacks on merchant vessels spread around the world—for example in the Matunas Islands, at Dar es Salaam and at Yanbu, China.

In most reported attacks the pirates have been armed, at least with knives. Sometimes they have operated in large numbers—for example the attack on mv *Benvalla* recounted below, and an attempt in June 1987 off Sri Lanka which involved 23 pirates in four boats. More often however they have attacked in small groups and favoured tactics similar to those used in the Malacca Straits area and, latterly, in West Africa. Sometimes approaches have been made at night, but sometimes during meal times when watches tend to be reduced.

Around 30 of the attacks have involved either serious losses of cargo, or crews being tied up or threatened. Other attacks have, as might be expected, been restricted to the loss of cash and personal property, or to relatively minor items of ship's equipment.

The "rest of the world" attacks include eleven incidents involving fatalities. Seven of these were yacht attacks in the Caribbean in the early 1980s, another was a reported attack on a yacht off Colombia in 1986. There was a grisly attack on a fishing vessel in the Bay of Bengal in 1982, when eight crewmembers were stuffed into sacks and drowned. The only report of a fatality resulting from an attack on a cargo ship is from the disputed story of the crew of mv *Pahlawan* in May 1986. The remaining fatal incident reported in the IMB Chronology is described below, although it may be a suspect candidate for definition as piracy, since it occurred on an inland river.

On 21 September 1984 the tug *Samual Antonio* was attacked whilst towing a barge *Gianina* carrying gasoline on the River Maranon, Peru. Three passengers and five crew were shot dead by an unspecified number of attackers. The sixth member of the crew saved himself by jumping into the river whilst the pirates were momentarily distracted. The gasoline was transhipped and the tug and barge were later found moored further down the river.

The pattern of injuries to crew of cargo ships corresponds to that of attacks in the West Africa and Malacca Straits areas—in other words, injuries are relatively rare, and normally occur only when pirates are confronted. However there were, notably, minor injuries inflicted in the course of some of the attacks at Santos.

The prevailing situation at Santos in the early 1980s may be judged by the following report from the master of mv *Durian*. His vessel was attacked during the night of 8 October 1983, and the ship's safe, containing $2,700 was taken from his cabin. It must be added that there is no firm evidence to support what the master says, and the problem does not appear to have developed in the way he feared.

> On arrival Santos I was warned by representative from charterers that in many ships alongside at Santos it have happened that armed burglars have attacked Captain's cabin to steal the safe or the contents, and therefore advisable that Captain lock up cabin carefully and sleep other cabin (in ships not in regular traffic to Santos). In several cases when Captain have tried to resist the attack and denied to supply key, he has been tortured and forced to do so and also in a few cases been shot at.

There follow two further accounts of piracy in different parts of the world, extracted from the IMB Chronology.

At 06.00 on 3 May 1985 mv *Stolt Heron*, was off Port Esquivel, Jamaica when the engineer on watch saw three armed pirates board the vessel. The master was informed and the entire crew were called to the bridge, where they remained until the pirates left, after taking most of the vessel's portable tools. This prudent reaction ensured that no one was injured.

At 19.40 on 23 October 1986 mv *Benvalla* was at Chittagong. The deck watch reported five boats, filled with between 80 and 100 men, approaching the stern. At least five of the occupants of these boats boarded at the stern, using poles with long hooks attached to the ship's rails, and were repelled with pressure hoses. Half the crew then went forward to find more pirates had boarded on the forecastle head. Before these intruders could be repelled they forced a hatch and took three mooring ropes, worth 500 each. A fourth mooring rope, which they did not have time to steal, was left hanging over the side.

Piracy Control—From on Board Ship

The control of piracy raises a pivotal question—what can be done about the problem? An attempt will be made in this chapter to review possible answers from three perspectives: on board ship, at the state level, and at the inter-governmental level. The special position of the yachtsman in preparing himself for a piratical attack, in particular with regard to firearms, is separately considered later.

There is no shortage of formal advice to masters on the measures they can take to reduce their vulnerability to attack. Recommendations from the US Maritime Administration (MARAD), the Baltic and International Maritime Conference (BIMCO), the International Shipping Federation, the Swedish Shipowners Association and the International Maritime Bureau (IMB) will be found at Appendices 16-21. The following paragraphs are based on, and amplify, these recommendations.

The emphasis in all five sets of recommendations is on keeping pirates off the vessel—once they are allowed to board any defensive action becomes very much more hazardous. It is also fundamental that, if any shipboard anti-piracy measures are to be effective, they must be part of a plan which is known and practised by the crew.

In dangerous areas a master should choose the point at which he anchors very carefully. At the West African peak, as defined on page 8, it was recommended that anchorages should be least 20 miles offshore. If possible masters should remain within the vicinity of other vessels and maintain radio contact with these vessels and with the shore. Agreed emergency signals, which could include pre-recorded messages transmitted at the touch of a button, were also recommended.

Most piracy against cargo vessels, apart from some blatant attacks in West Africa, has taken place in the dark and ships should if possible keep clear of known pirate areas—in particular the Malacca Strait—at night. Some masters are tempted to risk extinguishing their navigation lights.

These precautions should be combined with good watchkeeping, lighting of vulnerable areas, and, possibly, loudspeaker systems to listen for sounds on deck. As far as is consistent with fire precautions, all outer doors of deckhouses and the forecastle should be locked or welded shut. In port, access to these areas of the ship should be properly controlled. Portable and theft prone cargo should not be kept on deck, and valuable containers should be properly stacked.

It is important that all persons wishing to come aboard—including those purporting to be customs, immigration or security personnel—are properly screened. This is particularly true in West African ports, and official advice on these lines has been issued by the Nigerian Port Authority.

If pirates are suspected and, in particular, if a vessel in a dangerous area is hailed by an unidentified boat or canoe, the master should alert his crew and be ready to increase speed or take evasive action. Crews should be able to protect themselves from missiles with safety glasses and heavy clothing. They should also have equipment available to dissuade unwelcome visitors—particularly fire hoses, flares (essentially to frighten and disorientate rather than to cause injury), and personal fire extinguishers. Bags filled with paint can be used with effect to identify pirates and pirate vessels later—this is reminiscent of the tactics used by some European police forces against rioters on land. Beer bottles, filled with sand so that they break and cannot be thrown back, have also proved effective.

The West German authorities have recommended the use of a tear gas additive (Chiloroacetophenon) to the water in the fire hoses, and of personal tear gas atomisers. There is no doubt about the powerful disorientating and deterrent effect of gas, but it has to be properly used and this entails a significant training commitment.

Dogs have been used occasionally—but the trouble is, not only that they have to be fed and sheltered from storms, but also that they tend to lose their fighting spirit after the crew adopt them as pets.

Whilst the above measures can be implemented at little cost to the shipowner, there is more sophisticated equipment on the market. For example, trip wires or infra-red detectors can detect an approach in a blind area, and can activate a flare or floodlights as well as raise the alarm. Special wire barriers, including razor tapes, can be deployed along hand rails and combings and other vulnerable parts of the vessel. Automatic cameras can be installed which will photograph intruders. Other ideas are being developed, such as trailing fibres to snarl the propellers of small craft in close proximity.

Some pirates are more brave and determined than others, and examples of successful deterrence of intruders by crews will be found in the IMB Chronology at Appendix 1. However, most advice supports the US government view, stated in Chapter 16 and at Appendix 16, that heroics are generally inappropriate. It is most unusual for an unresisting crew to be harmed, but pirates can be ruthless if challenged.

Once pirates have boarded there must, as stated above, be a definite plan. Depending on the number of attackers, their determination and, in particular, whether they are armed, resistance may be neither advisable nor practicable after this stage is reached. The plan must therefore include a secure retreat for the crew. Positive action such as closing down the generators in order to impede the pirates may be appropriate in some cases.

It is not unusual, when the danger of piracy is aggravated, to meet it by the recruitment of professional guards. A notable example of these were the "bow and arrow men"—Hausa warriors—during the West African peak. Even if the arrows were often ceremonially tied and would have been difficult to aim in the confined spaces between containers, their owners promised protection both from gangs with which they themselves were in league, and from rival gangs. This said, their mixed effectiveness can be judged from the West African voyage of the *Nedlloyd Steenkerk*, related on page 10. Some commercial companies now offer anti-piracy services in the shape of men on board ships, and their presence has been noted in the Malacca Strait.

Most opinion, which the IMB wholeheartedly endorses, opposes the use of firearms for the following four reasons. One, the risk of escalation of violence, present in any type of resistance, will be enhanced. Two, the problems associated with anti-piracy training will become qualitatively different, and should involve psychological testing and selection. Three, laws of self defence are complex and, of course, vary between jurisdictions. Crew members using guns in earnest could easily find themselves facing criminal charges. Four, there is the question of sovereignty and the attitude of governments to merchant vessels defending themselves in this way in territorial waters—a vessel which is too heavily armed may even change her character and be regarded as a warship (although there would normally be an additional requirement that she was acting as an arm of a state). Moreover, firearms are of course subject to import regulations, and may be impounded as soon as a vessel reaches port—when they are most needed.

These arguments may not apply with the same force to Soviet and Israeli merchant vessels. Firstly, these vessels are crewed exclusively by their own nationals and, secondly, different external threats may be perceived which counterbalance the objections.

The following incident is related by Nigel Cumber, Director of Isis Security, in *Asia Wall Street Journal*, 12 June 1984. It is alleged that in 1982 a heavily armed Soviet vessel captured a group of Nigerian pirates and towed them out to sea, and that only one pirate returned. The bullet ridden bodies of his companions were later washed up on shore. A somewhat similar allegation has been made in connection with the Malacca Straits area. After this, pirates tended to ignore Soviet vessels in both areas—the case of the *Slutsk*, mentioned above, is a rare exception.

In any case, not everyone supports a "low level response" to piracy. Greek owner John Theodoracopoulos, said in a statement bearing a hint of desperation after his vessel, mv *Marianna*, had been attacked at high speed with heavy machine guns in October 1985: "Our ships are being attacked and the lives of our crews, as well as the safety of our vessels, are at stake." He had already installed long range flares as frightener devices on all his ships. He was convinced that the well aimed discharge of these would cause pirates to "turn tail", but nevertheless saw this only as an intermediate step towards the sanctioning of "automatic rifles, rocket launchers and mortars". A further comment on the use of firearms is made by the captain of mv *Grey Fighter*, who is quoted below.

In spite of the awareness of certain owners, some vessels fail to take the most rudimentary precautions. There are at least three reasons for this.

One, with reducing crew levels masters may not have the necessary manpower. It may not for example be reasonable to expect a crew of 25 to carry out anti-piracy night watches after a day's work. But there is scope for selectivity. As stated in Chapter 19 it is only necessary to make a watchkeeping effort for four or five hours in order to transit the Phillip Channel.

Two, initiatives are inhibited by the practical economic insignificance of piracy on world shipping, and the consequent temptation to "rely on insurance". This must however be balanced against, not only the possible immediate effects of a piratical attack on those on board, but also against the potential harmful commercial consequences for owners in increased insurance premiums and reduced revenue from interrupted voyages, which may exceed the cost of what the pirates actually take.

Three, seamen, and their unions, may oppose anti-piracy training partly because, as stated above, resistance may provoke pirates, and partly because of the possible identification of seamen as a physical security force. Even if the training is agreed, the unions may ask for danger money or qualification pay.

The experience of mv *Erodna*, at anchor off Madras on 6 April 1987, indicates that even the most conscientious and responsible master cannot guarantee immunity for his vessel. Extra precautions against piracy and theft had been planned at the weekly work meeting, before arrival at Madras. Among these were the stationing of two seamen on watch during the night. At 07.55 boarders were discovered, but they appeared to be in possession of no property and were ejected. Later it was discovered that fire hoses, a lifeboat painter, and other ship's equipment had been stolen.

The following two extracts from ship's logs—both from vessels off Bonny, Nigeria—will convey something more of the potential and limitations of shipboard anti-piracy action.

First, there follows an extract from the report of the master of mv *Grey Fighter*, a British oil tanker which was anchored ten miles off Bonny inshore terminal on 5 December 1985.

> Ever since anchoring, and in company with other ships, a continuous deck watch has been maintained with patrols reporting to the officer of the watch at 15 minute intervals by VHF walkie-talkies. On the watchman's reporting that there were about ten intruders on the forecastle, the alarm was raised and accommodation doors which were unlocked up to that time for safety purposes were secured. The forward whistle was blown repeatedly and I attempted to call for assistance from local naval and police authorities by VHF. I received no reply except from other ships in the anchorage who while appreciating the warning could do nothing to help.
>
> I cannot positively say whether the boarders were armed but was not prepared to send unarmed crew members forward to what would almost certainly have been an unequal contest. Had a rifle been available to me on the bridge, the intruders could have been effectively discouraged and I would have had no hesitation in firing on them. I eventually managed to contact the Shell Terminal and was advised, quite unbelievably, by the duty operator that my request for immediate assistance could not be passed to the local authorities until morning. The pirates took two mooring ropes which had been brought on to deck preparatory to berthing, then forced entry to the forecastle store and removed another three mooring ropes and a quantity of paint. No casualties were suffered.

Second, there follows an extract from the report of the master of mv *Omissis* on 24 May 1986.

> I report the following piracy act undergone at Bonny Roads, Nigeria. At sunset at about 20.10, the third officer on duty on the bridge noted the presence on board of foreign people on the forecastle. The alarm was on when we saw some negroes on board, probably having climbed up from the anchor chain or by grapnels. With hesitancy we approached the forecastle, but they first became angry and threatened, and then dived into the sea. Once we reached the forecastle we noticed that six mooring propylene ropes of nine inches had been stolen, almost all of them in fairly good condition. At that time one of the two anti-collision radars was on and in order to pick up any noise on board the vessel, the fore after interphone was on. We called Bonny's signal station for urgent help of the local police, but the only answer we got was to go away and not to follow the pirate's boat because it could have been possible that the pirates had arms with them. At 20.40 anchor up; we follow the pirates who are going to the shallow waters. At 21.30 the pirates' boat at 300 metres, we gave up with the chase for safety reasons and we went back to the open sea, resigning ourselves to the affront undergone plus the material damages suffered.
>
> The reasons why we did not leave earlier Bonny roads were:
> (1) Our agent in Lagos told us that Bonny Roads was a safe place as far as piracy was concerned
> (2) Our position in Bonny was ten miles from the nearest coast
> (3) On arrival at Bonny Roads another three vessels were there

(4) During our stay in the roads no suspicious boat was noted either during daylight or at night.

At 23.40 we stopped the engine at about twenty miles from the coast, and we remained adrift, watching everything with great care.

Piracy Control—At the Government Level

Governments are likely to take an interest in piracy for either of two reasons. One, a state may be the victim—because its flag vessels or interests are being attacked in distant parts of the world—this aspect is considered below in the international context. Two, a government's interest may be as coastal state—foreign ships are being attacked in its territorial waters and ports.

There is little doubt that the role of the coastal states is crucial. To an extent the shipboard measures discussed in the preceding paragraphs compensate for the, often inevitable, shortcomings in government control. It is clear from Chapter 2 that this has historically been the case.

Anti-piracy measures by two of the coastal states best placed to take them—Nigeria and Singapore—are fully described by their representatives in Chapters 18 and 19 below. Some additional comments are made here.

By the early 1980s piracy in Nigerian waters was inhibiting trade because shipowners were becoming reluctant to send their vessels to the area, crews were becoming reluctant to go there and insurance costs were rising. In addition, the apparent lawlessness was reflecting internationally on the government.

After some years of official denials that there was a real problem, and with the new government of Mohamed Buhari in 1983, the "piracy control regime" was developed. As stated in Chapter 18, this was intended as an intermediate solution before the establishment of a regular coastguard. This ultimate objective was prejudiced by, among other factors, constitutional difficulties surrounding the creation of a "third force", in addition to the defence forces and the police. Nevertheless, within its terms of reference the anti-piracy regime introduced much needed organisational changes which improved coordination and provided increased manpower and equipment, in particular fast patrol boats. A separate police ports division was established, and the traditional port security staff were replaced by trained police with full powers.

Emphasis from the start was placed on the important factors of training and publicity. Some of the training, for example for hovercraft pilots, took place in the United Kingdom. Publicity was important in this context because of its educative effect on other affected states and its deterrent effect on the pirates themselves.

Pirates' methods were analysed, and where possible legislative support was given to the control regime. For example, it became necessary to obtain a licence to operate communications equipment because, as stated above, the pirates were both monitoring and jamming radio channels; and small boats were prohibited within 200 metres of moored vessels, because these were often used to transfer the "loot" from ships attacked in port.

The Nigerian military regime introduced public execution for armed robbery in the 1970s. In July 1985 six Nigerian citizens were executed by firing squad for murder (as far as is known, not in public but inside Kirikiri maximum security prison), after being found guilty by a military court of attacking a vessel at Agbowa in early 1985, from which several passengers had drowned attempting to escape.

The Nigerian control regime had an immediate effect. It will be seen from the figures on page 8 that the number of piratical attacks in Nigeria roughly halved between 1981 and 1982. Since 1985, as explained on page 9, the nature of piracy in West Africa has altered.

This is partly, as also stated above, because of the decline in trade and decongestion of the ports. But the effect of the control regime is clear from comparison with some neighbouring countries where enforcement effort was less vigorous and pirates were more rarely arrested. In these countries the decline has been somewhat less marked and they have probably suffered from "shifting" of piracy from Nigeria. It must however be stated in this connection that the West German Bundeskriminalamt, in the course of their activities described below, were satisfied also with the cooperation they received from the authorities in Ivory Coast and Sierra Leone.

In spite of the Nigerian control regime an examination of the IMB Chronology at Appendix 1 will indicate cases, in addition to those of the *Grey Fighter* and the *Omissis* mentioned above, where masters have called on Nigerian authorities for assistance and received no response. This has happened on one or two reported occasions in most years since 1981.

The chronic problem of piracy in the Malacca Straits area is now being perceived by commercial interests as having an effect on trade comparable to that earlier provoked by Nigerian piracy. There is a danger that owners will begin to avoid Singapore for bunkers and victuals. The sharp increase in attacks in 1987 (29 reported, as opposed to 19 in 1986) caused the ASEAN Shipowners Association to resolve in November to "take positive steps to end this dreadful menace on the high seas".

This region has its particular problems, not the least of which is a certain confusion of jurisdiction between the neighbouring territorial states of Singapore, Malaysia and Indonesia. An examination of the IMB Chronology will identify three recent cases (in 1986) in which Singaporean authorities stated that they could not investigate because they could not establish the precise location of the incident, and therefore whether they had jurisdiction. A further complicating factor is the international law which states that the Malacca Straits are open to ships of all nationalities—although this international status was modified by an agreement in March 1970 under which Indonesia and Malaysia agreed to divide the straits along a median line. A similar agreement in May 1973 between Singapore and Indonesia defines a boundary separating their waters in the Strait of Singapore.

Singapore has the greatest economic incentive to do something—its port is the reason for the presence of many of the attacked vessels. And, with its developed institutions and high standard of living, Singapore is relatively well placed to take action. However, as stated on page 12, most attacks take place on the opposite, eastbound, lane of the local traffic separation system in the Phillip Channel, close to the Indonesian islands and therefore outside Singaporean territorial waters.

Reference is made in Chapter 19 to increased Singaporean patrols, and to a dedicated VHF channel to report attacks. It is believed that the Indonesian government patrols the Phillip Channel by means of a joint force of police, navy and customs. It is necessary in this context to draw attention again to the alleged activities of some Indonesian customs officials, as described on page 17. There has in the past been some disagreement between the Singaporean and Indonesian governments. The Singaporeans have claimed that the Indonesians have not done enough to protect their waters and locate pirates on their territory, although both tasks are immensely difficult. The Indonesians have accused the Singaporeans, not altogether realistically, of harbouring pirates.

The Indonesian authorities in 1983 scored an undisputed and notable success in breaking a gang which had attacked their own flag oil tanker in the Phillip Channel and taken $15,000 from the safe. They were subsequently traced to their base on Batam Island in the Rhio Archipelago. Police seized weapons, jewellery and other valuables, believed to have come from other attacks in the Phillip Channel.

An insight into the problems of government forces in controlling the varied forms of piracy in the south-east Asia region is offered at page 15.

As an indication that effective enforcement action is not confined to the Malacca Straits and West Africa, attention is drawn to the recent failed attack on mv *Sea Heron* off Colombo in June 1987. The master noticed 23 pirates approaching him in boats and radioed the authorities. Sri Lankan gunboats and customs boats arrived and arrested 21 of the pirates after a high speed chase.

In general, there is a need for landbased detective work. Pirates have to "live" somewhere, in spite of the suggestion on page 8 that some West African pirates relied on vessels as floating headquarters. Further, local law enforcement needs to develop a strategy for responding to piracy, which depends on more than everyone rushing to the scene after a report. In many parts of the world this reaction is in any case unlikely to be effective because of the distances involved, poor communications, and apathy.

Identifying a requirement for landbased detective work is of course usually very much easier than meeting it. For example, as mentioned above, Indonesian pirates have their own village sub-culture, not easily penetrated by police—and any attempt at intervention normally requires a large well armed force.

Enforcement effort by many coastal states suffers from lack of resources at least as much as from lack of commitment. For example, some West African police forces do not even have the facility to take photographs of suspects—not to mention their fingerprints. And there are other enforcement problems peculiar to the crime of piracy. Police attitudes may be compromised by the knowledge that losses will be met by insurance. More fundamentally, the real "victim"—that is to say the shipowner or cargo owner—is often located thousands of miles away from the scene of the crime. The West German initiative through Interpol, which is mentioned below, is an attempt to resolve the basic problem of coordination (and motivation) which can result from this.

Examination of all major efforts to control piracy, for example the Thai anti-piracy programme, cooperation between the US Coast Guard and the FBI, and the Nigerian control regime, will reveal considerable emphasis on the coordination of different enforcement agencies—in particular of "territorial" police and maritime services. It is crucial that professional maritime and police expertise are combined in some way.

Often the police approach can profitably also be combined with straightforward military measures. During the West African peak the French successfully protected their merchant vessels by deploying a warship close to Abidjan. In 1983, in the wake of the odyssey of the *Nedlloyd Steenkerk*, related on page 10, the Dutch Seafarers Union recommended stationing armed marines on a supply ship and transferring them to vessels as they entered Nigerian waters. There is supposed to have been established a US Navy SEAL commando unit standing by to protect American ships after the attacks in January 1983 on the *Sealift Arctic* and the *Spartan*.

The importance of efficient collation and dissemination of information, which is arguably most effectively done at an international or regional level, is emphasised below. However two governments—the United States and Greece—have instituted systems for their own flag vessels.

Greek masters are instructed to send an immediate radio or telex report of an attack to the Ministry of Transport. The matter is then assessed and diplomatic channels are used to register a protest or demand an enquiry if appropriate. The Anti-Shipping Activities Message (ASAM) system established by the Defense Mapping Agency and combined with other regularly updated information to mariners such as chart corrections and navigational warnings, is one aspect of the US government's efforts to combat piracy, described in detail in Chapter 16. The word "anti-shipping" is used to get around narrow definitions both of piracy and terrorism. A relatively sophisticated computer system allows on line speculative enquiries. However it will be seen from

Chapter 16 that for a number of reasons, not least of which is the absence on most vessels of the necessary expensive computer terminals and satellite transmitters, there are grounds for pessimism whether the system will "take off".

Piracy Control—At the International Level

Any international perspective on piracy will be complicated by the "confusion" of international law—both as codified in the Conventions of the Law of the Sea (UNCLOS), and as customary law—and domestic laws. The relationship between the different systems is carefully explored in Part 3 of this book.

Alongside the analytical desirability of reconciling international and municipal law there exists a practical requirement for international action for at least two reasons, reactions to each of which will be considered separately below. One, although piracy is essentially a local phenomenon, it tends to occur in parts of the world where resources to deal with it are scarce, and some international, or at least regional, mechanism is therefore necessary to enhance these resources. Two, as mentioned above, the victims of piracy are usually ship and cargo owners living in countries far away from those in which the offences took place.

The worldwide humanitarian reaction to attacks on Vietnamese refugees in the South China Sea led to the establishment of an international anti-piracy programme to assist the Thai government in protecting them. This is examined later in this chapter and in Part 2 of this book. This could be viewed as a "model" for dealing with piracy, by supplementing inadequate local resources on an international basis. However, in the absence of human consequences of the same dimension it is unlikely that it would be applied to attacks on merchant vessels elsewhere in the world. The incidence and importance of world piracy more realistically suggest a regional approach— in particular funding, seminars and publicity, and training of law enforcement personnel.

Almost every group which has met on the subject of piracy, including the Woods Hole meeting in 1985, has ended by highlighting the need for a dependable system of reporting and a centralised database. Reporting systems initiated by the US and Greek governments were described on page 25. A "prototype" Maritime Violence Incident Report, together with some notes about its possible use, appears at Appendix 22.

Two initiatives which have been made at an international level— by the UN International Maritime Organisation (IMO) and the International Criminal Police Organisation (Interpol)— also both depend on the collection and use of information.

At its 13th session, in November 1983, the IMO resolved to adopt a system where violent acts at sea would be centrally filed and accessed by the maritime community. Governments were accordingly requested to inform the IMO of any act of piracy or armed robbery against a ship flying their flag, indicating the location and circumstances of the incident and action taken by the coastal state. This "Resolution to prevent Acts of Piracy and Armed Robbery against Ships'' was proposed by the government of Sweden following a brutal piratical attack on their flag vessel *Tarn* (including the rape of a stewardess) and supported by seven consultative non-governmental organisations, and is reproduced at Appendix 21. In addition to calling for reports, it noted the serious situation which was developing and called on governments and their maritime industries to do something about it.

The General Assembly of Interpol in November 1987, in response to an initiative from the West German police, referred proposals ''for clarification'' to a working party. Envisaged is an early warning communications network to alert shipping to trouble spots. It is proposed to keep records of known pirates, and to analyse intelligence to identify particular cargoes or regions at risk, as well as the existence of any international links. This information, together with general expert advice, would be made available to the industry.

The provision of accurate intelligence about countries and cargoes will be valuable. Further, there is a role for an international organisation with the resources and status of Interpol in making coastal states aware of their responsibilities in ports and territorial waters, and, perhaps more arguably, in coordinating measures between ships' masters, owners, port authorities, police forces and international organisations.

However there are one or two apparent difficulties about the proposals. The approach is reminiscent of the measures taken against international air terrorism. These measures have of course been (generally) very successful, but it is by no means clear that they can appropriately be transferred to this type of maritime crime. Maritime piracy is more ''ordinary'', as well as being less genuinely ''international''— the international element is essentially confined to the fact that the victims are of a different nationality from the offenders. For example, it may be that masters can alert owners and port authorities more efficiently by communicating directly than through formalised channels.

Moreover, Interpol may encounter difficulties due to its constitution. It will have to tread a careful path to avoid interference in local jurisdictions, or the assumption of tasks which could more properly be done by bodies such as the IMO. In particular, there may be professional and other difficulties in releasing police information to commercial companies.

Interpol has also been approached for assistance by the government of Singapore—confronted as it is by the considerable jurisdictional difficulties which have been identified above.

A final comment is necessary on the subject of international (or any other type of) intelligence networks. However sophisticated the systems, their establishment will not alter the fact that many countries lack the police resources to act on, or contribute to, the information they provide. This point has been adequately made above. Neither will the systems do much to mitigate the effects of corruption—whether tribal, political or simply mercenary.

Before leaving the subject of supranational action generally, the role of the European Community should be mentioned. The Community works quite closely with the IMO, particularly through its Transport Group. For example, the Group sent protest notes to Nigeria in 1981 and 1983, during the West African peak.

The outstanding response of a "victim" state to protect its flag vessels from piracy in a different part of the world is that of the West Germany during the West African peak. Until 1986 there was a department of one or two specialist officers within the Bundeskriminalamt. This department liaised with German shipowners, in order to analyse attacks on flag vessels, and, on a diplomatic basis, with the authorities in Nigeria, Sierra Leone and Ivory Coast, in order to monitor enforcement.

In spite of the implications for sovereignty, there may also be valid precedents to be drawn from the bilateral agreements between the United States and some Caribbean governments to allow US enforcement vessels to enter Caribbean waters to defend US small boats. More is said about this on page 32.

Finally, the military responses by certain victim states, which do not necessarily involve collaboration, or even consultation, with governments in whose waters the attacks occur should be recalled here—the deployment of a French warship off Abidjan, the recruitment of a US Navy SEAL commando unit and the proposal to tranship Dutch marines on to vessels entering Nigerian ports.

Small Boats in The Caribbean

The recent history of attacks on small boats, particularly on US boats and particularly in the Caribbean, is related in Chapter 3. At Appendix 12 will be found a chronology of attacks on American small boats, or "yachtjackings", since 1969. The rationale behind this chronology is explained at page 66. Known attacks on yachts and small boats in the Caribbean also appear in the IMB Chronology at Appendix 1.

It was emphasised above that many piratical attacks are unreported—largely for "commercial" reasons. The likelihood of an attack on a small boat never coming to light is no less than that of an attack on any other type of vessel. Very often an attacked boat and its occupants are never seen again, and it is impossible to be certain what happened to them. Additionally, most marine insurance policies on yachts, as opposed to those on merchant vessels, do not pay in respect of piratical attacks. A yachtowner who wants an attack on his vessel to be investigated may therefore find himself in a difficult position. Clearly he will have to satisfy the appropriate law enforcement agency—for example the Federal Bureau of Investigation—that there has been a crime. However, if he wants his insurance company to compensate him, he may have to satisfy them that there has not been a crime.

Chapter 3 also provides a detailed insight into the attitude of the US government towards reports of attacks on small boats. Suggestions that Caribbean governments have also at times been reluctant to accept the full extent of the attacks should be evaluated in the context, first, of the importance of tourism to the area and, second, of its sheer size—the Bahamas alone consist of over 700 islands spread out over 100,000 square miles, and the entire Caribbean extends 1500 miles by 600 miles.

What evidence there is on the subject of piracy against small boats in the Caribbean suggests that it is often drugs related. For example, crews have been "eliminated" when they have accidentally witnessed trafficking activity, or because traffickers wished to use their boats—expensive vessels with modern equipment which would otherwise be beyond their means. Further, US registered vessels can of course re-enter the United States without attracting attention.

Attacks increased between the 1960s and the early 1980s as affluent but inexperienced mariners tried their hand at ocean cruising. As explained on page 64, this coincided with changes, in effect an "amateurisation", of the drugs trade.

Since the early 1980s, as can be seen from Appendix 12, the attacks have decreased. There are a number of apparent reasons for this. One, the US Coast Guard has, as part of the national fight against drugs, developed more effective countermeasures. As mentioned above there have been government agreements under which US Coast Guard and Navy vessels are able to take enforcement action in certain Caribbean waters. An operation mounted on this basis is described at page 171. Two, pleasure sailors are now more aware of the dangers and therefore more careful. Three, perhaps most significant, the drugs industry has reorganised and has generally again become more professional. It is now less likely to involve haphazard, brutal contact with yachtsmen. More smugglers now have their "own" vessels, not to mention helicopters and fixed wing aircraft.

Advice from the Coast Guard Operations Center on yachtjacking countermeasures will be found at Appendix 13. A yacht, threatened by piracy, is in a substantially different position from a merchant vessel. Crews are smaller and it is less likely that there will be anyone to turn to for help. With its low freeboard, a yacht can be boarded without difficulty, even by a swimmer. On a more sinister level, yacht pirates are not likely to be satisfied with taking the vessel's cargo. They usually wish to take the entire boat and very often, for the reasons mentioned above, they will kill the occupants.

It is therefore much more important for a yacht completely to avoid an attack. The most effective precaution is to stay away from "bad" areas. In any case overnight anchorages should be chosen very carefully and, if possible, yachts should not sail alone.

There is a requirement for good watchkeeping, so that the correct action can be taken in time. By day this is not too difficult. At night, when the occupants are likely to be asleep below, some resort to technology is necessary in dangerous areas. Radar can be a partial solution, supplemented for example by trip wires and tacks laid on deck to warn of intruders. There are also intruder alarms on the market, although they can be extravagant on the power systems of small boats.

If a yacht is threatened, decisive action is necessary, which will often involve moving as fast as possible towards a vessel which can assist. Any radio message should be discreet, and should not include details of defensive measures. If there is going to be a chase at night, lights should be extinguished.

There is a case, fully discussed by Villar in *Piracy Today* (Conway Maritime Press, London 1985), that yachtsmen in dangerous areas should take firearms with them. It must however be stated that the problems outlined on page 23 still generally apply here—in particular, the implications of sovereignty. When a yacht reaches port guns are likely to be confiscated, sealed or impounded—at the time when they may be most needed. And training will still be a problem, although it may be more easily overcome in view of the smaller crews.

If a yachtsman produces a gun he must be prepared to use it and, unless he is an expert shot, this means that he must be prepared to shoot to kill. The production of a gun as a "bluff", without this resolve, is likely to do no more than enrage an attacker. An example of the consequences of an ill advised "warning shot" is described below.

This said, drugs pirates in the Caribbean are likely to kill all the witnesses anyway. An attacked yachtsman may therefore have little to lose, and no choice but to fight back, and the fact that he enrages his attackers by producing a gun may not be particularly significant. In the opinion of the IMB, this differentiates yacht attacks from other forms of piracy and tips the balance in favour of carrying firearms in dangerous areas.

From a tactical point of view, it has been suggested that two guns are required—a long range rifle which can be fired at approaching pirates and persuade them to seek an easier target before they are committed, and a smaller weapon for defence after pirates have boarded. Pirates will often avoid a fight if possible—for one thing, they want boats in good condition, not bullet ridden hulks.

Examples will be found in the Chronologies at Appendices 1 and 12 of the successful use of firearms by crews of small boats to defeat attacks, more than one of which has had fatal results for the pirates. A tragic exception was the 1979 case of Lydia Tyngvald, who fired a warning shot at pirates approaching her yacht, the *Artemis de Pythgas*. The pirates responded with a fatal shot through Lydia Tyngvald's head. She probably fired too late, *after* the pirates were committed.

Finally, on the question of weapons, one experienced yachtsman relies on crossbows, which are of course very effective. Villar suggests that a bottle of drugged or poisoned whisky should be available, so that pirates can be invited to a drink. Although neither of these two techniques are subject to the same legal controls as firearms, they of course entail the legal risks associated with any type of "assault".

The Boat People

The reasons why a substantial section of the Vietnamese population wish to leave their country, and have done so since the end of the war in 1975, are varied. Some are motivated by a straightforward love of freedom. In the words of a refugee: "In Vietnam you cannot smile without a reason. You cannot sing without a reason. Always it must be for the good of the country, for the party." Others wish to join their families. Others are suffering persecution because of their association with the old US backed administration. Others wish to avoid draft into the army to fight in Cambodia. Still others—economic migrants as defined by the Thai Ambassador to the UN in Chapter 8, and now by the Hong Kong authorities, as will be seen on page 39—seek a more comfortable life in the West.

It is well known that many of the "boat people", Vietnamese refugees making their way across the South China Sea in small boats to other south-east Asian countries, have been attacked by pirates. A factual account of what has happened, and continues to happen, to them will be found in Chapter 4. There have been over 600,000 boat people since 1975. Estimates of deaths among them—including deaths from "natural" causes such as the weather and shipwreck, as well as from piracy—vary from 60,000 to 250,000.

All the evidence points to the fact that the pirates are Thai fisherman. It must however be emphasised that only a small proportion of Thai fishermen resort to piracy, and many have always helped refugees, rather than attack them. In 1986, for example, 67% of arriving boat people reported receiving assistance from fishermen, by, among other things, repairs to their motors and hospitality in villages. The motivation of the pirates, including their economic problems, and the traditional distrust which appears to exist between the Thais and the Vietnamese, are discussed in Chapter 4.

Detailed statistics of attacks on the boat people are no easier to compile than statistics of other piratical activity. For one thing, refugees, almost by definition, leave in secrecy. The best available figures appear in Appendices 3 and 4 and are analysed below and in Chapters 6 and 7.

The figures in Appendix 3 for Thailand alone indicate a sharp drop both in the number of refugees and in the number of attacks on them between 1981 and 1982. In 1981 there were 15,479 reported arrivals and 1,122 reported attacks. In 1982 these figures reduced to 5,813 and 373 respectively. Between 1982 and 1986 arrivals remained generally constant, at an average of 3,550, whilst the number of attacks declined steadily from 181 in 1983 to 87 in 1986. In the first eleven months of 1987 there was a sharp upward turn in arrivals, to 10,313, but no corresponding increase in attacks, which totalled 95.

Over this period 773 deaths due to piracy were reported. To an extent, these figures follow the pattern of attacks. In 1981 454 deaths were reported, 2.7% of all refugees. In 1982 the number of deaths declined to 155, but the percentage remained roughly constant. In the following three years, 1983 to 1985, there were 146 reported deaths, but the percentage declined sharply to an average of 1.4. In 1986 the percentage again declined sharply, to 0.4, and there were 18 reported deaths. In the first eleven months of 1987 there were no reported deaths.

Reports of rape are also roughly in proportion to reports of attacks generally. There are marked declines between the years 1981 (571), 1982 (176) and 1983 (95), followed by a steady decline in 1984 and 1985 to 57 in 1986. However, in contrast to the general figures, there was a small increase in 1987.

The percentage of boats attacked, perhaps the most reliable indicator of piratical activity, has declined progressively, and significantly, from 77% in 1981 to 8% in 1987.

Figures for countries other than Thailand, and regional totals, for 1985, 1986 and the first nine months of 1987, will be found at Appendix 4. It would be tedious to attempt to analyse these figures in detail here. However it should be noted that Malaysia, Indonesia and, to a lesser extent, the Philippines, received boat people in numbers comparable to those received by Thailand over this period. Hong Kong, Singapore, Japan and other countries received smaller numbers.

The percentage of boats attacked arriving in Malaysia was generally higher than for Thailand. With certain marked aberrations, the percentage was relatively insignificant for the other countries. In 1985 there were 28 deaths reported amongst arrivals in Malaysia and (an anomalous figure, since only three boats were reported attacked) 116 amongst arrivals in Indonesia. This contrasts sharply with 1986, during which there were no reported deaths amongst arrivals in the two countries, and with the first nine months of 1987 during which there was one reported death. The only significant reports of rape have been amongst refugees arriving in Malaysia, where the numbers in 1985 and 1986 (46 and 84 respectively) were generally comparable to those arriving in Thailand, but in 1987 reduced significantly to nine.

It was stated above that it is impossible to rely uncritically on any reported figures. But the figures concerning rape may be particularly underestimated. Some estimates indicate that in the early 1980s as many as 60% of women aged between 10 and 59 were sexually assaulted as they crossed the Gulf. However, as mentioned, in 1981 there were only 571 reports of rape amongst a total of 15,479 refugees reaching Thailand. For clear personal and cultural reasons the victims of this type of attack wish to conceal what has happened. There is a detailed psychological exposition of the effects of rape on page 86.

The fact that only one death in the entire region was reported in the first nine months of 1987 is symptomatic of a decline, not only in the absolute number of attacks, but also, to an extent, in the severity of those which do occur. Appendix 7 contains a chronology of incidents in the first nine months of 1987. The chronology still includes a number of violent and ruthless attacks, and provides depressing evidence that most pirates will take the opportunity to rape female refugees. Nevertheless, piratical attacks on boat people are at present *relatively* mild, compared with past years. A study of Appendix 7 will also reveal a number of cases in which pirates have robbed (and raped) refugees, but have then given them genuine assistance to reach land.

The Thai Ambassador to the United Nations justifiably states in Chapter 8 that the anti-piracy programme, operated by his government with the support of the UN High Commission for Refugees (UNHCR) and a number of donor countries, is unique. Its operational effect is carefully considered in Part 2.

It must be said at this stage that law enforcement in the South China Sea and the Gulf of Thailand will never be easy. It is a very large piece of water, exploited by tens of thousands of legitimate fishing boats, as well as by a few pirates, who may not be distinguishable from the legitimate fishermen. This latter problem is now eased, by compulsory computerised registration (with the clear attraction for foreigners of a supplementary requirement that the vessel's name in Thai script be supplemented by a numerical identity code).

In the first seven months of 1987 Thai patrol craft undertook around 200 missions and investigated nearly one thousand boats. The effectiveness of the patrols has been strengthened by improved ship navigation equipment, as well as by the installation of airfield lights to allow air surveillance by night.

The programme, although unique to Thailand, benefits from increasing liaison under UNHCR auspices with other countries in the region. In particular there is a system under which Kuala Lumpur provides "early warning" reports of attacks to UNHCR staff in Thailand.

In addition to this operational effort, there is a renewed emphasis on seminars for fishermen and vessel owners, explaining the government's policy and encouraging humane treatment of refugees. This type of educative crime prevention is considered to be extremely important in view of the opportunist nature of most current piratical attacks.

Detailed information about arrests, prosecutions and sentencing of pirates in the South China Sea will be found at Appendix 5. Some Thai trials are described in more detail, and some remarks are made about Thai justice, in Chapter 4. In the first few years of the anti-piracy programme arrests were relatively rare—in some years they were non-existent—although there may of course have been a deterrent effect. However in 1986 the Thai authorities made fifty arrests, followed by a further 16 arrests in the first nine months of 1987.

As stated in Chapter 4, a major problem in securing a conviction continues to be identification. Refugees may be unwilling, as well as unable, to testify against pirates, despite the support offered by the

UNHCR and the Thai government. They are glad to have "made it", and all they want is to be considered for resettlement without further legal delay—which can sometimes be extended for tactical reasons by defence counsel.

The sharp upward curve in arrests and convictions is, to an extent at least, the result of a welcome shift to landbased detective work. As explained in Chapters 7 and 8, the Thai police are fully involved in anti-piracy operation plans and receive an increasing share of the anti-piracy programme budget. There is also a paid informer system, under the guidance of US law enforcement professionals.

Nevertheless there are other factors, apart from the anti-piracy effort, which have contributed to the improvement in statistics in recent years.

One, it seems clear that the Disablement Resettlement Offers and Rescue at Sea Resettlement Offers schemes (DISERO and RASRO), which aim to reimburse masters the cost of stopping to pick up refugees and to ensure their resettlement once they are disembarked at the next scheduled port of call, are at last becoming more understood and effective. UNHCR guidelines for disembarkation are reproduced at Appendix 8 and the schemes themselves are fully discussed in Chapters 6 and 7.

Many flag states (for example Liberia) threaten to cancel registration and withdraw masters certificates in cases where vessels have failed to act correctly. However. there are other flag states, for example Bermuda as mentioned on page 122, which seem, at least in the past, to have been less supportive.

It is estimated that, by July 1986, West German vessels had picked up 1,000 refugees. Details of Belgian ships which have distinguished themselves in this way will be found on page 91. The award of the Nansen medal to a US vessel is mentioned on page 109.

Details of the flags flown by vessels reported as picking up refugees between 1980 and 1984 will be found at Appendix 9. Comparable totals for the years after the introduction of RASRO in 1985 are 2,890 (1985), 2,591 (1986) and 2,429 (1987). These totals, as will be seen from Appendix 9, are generally lower than the figures for the earlier years. However the more significant statistics, in judging the immediate effect of the resettlement schemes, are the numbers rescued expressed as a percentage of all arrivals. This rose from 8.8% in 1984 to 13.0% in 1985 and 12.9% in 1987 (although it has not reached the levels of the earlier years, as indicated in the appendix).

Two, in 1979 the "Orderly Departure Programme" (ODP) was established as an alternative method of leaving Vietnam to crossing the South China Sea in a small boat. The ODP allows those with relatives abroad to apply to the authorities in Hanoi for permission to leave by air. By 1984 it had established itself as the main method of emigration. In spite of its dependence on political factors, which provoked a brief interruption in 1987, 132,000 people have already left under the ODP.

The total for 1987, despite the interruption, was around 13,000. Further figures will be found on page 111, and detailed figures from the start of the programme until January 1988 are available at Appendix 10.

Three, today's refugees may be less inviting, because the wealthiest were the first to flee. It is likely that there are no longer sufficient rich pickings for the "career" pirate, of which there were a few in the early 1980s. He has been replaced by the amateur who attacks refugees in boats as he chances upon them.

Four, more refugees now head for the east, partly in the hope of meeting clandestine ferries operating from Cambodia. This route is less dangerous than the traditional voyage to the southern coast. In 1986 and the first nine months of 1987 only 4% of vessels taking the route were attacked. However in 1986 as many as 46% of those boats still making for the southern coast were attacked—but it is significant that even this figure reduced to 28% in the first nine months of 1987.

The above factors are all arguably compromised by the phenomenon of the "pull factor". If the crossing is made safer, more people may be tempted to risk their lives by making it. The factor is difficult to prove, but it is not supported, for example, by the fact that in 1985, the first year of operation of RASRO (see page 110), arrivals *dropped*, although the rescue rate was the highest recorded.

The pull factor was one of the problems affecting the "magnet" charity ships, listed on page 89, which used to be stationed in the South China Sea to assist boat people. It was not of course their main problem—this, as stated on page 122, was political. It will be seen from Chapter 5 that none of the problems experienced by earlier vessels will deter Maurice Vitty from taking mv *Seacare* to the South China Sea.

It is believed that a directive originally made by President Carter that the US Navy should actively search for refugees is no longer in force—because it is not thought cost effective with the decline in their numbers. It may also of course be due to fear of operation of the pull factor. Very considerable US government financial resources, and expertise, are of course still applied to, among other things, RASRO, the ODP and the anti-piracy programme.

More vigorous law enforcement may have a further negative effect—pirates may be more anxious to ensure that there are no witnesses. Like the pull factor, this theory is difficult to prove or disprove. It has been indicated above that deaths due to piracy have certainly *not* increased in recent years. One indication to support the theory can however be deduced from Appendix 3. Between 1985 and 1986, when more people were arrested for piracy by the Thai authorities than ever before, the percentage of abducted women *recovered* fell from 54% to 33% (however the absolute number of abductions between these two years fell even more sharply).

Even after they have survived the crossing, the problems of the boat people are not over. They have never been welcomed anywhere with open arms, and it has been related above that the missions of the "mercy ships" eventually failed mainly because of resettlement difficulties. Things are certainly becoming no easier for them. For example, in spite of the US commitment to the problem generally, its resettlement quota for 1987 was 32,000—5,000 fewer than for 1986.

A map indicating the location of Indo-Chinese in camps, a total of 138,000 at the close of 1987, will be found at Appendix 11.

Hong Kong was proud of the fact that it had never turned a refugee away. Nevertheless concern grew about the increasing numbers—2,087 arrived in 1986, double the number for 1985—and the overall cost— US$ 79 million by 1987. Moreover, there was a perceived incongruity between the reception given to Vietnamese refugees and that given to the, ethnically more closely related, refugees from the Peoples Republic. The latter are of course immediately repatriated if detected.

In June 1988 the policy in Hong Kong, which is controlled by the United Kingdom, therefore changed. A distinction is now drawn between economic migrants and genuine refugees. All arrivals are now taken to a former leper colony on Hei Ling Chau island for screening. Political refugees will then go to closed camps, as before. But the economic migrants—an estimated 90% of arrivals—will be sent to detention centres, and will face repatriation as soon as the Vietnamese government agrees.

Refugees arriving in Hong Kong have always been offered food supplies and boat repairs, if they will sail on. These offers will be maintained, whatever the apparent status of new arrivals.

The intention is to send a clear signal to those considering leaving Vietnam—in the words of a Hong Kong official: "Do not come here. You will only face years of detention." This message has disturbed the UNHCR, although it has no objection in principle to screening refugees. The UNHCR considered that the timing was bad, because it could harm negotiations with the Vietnamese government to allow boat people home "under acceptable conditions." Further, the UNHCR was disappointed only to have been allowed observer status in the screening process. Finally, it is feared that other governments in the region may follow the UK's lead.

The Thai government indeed at one time operated a policy of "humane" deterrence, now discontinued. The intention of this was to make the stay of refugees in Thailand as long and uncomfortable as humanely possible. A valuable insight into life in a Thai camp appears in Chapter 5.

The Thai government has had to tolerate rumours of abuse of UN money, and of its own judicial and police procedures, and rumours that its fight against piracy has been half hearted because successful pirates control the influx of refugees to their territory. Any suggestions of this type must be balanced against an understanding of Thailand's own problems and poor resources, and the real possibility that some "refugees" are really communist infiltrators.

The Vietnamese boat people present an international problem which requires an international solution. The involvement of the UNHCR is a recognition of the fact that it is not practical or correct to place the responsibility for it on other states in the region. Most observers agree that the problem must be addressed at several levels but, above all, it must be attacked at its source—in Vietnam itself. Some reassurance can be taken from the re-establishment of the Orderly Departure Programme in 1987 and a general move towards openness, particularly in the economy, within the country in the same year. These questions are explored more fully later in Part 2.

Also developed elsewhere in this book is the question whether the type of international and regional action being taken in the South China Sea can appropriately be applied to other facets of the piracy problem throughout the world.

CHAPTER 2

AN HISTORICAL PERSPECTIVE ON THE INCIDENCE OF PIRACY

M J Peterson

Introduction

Piracy has existed as long as legitimate maritime trade, though historical records show that its incidence differs from locality to locality and from time to time. This suggests that some conditions or clusters of conditions favour piracy while others discourage it. An understanding of the circumstances which favour piracy is useful to law enforcement authorities, seamen, and shippers alike since this permits concentrating attention on those areas at those times when it seems most likely to occur.

Piracy, like any other form of crime, requires both a motive and an opportunity. In almost all cases of known piracy, the motive is personal gain. Most pirates take ships and marine equipment for their own use. Some even take goods for this purpose. The Chinese pirates that ranged along their country's southernmost coasts between 1799 and 1850 began their operations taking cargoes of food to feed their starving families, though branched out later (Snow, 1963, pp 35-37). After the battle of Evesham in 1265, followers of the defeated Simon de Montfort took their families to sea and subsisted by piracy until royal policy changed from prosecution and dispossession to clemency (Costain, 1951, pp 320-1). Many Caribbean pirates of the late eighteenth century, lacking ready markets, took their loot to isolated islands and dissipated it in riotous living. However, most pirates hope to sell the cargoes they steal and get ransom for or (where slavery is permitted) sell any captives they take. This requires access to places where loot can be sold or held pending sale or ransom.

There is always a fairly large number of people seeking personal gain. Whether they do so through activities accepted as legitimate or through those defined as crime depends on the opportunities presented. In the case of piracy, it flourishes when there are plentiful sources of booty, ready markets for the booty, and secure bases where pirates can rest and resupply between voyages.

The following analysis will avoid taking sides in the current debates among international lawyers about defining the term "piracy". Rather, it will pay attention to all forms of robbery at sea—attacks on one ship by persons aboard another on the high seas, raids on ships lying in harbours or roadsteads, captures of ships by persons originally aboard as passengers or crew, and even raids on coastal towns by ship borne groups of marauders—without attention to the distinctions among the various offences used in most legal systems. This may be heresy to modern lawyers, but there are precedents for treating all forms of maritime marauding together. The seventeenth century English jurist Sir Charles Hedges said:

> Now piracy is only a term for sea robbery, piracy being a robbery committed within the jurisdiction of the Admiralty. If any man shall be assaulted within that jurisdiction and his ships or goods violently taken away without legal authority, this is robbery and piracy. If the mariners of any ship shall violently dispossess the master, and afterwards carry away the ship itself or any of the goods, or tackle, apparel or furniture, in any place where the Lord Admiral hath or pretends to have jurisdiction, this is also robbery and piracy. (Trial of Joseph Dawson *et al*, 1696, quoted in Lucie-Smith, 1978, p 8)

A similar understanding appears in the German language, where the older word for piracy, *Seeraub*, can be translated literally as "sea robbery".

Loot

Piracy cannot exist without loot. Historically, pirates have been interested in taking specie, high value merchandise, captives, ships, and ship stores. The last two were kept for pirate use; unless pirates had very powerful sponsors ashore they were not able to equip themselves by visiting the local shipyard. The rest was usually intended for resale. Making loot difficult to get discourages piracy, and this can be done through either private or government activity.

Private Defences

Private parties—shippers, ship owners, mariners, and marine insurance companies—can affect the supply of loot in many ways. This self-protection has always been important because governments pay uneven attention to the problem. Until quite recently, they have usually lacked the resources to provide very much security against pirate attack, even in their chief ports.

Marine insurance may seem somewhat removed from the problem, but it has had two definite effects on the relation among the legitimate maritime community, pirates, and governments. First, by spreading the financial risks, it meant that an individual shipper or ship owner would not be bankrupted by a single pirate attack. Banded together in this way, the legitimate maritime community as a whole could bear the financial burden of a low level of piracy. This meant that the maritime community did not have to call upon what were often inefficient or uncertain government efforts all the time simply to stay in business. Obviously, it also meant that governments could ignore piracy a little longer than would otherwise have been the case. When, however, piracy attained high levels, the insurers were important in focusing government attention on the problem. Through their own records and exchange of information, insurers had the broad based information about losses from pirate attacks necessary to showing that it was indeed a serious menace. Insurers have always been important in efforts to secure government action against pirates, both indirectly through increases in rates that led shippers and ship owners to protest and directly through representations to the government.

Private individuals and firms need not rely solely on insurance. Ship owners and ship crews can take a variety of measures to discourage or fend off pirate attack. This requires learning pirates' likely tactics and taking countermeasures.

Though popular images from the eighteenth century picture pirate attack as one ship overhauling another on the high seas, most piracy has been a coastal operation. This makes sense. It is far easier for pirates to find victims if they operate in straits or other narrow areas of the sea, and to get away after committing their crime if they do not venture too far from base. The best areas for pirates are coasts which offer plenty of hiding places in the form of covers, streams, or islands to which pirates may retreat between raids to store or divide loot, recover from wounds, repair ships, and rest. The combination of narrow passages and numerous hiding places mean that the Indonesian and Malay archipelagos, the Caribbean, the English coast, and the Mediterranean have all been areas of considerable piratical activity over the centuries.

Particularly in the days of sail, when ships had less choice in the matter, knowledge of major navigation routes also suggested good locations for pirate bases, and hence spots of greatest danger. Ships going between Europe and India, for example, generally put in at Cape Town for fresh supplies. Pirates based on Madagascar could then sally forth and be fairly sure of finding victims as the merchantmen sailed between Cape Town and ports on the Indian coast. Similarly, pirates operated in the Straits of Malacca not only because of the narrow waters, but because the patterns of prevailing winds meant that trade between Asia and India went in stages. Chinese and Japanese ships came down and put into ports on Sumatra and the Malay Peninsular. Indian ships came across the Indian Ocean with the monsoon bearing cargoes of their own. While waiting for favourable winds to complete the voyage to India or the Far East, the merchants involved also took time to trade in the ports they visited. Pirates needed only to wait near the Straits of Malacca for rich prizes.

Harbour piracy and similar operations have always been common. Seventeenth century London was plagued by pirates operating in the Thames. In the early nineteenth century, a number of West African tribes made a regular practice of rowing out to attack and rob ships lying at anchor off the coast. There were few good harbours, so many captains simply dropped anchor near a settlement and lightered cargo in and out. Being at anchor made the ships a tempting target for robber bands. Harbour raids were also a common feature of piracy along the Arabian Coast, while nineteenth century pirates in south-east Asia often attacked just outside harbours or when ships had dropped anchor to trade with coastal villages.

In many instances, coastal piracy was simply the first step in the creation of a new pirate venture. Many of the pirates operating off the English coast in the seventeenth century did so only long enough to steal a large enough vessel for high seas operations (Senior, 1978, p 20). This method allowed beginning operations with a smaller initial stock of capital (ie, a smaller ship) than would otherwise be the case. Some pirates developed a method requiring even less initial investment. In 1826, a group of Malays boarded the Dutch schooner *Anna* as passengers, then attacked the crew soon after the ship had left harbour (Course, 1966, pp 86-7). Though this attack failed because the crew and passengers succeeded in killing or driving overboard all of their attackers, the method was used again. In the 1920s, there were at least three incidents a year of pirate bands boarding steamers heading upriver or out to sea from South China ports then taking over the ship at an opportune moment. (Lucie-Smith, 1978, 106-7.)

All this suggests several defensive measures. The first was avoiding pirate attack altogether. For this, speed would suffice; a merchant vessel able to outrun pirates would not be attacked. In most cases, however, speed was on the side of the pirates. Merchant ship owners wanted maximum cargo capacity. This means slower ships either because they are broader of beam or more heavily laden. The European pirates operating in the broad oceans during the late seventeenth and early eighteenth century favoured 350 ton three masted square riggers and 150 ton two masted brigantines. Once lightened by removal of most fore and after castle, they could outsail comparably sized ships. The larger ships could also be modified to carry up to twenty cannon, which gave them armament close to that carried by naval frigates. Coastal pirates favoured smaller craft, anything with a shallow draft, reasonable speed under sail, and fittings for oars when the wind failed. Pirates were also careful to maintain their speed advantage by frequent careening of the hull to remove seaweed, barnacles, and wood boring worms. Those operating in tropical waters tried to careen their hulls three times a year; the average merchant ship was careened no more than once a year and sometimes went several years between careenings.

Outrunning pirates was even more difficult in straits or poor winds. Many pirate attacks, particularly in the Caribbean and Mediterranean, came when a merchant vessel lay becalmed and the pirates took advantage of better sailing qualities or of oars to make an attack. Outrunning became much easier with the development of steam power because merchantmen no longer had to depend on the wind. Of course, this gave pirates an incentive to acquire steam vessels of their own and simply changed the terms of an old competition.

Since most merchant ships could not outrun pirates, they had to adopt other defences. Size alone was not a decisive advantage; it was a defence only when used in conjunction with other anti-pirate measures. A frigate-built merchant ship had fore and after castles which could be given stout walls, barred doors, and holes for firing muskets and small cannon. Should pirates board, the crew could retreat inside and resist for hours if the ship was not sinking. The crew of the English ship *Bauden* beat off pirates after a four hour battle using these tactics in 1686 (Botting, 1978, pp 58-59).

Most of the time, however, pirates were able to win because they had larger crews and greater numbers of cannon. Most merchant ships were designed to sail with relatively small crews to save labour costs. Even a 280 ton three masted square rigger could be sailed by a crew of 19, while pirate ships carried as much crew as could be crammed abroad—even a 100 ton sloop would commonly carry 75. Few merchant vessels carried as many cannon as they could since cannon took up space more profitably used for cargo, and their smallish crews could not work very many cannon anyway (a crew of 19 might manage three). Pirates tended to carry as many cannons as they could, often adding gunports to their ships to accommodate additional armament, and had the manpower to use them all.

Only the very largest ships carrying the most valuable cargoes took full advantage of size. The ships of the British, Dutch, French, and Portuguese East India Companies carrying goods from Asia to Europe were the largest merchantmen of their time. In the eighteenth century, a Dutch Indiaman was a 700 ton ship capable of carrying 54 cannon and 300 crew. In the first half of the eighteenth century, British Indiamen ranged from 850 to 1000 tons. By 1810, 34 of them weighed in at more than 1200 tons. By 1880, most British Indiamen were built with 30 gunports and, even when not carrying a full set of cannon, had armament comparable to that of a naval frigate or the largest and best equipped pirate vessel. They were so large and well armed that the Royal Navy occasionally pressed them into service. In 1804 a group of 16 British East India Company ships sailing together even evaded attack by a French force consisting of a 74 gun ship of the line, two frigates, and a brig. When the French force came into view the largest of the Indiamen raised the Royal Ensign. This deceived the French into thinking the group had naval escort and led them to veer off (Crowhurst, 1977, pp 215, 223, 229, and 241). Yet even with these advantages, the East India Company found it prudent to seek naval escort whenever large groups of European or well equipped Arab or Indian pirates were operating in the Indian Ocean. Against most native pirates, group sailings of Company ships usually provided sufficient protection for the large ships, though the company's smaller craft often suffered capture (Course, 1969, ch 4).

Even group sailing did not guarantee freedom from capture; cowardice or ill luck might intervene. In August 1720, the British Indiamen *Cassandra* and its smaller companion *Greenwich* were caught by pirate ships under Edward England and John Taylor off Johanna Island near Madagascar. The pirates were able to capture the *Cassandra* because the *Greenwich* first stood off and then sailed away while combat raged. Taylor then took a refurbished *Cassandra* as his own ship and, with a French pirate ship under La Buze, caught the Portuguese

Indiaman *Nossa Senhora do Cabo* at St Denis in the Mauritius island group, where it was undergoing repairs. The pirates sailed in on either side, fired broadsides, and boarded simultaneously from both sides. This attack yielded them £500,000 worth of diamonds and £375,000 worth of other merchandise (Botting, pp 63-65).

Greater size was also no defence if pirates attacked in groups. Malay pirates of the nineteenth century, like most of their Arabian counterparts in the eighteenth, operated with flotillas of small ships. In the 1830s, the Malays favoured prouws (prahaus) about 56 feet long. Though the hull was about six feet deep altogether, these craft could carry one cannon, eight swivel guns, up to 72 oarsmen (some of whom were captives), and a boarding party. Single or, more usually, in groups, the Malays were ready to attack 300 ton junks and European brigs (Course, 1966, ch 5).

Pirates operating near shore could also be combated through coordinated private efforts in and near seaports. Both the Cinque Ports of England and the Hanseatic League took on anti-piracy activities as part of their mutual association (Lucie-Smith, 1978, 39-42). In 1832 Chinese merchants resident at Singapore outfitted four ships carrying four guns and a crew of 30 well armed men to attack pirate prouws lurking just outside the port, an effort the Singapore government supplemented with two additional vessels (Course, 1966, p 87). The British East India Company was expected to combat pirates as part of its normal activity.

Government Activity

Such private activity is only a first line of defence. It has never been sufficient against the larger and better organised pirate groups that have often plagued the seas. Getting governments to act effectively has not been easy, however. Piracy is only one of many problems, and even when it is rampant governments often pay attention to other things. Then, too, effective suppression of piracy requires both substantial naval power and the will to use it effectively against pirates.

In the ancient Mediterranean piracy waned whenever a strong naval power decided to take action. The Cretan state of Minos was able to suppress piracy in the Eastern Mediterranean during the fifteenth century BC. Athenian naval power was applied effectively to the problem between the end of the Persian War in 479 BC and the beginning of the Peloponnesian War in 431 BC. However, the Peloponnesian War diverted Athenian attention to other enemies who eventually succeeded in destroying Athenian fleets. Though Athens later recovered some of its power, this left a vacuum permitting pirates to resume operations all around Greece. The task of suppressing pirates in the Eastern Mediterranean was then taken up with some success by Rhodes, which employed a combination of armed merchantmen, anti-piracy patrols, and agreements with other states for mutual aid against pirates. Yet Rhodes proved too weak for the task, especially after Rome clipped its naval power in the mid-second century BC (Ormerod, 1924, pp 110-13 and 137-39). Egypt was active against piracy in the Eastern

Mediterranean until Anthony's alliance with Cleopatra led Octavius to crush Egyptian power. Once the Roman civil wars ended and the new imperial government turned its attention to the pirates, they were suppressed in 40 years (Ormerod, 1924, chs 6 and 7). Pirates did not become a serious menace in the Mediterranean again until the fifth century AD, when the weakening of Roman power under various barbarian invasions led to a breakdown of the fleets that had provided efficient policing of the whole sea.

The importance of government action, as well as the choice of methods governments might use, are demonstrated again in Korean efforts to suppress the Wako in the fourteenth and fifteenth centuries AD. These efforts combined force, agreements with foreign governments, and conciliation of particular pirate leaders. Kings T'aejo and T'aejong of the Yi dynasty, who reigned from 1392 until 1418, greatly reduced the number of Wako raids by offering pardon to those who would desist while chasing down those who refused. At the same time, they sought to deal with the source of the problem by entering into a cooperative arrangement with the So daimyo of Tsushima. In return for giving the So a monopoly on Japanese trade with Korea, the Korean kings expected the So to control their countrymen and ensure that only legitimate traders made voyages to Korean ports (Tanaka, 1977, pp 173-4).

The same combination of clemency and force was used in many campaigns to suppress pirates. The British naval squadron detailed to clear pirates out of Madagascar in the first decade of the eighteenth century had orders to offer the pirates (except Captain Kidd) amnesty in return for future good behaviour, then to capture any who refused the amnesty (Nutting 1978, p 209). Woodes Rogers used the same combination in bringing order back to the Bahamas in 1718-21 (Botting, 1976, pp 154-56).

The campaign to clear the Caribbean of piracy in the 1820s combined diplomacy and force in a more complicated manner. In 1820, the United States government persuaded Simon Bolivar and other leaders of Latin American independence movements to restrict the number of commissions they gave to privateers and to cease issuing blank letters of marque and reprisal. At the same time, the Spanish government came to accept the independence of its former colonies, so shifted away from its earlier toleration of pirate activity. From 1823 on, the local authorities in Cuba and Puerto Rico were cooperating in anti-piracy efforts by rounding up many pirates ashore and hanging those turned over to them by US squadrons. In 1822, the US Navy Department established a separate West Indies Squadron to operate against pirates. Equipped with sailing ships of the line, ship's boats, eight small Chesapeake schooners converted for naval service, and a small paddle wheel steamer, the squadron was able to suppress piracy by sailing close to shore and sending the small boats against pirate vessels lying at anchor or run aground in their bases. The steamer also permitted the squadron to catch becalmed pirates and go up creeks where many hid (Morison, 1967, pp

81-82). By 1825, those pirates who had not been caught had quit the profession.

Lack of sufficient naval power frustrated many government efforts to suppress piracy. The various rulers along the Persian Gulf were powerless to stop the European (mainly Portuguese) freebooters of the sixteenth century (Serjeant, 1963, p 112). Though sultans of Oman wanted to cooperate in suppressing piracy during the late eighteenth and early nineteenth centuries, their efforts were inhibited by the fact that the pirates enjoyed tacit protection by the Wahabis, a strict Moslem sect from the interior often threatening the coastal states' existence (Belgrave, pp 22-38). In the early eighteenth century the Mogul Empire freely admitted its lack of naval power and relied on the British East India Company or the British navy for protection (Nutting, 1978, p 205).

Yet even a strong naval power might not be able to deal with pirates because of domestic weakness or inefficiency. Both long bedevilled English efforts to deal with piracy. Fourteenth century English kings, like many rulers later, found that it was impossible to punish pirates because sympathetic juries let them off. Frustrated with this, Edward III decided in 1361 that pirates should be tried by the Admiralty Courts under civil law rather than in the common law courts. Jealous of their authority, common law judges worked hard to limit the authority of Admiralty courts. They succeeded so well that by 1500 pirates were convicted only when they confessed, and possession of stolen goods or ships was deemed inadmissible evidence. In 1536, the government tried to deal with the problem by transferring jurisdiction to special Commissions of Oyer and Terminer appointed by the Crown. These operated under common law with a jury but were able to admit circumstantial evidence. Even this failed to stop the problem. The Commissions, too, were heavily influenced by the very local gentry who were providing pirates with harbours and markets in return for a share of the loot. In the seventeenth century pirates were extremely active in the Thames between London and the Channel. Rapid urban growth had overwhelmed the capacity of local administrative structures. There were no real police forces, and few naval units available for operation against the robbers. Widespread poverty encouraged resort to crime, and the difficulty of securing convictions on charges of receiving stolen goods only increased the already large market for pirate loot (Senior, 1978, 110-23). The situation did not improve until the Piracy Act of 1700. This put high seas piracy under the jurisdiction of special commissions appointed by the Crown, applying the rules of admiralty and civil law, and deciding by a majority without a jury (Nutting, 1978, p 209).

The port of Baltimore in the United States provided another example. Many Baltimoreans took up commissions as privateers during the War of 1812 and made a large profit. When the war ended, they simply shifted services to various Latin American republics. Though many ignored the limits of their commissions—even to the point of attacking fellow Americans—the United States government found it difficult to act against them because of their local popularity. For many years it was impossible to secure convictions in the Federal District Court at Baltimore because judges, prosecutors, and juries all sympathised with the pirates (Lewis, 1981, p 1012).

Where there was no effective central power, piracy had even freer rein. It flourished in China any time the central power was weak. The early nineteenth century pirates on the southern Chinese coast operated at a time when Imperial power was waning. Their equally daring river successors of the early twentieth century operated at a time when China lacked any effective central government because of the civil wars among regional "warlords".

Even with plenty of power and well functioning domestic institutions for suppressing pirates, governments pay uneven attention to the problem. Piracy is only one of many issues before governments, which have to distribute their time and resources across a whole range of matters. Serious efforts to suppress pirates tend, therefore, to come in bursts when complaints by nationals or friendly governments become too loud and numerous to ignore. The late seventeenth century provides one of the more striking examples. By 1690, the Mogul Empire was feeling the effects of European piracy in the Indian Ocean severely. Mogul accounts credited the Madagascar based pirates with more than 400 seizures of ships in the early 1690s, a figure modern historians consider exaggerated (eg, Nutting, 1978, p 205). The British government and the East India Company were not particularly concerned since most of the attacks fell on locally owned vessels. Their attitude changed dramatically after the uproar caused by Henry Avery's capture of the *Gunj-i-Suwaee*, a large ship owned by the Mogul Emperor himself, in the autumn of 1695. Avery and his crew stole the cargo (worth some £180,000) pillaged the ship, and raped the women aboard. The women included a number of nobles returning from a pilgrimage to Mecca. Despite all this, the ship managed to make its home port of Surat. Once news of what occurred spread, there was large scale rioting. The local agents of the East India Company were jailed and the Moguls refused to release them until the Company posted a large bond as surety for its promise to protect Indian shipping. Though the Company did maintain armed ships of its own, these were not sufficient to the task. It, in turn, asked the British government for help from the Royal Navy. Despite the fact the East India Company was in political trouble at home, the government was sufficiently concerned about protecting the Indian trade to consider rendering assistance. The British Admiralty was stirred to action in 1698 when continued pirate activity led the Mogul Emperor to declare an embargo on all European trade. This induced the British government to stop talking and actually dispatch a naval squadron to Madagascar (Nutting, 1978, pp 202-9).

In many instances, governments shifted from toleration or indifference to active suppression of pirates when legitimate trade was severely disrupted. British attention focused on the Caribbean in the 1680s and 1720s because pirates had succeeded in virtually stopping trade (Newton, 1933, ch 22; Botting, 1978, p 136). Singapore began its anti-piracy activity in the 1820s because the Chuliaks of the Coromandel Coast refused to sail southward of Penang. This meant that at least 60 fewer ships a year were coming to Singapore, a real dent in the port's revenues (Course, p 84).

At times other policy considerations reinforced efforts to suppress piracy. British efforts to suppress the pirates based in Madagascar, the Caribbean, and the North American coast in the late seventeenth and early eighteenth centuries were assisted by a number of officials in London using the issue for other purposes. The Board of Trade was particularly keen on uniting the Empire politically and economically. They and others also wanted to improve central control of colonial policy by getting the proprietary colonies established in the early seventeenth century brought under direct rule by the Crown. Both groups used the fact that the pirates causing so many difficulties in relations with the Mogul Empire came from or found markets in North America to advance their wider cause (Nutting, 1978 206-10).

Nineteenth century efforts to abolish the slave trade between Africa and the Americas, and then slavery itself in all parts of the world, also contributed to the suppression of piracy. Abolition meant cutting off the market for captives, always a major pirate commodity. Second, suppressing the slave trade led several maritime powers to establish more regular naval patrols in the southern Atlantic, the Indian Ocean, and the Caribbean. This made piracy in those areas more hazardous by increasing the likelihood of being caught.

Markets for Loot

Though pirates operate at the fringes of society, they depend on society to provide a market for their goods. While there are always people ready to deal in stolen goods, the extent to which this activity spreads depends heavily on government policy. Three aspects of policy are particularly important: a) the extent to which governments themselves sponsor sea robbery against vessels flying the flags of other states as a war measure, b) the ability of governments to maintain order and prevent corruption in their ports or roadsteads, and c) the extent to which government economic policies encourage or discourage sea robbery as an alternative to legitimate trade.

Government Sponsorship

A considerable amount of the robbery at sea committed historically was not labelled "piracy" because it was undertaken by crews acting on formal or informal government commission. Though the consequences for victims were little different than an attack by pirates, government sponsorship meant two things for the sea robbers involved. First, as commissioned agents of the state, they were not liable to punishment so long as they obeyed the limits of their commissions by confining attacks to enemy shipping. Second, prize courts or other government procedures enabled them to sell their loot legally and openly, a boon worth the usual requirement that the sponsoring government receive a share of the proceeds.

Such government commissioned sea robbery, known as privateering among European nations, was simply a method of expanding government resources for the conduct of hostilities. While the regular fleet concentrated on defeating the enemy's fleet, bombarding coastal targets, and ferrying troops across salt water, privateers were commissioned to harass, if not stop, enemy commerce by capturing any merchantmen flying the enemy flag that they could find. In Europe this practice began in the thirteenth century and ended only in the mid-nineteenth. Under other names, and with less formality than the letters of marque and reprisal used by European powers, privateering was common in other parts of the world. Until the late nineteenth century, state finance everywhere was so weak that recruiting private auxiliaries for land and sea warfare alike was common. Commerce raiding was also an easy way to garner more for one's own war chest while disrupting the enemy's finances. Nutting's description of the seventeenth century can be generalised to other eras:

> For Englishmen of the colonial era identifying a pirate was easier than defining one ... As we have seen, not all persons who committed violence on the seas were pirates. Privateers acted under lawful warrant; English buccaneers of the Caribbean, having tacit government support, were deemed neither pirates or privateers. Pirates were those whose maritime violence was unjustified by either written commission or unwritten policy. Unfortunately such categories became confused when privateers lapsed into piracy or government policy changed. Definitions notwithstanding, in the long run a pirate was "adjudged" a pirate because the law and the government's interpretation of the law said he was (1978, p 204).

Many ancient rulers, including Demetrius Poliorcetes of Macedon (reigned 294-288 BC), Mithradetes VI of Pontus (reigned 120-63 BC), and several Roman governors during the Civil Wars of the last century BC, used pirates as naval auxiliaries as the need or opportunity arose (Lucie-Smith, 1978, pp 30-33).

Piracy had long been a problem in the Baltic, but rose to new heights during the alliance between the Victalienbruder (Victualling Brothers) and the House of Mecklenberg. Charles Albert of Mecklenberg was chosen as King of Sweden in 1364, but deposed in 1389 by his cousin Margaret. This led to a civil war in which the Victalienbruder acted as Charles Albert's main naval force, keeping Stockholm supplied and capturing other ports. When Margaret won in 1397, imposed the Union of Kalmar, and pushed the Bruder out of Sweden, they reverted to piracy in the North Sea. They harried commerce from their bases in East Frisia until suppressed by the Hanseatic League in 1402 (Lucie-Smith, 1978, 43-44).

The Mediterranean was so heavily infested with maritime raiders between the sixteenth and eighteenth centuries because rulers on both sides of the Christian-Moslem divide employed or encouraged them. Moslem corsairs operated mainly out of the Barbary states of Tunis, Tripoli, and Algiers in North Africa, while Christian ones operated first out of Rhodes and then out of Malta under the protection of the Knights of St John. Initially, this struggle had all the features of regular naval warfare. After Christian fleets won the Battle of Lepanto in 1571, Moslem power was so weakened that the Barbary States had to resort to the piecemeal operations known as "corsairing" (Lucie-Smith, 1978, 56-59).

The Moslem corsairs operated more widely, raiding island and coastal areas to capture slaves, stopping ships anywhere in the Western Mediterranean, and even, in the first decades of the seventeenth century, attacking ships as far away as Iceland and the West Indies. Yet Christian corsairs caused their share of damage. Both sets of corsairs were able to operate steadily because their activity was justified in religious rather than political terms. As Earle noted:

> Normally the corsair's licence was good only in wartime. In the Mediterranean, however, human ingenuity had solved the problem of such arbitrary interruption of what was a very profitable business. For while political wars, though commonplace, were intermittent, there was one war that was eternal. And that was the Holy War (1970, p 7).

All governments concerned treated Mediterranean corsairs as state agents. When Maltese activities near Levantine shores seemed likely to disrupt growing European trade because local rulers threatened to retaliate against merchant ships for corsair attacks on Levantine vessels, Popes and Kings of France combined to force the Grand Master of the Knights of St John to prohibit corsair operations in the Eastern Mediterranean. In the eighteenth century British, French, and Dutch governments dealt with Arab corsair attacks on their merchantmen by sending fleets to bombard North African ports and then agreeing to pay the local annual tribute in return for immunity of their merchant ships from attack. When the corsairs ignored the treaty stipulations too often, as occurred periodically because revenue from tribute always fell short of the Barbary states' needs, the European fleets would reappear and reimpose the treaty.

Much of Caribbean piracy in the seventeenth century stemmed from government policy. The English tolerated the Buccaneers based at Jamaica as long as they concentrated their energies on Spanish vessels. This was simply a continuation of Queen Elizabeth I's policy of carrying on undeclared war with Spain by tolerating and sometimes helping finance the activities of the "Sea Dogs". The Buccaneers' activities also permitted defence of British settlements at a time when the Royal Navy had no ships to spare for that purpose. The French also tolerated maritime attack on enemies, though usually only during declared war and if the raiders had secured a privateer's commission. However, French authorities in the Caribbean were quite willing to grant such commissions. In the 1670s it was possible for the same captain to carry an English commission authorising attacks on Dutch shipping and a French commission against Spanish shipping (Lucie-Smith, 1978, p 173). Haiti was a French possession because French pirates had set up at the uninhabited western end of Hispaniola in 1664, and their occupation was regularised by Spanish cession of the area in the 1697 Treaty of Ryswick.

The Caribbean again became a world centre of maritime lawlessness in the first decades of the nineteenth century because of government policy. Simon Bolivar and other leaders of the Latin American struggle for independence against Spain needed naval forces quickly, and were not particular about how they were recruited. As Samuel Eliot Morison put it, "the liberated South American nations' practice of issuing letters of marque in blank to armed vessels manned by desperadoes of all nations (including the United States) was causing havoc to peaceful American merchantmen" (Morison, 1967, p 77).

At the same time, Spanish authorities in Cuba and Puerto Rico, who resented US support for the rebelling Latin Americans, winked at piratical activity. The result was quite hazardous to commerce. In December 1819, six Boston insurance companies complained to the US government that 44 US flag vessels had been captured or plundered in the Caribbean during the preceding eleven months alone (Morison, 1967, p 77).

The use of privateers and other informal naval auxiliaries was not confined to Christian and Moslem governments. Indian rulers often used Arabic, Indian, and European pirates in their local wars. The Kings of Arakan on the eastern Indian coast employed a succession of adventurers (Hall, 1970, pp 390-1). The Dutch pirate Herbert Hugo was hired at different times by a number of rulers along the Indian coast between 1659 and 1663 (Serjeant, 1963, pp 117-29). Many rulers of small states in Arabia and south-east Asia used pirates as auxiliaries and in return provided them havens (Belgrave, 1966; Course, ch 5).

Privateering helped increase piracy—that is, sea robbery not commissioned by states—in two ways. First, privateers often ignored the limits stated in their commissions and attacked neutral or even friendly shipping. Second, the end of a war usually left many armed ships and experienced crews loath to return to the low pay of ordinary merchant service. Once their commissions lapsed, many ex-privateers became pirates. This can be seen in the history of European conflicts between 1600 and 1850.

The end of formal British-Spanish hostilities in 1603 led directly to Caribbean piracy. As privateers lost their commissions, they took their ships to the West Indies and continued to attack Spanish commerce on their own. Subsequent renewals and cessations of formal hostilities had little effect on pirate activity. Periods between wars were fairly short; pirates getting into trouble could usually find a new commission before long. The Peace of Utrecht in 1713, and the end of the Napoleonic Wars in 1815 were all followed by an increase in piracy as privateers found few opportunities for legitimate employment at terms they found appealing.

Governments were aware of this relation. The Spanish were loath to commission privateers in the seventeenth century lest this weaken their trade monopoly in the Americas. They did issue commissions in 1674, during King William's War, but only for coastal craft. The British used privateers whenever they were at war in the seventeenth and eighteenth centuries even though the Admiralty was not enthusiastic about the practice. The French were more enthusiastic about using privateers. They were unable to maintain as large a fleet as the British because of weaker state finances and the great drain on them caused by having to maintain a large army. However, the French regulated privateer activity fairly rigorously. The navy worked closely with privateer squadrons. Some mariner families provided five and six generations of privateers, while the outfitting of privateers was an important industry in several ports, particularly St Malo (Lucie-Smith, 1978, p. 175). Even with these stronger state-privateer connections, though, a significant number of Frenchmen became pirates in the Caribbean and the Indian Ocean.

By 1800, government attitudes toward privateering were beginning to change. British naval officers had long felt that privateering was simply a school for indiscipline making sailors unfit for service in the Royal Navy. In 1775, Edward Rutledge of South Carolina expressed the hope, disappointed in the War of Independence, that the Continental Congress would not authorise privateering because such activity would "ruin the character and corrupt the morals of all seamen", making them "selfish, piratical, mercenary—bent wholly on plunder" (quoted in Page, 1962, 1: 217). However, between 1790 and 1820, a number of governments concluded treaties stipulating that they would only permit their nationals to accept third state privateering commissions against the shipping of the other party when they were also at war with the latter. Proposals for complete abolition of privateering began to circulate among statesmen in the 1820s. These were finally acted upon by the Great Powers in the Declaration of Paris of 1856. Though some other states did not agree until the end of the century, the example of the Great Powers had considerable influence. Of course, the Declaration was not solely an anti-piracy measure. Large navy states preferred it because it prevented smaller fleets from informally augmenting themselves in wartime. Yet,whatever the motive, an important link between government and pirates was broken.

Integrity of Law Enforcement in Ports

The vigour and honesty of law enforcement in ports and along coasts has a great effect on markets for pirate goods. Lax, corrupt, or locally minded officials often permitted pirates great liberties in the storage and sale of goods. The West Indies and North America were preferred markets for pirate goods because of the toleration shown by colonial governors and port officers. Jamaica was run by pirates between 1660 and 1681. When the American colonial council was persuaded to take serious measures against piracy, the pirates simply shifted their bases to the Bahamas and North American ports, New York was a major pirate market in the 1680s and 1690s. Nearly all the port officials had some share in trade of pirate loot. Leading merchants, including members of the Colonial Council, were involved as financial backers or suppliers of equipment (Nutting, 1978, pp 204-10). Even after being converted into a Royal Colony, which meant that the leading officials were appointed from London rather than selected locally, New York continued its pirate trade. The new Royal Governor, Colonel Benjamin Fletcher, issued privateering commissions rather freely. Most of those so commissioned ended up joining the pirates based in Madagascar who were raiding Mogul commerce (Nutting, 1978, p 205). Only with the appointment of new officials and stricter measures in ports in the 1720s was the North American connection broken. Spanish officials on Cuba and Puerto Rico let pirates sell their loot in market towns during the early 1820s, where leading merchants figured among the purchasers (Morison, 1967, 79). Singapore faced similar problems in the 1820s. Knowing that they could trade loot for money or ammunition there encouraged pirates to congregate nearby (Course, 1966, p 85).

Effect of Economic Policies

While many accounts of seventeenth and eighteenth century pirates suggest that most individuals engaged in piracy specialised in that occupation, the fact is that piracy has generally been only one of several choices available to maritime peoples. The same ships and crews could be used for legitimate trade, coastal raiding, smuggling, privateering, slave trade, or piracy depending on the balance of opportunities at any moment.

The connection between piracy and coastal raiding is particularly clear with the Wako and the North African corsairs. The Wako ranged up and down the Korean coast in the fourteenth and fifteenth centuries. Though they occasionally preyed on ships at sea, their most numerous, and spectacular, activities were raids on Korean ports and surrounding countryside (Tanaka, 1977, pp 161-62). The North African corsairs were sufficiently active in the seventeenth century to force abandonment of many coastal areas along the Mediterranean (Earle, 1970, p 67). Most south-east Asian pirates also shifted energy among piracy, coastal raiding, and the slave trade (Hall, 1970, pp 528-30; Course, 1966, ch 5).

Governmental efforts to restrict previously established legitimate trade often bred priates as well as smugglers. The clearest examples occurred in East Asia, where various Chinese Emperors sought at different times to restrict international trade to a trickle. This can be seen in Sino-Japanese relations during the early fifteenth century. The Ashikaga Shoguns Yoshimitsu (reigned 1368-94) and Yoshinori (reigned 1433-39) accepted the Chinese tributary system and regulated Japanese trade within it, hoping that the Chinese would then allow a level of trade sufficient to meet Japanese needs. However, the level of Japanese trade grew more than the Chinese liked. In 1451, they reacted by specifying tighter restrictions on the size and composition of Japanese tribute trade. The Japanese were restive and certain daimyo were willing to support pirates and raiders. The Japanese also wanted trade with Korea, in order to purchase cotton textiles and copies of Buddhist scriptures. Yet Korean kings were no more interested in foreign trade than Chinese emperors. They restricted legitimate Japanese trade to three ports (Fusan, Naeji and Empo). After a period of laxity in enforcement of regulations, the newly acceeded King Chunjong ordered strict enforcement of all regulations limiting trade. This inspired the Japanese community in the ports to join in a Korean revolt against his rule. When Chunjong succeeded in supressing the revolt, he closed off all Japanese trade for two years. In 1512 he agreed to reopen it on a more limited basis and gave the So diamyo of Tsushima a monopoly. This in effect transferred costs of enforcement to the So since thay had to protect their monopoly from other Japanese.

From this experience, Tanaka concluded that:

> It is clear that foreign trade had not yet been accepted as a normal and desirable economic activity. Neither China nor Korea looked upon it as a national asset but rather tolerated trade for political reasons. Thus Japanese traders faced unusual difficulties in establishing secure commercial opportunities and for various lengths of time trade could only be accomplished forcibly or illegally (1977, p 178).

The British learned the same lesson in the late seventeenth century. Passage of successive Navigation Acts, the first in 1651, opened markets for pirate goods in the West Indies and North America. The Acts required that British colonies sell all their exports and buy all their imports in London. This raised the price of colonial imports by increasing shipping costs and taxes, lowered the price of colonial exports by cutting the colonies off from competing markets, and drained the colonies of specie since the difference in export and import prices had to be made up by transferring gold and silver to London. All this created many opportunities for pirates, who could supply specie and lower priced manufactured goods. Therefore it is not surprising that many of the leading merchants in the West Indies and North American ports handled pirate cargoes (Nutting, 1978, pp 204-10).

The role of economic policy in encouraging piracy is also evident in Western European dealings with the Moslem corsairs during the eighteenth century. At this time, all European governments accepted some form of mercantilism. This economic doctrine assumed that international trade is a zero sum game in which one state could get richer only by taking trade away from others. The British, Dutch, and French treaties with Barbary states simply shifted corsair attacks to ships flying the flags of weaker Christian states. This consequence did not trouble the great power. At that time no government was ready to view the corsairs as a general nuisance. Rather, redirecting their activity was seen as useful in efforts to garner a greater share of the Mediterranean carrying trade. Encouraging corsairs to raid other states' ships resulted in more work for one's own since having a treaty meant fewer losses, lower insurance rates, and savings from being able to dispense with extra guns and crew for anti-corsair defence. In fact, the Moslem corsairs were so useful to British and French policy that both included in their tribute masts and other naval stores the Barbary rulers could not obtain at home (Earle, 1970, pp 265). Only with the shift to liberal, positive sum views of international trade in the late eighteenth and early nineteenth centuries did European governments come to view the corsairs as a general menace that should be eradicated.

Piracy flourished so mightily in Asia during the sixteenth century because of several governments' policies. Even before the Europeans arrived, Chinese efforts to restrict trade had encouraged piracy along the China coast and in south-east Asian waters. Piracy also existed in the Indian Ocean, where gangs from the Arabian Peninsula and the Indian coast plagued local shipping. All of this local activity got another boost from rival European efforts to gain control of trade in the seventeenth and eighteenth centuries. Both Chinese restrictions and European attempts at monopolisation disrupted prevailing patterns of trade, pushing native seamen and traders out of work. Many responded by taking up piracy against any available target, usually the native traders still operating (Hall, 1963, pp 338-39 and 528; Belgrave, 1966, p 16). The seventeenth and eighteenth century European pirates thus did not enter hitherto peaceful seas; they did, however, bring a new set of technologies that the locals adapted to their needs.

Secure Bases

Successful piracy also required possession of a secure base where the pirates may store loot, refit or repair their ships, and rest between voyages. Though a base may be anything from a large island or remote stretch of coast to a small cove on an isolated private estate, the most formidable groups of pirates had large bases. Historically, islands were preferred; pirates could run them without interference and fend off attacks more easily.

Though it is possible for private individuals and firms to sponsor attacks on pirate bases, the task of clearing out a well entrenched pirate base almost always required commitment of some government resources. Though private merchants leased the Bahamas from the Crown and promised to finance part of the costs involved, the British government contributed 100 foot soldiers and naval escort for the initial landing and taking over of the pirate harbour at Nassau (Botting, 1978, pp 139-40). The British East India Company did have navy-like forces of its own (the Bombay Marine) in the eighteenth century, but had to call on Royal Navy assistance to wipe out the largest groups of pirates. This was particularly true with the Angrian pirates of the Malabor Coast, the Coolee Rovers on the Coorla River, and the Joasmee pirates of Ras-al-Khyma.

Some pirate groups gave as good as they got in battles with government forces. In the mid seventeenth century, large numbers of pirates operated out of the Sulu archipelago. They so disrupted commerce that the Spanish governor of the Philippines tried to destroy their bases in 1751. Not only were Spanish forces beaten off, but the pirates then ravaged the Philippine coasts for the next three years. In 1756 another group of pirates, the Bugis based in Riau and Selangor, even attacked Malacca, one of the major transhipment points on the China-India trade routes (Crowhurst, 1977, p 234).

Once piracy has reached large dimensions, rooting out of pirate bases is the only way to assure its suppression. The ending of the "Golden Age" of European pirates in the early eighteenth century demonstrates just how difficult this can be. The British campaign against these pirates began with clearing Madagascar in 1698-1701. The pirates then shifted activity to the Caribbean and western Atlantic, where the British had to replace many colonial officials and dispatch squadrons of small, fast naval ships (mainly frigates and sloops) to deal with the problem. A number of pirates then shifted operations to the West African coast until the Royal Navy chased them down there.

Campaigns to eradicate piracy in south and south-east Asia proved as difficult, requiring combined efforts of local rulers and the Royal Navy over four decades. Again, bases had to be reduced and pirates chased from area to area as their activity waxed and waned. Here, operations were greatly complicated by local wars and European diplomatic rivalries (Course, 1966, chs 5 and 6; Hall, 1963, pp 530-38 and 576).

Conclusion

Piracy has been a problem for seaborne trade throughout recorded history. Having surveyed the ups and downs of historical piracy, it is possible to quantify factors which encourage it: easy availability of loot, ready markets for captives and stolen goods, and secure places for rest and resupply.

Both private and governmental activity can reduce the supply of loot. Shippers, ship owners, and ship crews can take measures on their own to avoid attack or beat it off. These measures can be anything from avoiding areas where piracy is rife to carrying and being ready to use arms.

Governments can contribute by maintaining order effectively, particularly in their ports and along their coasts. Piracy, like all other forms of crime, flourishes during times of disorder. Disorder may result from war, civil strife, local riot, or a breakdown of law enforcement institutions. Wars between naval powers not only caused disorder while the war was on, but often continued to do so afterward, particularly if a once strong fleet was weakened to the point it could no longer continue anti-piracy operations on its former scale. Both Athens and Rhodes in the ancient Mediterranean provide examples of this process.

Government policy is particularly important in determining the size and availability of markets for pirate loot. Governments have often contributed directly to creation of markets for pirate goods, particularly by allowing slave markets and privateering. Since few individuals ever put themselves on the slave market voluntarily, pirates' captives were always an important source of supply. Abolition of the slave trade and then of slavery itself thus meant closing off one of the major traditional sources of pirate revenue. Until the abolition of privateering in the late nineteenth century, government methods of pursuing naval war also contributed directly to piracy. Authorising privateers not only made certain sea robberies legitimate—and indeed heroic—actions, but contributed to piracy by equipping crews with ships and giving them experience that could be used simultaneously or later for private ends. The abolition of privateering, then, took governments out of the business of encouraging pirates. Finally, all measures to assure order in ports and to prevent corruption among port police and customs officials make selling loot more difficult.

Governments also contribute indirectly to creation of markets for pirate goods. Historically, disorder followed from the meeting of European and non-European cultures from the sixteenth century onward. Particularly in the mercantilist era when monopolisation of trade was a major goal, the better equipped Europeans created considerable disruption in previously established local trade patterns. This drove many groups which had depended on trade into piracy and encouraged traditionally piratical groups to continue their activity.

Severe restrictions on trade, whether general or limited to certain categories of goods, can also encourage piracy. Restrictions do not end trade; they usually only inspire efforts to evade them. Smuggling is one way; piracy is another. As long as people will pay for goods, smugglers and pirates have a market. Highly restrictive trade policies, whether Ming Empire limits on all foreign trade, or European mercantilist attempts to control the patterns of colonial trade, thus breed lawlessness at sea.

Governments may have good reason to make trade in particular goods, such as alcohol or narcotic drugs, illegal. Yet this analysis suggests that whenever they adopt such a policy, they must be prepared to deal with an upsurge of smuggling and piracy. Efforts to prevent or suppress this upsurge of maritime lawlessness will succeed only if two conditions are met. First, the government has to be willing and able to catch and punish pirates and other criminals. Second, government policy needs popular support. If large segments of society continue to view a particular good as legitimate despite what the law says, suppressing trade in it will be difficult—if not impossible. This can be seen by contrasting late nineteenth century attitudes towards the slave trade with American attitudes towards alcoholic beverages during Prohibition.

Finally, pirates always need bases. Any time it becomes obvious that a particular government lacks the will or the resources to take piracy very seriously, pirates will congregate in places within or near its territorial jurisdiction. England was so long a home of pirates because courts could not convict them. Jamaica became a buccaneer headquarters because the colonial governor winked at their activities. Only vigorous measures by the government can root out established pirate bases; only continued readiness to maintain order in all parts of a state's territory will prevent their reemergence.

Keeping piracy suppressed takes constant effort. A low level of piracy always exists because there are always individuals who find a life of crime more attractive, for financial or non-financial reasons, or both, than legitimate activity. When piracy is at a low level, the self-protective measures of private shippers, ship owners, ships' crews, and marine insurance companies can provide an effective first line of defence. When, however, piracy rises beyond low levels, governments must act to suppress active pirates and remove the incentives that encourage others to join them.

This paper benefited greatly from suggestions and comments by Bernhard Abrahamson, Burdick Brittin, Melvin Corant, Giulio Rontecorvo and Robert Solow.

REFERENCES

Belgrave, Sir Charles D 1966. *The Pirate Coast*. London: Bell.

Botting, Douglas. 1978. *The Pirates*. Alexandris, Va.: Time-Life Books.

Costain, Thomas B 1951. *The Magnificent Century*. Garden City, NY: Doubleday.

Course, Capt A C 1966. *Pirates of the Eastern Seas*. London: Frederick Muller, 1966.

Crowhurst, Patrick, 1977. *The Defence of British Trade, 1689-1815.* Folkestone, Eng.: William Dawson & Sons.

Earle, Peter. 1970. *Corsairs of Malta and Barbary.* Annapolis: United States Naval Institution.

Hall D G E 1970. *A History of South East Asia.* 3rd edition. New York: St Martin's Press.

Lewis, Walker. 1981. "John Quincy Adams and the Baltimore 'Pirates'". *American Bar Association Journal*, 67: 1011-14 (August 1981).

Lucie-Smith, Edward, 1978. *Outcasts of the Sea: Pirates and Piracy.* New York: Paddington Press.

Morison, Samuel Eliot. 1967. *"Old Bruin": Commodore Matthew Calbraith Perry.* Boston: Little, Brown.

Newton, Arthur P 1933. *The European Nations in the West Indies*, 1493-1688. London: A & C Black.

Nutting, P Bradley. 1978. "The Madagascar Connection: Parliament and Piracy, 1690-1701." *The American Journal of Legal History*, 22: 203-15.

Ormerod, Henry A 1924. *Piracy in the Ancient World.* Liverpool: University of Liverpool Press.

Serjeant, R B 1963. *The Portuguese off the South Arabian Coast: Hadrami Chronicles.* Oxford: Oxford University Press.

Senior, C M 1978. *A Nation of Pirates: English Piracy in its Heyday.* London: David and Charles, and New York: Crane, Russak.

Smith, Page. 1962. *John Adams.* Vol. 1: 1734-1784. Garden City, N.Y.: Doubleday & Co.

Snow, Edward Rowe. 1963. *Women of the Sea.* London: Alvin Redman.

Tanaka, Takeo (with Robert Sakai). 1977. "Japan's Relations with Overseas Countries." In John Whitney Hall and Toyoda Takeshi, eds, *Japan in the Muromachi Age*, pp 159-178. Berkeley: University of California Press.

CHAPTER 3

THE UNITED STATES AND POST-WAR PIRACY

Samuel P. Menefee

She was boarded, she was looted, she was scuttled till she sank. And the pale survivors left us by the medium of the plank.

John Masefield, "A Ballad of John Silver"[1]

In yesterday's opening statement, US Attorney Elliot Enoki told the jurors that Walker had boasted in federal prison that he had "toyed" with the Grahams and later said he had forced Mac Graham to "walk the plank".

San Francisco Chronicle, 29 May 1985[2]

We read of "classic" piracy in the works of Alexander Esquemeling and Captain Charles Johnson, Stevenson's *Treasure Island*, and in Masefield's poetry. The pirate ship, *Whydah*, foundered off Cape Cod, Lieutenant Maynard braved Blackbeard among the inlets of the Carolina coast, Baratarians aided Jackson at the Battle of New Orleans, and Captain Kidd, who hung at Execution Dock for his piracies in the Indian Ocean, had more than a few New York backers. Nonetheless, as contemporary reports of robbery at sea and in port drift in from the far points of the globe—Santos, Brazil, the coasts of West Africa, the Gulf of Thailand, the Strait of Sunda—one is tempted to ask, "What has all this to do with the United States? How do these manifestations of post-war piracy affect American interests and American lives?"

In considering this topic, it is necessary to go beyond the somewhat unsatisfactory definitions of the US Code[3] . Therefore, for the purpose of this discussion, "piracy" may be thought of in terms of "illegal acts of violence, detention or any act of depredation" directed against a ship, its passengers, or cargo, for "private ends."[4] With this as a guide, it is possible to isolate several patterns of piratical behaviour which have affected post-war American interests. These include: a) cruise ship extortion, b) scams involving government maritime targets, c) yacht jacking and related small boat violence, d) labour problems, e) immigration related violence, f) "eco-terrorism", and g) "classic" piracy.

Cruise Ship Extortion

Individuals involved in cruise ship extortion may operate either passively, by threatening an explosion unless ransom is paid, or actively, by seizing control of a vessel. Bomb threats have undoubtedly derived from the success of similar tactics against businesses and aircraft.[5] Often, it is unclear whether such menaces are for private or political ends.[6] One good example, however, is the 1973 arrest of ex-New York

Yankee, Gerry Priddy, for attempting to extort $250,000 from Princess Cruise Lines. The *Island Princess*—with 850 passengers and crew—was at sea when Priddy called cruise line offices in Los Angeles. He threatened destruction of the vessel unless the money he demanded was delivered. The Captain of the liner, then off Baja California, was notified, and a discreet search for explosives turned up only two cigarette sized packages wrapped in brown paper. The cruise continued without incident or disturbance. Meanwhile, the FBI arrested Priddy at the arranged drop site for the money. He was convicted and sentenced to nine months in prison.[7]

Active vessel takeovers have probably been inspired by the successful capture of the cruise liner, *Santa Maria*, in January 1960[8] and by popular novels and movies with similar plots.[9] One American case, which has been largely ignored, was a May 1978 plan to seize the 24,000 ton Panamanian registered liner, *Emerald Seas*, owned by Eastern Steamship Lines. The four individuals arrested—three from Chicago and one from New York City—were all unemployed and shared a common bond as readers of *Soldier of Fortune* magazine. They apparently intended to hijack the Miami based liner, sail to South America with the passengers and crew, and hold them for a $6 million ransom.

> According to information supplied at a bail hearing... the four men had completed their plans and were packing for a trip to Miami to book passage on the SS *Emerald Seas* when agents of the FBI stormed their Staten Island hide out and arrested them.
>
> In the raid, the agents reportedly seized brochures on the ship, including deck plans, and a script of a 1966 movie, "Assault on a Queen", that allegedly served as a manual for the suspects' plans to seize the *Emerald Queen* (sic) during a three day cruise from Miami to Nassau.
>
> Federal agents said... that the FBI learned of the plot ...when a fifth member of the conspiracy defected and told them of the scheme.
>
> With the aide (sic) of the defector ... a bureau agent ... went to the alleged hide out at 3 Van Duzer Street in the New Brighton section of Staten Island and managed to convince the suspects that he could supply M-16 automatic military rifles and .45 calibre pistols to be used in the takeover of the ship.
>
> Unfortunately for the aspiring hijackers, the agent was wired for sound, and they were charged with conspiracy to commit kidnapping.[10]

Scams involving Government Maritime Targets

Certainly the most notorious scam of this type was the reported attempted hijacking of the USS *Trepang*, a nuclear powered submarine armed with nuclear tipped ballistic missiles. According to G O W Mueller, "the plotters were an assortment of revolutionaries, dropouts, and adventurers, including a former crew member of the *"Trepang"*."

> The plan was simple: The terrorists were to blow up the *Trepang's* tender, thereby diverting attention from their principal object. They were then to board the *Trepang*, kill her crew, and sail her out of New London Connecticut... Once out at sea a nuclear tipped missile was to be fired at an East Coast city, and then demands were to be made. There also was a hazy plan to sell the *Trepang* to an undisclosed buyer.[11]

If this seems to read like a thriller, there could be reasons why. "North

Star Crusade", by William Katz, concerns "crew members who mutiny, take control of a nuclear submarine and launch its 15 ballistic missiles against American cities in an effort to start World War III." While acknowledging a general similarity, the author doubted that his novel had influenced this plot. "If they had read my book, they would have seen how difficult it was to seize a ship even under ideal conditions..." He concluded, "I prefer to get publicity in more conventional ways."[12]

The reaction of sailors involved with the sub was disbelief. "It's ludicrous." "Unbelievable." "It's just impossible."[13]Nor were they far from wrong. Although initially arrested and charged with "unlawfully conspiring and agreeing to steal and purloin a thing of value from the United States. To wit, the USS *Trepang*, a United States Navy Nuclear Submarine," the charge was later revised to wire fraud.[14]According to the testimony of Curtis Schmidt, a prosecution witness, Edward J Mendenhall "related to me... that the true intention, in fact, was not to steal the submarine but was to rip off the front money..." Based on the videotape of a meeting between the conspirators, a St Louis businessman, and an undercover FBI agent (who was posing as a potential buyer for the sub), Mendenhall was convicted of wire fraud and his accomplice, James W Cosgrove, pleaded guilty to a similar charge.[15]

A subsequent (1982) plot had more serious ramifications. While on patrol in the Gulf of Alaska, the Coast Guard cutter, *Boutwell*, seized a 39 foot sloop, the *Orca*, carrying 3,100 pounds of marijuana. On the return trip to Kodiak with this prize under tow, the *Boutwell* began to experience a series of mechanical breakdowns which were eventually identified as sabotage. "A 19 year old Coast Guardman was formally charged with two counts of damaging machinery, one count of damaging military property, one count of conspiracy to endanger the cutter and one count of attempting to steal the sailboat." The conspirators had planned to immobilise the *Boutwell*, put on wet suits, and abscond with the *Orca* and her cargo. Another crewman was implicated, while a third, found drowned in his wet suit, may also have been involved.[16]

Yachtjacking and related Small Boat Violence

In 1974, Congressman John M Murphy reported to the House Merchant Marine and Fisheries Committee:

Since 1971, there has been a sharp increase in the hijacking of yachts, and other pleasure craft privately owned by US nationals. Literally hundreds of crews, passengers and boats have since mid 1971 disappeared in the south-eastern Atlantic, the Gulf of Mexico, along the Pacific Coast and in Hawaii. A great percentage of the victims were actual or suspected targets of drug smugglers who have found hijacking can be accomplished easily and the owners disposed of without much fear of apprehension. (None of the owners of the missing vessels have been found and law enforcement officials assume most or all have been murdered.) The cabin cruisers are disposed of after lucrative drug hauls and only one or two hulks have been recovered after attempts to destroy them failed. With the exception of one case, the Coast Guard has yet to find survivors to help pinpoint the drug peddlers and their operations.

To understand this problem in context, it is necessary to recall that anti-drug efforts in the late 1970s broke up many of the professional importing rings, which were replaced by amateurs operating out of Central America, Mexico, and on the east and west coast of the United States.[18]

> Corresponding to these changes in the drug flow pattern was an apparent change in the incidence and type of boats lost in certain areas.
>
> In the early 1970s a possible pattern of losses involving smaller powered vessels began to emerge in the lesser Antilles Islands.
>
> Perhaps by coincidence, a significant amount of hard drugs were making their way from the South American Continent (sic) to the United States via the Lesser Antilles, the Virgin Islands and Puerto Rico.
>
> Martinique, Guadeloupe and Grenada are believed to have served as staging bases in such deliveries made in fast runs between the islands by small boats.
>
> Later as marijuana began to predominate, marine transport in the Caribbean from Jamaica, Venezuela, and Colombia, and along the Pacific west coast of Central America began to develop in earnest.
>
> Due to the long distances involved in the enterprise and the desirability of making a non stop trip the vehicle of choice was, and still is to a degree, the auxiliary powered sailing vessel.
>
> As demands grew, the cargo carrying limitations of the sailboat forced a shift toward the heavier displacement type vessel. Either a true fishing craft or the emerging luxury trawler yachts would serve; however, the cost and availability of the latter, usually outfitted with the latest in electronic navigation equipment, definitely limited its legitimate accessibility to the run of the mill amateur drug trafficker.
>
> Losses of these types of vessels also began to increase in the southern waters. In the Atlantic the drug traffic route has generally been via the Bahama Islands, east of Cuba, through the Windward Passage and into the Caribbean to Jamaica or the South American coast and return...[19]

While the evidence of hijacking in most instances was circumstantial, it was noted that most of the cases involved shared several of the following traits: a) a "long legged" or capable sea boat which could carry large cargo some distance, b) one or more hired crew whose identity was questionable, c) an owner operator known to carry a large sum of money aboard, d) a vessel outfitted for a reasonably long voyage, and e) departure of the vessel from its last port without being observed.[20] Out of some 610 instances in which American vessels vanished between 1971-74 in mysterious circumstances, in good weather, and without subsequent recovery, 44 matched this profile, and 202 missing individuals were involved.[21] Admiral Siler, Commandant of the Coast Guard, testified that he agreed with this characterisation of these cases and that he had issued a press release warning the boating public of the problem along with recommendations.[22] Yet, at an October hearing, Congressman Murphy noted that controversy had arisen over the number of yachts hijacked and individuals allegedly murdered.

> Certain members of the Coast Guard chose to play down the problem and initially attempts were made to limit the number of craft and seagoing Americans that had been eliminated by drug runners or other criminals...
>
> It would now appear that this figure is quite conservative.

Since the 28 August hearings, the committee has received mail and telephone calls from across the Nation from the surviving families or friends of persons apparently eliminated in a similar manner.

Many parents have written concerned about youthful sons or daughters who had previous histories of drug involvement, drug trafficking, and so forth, where there was strong evidence of foul play on the high seas.

A dozen or more such cases have been checked out and have been verified by the Coast Guard adding to our list which is growing daily.[23]

It is interesting to note that Congressman Biaggi's summary of Coast Guard statistics in November of 1977 yielded a potential figure of 44 boats hijacked between 1971 and 1977,[24] the same number given three years before. According to Admiral Barrow, Commander of the Coast Guard's Eighth District, four further cases had been added in the three months preceding the 1977 Hearings. "I believe that, in the summary, 48 fit the profile and there were 6 known hijackings. There are 12 listed as possible hijackings; another 9 as possible sinkings; and 21 where there was insufficient information for determination."[25] That some hesitation in dealing with such cases remained is shown by testimony before the Subcommittee:

Mr PATTERSON. You have indicated the Coast Guard has some reluctance to get into the investigative criminal activities. I think that is correct. Is that correct?

Admiral BARROW. I think the reluctance is to get involved in law enforcement efforts wherein we feel that the State is the appropriate jurisdiction. Outside of criminal investigations within the Coast Guard itself, we do not have the personnel, nor do I think we would seek personnel, to engage in investigative activities wherein the FBI has the capability and the staff and the willingness to undertake it.

Mr PATTERSON. Do you think the Coast Guard should take a greater position in terms of the investigative matters dealing with possible hijackings than they are now?

Admiral BARROW. No, Sir. I think that our efforts are well balanced now to at least do the preliminary investigation to determine whether or not we feel a different type of response is needed earlier on. But once this case has gone—we have searched for them, we can't find them, we have developed as much as we can—I do not think that we should have a further responsibility for it, insofar as active investigation is concerned. We have a perfectly appropriate Federal investigative agency to deal with that and I can't really see getting involved in that.[26]

The Coast Guard has nevertheless produced some useful research on yachtjacking. Commander Phillips, who was responsible for the trait list, has also produced a yachtjacker profile, based on available evidence; "He is a youth between 21 and 32 years old and has a narcotics record. He is rootless, but often intelligent and personable enough to charm his way onto a vessel. Once out to sea, he turns into a cold blooded killer."[27] There are still complaints. According to one reporter:

Circumstances suggest that the Coast Guard, like some ostrich, is burying its head in sand. The agency, for instance, is willing to classify as a hijack only those yacht disappearances in which the yacht was found or the captain and crew returned alive. As the murder of the crew and the scuttling of the vessel are implicit in successful yachtjacking, Coast Guard seems prepared to classify as successful crimes only those which by definition are not.[28]

Obviously, this is one form of American piracy which could still bring men to blows!

But what of the actual evidence? The following chronological discussion will be both more restrictive and more expansive than the list of 48 possible hijackings mentioned above. While not covering many of the "vanishings without trace," it *will* consider *crimes other than hijacking* if these appear to have been piratical.[29] The following examples should be considered representative rather than comprehensive in nature.

In June 1971, the *Nina*, an American yacht bound from Mexico to Tampa, Florida, was hijacked, along with its American owner and two elderly friends, by two American crew members hired in Yucatan. The hijackers, both drug users, were a father and son, aged 16 and 42, who wished to sail the vessel to Central America. This attempt was stymied when the elder hijacker suffered a heart attack during the takeover and was evacuated by Coast Guard helicopter to New Orleans.[30]

August of the same year saw another providential deliverance. The *Kamalii* was boarded and seized in Honolulu harbour by two Vietnam veterans (Mark Maynard age 27 and Kerry Bryant age 25) and an ex-Coast Guardman (Michael Melton age 24). With the real crew (Bob Weshkeit age 49, Frank Power age 47 and John Freitas age 52) bound and gagged, the boat was sailed to pick up drugs in Thailand. Two days into the Pacific, the original crew, despite their pleas, were forced overboard. The hijackers paused only to throw them a liferaft along with the dime whose "flip" had won them this concession. Although outside normal sealanes, the castaways incredibly were picked up five hours later by the Italian freighter, *Benadir*. Coast Guard headquarters in Honolulu was radioed and, after pursuit by the cutter, *Point Corwin*, the *Kamalii* was overhauled and the hijackers arrested.[31]

In July 1972, the yacht, *Whirlaway*, was stolen from her berth in San Pedro, California, by four adults and three juveniles. While their intention—to sail to a deserted island and live there—may appear to have been idealistic, six of the party had previous arrests for burglary, possession of dangerous weapons, and yacht theft, and one was AWOL from the Untied States Navy. When the Coast Guard and Los Angeles police refused to search for the vessel, its owner chartered a plane and did so himself. Eventually, the cutter, *Cape Hatteras* was despatched, manned by the Coast Guard, two FBI agents and assorted Los Angeles police. The cutter overtook and boarded the *Whirlaway*. The hijackers were disarmed of knives and a machete. They had a four day supply of food stolen from other boats. Four adults pleaded guilty to federal larceny charges and the juveniles were handed over to local authorities.[32]

Sometime in 1972, according to a communication received by the House Merchant Marine and Fisheries Committee, the captain of the yacht, *Ta'aroa* in the Caribbean, and a female member of the crew "were murdered by an ex-Nazi who operated a drug and gunrunning operation in Central America... and the yacht hijacked." The woman's body was subsequently recovered. This appears to be the same German mentioned by Mueller as "serving thirty months in a Martinique jail for commandeering two American yachts. It is known that he was involved in the hijacking of at least two other ships—all four were stolen for resale."[33]

May of 1973 saw the disappearance of the American yacht, *Imamou*, on a voyage between Cartegena, Colombia and the Mexican San Blas Islands. Of the four individuals aboard, the owner and two Frenchmen on his crew had a history of drug involvement. The vessel was reported overdue, and a search was begun. It was not until 28 January 1974 that the *Imamou* was located at Pointe-a-Pitre, Guadaloupe. Only the two Frenchmen, who claimed that the vessel had been given to them, were aboard. They were seized and held by the French authorities for possible piracy and unlawful possession of the vessel. Another source states that an investigator on the case was murdered.[34]

On 26 October the Colombian registered yacht, *Hedonist*, sailed from Marina del Rey, California, despite the fact that the live-in owner, Normal Finkbine, was believed to lack the necessary sea experience. Six months later, a drug addict and drifter (Gary Duncan age 25) confessed, after being granted immunity, that he and a fellow addict (Russell Weisse) had boarded the boat and forced Finkbine to get it underway. Finkbine had been killed at sea, his body weighted and disposed of in the San Pedro Channel. The yacht was sailed to Ventura, California, and sold for $47,500 after a bill of sale had been forged. Duncan was convicted of assault and accessory to murder, Weisse of murder and grand theft.[35]

A *possible* 1974 piracy was the July hijacking of the charter boat, *Spook*, to Havana.[36] Also mentioned in the August Hearings of the Subcommittee on Coast Guard and Navigation are a number of incidents of uncertain fate. These include the possible hijacking of the *Tecumseh* and the *Kat Mei*, both well equipped boats, which disappeared after leaving Caribbean ports with a pick-up crew.[37] The *Lupita*, leased in Mexico by two American couples, was later found stripped on San Jose Island. The pick-up crew is believed to have murdered the charterers and used the vessel for a drug run.[38] The *Perregrine* was slated for a voyage from Acapulco to Grand Cayman Island through the Panama Canal, and took on a six man crew of Southern Californians. The boat vanished without trace, but investigators determined that extra quantities of supplies had been taken on before the departure. Again, a drug connection is suspected.[39] Perhaps most curious are the cases of the *Puerto Limon* and the *Como No*. The former left Houston for Costa Rica, after known drug traffickers had been seen on board. The vessel and its crew of twelve never arrived. Nor, more surprisingly, did its marker beacons (automatically activated upon contact with water) ever broadcast a position. Federal agents view the disappearance as a drug hijacking.[40] The *Como No* was to be sailed by a retired couple from Fort Lauderdale, Florida, through the Panama Canal, to their west coast home. In Nassau, a Dutch national was hired to work the boat and upon his recommendation, a West Indian was added in Barbados. As the boat continued on to Venezuela and the Canal, letters home from the wife began to express concern and apprehension in regard to the crew. The *Como No* did not arrive. Subsequent investigation revealed that the crewmen's identities had been falsified and suggested that a drug hijack had taken place.[41]

More certain in date is the August 1974 disappearance of the ketch, *Seawind*, from its anchorage at Palmyra Island in the Pacific. While at anchorage the owners failed to make a pre-arranged radio contact with an amateur radio operator in Hilo, Hawaii. In previous contacts the couple had expressed suspicions of a couple on board the yacht *Iola*. After waiting three weeks, the ham operator reported the *Seawind* to the Coast Guard as missing. A search was under way when the *Lokahi*, a boat meeting the *Seawind's* description was spotted in Honolulu in late October by an off duty Coast Guardman who called for a boarding party. When the Coast Guard and an FBI agent approached a man jumped overboard and swam to shore. A woman attempting to row ashore, Stephanie Sterns, a convicted drug trafficker, was apprehended. The man, who was arrested later, was Buck Duane Walker (alias Roy A Allen), an escaped federal prisoner, bank robber and drug trafficker. Both were convicted of grand theft. Some years later, after Mrs Graham's bones were washed ashore, Walker was convicted of murder—he had boasted that he had shot the couple after making Mr Graham walk the plank.[42]

The Panamanian vessel, *Feisty* while anchored with engine problems off the Colombian coast, was boarded on the night of 18 July 1976 by four Spanish individuals who shot and killed Wayne Dahling and Robert Fischer, both of Miami. Two other Americans on board, Steve Johnson and Dave Kjolner, saved themselves by securing the hatches and remaining below deck. When the attackers, unable to open the hatches or lift the anchor, returned to their rowboat, to follow the anchor line, the Americans started an auxiliary engine, cut the line, and outran the rowboat. Roused by a distress call, the *Esso Lincoln* picked up Johnson and Kjolner. Initial Coast Guard and FBI investigation of this case was dropped in view of the registration of the yacht and when questions arose as to whether it had occurred in Colombian waters.[43]

The *Flying Dutchman*, owned by John Dijt of Montgomery, Alabama, vanished on a voyage from Fort Walton between 26 and 27 October 1976. Also on board were Jerry Stone, Jeannie Kelly, Ruth Easterly and possibly two others. There is evidence that a "natural" disaster may have taken place—an enquiry revealed prior generator problems and that the parties had been drinking. Nevertheless, an unauthenticated note in a bottle, found three months later on a Gulf Coast beach, read: "Flying Dutchman. Three Cubans on board. Heading due east."[44]

Certain areas received particularly bad press. Yachtsman Chuck Tobias writes:

> We'd been warned, too, about crime in Colombia by many of the boats we met at

the Panama Canal Yacht Club in Cristobal at the eastern end of the canal. They cautioned us to be especially alert during our first night into port (at Cartagena). It seemed the thieves were making it a regular practice to hit new boats on that first night—their crews tired and relaxed with a few beers in their bellies, and not yet aware of the dangers around them.

Even though we discounted much of what we heard, the warnings were to numerous to ignore.

And well it was that Tobias and his crew set a look out on board the *Mar*. Their February visit resulted in the 4.00 am shooting of two Colombian bandits, escaped murderers, who had planned to kill the crew and escape the country on the yacht.[45]

Another problem area was the Bahamas. When sailing between Chub Cay and Nassau, Richard Martin's yacht was shadowed by a workboat which only desisted when he showed them his 12 gauge shotgun.[46] Bob and Marilyn Bohemier had a similar experience with their boat, *Sunchaser*, in August of 1978—pirates attempted to board several times and were only turned back when Bohemier fired a gun over their heads.[47]

In May 1979, the five American crew members of the Panamanian freighter, *Nooderkroon*, en route from Colon, Panama to Tampico, saw a shrimp boat's distress signal. "We went to render assistance and they said they were sinking... so I invited them on board and all hell broke loose." The pirates cast the freighter's crew adrift in a rubber raft and took command of the vessel. The crew came ashore in Texas. On 15 June, the *Nooderkroon* "was found ablaze at the mouth of the Mississippi River" with "five bales of marijuana floating in the ship's flooded hold."[48]

In the same year, the *Rig-n-Tom* received a false SOS near Chub Cay in the Bahamas, a call which asked for the vessel's *own* position. Advised by someone on board (who fortunately was reading Peter Benchley's "The Island") the skipper, Mr Laburg and his wife, asked for the broadcaster's position. There was no answer, but a high powered fishing boat appeared, which chased the *Rig-n-Tom* until it reached the safety of another boat.[49]

Two other Americans, Peter Deambrogio (or Beamborough) and Michael Kallestad (or Collesta), aboard the *Snowbound* were attacked by men in four speedboats in June 1980 off Williams Island (Bahamas). The attackers demanded drugs and sank a dinghy with gunfire, but neither yachtsman was hurt.[50]

In perhaps the most notorious case of recent piracy in the Caribbean, Mr and Mrs William Kamerer (age 55 and 46) were killed aboard their boat at Pipe Cay in the Bahamas. On 31 July 1980, Illinois State Representative Henry Yourell found the *Kalia III* riddled with shotgun pellets and spattered with blood. A bloated body lay in the stern. Yourell radioed the Bahamian authorities who sent a spotter plane and, one day later, the police. They claimed that no body existed until Yourell supported his testimony with photographs and movies of the scene. The area was known for drug transfers, and, indeed, one trafficker is claimed to have boasted subsequently that he had ripped the Kamerers off.[51]

The rest of the year was almost as wild. October and November saw three other sailboat robberies by bandits in high powered boats, backed with guns.[52] In December 1980 (one source gives the date as early 1982), the *Bell-Esprit* was chased by five men in a speedboat near Nichollstown, Andros. Although claiming to be customs officers, the motorboat's occupants fired at least fifteen shots after owner Austin Evans had displayed a shotgun. The attackers fled when Evans radioed for help and a Bahamian police plane appeared overhead. One source states that fifty bullet holes were found in the hull.[53]

On 2 June 1981, four men (two of whom were American) were arrested after harassment and attempts to board two unidentified US vessels—a houseboat and a sailboat—at Honeymoon Harbour, Gun Cay, in the Bahamas. The owners of both vessels fired rifles to scare the attackers off. Bahamian officials announced that four men, including two Americans, were subsequently arrested and that marijuana, quaaludes and $35,000 in cash was seized. Five American vessels were given a US Coast Guard escort out of Bahamian waters.[54]

A more unusual case was that of *The Threesome*. Dennis Wilson, the skipper, Anthony Ventsias and Paul Cates were fishing between five and 20 miles from Andros Island, Bahamas, when they were attacked by two boatloads of pirates, each with four or five men on board, firing a variety of weapons. Wilson, who was aged 30, was killed. Strangely, the pirates left without taking or saying anything. Neither survivor could operate the boat, and they therefore called the Coast Guard by radio. The boat was located after an air search and taken to Islamorada, Florida. Ventsias and Cates claimed not to have used a rifle that was on board, but a Coast Guard spokesman later said that it was believed that the two had fired back. *The Threesome* was seized by US Customs, pending an investigation.[55]

In April 1982 retired Pan American pilot Lawrence Holloway, age 62, and his wife Audrey were on board their yacht, *Whip Ray*, off Joulter's Cay, near Andros Island. A 40 year old man and two teenage boys came aboard "asking for matches, water and food in exchange for fish they had on board ....(their dinghy)." The man took out a knife and started cleaning fish on the yacht's deck; "I was very uneasy throughout all this," said Mrs Holloway,"they were asking so many questions. They wanted to know how the boat was steered, how much fuel it used and how far it would go." Mrs Holloway went below and got a .45 calibre pistol. The men attempted to lure her on deck. Eventually, the older man grabbed Mr Holloway and put a knife to his throat. Mrs Holloway then came up the companionway and yelled, diverting the Bahamian's attention. Mr Holloway grabbed the pistol and shot him dead. When he was rushed by the teenagers, he killed them too. Judging that the American had acted in self defence, Bahamian police refused to press charges.[56]

As recently as 1987, an incident occurred in Antigua during Race Week. Jean W Solomon, co-owner of *Zoom*, reports:

> One evening, four of our crew were returning to our boat after dinner and encountered two men who had broken into the boat and were then leaving. Our captain tried calmly to negotiate the return of our stolen property of $2,000 in traveller's checks. Suddenly one of the thieves panicked, pulled out a knife and slashed out wildly, severely injuring our captain and cutting two of the other crew. Our captain had three tendons in his hand cut, two fingers slashed open and required major surgery and hospitalisation. Another crew member also had two tendons cut in his hand.
>
> While yachtsmen have in the past suffered the theft of dinghies and outboard engines (which also occurred during the week), personal violence of this sort in a vacation environment is an outrage...
>
> We have demanded the Antiguan authorities pursue and prosecute the assailants. They have given us passive assurance that they will do so; yet, to date, the local police haven't uncovered a single clue. One parliamentarian even requested that the incident be kept quiet.[57]

Labour Problems

Other quasi-piratical violence can be traced to the underlying strains of labour disputes. Take the case of the (inappropriately named) *Easy Rider*. On 12 January 1980 this vessel was anchored approximately 25 miles south-west of Morgan City, Louisiana. At this point, crew member Robin Stansbury decided that he "wanted to go home right now..." According to Captain Jack Waller Jr:

> I came upstairs and Robin had a pistol and a rifle ... He said he wanted to go to Brownsville (Texas). He said he had an emergency, which didn't make any sense since we had a radio.
>
> Waller said he weighed anchor and headed toward Brownsville. He put out a mayday call, saying he was being held at gunpoint.
>
> During the course of an all night chase by the Coast Guard, Waller and another crewman were locked in an ice locker ("It sure was cold down there"). Although firing at both a Coast Guard airplane and the pursuing cutter, *Point Noel*, Stansbury surrendered peacefully when the crew regained control. He was arrested and taken to Freeport, Texas.[58]

More widely known was the "mutiny" on board the Liberian flag tanker, mv *Ypapanti*. After having been denied entrance to the port of Philadelphia, for pollution and safety reasons, the ship anchored in international waters near Delaware Bay while the owners negotiated for admission to the port.

On 23 May, while negotiations were ongoing, the crew, in the dispute over wages and the alleged poor condition of the vessel, mutinied. The leaders of the meeting were the bosun and the chief officer. A decision was made by the Coast Guard not to intervene at that time, since no danger to navigation existed and the crew was not violent or attempting to take over total control of the vessel. The Liberian government was contacted by the United States and was asked to negotiate with the crew. Over the next several days negotiations continued ashore between the lawyers for the owners, the Liberian Government, attorneys for the mutineers and others. The results were generally negative.

> On 25 May the Coast Guard was advised by the master of the *Ypapanti* that the crew had rioted, taken hostages and was threatening to set fire to the vessel...[59]

Indeed, according to one man who managed to escape the vessel, the mutineers had threatened to fill the engine room with oil if their demands were not met. On 29 May, the Coast Guard cutter, *Alert*, arrived on the scene, and was to remain in touch with the vessel until the close of the mutiny. During the next few days, the Liberian government officially requested the United States to intervene in the situation and an assault plan was drawn up with the FBI. After a final effort at negotiation, the vessel was to be seized and the hostages rescued if no agreement had been reached. On 22 June, when the mutineers and government negotiators failed to agree on the issue of wages, the *Ypapanti* was successfully stormed by a Coast Guard-FBI team.

> The Coast Guard and the FBI were able to act together outside the territorial limits of the United States due to the unique enforcement responsibilities and capabilities of each agency. Title 14 of the US (sic) Code provides for assistance by the Coast Guard to other agencies, in this case, the State Department, and further provides the Coast Guard with the authority to request assistance from other agencies. A Memorandum of Understanding between the Coast Guard and the FBI covering incidents of this type has been in effect for a number of years. In this case the Federal Bureau of Investigation had the tactical expertise in assault and hostage rescue and the Coast Guard the expertise and experience with ships. Combined the talents and authority of the two agencies accomplished the first significant maritime hostage rescue in modern history.

And certainly, the only one recorded live for posterity on videotape.[60]

Immigration related Violence

There is also evidence of violence directed against illegal immigrants attempting to enter the United States. In August 1979, the captain of a speedboat smuggling Haitians into Florida forced 18 passengers overboard at gunpoint. A mother and five children drowned.[61] In July 1980 the crew of the *Dieu Qui Donne I* threw another refugee overboard, because they believed he was possessed by evil spirits.[62] The FBI investigated reports "that as many as 16 Haitians were murdered with machetes, knives and ropes and that dozens of others were deliberately starved to death" on board the *Jesula* in July of 1981. In commenting on the investigation, the Assistant United States Attorney in Miami noted that "although there had been other stories of murders on refugee boats from Haiti, this was the first instance in which witnesses had come forward."

> The passenger reported that the boat had left Haiti with from 200 to 250 people on board...The boat captain had demanded money for food and water and... those unable to pay had been forcibly starved and made to die of thirst. Those who objected to the way the trip was being conducted were hacked to death with machetes or killed with knives and ropes...

The investigation was hampered because of the Haitian nationality of the *Jesula*, its crew and passengers and the fact that it was unclear whether any crimes had taken place within US territorial waters.[63]

A similar jurisdictional problem complicated prosecution for an October 1981 voyage. "Two passengers on the wooden sailboat have said that two men were thrown overboard in a sacrifice ordered by a voodoo priest''; the indictment handed down by Federal grand jury, however, dealt only with charges of conspiracy and alien smuggling.[64]

Ecoterrorism

Acts of violence based on *environmental* concerns fall between the twin poles of political activism and the lucre of classic piracy. While a good case may be made that these activities are an evolving form of terrorism,[65] the possibility that they might be considered ''private acts'' calls for a short discussion of American examples. In the maritime field perhaps the most outstanding acts of ecological violence are connected with the campaign to save the whales. Thus, on 15 July 1976, FBI agents raidcd the house of a former Navy diver, and seized C-4 explosives, blasting caps, detonator cord, diving gear and a two man submarine intended for use in a attacks against Soviet and Japanese whalers.[66] Paul Watson, when he rammed the pirate whaler, *Sierra*, on 16 July 1979, was assisted in his assault by an American.[67]. While it is difficult to trace responsibility for the subsequent explosion of the *Sierra*, the *Ibsa Una*, and the *Ibsa Dos*, for which Watson's Sea Shepherd organisation claims credit, there is no denying the fact that an American, Rodney Coronado, was involved in the destruction of the Hvalur Whaling Company's whale oil processing plant,[68] and the scuttling of the *Hvalur 6* and *7* in Reykjavik harbour on 8 November 1986.[69] Watson's recent move from Vancouver to California means that now, more than ever, Sea Shepherd's activities will depend upon United States resources and support.[70] If such activities are piracy, they will be viewed as American responsibilities.

''Classic'' Piracy

There must also be some place in this discussion for those reports which drift in form the far corners of the globe, some of which *do* involve American interests. The *Joseph Lykes*, for example, a US flag cargo ship, was boarded by pirates at Guayaquil, Ecuador, on 12 April 1982, and its cargo robbed.[71] A similar fate befell its sister ship, the *James Lykes*, at Cartagena, Colombia, the next day.[72] In Lagos, Nigeria, four bandits, wielding knives and pistols, robbed the master of the *American Camellia*.[73] The ill fated *Export Challenger* was pillaged at Monrovia, Liberia,[74] and again at Lagos, where tinned milk was stolen.[75] At Takoradi, Ghana, locals filched food supplied from the US cargo ship, *Del Monte* while it lay at anchor.[76] The situation is much the same off Asia. The *Spartan*, true to her name, repulsed a pirate attack in January 1983.[77] The *Sealift Arctic*, however, was not so lucky. Seven men—one armed—boarded the ship and looted the Master's cabin, taking a closed circuit television and ... his credit cards![78] So long as America retains *any* merchant marine, American cargoes, American vessels, and American lives will be vulnerable to piratical attacks throughout the world.

Conclusion

Post-war piracy is here with us today. Its practitioners, while not as notorious as "Gentleman Stede" Bonnet or Teach, are just as deadly. Whether they be extortionists with hare brained schemes of riches, self styled scam artists, aspiring drug runners, or mere beach flotsam; whether they represent the rights of labour, of immigration, or a preserved environment; their violent excesses brand them as pirates. Many of the crimes herein described are not considered piracy. They should be. I argue this further in Chapter 13. The revision, as the US Code's reporter notes, is long overdue. It is only by addressing this problem of piracy, or violence at sea, off our coasts, that we can hope to influence farther shores. Until then, American cargoes, vessels, and lives will remain at risk.

NOTES

1. John Masefield, Salt-water Poems and Ballads 64 (1936).

2. C Castillo, SF Testimony Begins In Piracy-Murder Trial, San Francisco Chronicle, May 29, 1985, at 2, col 1.

3. In addition to recognising "piracy as defined by the law of nations," 18 USC 8 1651 (1983), Chapter 81, which deals with "Piracy and Privateering", defines "piracy" as follows:

> Whoever, being a citizen of the United States, commits any murder or robbery, or any act of hostility against the United States, or against any citizen thereof, on the high seas, under colour of any commission from any foreign prince, or state, or on pretence of authority from any person, is a pirate,...
>
> 18 USC 8 1652 (1983)
> Whoever, being a citizen or subject of any foreign state, is found and taken on the sea making war upon the United States, or cruising against the vessels, and property thereof, or of the citizens of the same, contrary to the provisions of any treaty existing between the United States and the state of which the offender is a citizen or subject, when by such treaty such acts are declared to be piracy, is a pirate,...
>
> 18 USC 8 1653 (1983)
> Whoever, being a seaman, lays violent hands upon his commander, to hinder and prevent his fighting in defence of his vessel or the goods intrusted to him, is a pirate,...
>
> 18 USC 8 1655 (1983)
> Whoever, being engaged in any piratical cruise or enterprise, or being of the crew of any piratical vessel, lands from such vessel and commits robbery on shore, is a pirate,...

This gives rise to several problems. First, although "high seas" is to be taken in its "popular and natural sense" as being *any* waters on the coast *outside* the low water mark, even if these are under a foreign jurisdiction, see *US v Ross*, 27 F Cas 899 (CCRI 1813) (No 16,196); *US v Gourlay*, 25 F Cas 1382 (CCNY 1823) (No 15,241); *US v Wilson*, 28 F Cas 718 (CCNY 1856) (No 16,731), there is an obvious *geographical* gap in coverage. Sections 1652 and 1653 deal with the "high seas," and 8 1661 with robbery on shore, but what of pillaging *within* the low water mark? See: Britannica Shipping Corp v Globe & Rutgers Fire Insurance Co, 138 Misc 38, 244 NYS 720 (1930) (theft from tug moored to harbour pier was not piracy as it did not take place on the high seas). Second, there are a number of "occupational" gaps in coverage which may best be illustrated by a series of hypotheticals. Should not American citizens engaging in piratical acts *without* colour of commission or any practice of authority be considered pirates? How about foreigners whose states have *no* treaty provisions with the United States concerning piracy? How about the seaman who interferes with his *crew* rather than his commander? And why should robbery on shore be classified as piracy, and murder *not*? One is therefore inclined to agree with the Reviser that:

> The law of piracy is deemed to require a fundamental reconsideration and complete restatement, perhaps resulting in drastic changes by way of modification and expansion. ... It is recommended... that at some opportune time in the near future, the subject of piracy be entirely reconsidered and the law bearing on it modified and restated in accordance with the needs of the times.
>
> 18 USC ch 81 (1983) (Reviser's Note).

4. This is *generally* based on the definition of "piracy" in Art 15 of the Convention on the High Seas, Geneva, April 29, 1958, 13 UST 2313, TIAS No 5200, 450 UNTS 82. It *differs* from the Convention definition, however, in not limiting the actors to the crew or passengers of a private ship or aircraft (or a mutinous warship, government ship, or government aircraft), mandating that the activity must take place on the high seas (more restrictively defined than in the USC) or outside the jurisdiction of any state, or requiring the presence of *two* vessels or aircraft.

5. See Edward F Mickolus, Transnational Terrorism: a Chronology of Events, 1968-1979 (1980), esp 225 (Oct 11, 1970: Threats to destroy local buildings in Oslo, Norway, unless money paid), 265 (May 26, 1971: Demand for money in exchange for directions on how to dismantle a bomb on a Qantas airliner in flight. May 27, 1971: similar demand), 272 (July 16, 1971: Demand for money in exchange for information to deactivate a bomb on a transatlantic flight), 272 (July 17, 1971: Demand for money in exchange for information on a bomb on Aer Lingus), 273 (July 23, 1971: Demand for money in return for information on a bomb on Ansett Airlines (Australiai), 273 (July 28, 1971: Demand for money for information on a bomb on Air Canada flight), 273 (July 28, 1971: Demand for money for information on a bomb on a TWA transatlantic flight), 277 (Sept 8, 1971: Demand for money for information on a bomb on a CP Air flight), 298 (Jan 28, 1972: Threat to bomb BOAC flight unless ransom paid), 299 (Feb 4, 1972: Threat to blow up planes in Vancouver unless ransom paid), 303 (March 7, 1972: Threat to blow up four TWA planes unless ransom paid), 304 (March 11-12, 1972: Threat to blow up Pan Am's New York facilities unless ransom paid), 304 (March 13, 1973; Threat to blow up Salt Lake City airline facilities unless ransom paid), 327 (June 16, 1972: Joseph Anthony Landisi threatened in a series of letters to blow up the planes and New York terminals of American Airlines, and to damage the *Queen Elizabeth II*, unless he was paid $300,000), 329 (June 26, 1972: Threat to blow up Ozark Airlines plane unless ransom paid), 337 (Aug 30, 1972: Threat to bomb Milwaukee airport unless money paid), 348 (Sept 20, 1972: Threat to bomb Lufthansa Airlines plane unless ransom paid), 350 (Sept 28, 1972: Threat to bomb Delta Airlines aircraft unless ransom paid), 358 (Nov 6, 1972: JAL hijacker threatened to blow up the plane unless ransom paid), 369 (Jan 4, 1973: Threat bomb would explode on TWA flight unless ransom paid).

6. See Brian M Jenkins *et al*, A Chronology of Terrorist Attacks and other Criminal Actions against Maritime Targets in E Ellen, Violence at Sea 63 (1987), esp 83 (1982 bomb threat against *Queen Elizabeth II* in New York Harbour), 84 (1982 bomb threats against Canadian passenger ferry *Princess Marguerite* in Puget Sound; G O W Mueller and Freda Adler, Outlaws of the Ocean 165 (1985) (Bomb threat in Jan 1983 to cruise liner docked in Miami, Florida). For bomb threats of a *political* nature against other vessels see Brian Jenkins *et al, supra* at 79 (1979 Threat against HMS *Hermes* at Fort Lauderdale, Florida, resulted in a brick being found labelled "Bomb by IRA"), 85 (1983 bomb threat against HMS *Hermes* in New York Harbour).

7. See Brian M, Jenkins *et al, supra* note 6, at 71-72.

8. See Samuel P Menefee, Terrorism at Sea: The Historical Development of an International Legal Response, in E Ellen, *supra* note 6, at 198-200, 210-18, Samuel P Menefee, Piracy, Terrorism and the Insurgent Passenger: A Historical and Legal Perspective, in N Ronzitti, The *Achille Lauro* and International Law (forthcoming); Warren Rogers Jr, The Floating Revolution (1962); Beth Bay, Passage Perilous (1962); and H Galvao, Santa Maria: My Crusade for Portugal (1961).

9. Including Ernest Lehman, The French Atlantic Affair (1977) (American adventurers

seize a ship and wire it to explode unless $35 million in gold is delivered to them), and Jack Finney, Assault on a Queen (1959) (Adventurers board and rob the *Queen Mary*, escaping with $1 million stolen from the ship's bank). See also G O W Mueller and Freda Adler, *supra* note 6, at 162; Four Held in Plot to Hijack a Cruise Ship and Hold It for $6 Million Ransom, The New York Times, May 2, 1978, at 13 col 4. For a discussion of the influences of fiction on maritime terrorism, see Samuel P Menefee, Maritime Terror in Europe and the Mediterranean 12 Mar Pol'y.... (forthcoming).

10. Charged were Robin Ernest Hayes (50; New York City), Jacob Raphael Goldstein (47; Chicago), Robert Wayne Prickett (20; Chicago), and Richard Nelson Reilly (18; Chicago). The defector was identified as Paschal Cascio (Chicago). See Four Held, *supra* note 9, at 13; Four accused of plotting to hijack Luxury Liner, Chicago Tribune, May 2, 1978, at 1, 14; A Plot to Hijack Ship and 800 Passengers, San Francisco Chronicle, May 2, 1978, at 2.

11. G O W Mueller and Freda Adler, *supra* note 6, at 172-73. See also Brian M Jenkins *et al, supra* note 6, at 78.

12. The New York Times, October 12, 1978, at 66 (strike edition).

13. *Id*, October 9, 1971, at 39 (strike edition). In another article the New York Times noted that the *Trepang* "although nuclear-powered, did not carry nuclear warhead missiles. The sub is armed with nuclear-tipped anti-submarine weapons which would be ineffective against land targets." *Id*, October 12, 1978, at 66 (strike edition).

14. See G O W Mueller and Freda Adler, *supra* note 6, at 172-73; Charges Are Changed for two men In Alleged Submarine Theft Plot, The New York Times, December 7, 1978, at 15, col 1 (noting that there was no difference in penalties between the two charges).

15. Salesman Is Guilty in Hijack Plot. The New York Times, December 15, 1978, at 20, cols 3-4. Mendenhall (24) was an insurance agent from Rochester, New York, Schmidt (22) an unemployed carpet cleaner from Kansas City, Kansas, while Cosgrove (26), from Geneva, New York, had served as a clerk-typist aboard the *Trepang*. St Louis businessman Charles Rosene had tipped off the FBI about the plot. Charges against Schmidt were dropped, presumably in return for his co-operation. See The New York Times, October 9, 1978, at 39 (strike edition); *id*, October 20, 1978, at 1 (strike edition); Salesman is Guilty, *supra*; Man Pleads Guilty in "Plot" To Steal a Submarine, The New York Times, December 19, 1978, at A-18, col 6. See also Two in Submarine - Theft Plot Will Undergo Mental Tests. The New York Times, December 23, 1978, at 7, col 5 (listing Mendenhall as of North St Louis County and Cosgrove as of Ovid, NY).

16. See G O W Mueller and Freda Adler, *supra* note 6, at 184; Brian M Jenkins *et al, supra* note 6, at 84; Chronology of Attacks - Gulf War and Terrorist, in E Ellen, *supra* note 6, at 242.

17. Report of Congressman John M Murphy to the House Merchant Marine and Fisheries Committee on the Hijacking of US Pleasure Yachts and Cabin Cruisers, August 27, 1974, in Coast Guard Miscellaneous - Part 2: Boating Safety: Hearings on HR 12848, 13259, and 15851. Before the subcomm. on Coast Guard and Navigation of the House Comm. on Merchant Marine and Fisheries, 93d Cong., 2d Sess. 156-57 (1978) (HR No 43) (hereinafter "1974 Hearings")

18. Testimony of Commander M K Phillips (US Coast Guard), in 1974 Hearings, *supra* note 17, at 166.

19. *Id* at 167.

20. See *id* at 168.

21. This was out of a total about 200,000 boats which had disappeared during this period. Alex Finer, Yachtjack! in Sunday Times Magazine (London), November 27, 1977, 40 at 42. See also Statement of Commander M K Phillips, in 1974 Hearings, *supra* note 17, at 166-68.

22. Exchange between Congressman Murphy and Admiral Siler, in 1974 Hearings, *supra* note 17, at 168, See also Appendix 13: Proposed Yachtjacking Countermeasures From a

Document Proposed by the Senior Deputy Officer, Coast Guard Headquarters Operations Center.

23. Statement of Congressman Murphy, in 1974 Hearings, *supra* note 17, at 205.

24. Statement of Congressman Mario Biaggi, in Yacht Hijacking and Drug Smuggling: Hearings Before the Subcomm. on Coast Guard and Navigation of the House Comm. on Merchant Marine and Fisheries 95th Cong. 1st Sess. 2 (1978). (hereinafter "1977 Hearings"2) Congressman Biaggi goes on to note:"When all unresolved "SAR" (Search and Rescue) cases were further studied, it was determined that the outside figure of potential hijackings would be significantly greater." *Id*

25. Testimony of Rear Admiral Winford W Barrow, in 1977 Hearings, *supra* note 24, at 34-35. See also Alex Finer, *supra* note 21, at 45.

26. Exchange of Congressman Patterson and Rear Admiral Barrow, in 1977 Hearings, *supra* note 24, at 35-38. See also G O W Mueller and Freda Adler, *supra* note 6, at 133 (speaking of the Coast Guard's "summary of cases in which evidence of hijacking or an actual hijacking existed.")

27. G O W Mueller and Freda Adler, *supra* note 6, at 140.

28. Alex Finer, *supra* note 21, at 45.

29. For a fuller listing of instances of possible yacht piracy, see Appendix 12: Some instances of Possible Yacht Piracy Involving United States Vessels and Nationals.

30. See G O W Mueller and Freda Adler, *supra* note 6, at 134 (identified as "Case 2" in the Coast Guard Summary); testimony of Admiral Siler in 1974 Hearings, *supra* note 17, at 169 (identifying the hijackers as drug users).

31. See G O W Mueller and Freda Adler, *supra* note 6, at 134 (identified as "Case 3" in the Coast Guard Summary); Report of Congressman John M Murphy, in 1974 Hearings, *supra* note 17, at 159-60 (identifying the vessel as the *Kamilii* and noting that the *Esprit*, a vessel in the same race, was hijacked from Honolulu, Hawaii, by three other men); Why a Big Surge in "Boatnapping", 84 US News and World Report, February 7, 1978, at 41; Alex Finer, *supra* note 21, at 42. Sunday Times Magazine November 27 1977 at 42.

32. Herbert L Markow, Small Boat Law 2/14-15 (1977), (citing Coast Guard Boating Safety Newsletter, October, 1973, at 3).

33. See Statement of Mr Murphy, October 11, 1974, in 1974 Hearings, *supra* note 17, at 205-06; G O W Mueller and Freda Adler, *supra* note 6, at 140.

34. G O W Mueller and Freda Adler,*supra* note 6, at 133-34 (identified as "Case 1" in the Coast Guard Summary and as FBI case no 45-1599); Report of Congressman John M Murphy, in 1974 Hearings, *supra*note 17, at 160-61; Why a Big Surge in "Boatnapping", *supra* note 31.

35. G O W Mueller and Freda Adler, *supra* note 6, at 135 (identified as "Case 4" in the Coast Guard Summary).

36. It is unclear whether the motivation for this act was political. See *id*, at 135 (identified as "Case 5" in the Coast Guard Summary); United States v McRary, 665 F 2d 674 (5th Cir, 1982); M Leigh, Judicial Decision: Federal Kidnapping Act - foreign commerce jurisdiction - high seas jurisdiction, 76 AM J INT'L L 619 (1982).

37. Report of Congressman John M Murphy, in 1974 Hearings, at 160.

38. *Id*, at 159

39. *Id*

40. *Id*, at 160.

41. *Id*

42. See G O W Mueller and Freda Adler, *supra* note 6, at 135-36 (identified as "Case 6" in the Coast Guard Summary); C Castillo, *supra* note 2; G E Swan, Conviction in South Sea Murder, San Francisco Chronicle, June 12, 1985, at 3; W Carlsen, Life Prison Sentence For South Seas Murder, June 29, 1985, at 12; Roger Villar, Piracy Today 150 (1985) (incorrectly stating that yacht found abandoned at atoll).

43. See Two Survivors Tell of Piracy Raid on Boat, The Times-Picayune, July 20, 1976, at I/2; Pirates Probe Blocked, The Times- Picayune, July 22, 1976, at III/3; US Dropping Probe of "Pirate Raid" on Boat, the Times-Picayune, July 23, 1976, at II/2 (giving the names "Daltrey" and "Fisher"); exchange between Congressman Patterson and Mr Coulton, in 1977 Hearings, *supra* note 24, at 68-69.

44. See 1977 Hearings, *supra* note 24, at 12-14; Average Yachtsman A "Sitting Duck": Fear Curtails Boating in Bahamas, Los Angeles Times, December 5, 1980, at X/9.

45. C Tobias, Intrigue on the Spanish Main: 1: High Noon in Columbia, in Motor Boating & Sailing March, 1979, at 62.

46. Letter from Richard Morton, Mailboat, in Motor Boating & Sailing, December, 1979, at 4.

47. B Lauren, Close Encounter on the Bahama Banks, in Motor Boating & Sailing, September, 1979, at 47.

48. Five Sailors Seized by Pirates Told Survival was Chancy, The New York Times, June 22, 1979, at A-10, col 6

49. Drug and Death on the High Seas, 116 Time, September 22, 1980, at 24.

50. See C Hiassen, Bahama pleasure boaters pack pistols, Chicago Tribune, July 5, 1981 (giving the yachtsmens' names as "Michael Kallestad" and "Peter Deanbrogio"); Roger Villar, *supra* note 42, at 149 (giving their names as "Michael Collesta" and "Peter Beamborough").

51. See A Knott, Legislator sails into pirate puzzle, Chicago Tribune, August 3, 1980, at I/1; B Price. Legislator won't buy ruling on "death boat", Chicago Tribune, August 11, 1980, at I/5; W Robbins, Legislator Tells of a Bahamian Sea Mystery, The New York Times, August 30, 1980, at 6; Drugs and Death, *supra* note 49; Roger Villar, *supra*note 42, at 147, 149 (treated as seperate incidents); D Bradley, The Out Islands, Chicago-Style, in Motor Boat & Sailing, December, 1980, at 10; Hijack Forum, in Motor Boat & Sailing, April, 1981, at 54 (Yourell's response to Bradley); Average Yachtsman, *supra* note 44.

52. See C Hiassen, *supra* note 50; Roger Villar, *supra* note 42, at 148 (giving the date as December).

53. See C Hiassen, *supra* note 50; Roger Villar, *supra* note 42, at 148 (giving the yacht's name as *Belle Esprit*, and stating that five speedboats were involved in the attack).

54. C Hiassen, *supra* note 50.

55. Pirates blamed for Shooting Death of Boat Captain, The Times-Picayune, October 27, 1981, at I/3.

56. See Self-defense Ruling in three Yacht Deaths, Chicago Tribune, April 16, 1982, at I/16; Bahamian Police clear Boat Captain of killing three Pirates, The Times-Picayune/The Staes-Item, April 16, 1982, at I/3; R Marston, Yachtsman Cleared in Bahamian Shooting, in 151 Yachting, No 6, June 1982, at 24.

57. See Letter of Jean W Solomon in 21 Sailing, No 12, August, 1987; L Gosselin, Reality in Paradise, in 162 Yachting, No 1, July, 1987, at 36.

58. See G O W Mueller and Freda Adler, *supra* note 6, at 136-7 (identified as "Case 7" in the Coast Guard Summary); Shrimp Boat Hijacking: Hostages on Ice, San Francisco Chronicle, January 14, 1980, at 2.

59. Transcription of narrative of videotape of the seizure of the mv *Ypapanti* (1) (obtained from International Maritime Bureau).

60. *Id*, esp (15)-(16). See also After Action Report; mv *Ypapanti* (LI) Labour Dispute and Restoration of Control to the Master, May-June 1982.

61. G O W Mueller and Freda Adler, *supra* note 6, at 240.

62. *Id* at 239-40.

63. J Thomas, 16 Murders and Starvation Reported on Haitians' Boat in The New York Times, October 16, 1981, at A-16. See also G O W Mueller and Freda Adler, *supra* note 6, at 239.

64. 10 From Ship Indicted in Voodoo Killings, The New York Times, July 11, 1982, at 16, col 6.

65. See Samuel P Menefee, *supra* note 9; Samuel P Menefee, "Green Terror at Sea; The Unrecognised Threat of Marine Ecological Terrorism," *ms* (hereafter "Green Terror").

66. See Samuel P Menefee, Green Terror, *supra* note 65; B Richards, Whale War, The Washington Post, September 5, 1978, at A-1; T Matthews and R Sympson, A Whale of a Tale, 92 Newsweek 35 (Sept 18, 1978).

67. See Samuel P Menefee, *supra* note 9; Samuel P Menefee, Green Terror, *supra* note 65; David Day, The Whale War 53-57 (1978); Paul Watson, Sea Shepherd: My Fight for Whales and Seals 207-36 (1982).

68. See Samuel P Menefee, *supra* note 9; Samuel P Menefee, Green Terror, *supra* note 65, David Day, *supra note 67, at 57-59, 62-62; Paul Watson, supra* note 67, at 246, 249-50.

69. See Samuel P Menefee, *supra* note 9; Samuel P Menefee, Green Terror, *supra* note 65; David Day, *supra* note 67, at 132-24.

70. B Stumbo, Sea Shepherd Society; Modern-Day Pirates Fight the Whalers, Los Angeles Times, June 13, 1987, I-1.

71. Roger Villar, *supra* note 42, at 142-3.

72. *Id*, at 143.

73. August 3, 1982, *Id*, at 112.

74. *Id*, at 115, 116 (August 31, 1983).

75. January 17, 1983, *Id*, at 115.

76. February, 1986, *Id*.

77. *Id*, at 125.

78. January 10, 1983, *Id*, at 125-26.

Part 2. An Aspect of Piracy – The Boat People

CHAPTER 4

THE GULF OF THAILAND

Pascal Boulanger

(Translated from the French by I R Hyslop)

The Facts

During the last ten years the Gulf of Thailand has acquired a sad reputation, not for attacks by pirates on merchant ships although there have been several incidents of this type around Bangkok, but rather because of the nightmares suffered by refugees. Since the end of the Vietnam war hundreds of thousands of people have tried to flee from their own country and to reach Thailand or Malaysia by crossing the Gulf of Thailand. Unfortunately, once they are at sea, their hopes of freedom quickly disappear and few of them complete the crossing without harm. Left to themselves in fragile small boats, many have died—drowned, starved or killed by pirates with unprecedented cruelty.

Everyone has heard of these boat people. The newspapers took an interest in them for a year or two and then turned away as if the suffering of these unfortunate people had gone out of fashion. However these refugees are still today being massacred by unscrupulous pirates.

Fortunately there are people prepared to devote their lives to attempting to save them from death. There are vessels chartered by bodies such as the Red Cross and other private organisations. A number of governments participate in an important programme to control piracy in the Gulf of Thailand, examined in detail later in Part 2.

An and Linh

The account which I reproduce in large part below was obtained by Al Santolli, a Bangkok journalist, and was sent to me by the United Nations High Commission for Refugees (UNHCR). It was published in March 1985 in the book "The Boat People Flee to Death or Worse in the Pirate Sea".[1]

On 26 September 1983 two Vietnamese girls, Duon Thi An and Kim Thi Linh, were found on a Thai beach close to the Malaysian border. After a week's medical treatment and having been interviewed by the police, they were placed in Songkhla camp where Al Santolli met them. An's and Linh's parents, Vietnamese farmers, had arranged their escape by paying four ounces of gold (the equivalent of US$ 1000) to an entrepreneur who organised departures of this type. He provided a boat, paid off the local police, and guaranteed a direct arrival in Malaysia, avoiding the dangerous Thai waters.

To obtain an idea of what this sum of $1000 represents, it is necessary to understand that the average monthly income of a Vietnamese farmer is between $10 and $15.

On 26 August 1983 a ten metre long boat left the Mekong Delta under sail, carrying 45 passengers and steered by a schoolteacher who had not the slightest experience of the sea. All prayed to their ancestors that they would not meet a coastal patrol, which would have sunk them without further formality.

By sunset they had left the coast. After two days they had exhausted their supplies of food and drinking water. The sun was burning their skin and was particularly affecting the children who were huddled together on the deck.

On the morning of the third day they were surrounded by seven trawlers and attacked by seamen with hammers, knives and steel bars. These seamen ripped open their luggage in the hope of finding gold and savagely beat anyone who tried to resist them. Finally they left the boat adrift after abducting Linh, her sister and three other girls.

They were beaten until they submitted to rape. One of the abducted girls, a young mother of 20, who could not tolerate being separated from her baby, tried to escape by diving into the sea. The pirates then separated her from the others and she was never seen again.

During ten days of continuous rape and humiliation they resisted the temptation to commit suicide because, according to Vietnamese tradition, a child must not die before his or her parents.

After ten days another group of boats appeared and An and Linh were offered to them. For three days they were raped night and day. Then they were returned to the original boat and the torment continued for a further week.

One night, after 20 days of captivity, the pirates threw them into the sea with a plastic drum as their only means of support.

Even though they did not know how to swim, they managed to keep their heads above water. At dawn there was still no land in sight. There were boats but they were too far away to hear their cries.

In the middle of the afternoon, after being thrown about for fifteen hours by waves which constantly threatened to engulf them, they were rescued by a kindly fisherman who looked after them and fed them.

A week later the boat came into sight of the Thai Coast and the fisherman landed the two girls on Songkhla beach on 26 April 1983, one month after their departure from Vietnam.

Lien

Lien, 21 years, and her two brothers left a Vietnam beach on the evening of 9 August 1982 on board a wooden motor boat. There were 79 people—35 men, 21 women and 23 children—on board the boat which was 13 metres long and 3.5 metres wide. They took some stocks of rice and water but these were very quickly exhausted and their only resource was then the rain water which they were able to collect.

The first pirate attack took place on 19 August, around 7.00 am. The refugees' motor had long ceased to function after running out of fuel. They saw the pirates a long way off. They signalled and, in contrast to other boats which had ignored them, the pirates changed course towards them. Around ten men armed with knives and hammers boarded the refugee boat and searched everywhere. They threatened the travellers and took everything they found. They also forced several of the men and women to remove all their clothing so that they could search it better.

Several days later the refugees were approached by a fishing boat. The three men on board seemed honest and offered to sell them food. The boat people pooled their possessions to find the price required. But as soon as they had been paid the fishermen started their engine and left, handing nothing over.

The second pirate attack took place on 1 September. Twelve men, two armed with guns, searched the boat for half an hour and raped Lien and another 18 year old girl.

They were finally picked up on 5 September by a Panamanian cargo vessel, the *Catamac II*, which landed them at Bangkok from where they were able to reach the refugee camp of Ponat Nikhon. Altogether, they saw fifty commercial boats, none of which stopped.[2]

The Island of Koh Kra

Unfortunately there is no lack of evidence. For example, some people have described how they had their jaws fractured by blows from clubs, because pirates wanted their gold teeth; others how they survived by eating a mixture of rice and human flesh and by drinking blood.

The wreckage and bodies washed up on the shores of several South East Asian countries give an indication of the disaster. The stories rival each other in horror, and it would not be correct to dwell too long on the suffering of these unfortunate people. Nevertheless, this account would not be complete without mention of the island of Koh Kra.

Acting on information from an oil company helicopter pilot, Theodore Schweitzer, a UNHCR representative at Songkhla transit camp, went several times, both alone and accompanied by Thai police, to Koh Kra. Between 1980 and 1982 he saved 1,250 people from certain death.

This island had been transformed by Thai pirates into an immense and repugnant brothel. On one flight Schweitzer counted 47 boats anchored in a bay. Bodies were floating around them. Some bodies were hanging and others, mutilated, lay on the beach. As pirates approached the island, the refugees tried to hide themselves as best they could. However the pirates set fire to the long grass to force them out. One woman preferred to endure the flames with stoicism, rather than give herself up to the pirates.

The Fate of the Refugees

Hundreds of victims have been killed, wounded and beaten. Others who have lost hope and feared a further attack have committed suicide by throwing themselves overboard. Many refugee families have been torn apart. however, those worst affected by the attacks have certainly been the women and children.

Children who have been abused or terrorised by armed and savage pirates are likely to suffer the effects for a long time. A child does not forget the rape and abduction of his or her mother.

Although Si Trasn, a little eight year old refugee in Songkhla camp has only a vague recollection of being attacked, she is haunted by it and it will always inhibit her personality. When the pirates boarded the boat she huddled up to her mother, closed her eyes and heard only screams. Then a pirate snatched her from her mother and she never saw her again.

Even young girls of six years have been sexually attacked. The distress can be deduced by this remark from an eleven year old girl: "It's as if they've stolen my childhood".[3] And there are psychological consequences. Tu Khuong Schroeder-Dao, a psychologist, has published a study on rape victims amongst the refugees on the island of Pulang Bidong.[4] The extract which I reproduce below is from an article which appeared in the journal *Refugees*.[5]

> *A priori*, rape is looked upon as an act of fate, and a certain resignation can be observed in confrontation with this "unavoidable accident"—a lesser evil in comparison with the risk of death which the boat people undergo when they are attacked by pirates. Then too, a woman will find it easier to "sacrifice herself to rape", if one may so express it, as a scapegoat in order to save other members of her family who are fleeing. She also knows that if she offers resistance, cries or struggles, she risks being thrown into the sea or being killed. In this case, her system of self-defence during a rape may consist of a loss of consciousness or memory which makes her fail to recall the event. The strongest urge, both conscious and instinctive, is to survive, even at such a high price. Nevertheless, this causes the woman to enter immediately into contradiction with the Sino-Vietnamese value system, which traditionally demands that she protect her body and her virginity. Hence rape destroys her socio-cultural heritage, debases her, sets her apart and besmutches the honour of her family. A significant fact is that the victim will never speak about it to her relatives back in Vietnam. In one way or another, the woman feels herself to be cast out of society. A traveller without baggage and lacking any material possessions, she is thus deprived of her cultural identity.
>
> Since the rape takes place before the eyes of the other boat people, the victim feels herself to be rejected by those who have failed to intercede and were unable to do so. The fact is that the boat people never take proper measures to prevent rape, nor do they carry arms on board. One rather useless precaution which they take is to prepare a mixture of saffron and motor oil, which the women smear on their faces, hoping thereby to appear ugly and repulse the pirates.
>
> An additional torture for the woman is that she suffers from having witnessed the helplessness of her husband, fiance or others close to her. The latter are made to feel guilty and humiliated by not having been able to protect her.
>
> Nevertheless, there is one ambiguity in this respect which should be mentioned. To a certain extent the woman is used to appease the pirates, who go so far in their cruelty as purposely to transform witnesses into accomplices. Moreover, a certain amount of bargaining may take place. A young girl may be offered in exchange for the liberty of the group of boat people.
>
> Rape is also felt to be an insult to the husband, whose authority has been shaken. The future life of the couple will be disturbed and previously existing conflicts may again come

to the surface. And if the husband maintains that it is an accident which is beyond the control of either of them—that they must "forget everything and begin anew"—this implies to some extent an accusation against his wife, as if she had committed a sin.

Left alone and in deep distress, a woman who has been raped finds that her whole world of human relationships has been upset. This includes her husband, her fiance, her social group and her society, by which she feels herself to have been condemned. Rape may even have an impact on the children which she brings into the world.

Other after-effects include nightmares, insomnia, phobias concerning men resembling the aggressor in appearance. Finally, her suffering may be masked by a frantic desire for revenge, pathological aggressiveness or simple apathy of the "I've got nothing to lose" type, which may lead her into prostitution or even to a kind of voluntary infantilism.

Although some women try to take advantage of their ordeal by deciding to be counted among the special cases for which the formalities involved in finding a country of asylum are facilitated and accelerated, most of them convince themselves that they are no longer entitled to a normal life and a family.

The Motives of the Pirates

The pirates who attack the boat people are, for the most part, Thai fishermen who see piracy as no more than a solution to their financial problems. They do not have an easy life. The price of fuel has risen considerably; and the Gulf of Thailand is crowded—especially since new nets with fine mesh have been taken into use, and Malaysia and Burma have extended their fishing zone to 200 miles.

The Thais have a traditional hatred of the Vietnamese. Pascal Dupont, Chief Reporter for *Actuel* describes the situation in the following terms:[6]

> Because they have scoured their own waters and the fish have not had time to reproduce, Thai fishermen have ventured elsewhere to cast their nets, including into Vietnamese waters. Some have been captured and rot in Vietnamese jails. This does not go to improve relations between the two countries. Further, the Vietnamese army occupies part of the territory of two close neighbours of Thailand—Cambodia and Laos—and launches from time to time raids against Thai border villages. The refugees are considered by Thai public opinion to be part of a mass invasion plan—the fact that in these conditions some people become pirates may be perceived as not such a bad thing. Pirates therefore possibly form a first line of defence for the Thais against Vietnam.

The Thai Authorities

Mr Dupont also accuses the Thai authorities of "covering for" the pirates and encouraging them.

He alleges that in 1979 a representative of UNHCR witnessed the shooting at Songkhla at a boat full of refugees by Thai police as a result of which several Vietnamese were killed.

Mr Dupont also alleges that in the Spring of 1981 19 refugees fought back, killing several pirates and taking their boat, and were then boarded by the Thai Navy. When three of the surviving pirates complained, the Thai authorities decided to make an example of the 19 Vietnamese and the procurator demanded the death penalty.

It is also alleged that on 11 July 1982 the Thai Authorities towed two boats full of refugees out to sea in bad weather. The first of the boats ran aground on a Malaysian beach with all its passengers unharmed. The second boat capsized and sank with 23 people on board. The rope which had been towing the boat broke, but it is alleged by a man who managed to swim to the coast that the Thais then decided to be rid of it and rammed it.

The Thai authorities reject these accusations. Mr. Prasong Soonsiri,

Secretary General of the National Security Council, has insisted, in reaction to articles by Henry Khan, an American journalist expelled from Thailand, that, although the Thai authorities welcomed constructive comment, certain articles were "prejudicial, distorted and irresponsible", He concluded that "...Thai officials regret the practice of some journalists of pursuing their personal prejudices rather than upholding their ethics."

Mr Nitya Pibulsonggram, Director General of the Department of International Organisations (or the Ministry of Foreign Affairs) supports this view:

> It is unjust and unacceptable for the international community and the media to judge Thailand and to throw doubt on her entire anti-piracy effort, basing their judgement only on certain extreme cases of misfortunes experienced by the boat people. For the same reason Thai officials are bitter when they see their efforts underestimated and again judged by reference to exceptional cases.

I would make no judgement on these arguments. Nevertheless, I have to accept that, even if these Far Eastern countries have not openly encouraged piracy, their attitude at the start of the exodus from Vietnam was hardly a deterrent to those attracted to it. Boat people are all the more easy prey because they generally offer little resistance—they are exhausted after days adrift with meagre, or no, rations. Practically all of them sail without weapons, particularly in view of the fact that since 1975 it has been extremely difficult to get weapons in Vietnam, especially for those considered suspect by the Government.

In any case the boat people are convinced that weapons would be of little use to them. They are afraid above all of aggravating attacks which are already violent enough. Pirates are capable of taking vengeance by killing the children, or by killing everyone on board. In addition, boat people know that the pirates can communicate by radio and call reinforcements.

Pirates enjoy the certainty of profiting by their attacks. Apart from the bestial satisfaction of terrorising, raping and even killing at no great risk, they can expect to abduct many women or girls for sale into prostitution networks.

In May 1986 two humanitarian Associations, the West German and French committees Cap Anamur and Médecins du Monde, stated to the press that Vietnamese women abducted by pirates in the South China Sea were being transported to brothels in Bangkok. A small number were sent directly, however a larger number went through Koh Kra before being sent in small groups to Thailand.

Basing his remarks on statistics of 136 women abducted in 1985, which are thought to be lower than the truth, Mr. Ruper Neudeck, president of the Cap Anamur Committee, accused the Bangkok Government of "not even having responded to" the approaches of UNHCR or of Cap Anamur. He requested facilities for on the spot investigations and for the return of the women.

International Public Opinion

At the beginning of the 1980s public international opinion became aware of the daily tragedy of the Indo-Chinese refugees. Several committees were formed with the aim of collecting funds to help these refugees and to campaign to apply pressure on certain South East Asian governments. As a result, these governments received thousands of letters from sympathisers.

Moreover, the committees, assisted by official organisations such as the Red Cross International and Médecins sans Frontières, have collected funds to help the refugees. In particular these funds have allowed them to charter vessels which have, sometimes together with American, French and Thai naval vessels, picked up thousands of boat people adrift at sea. Below are the names of some of these vessels chartered by private organisations to help the refugees:

1978	USA	Akuna I
1978-1981	USA	Seasweep
1979-1980	France	Île de Lumière
1980-1982	France	Goelo
1979-1980	Norway	Lysekild
1980-1982	West Germany	Cap Anamur
1980-1981	West Germany	Flora
1981-1984	USA	Akuna I; Akuna II; Akuna III
1981-1983	Switzerland	Akuna II; Akuna III; Herta S
1982-1983	France	Goelo

An example of a new, projected venture of this type will be found in Chapter 5.

Some naval vessels have also been put at the disposal of humanitarian organisations. I would mention in particular two French naval vessels, the *Jean Charcot* and the *Victor Schelcher* which had to terminate their mission in June 1985 because other countries would no longer accept refugees.

Before closing this section on humanitarian organisations it should be noted that some have the secondary aim of finding soldiers lost during the Vietnam War. As Colonel Jack Bailey, the commander of the *Akuna II* mission and a Vietnam veteran, stated: "First and foremost we want to save lives but we also want to find out anything we can about MIAS (missing in action servicemen)." Many refugees from Vietnam have been detained for a long time by the communist regime in re-education camps and are in the best position to provide information about missing Americans.

Anti-Piracy Programmes

Although the UNHCR first provided the Thai Government with a non-armed surveillance vessel in May 1980, the first anti-piracy programme commenced in February 1981 and continued until September the same year. It was the result of a bilateral American and Thai initiative and relied on a $2 million subsidy from the United States. The subsidy allowed the Royal Thai Navy to acquire reconnaissance aircraft and a patrol boat, and to cover operational expenses in 33,000 square kilometres of the South China Sea. The reconnaissance aircraft allowed pirates to be identified and help to be summoned. Decoy vessels, disguised as refugee boats, were subsequently introduced. A map indicating the extent of anti-piracy activities is reproduced at Appendix 6.

The programme ended when the USA and Thailand could not agree on how to maintain the initiative, apparently because of the insistence of the Thai Government on a further credit of $30 million.

Because these tragedies occur on the high seas and affect the entire international community, the UNHCR referred them to its Executive Committee, to the General Assembly and the Secretary General of the United Nations and to the International Maritime Organisation. Negotiations begun on this basis led to the introduction of the second anti-piracy programme. This programme started in July 1982 and details will be found on pages 102 and 108.

In June and July 1983 a team of three international experts were sent to Thailand with the purpose of overseeing the programme and improving it. Some of their suggestions were implemented—in particular the introduction of unexpected night patrols, the creation of an anti-piracy commando, and the establishment of a regional centre of information to register, coordinate and disseminate information about pirates.

Since the introduction of the programmes, the Thai Authorities have received through the UNHCR $17.8 million in specialist services, equipment and cash.

The Saving of Life at Sea

It is clear from the accounts of the boat people that many commercial vessels have failed to help them. A number as high as 50 was quoted above. But have these boats, suspected of deliberately ignoring people in distress, ever really even seen them?

Small refugee boats are very difficult to locate in the open sea, even if the refugees themselves can see a large ship ten miles away. Further, the boats, made of wood and not equipped with deflectors, are difficult to detect by radar. Finally, the attention of the crew on watch will not necessarily be attracted to a small boat off their course showing no signs of distress. How many fishermen on board such boats signal to others merely as a greeting?

All the same, many vessels have deliberately refused to help refugees in boats, some of whom were dead or in agony, thereby breaking maritime tradition and international law. The duty to save life at sea has been universally recognised since antiquity and depends on an unquestionable moral obligation. It is possible that captains have deliberately avoided refugee vessels in distress because of the possibility of heavy expense, and a prolonged stay in port.

For several decades legislators have tried to codify the law of the sea and have many times underlined the duty of rescue. However they have never envisaged situations other than traditional wrecks involving seamen, whose repatriation will cause no problems and can normally be put in motion at the first port of call. The boat people are asking for asylum, and cannot therefore expect help or protection from their countries of origin.

Faced with the continued arrival of boat people on their shores, Asian countries sometimes refuse to allow them to disembark without formal guarantees that they will be re-settled abroad after a very brief delay.

In August 1985 Mr Paul Hartling, High Commissioner of the UNHCR, launched an appeal to all masters of vessels crossing the South China Sea, and messages are regularly broadcast in the South China Sea, encouraging masters and fishermen to help boat people and promising that they will be compensated for doing so.

The UNHCR has developed the DISERO (Disembarkation Resettlement Offers) and RASRO (Rescue at Sea Resettlement Offers) schemes. The aim of the schemes is to allow masters to pick up and discharge refugees without difficulty or expense. Their operation is described on page 110. More than 15,000 copies of a booklet *Guidelines for the Disembarkation of Refugees* (reproduced at Appendix 8) have been distributed.

Several Belgian ships have distinguished themselves in helping refugees in distress in the South China Sea:

Vessel	**Master**	**Owners**	**Date**	**Number Saved**
Maaskroon	A Noirot	Nedlloyd Bulk	19.09.79	61
Fina Belgique	J M Arendt	Fina Marine	08.10.80	19
Maaskade	W Dubart	Nedlloyd Bulk	06.06.81	35
Titus	P Mandeville	UBEM	03.08.81	15
E R Brugge	J Pierloot	Ahlers Shipping	13.08.81	63
E R Wallonia	H Vereecken	Ahlers Shipping	25.04.82	16
Maaskroon	J Allard	Nedlloyd Bulk	13.05.82	19
Amazon	G Quivreux	UBEM	30.05.82	56
E R Wallonia	H Vereecken	Ahlers Shipping	11.08.83	88
Osa Gent	D Geirnaert	Ahlers Shipping	02.06.84	13
Nuptse	W Dubart	UBEM	07.07.87	7
Nuptse	W Dubart	UBEM	02.08.87	42

What has been Achieved

The measures described above have had diverse but significant results. Firstly, thousands of refugees have been picked up at sea, by private ships, warships, merchant ships and fishing boats. Secondly, many maritime and other institutions have cooperated in initiatives to pre-empt the risk of pirate attack. The following have been prominent in this respect—Baltic and International Maritime Council (BIMCO), International Chamber of Shipping, International Group of P & I Clubs, as well as the UNHCR, government bodies and press organs.

Thirdly, many pirates have been arrested and imprisoned. Statistical summaries will be found at Appendix 5, but more detailed information about selected events is provided below:

Nov 1979: Seven Thais arrested for rape on Koh Kra. Sentenced on 22 June 1980 to terms of imprisonment ranging from eight to 20 years.

Aug 1980: Royal Thai Navy boarded two fishing vessels—this was the first known case of such a boarding.

1981: Six Thai pirates arrested by a Thai Navy decoy vessel.

Apr 1981: Seven out of the nine pirates who had seized a trawler arrested at the fishing port of Chaimongkol. Amongst them were four crewmembers who had killed the master, an engineer and the cook.

Aug 1981: 54 boats boarded in the course of a joint campaign by Malaysia and Thailand.

Oct 1981: The captain of a fishing vessel arrested as he was raping a Vietnamese girl of 15 years.

Oct 1981: Eight people arrested at Prattini for having stolen the boat *Pro Darunee* by armed force and having attacked refugees.

Oct 1981: Suspect arrested.

Jan 1982: Five Thai pirates arrested by Malaysian police.

Nov 1983 : A Malaysian warship fired warning shots at Thai boats in order to protect two Vietnamese boats.

Jan 1984: Two pirates arrested.

Sept 1984: Nine pirate fishermen arrested. Their vessels had been identified by seven of their victims.

Sept 1984: Pirate fisherman arrested—later sentenced to three years prison—This was the ninth sentence imposed by a Thai court.

Oct 1984: Two pirate fishermen arrested.

And so on....

Between 1982 and 1984 the anti-piracy activity financed by the international community led to the arrest by the Thai Navy and police of 30 people suspected of piracy in connection with refugees. However in 1986 alone 50 suspects were arrested and charged. Of this total of 80 people arrested, 15 had charges dropped against them. During the last weeks of 1986, tribunals pronounced particularly severe penalties, such as the death penalty and sentences to 448 years (later reduced to 50 years) in prison. Some examples appear below. These exceptionally long penalties were "justifiable in view of the gravity of the crime", as Judge Ranysam Wijitkraisan stated to journalists.

The Thai government has compiled details of fishing vessels, using a new system of numerical registration and a computer donated by the Norwegian government. This should greatly assist the identification of boats suspected of piracy.

Unfortunately, hardly anything seems yet to have been done to dismantle the prostitution network and recover the hundreds of women abducted.

Thai Jurisprudence

It is useful in this connection to examine a few Thai judicial cases. Again, fuller statistical summaries are available at Appendix 5.

The First Trial—25 June 1980

Seven Thai fishermen from the boat *Krisada 20*—were accused of gang robbery, false imprisonment and rape. Their victims were five Vietnamese girls abducted from a refugee boat. Recourse was made during the trial to other statutes—the defendants were also accused of having brought the girls illegally into Thailand in contravention of the Immigration Act 1979. The word "pirate" did not appear in the indictment.

Although it was not clearly established whether the incidents had taken place in Thai territorial waters or on the high seas, the court seems to have deduced that, at the critical time, both the Thai and Vietnamese boats were in Thai territorial waters, and therefore under the jurisdiction of the Thai Penal Code. The accused were found guilty of the charges against them and were sentenced to terms of imprisonment varying from eight to 24 years.

The Second Trial—26 June 1980

Three fishermen from the Thai fishing boat *Saeng Sri* were accused of theft, rape and having illegally brought 47 Vietnamese boat people into Thailand, contravening the Immigration Act 1979.

The first two charges were dismissed but the Songkhla Tribunal found them guilty of the third offence and sentenced each to six months imprisonment.

The Third Trial—13 August 1980

Three fishermen from the fishing boat *Sap Asoon Chai* were suspected of rape, indecent acts and attempts related thereto against two Vietnamese women from a Vietnamese boat. Further charges were held on the file against them, notably having brought the foreigners to Thailand contravening the 1979 act.

It was again not clearly established whether the initial contact between the two boats had taken place in Thai territorial waters. It was nevertheless established with certainty that, after having given food and water to the occupants of the Vietnamese boat, the crew of the *Sap Asoon Chai* took it in tow towards the Thai coast. After abducting the two Vietnamese girls, the accused cut the tow wire and abandoned the others to their fate. The accused were arrested as they committed the offences mentioned above in a hotel on the Thai coast.

The court sentenced two of the accused to six months imprisonment for indecent acts but the third fisherman, who had not taken the girls to the hotel, was acquitted.

The Fourth Trial—21 November-15 December 1980

Six cases were combined. They concerned six Thai fishermen from the boat *Suchinnawa* , accused of rape, indecent acts, abducting a woman for indecent acts and false imprisonment of seven Vietnamese women. It was alleged that these incidents had taken place on the island of Koh Kra in Thai territorial waters (mentioned above).

The Court found there was no case to answer as the identity of the offenders was not clearly established.

The Fifth Trial—15 December 1980

This case was a continuation of the first one mentioned. The same accused were now indicted for conspiracy to murder. Vietnamese witnesses had testified at their first trial that some of their relatives—15 altogether—had been killed during the theft committed by the accused.

The tribunal seemed no more clear on this occasion whether the facts had arisen in Thai territorial waters, but this did not prevent it from rejecting a defence on this basis by the accused. However, according to the Code of Criminal Procedure, the right to prosecute the accused was extinguished because there had already been a definitive judgment on the facts. The tribunal decided that it did not have the jurisdiction to compromise this principle in view of the fact that the accused had *not* previously been charged with murder or attempted murder.

The Sixth Trial—16 December 1980

The captain of a Thai boat was accused of having participated in gang robbery on board a boat close to Koh Kra and of having caused several Vietnamese to drown by robbing and sinking their boat. He was not however accused of murder.

The tribunal found no case to answer since the identity of the offender was not clearly established.

The Seventh Trial—14 July 1981

Five Thai fishermen were accused of attempted gang robbery. They had been arrested when they attacked a Thai Navy decoy vessel. It was established without doubt that the incident had taken place in Thai territorial waters. The accused had rammed the camouflaged boat after which they had boarded it with the intention of stealing. Further, during the trial the accused admitted that they had confused the boat with a Vietnamese boat.

The court found them guilty and pronounced sentences of imprisonment from four and a half to eleven years.

The Eighth Trial—November 1986

On 20 May 1986, the Sri Racha Marine Police arrested two fishermen and charged them with gang rape and deprivation of liberty. On 2 January 1986 the fishermen had attacked a group of eight boat people during which two girls (aged 15 and 18) were abducted. Both girls were subsequently set adrift in the sea near Kut Island on 21 February and swam ashore the same day.

The Court hearings were concluded in October and the verdict was handed down in November.

Thai law fixes the maximum term of imprisonment at 50 years but Judge Ranysam Wijitkraisan took the unusual measure of counting each of the 28 days of rape as an offence punishable by 16 years.

The first defendant was sentenced to 448 years imprisonment, reduced however by half due to his confession of guilt, and later further reduced to 50 years in order to comply with the Penal Code. The second defendant was sentenced to 453 years and one month, which was similarly reduced by half and then to 50 years.

The Ninth Trial—12 December 1986

Two verdicts were announced by the tribunal of the southern province of Songkhla.

At the end of the first trial a man was condemned to death. He was a member of a group of four pirates; the three others were sentenced to eleven, 15 and 22 years imprisonment. They were found guilty of ramming a refugee boat at the end of 1985, causing the death of at least one refugee. In addition, eight refugees had been reported missing, presumed dead.

At the end of the second trial, two men were sentenced respectively to eleven and 38 years in prison for an attack with rape but without murder.

Deductions from these Trials

Relatively few prosecutions have been undertaken for crimes against the boat people. This is explained principally by the difficulty of identifying the offenders, and by the fear of witnesses and victims to testify. However in most cases theirs is the only available evidence. It is generally always difficult to establish what happens at sea—with the exception of cases in which pirates have been lured by Royal Thai Navy decoy boats.

There is one interesting conclusion to be drawn. Recourse to immigration law has made it possible to convict defendants against whom there is insufficient evidence of piracy, abduction or imprisonment, for having "connived at" the illicit immigration of foreigners.

As seen, it is impossible in many cases to determine with certainty whether facts have arisen on the high seas or in territorial waters. Courts however have been able to assume jurisdiction because either they had partly done so, or because a Thai boat had been involved.

NOTES

1 *Atlantic Magazine*, March 1984

2 A Billiard: Pirates dans le Golfe du Siam, *Refugees* magazine, 1983 no 2

3 H C Amar: Boat Women: Piracy's other Dimension—Rape and its Consequences, *Refugees* magazine 1985 no 18.

4 Schroeder Dao T K: An experience in counselling women refugee Boat People

5 Amar H C o.c.

6 Dupont P: Pirates d'Aujourd'hui, Editions Ramsay Paris 1986

CHAPTER 5

TWO PERSONAL INSIGHTS INTO THE SOUTH CHINA SEA

Maurice Vitty and Francis Wiyono

MV Seacare—Maurice Vitty

When my wife Hilary, and I flew out to Bangkok in 1980 to join the mv *Logos*, we little realised that the days and weeks that followed were going to have such a profound effect on our lives. In fact we would never be the same again.

The *Logos* had just rescued 93 Vietnamese Boat People and when we arrived we found them all camping out on the poop deck. The ship was marooned in Bangkok because neither Britain, where the company was based, nor Singapore, where the ship was registered, would agree to take the refugees. For us it was like stepping into a television documentary. We could hardly believe some of the horror stories that these defenceless boat people were telling us about the activities of pirates who made a living by preying on them.

The more we looked into the piracy problem, the more horrified we became. We heard of a tiny island, off the Thai cost, called Koh Krah, where thousands of refugees, mainly women and young girls, had been imprisoned. Young girls hardly even in their teens were being raped, abducted and sold into prostitution. Others were simply mass raped and then murdered. Some children had been violated in full view of their parents, and parents had been beaten and murdered in front of their children. One boat we heard about was simply rammed by the pirates until it broke into two and sank. Then the pirates sailed through the survivors, cracking them over the heads with hammers. This story only came to be told because one young boy miraculously managed to escape on a makeshift raft and was later rescued by fishermen.

My wife and I have since visited south-east Asia twice in recent years. On these occasions our purpose was to visit refugee camps as leaders of Christian Care Projects, an organisation that we formed in response to the Boat People problem. I'll never forget the looks on the faces of one particular Vietnamese couple who we met in a camp in Malaysia. "Please help us to find our daughter." they pleaded, "Pirates take her, pirates take her. She gone, please help." We felt totally helpless but decided that we must try to find the girl if at all possible. It transpired that she was only 13 years old and one of a number of young girls abducted from this particular boat.

Our search took us to eleven different refugee camps in three countries. We also, of course, contacted the United Nations High Commission for Refugees, who put out a trace for the girl in all the refugee camps where she could possibly be. We came up with a total blank—nothing. She was nowhere to be found. Writing and telling the parents was one of the hardest things that I've ever had to do.

Later on, as I paced up and down a deserted beach in Songklha, Southern Thailand, I began to dream about the impossible. "What's needed here," I thought, "is a ship. And what's more, I'm a seaman. How can I ignore the plight of these people?" I remembered photographs I had seen of this very same beach that I was walking on, but on the photographs it was littered with bodies—half eaten, half rotten carcasses that had once been men, women and children who had set out from Vietnam full of hope for a better life. My mind thought back to the parable of the Good Samaritan. How can the world cross over to the other side? Doesn't anybody care?

The next two years saw me travelling the world, visiting the experts. In the earlier days when the Boat People were in the headlines, there was much more support for rescue work. President Carter was particularly sympathetic. Various ships were then in use; World Vision had *Seasweep*, Food For the Hungry had *Cap Anamur*. The *Cap Anamur* was the last ship to be used in this rescue work. Ein Schiff für Vietnam also tried using a spotter plane to pinpoint positions of refugee boats to pass on to Merchant ships. They had all had to stop because the situation became too hot politically. If you did pick the refugees up, nobody would take them. In theory (perhaps even in practice) a ship like the one we are planning to get could find itself exiled at sea, completely untouchable, simply for rescuing Boat People. I hope it won't come to that, but I am afraid that I cannot be put off by that possibility either. No civilised society should turn its back on those who are dying, and if it does, then it's up to civilised citizens within that society to do something instead. I think Bob Geldoff demonstrated this very well, didn't he?

So in 1986, Seacare was set up and we are now in the process of purchasing the *Seacare*, a ship, soon and to start patrolling the South China Seas. Our aim is not to pick up the refugees for the sake of it. If they seem all right, we will just give them fuel, food, medical help, etc. and then watch over them from a distance. If however, we see that their lives are in danger of being lost, we will pick them up. Our aim is to run the whole operation with the minimum of publicity so as not to create a "pull factor". (It is argued that refugees who would otherwise not leave Vietnam, might be encouraged to do so if they knew of such a ship. This is a valid point of course, and one that we are sensitive to.)

The crew of the Seacare ship will all be volunteers recommended to us by different Churches of all denominations. Seacare also has representatives in America, Canada and Singapore.

For more information please get in touch with me.

The Paulo Galang Refugee Camp—Francis Wiyono

I worked in Paulo Galang Refugee Camp, Indonesia for one year from mid-1983 to mid-1984. The camp was provided by the government and situated on a small island near Sumatra, about half an hour by speedboat from Singapore. I was sent there, mainly as a "social adviser" by the Conference of Bishops in Indonesia, a charity organisation. I worked with Father Dimitri, an Italian priest who had lived in Vietnam for about nine years until the end of the war when he went to work at Paulo Galang.

The camp held around 11,000 refugees. My task was to identify family problems, to comfort the refugees and if possible to find them sponsorship in a third country.

The refugees used to tell me how they had secretly left Vietnam by building themselves boats which were just big enough—about twelve metres by 2.5 metres. The boats had no names. Sometimes they were painted black, I think for camouflage. I saw many boats which were really suitable for a dozen people coming into Paulo Galang carrying 75 or more. This was a terrible problem as far as seaworthiness was concerned.

The crossing was very dangerous. If the refugees went too far east they met bad weather, particularly the Russian typhoon. If they went too far west they met the pirates.

The pirate boats were very fast. They could manoeuvre very well. And the people handling them were very experienced, and clever. There were patrols, but they could escape from them. They may have been fishermen, at least they sometimes posed as fishermen to avoid the patrols.

Piracy was very sporadic. Sometimes there was no piracy for very long periods, but sometimes there were frequent attacks.

The refugees concealed their money by stitching it into their clothes. So they never took their clothes off, and they became very dirty. Also, the pirates knew this and sometimes stole their clothes and they arrived at Paulo Galang with nothing.

The pirates were armed with knives. The refugees had no weapons, at least not when they arrived at the camp. They may have thrown weapons away before arriving, because the police would confiscate them.

Many died because of the weakness of their health, as well as from pirate attacks. Many were very old, or very young. When a boat was ready to go, but too crowded to take the whole family, the parents would just send their children. So many children arrived without their parents. It was very, very hard for them. It was one of my responsibilities to take care of them.

With an experience like this children were always frightened and we tried to comfort them. Because they had been unprepared for the dangers and hazards they sometimes screamed with fright, even after they reached the shore.

We tried to get families together again, but it was difficult. We tried to maintain contact with letters.

But it was difficult for everyone in the camp, especially for those who had suffered from piracy. It took them a long time to settle—especially the young ladies, and families where the husband had been killed by pirates. But if a sponsor could be found in a third country, this made it easier for them to recover.

Sometimes the women were made pregnant by the pirates, and did not want to keep the baby. So we had to find a way out, a way to solve the problem. As Catholics we could not encourage abortion, but it may have been done in secret—there were medicines and doctors available. We tried to encourage unmarried mothers to find a sponsor to keep the baby.

The most urgent problem of the refugees was to leave the camp as soon as possible. This concerned them even more than their experiences regarding piracy. In any case we tried to comfort them, to tell them that it was in the past. We also tried to help psychologically and financially.

As a Christian, I told them that piracy was one of the consequences of their leaving the country. They must have realised the danger and decided to face it. I tried to give them confidence again and to prepare them for their future.

There was some crime in the camp—mainly concerned with money, and with jealousy provoked when some refugees received money from their relatives. I do not recall a problem with drugs.

Other problems were typhus and the existence of two groups of people—Vietnamese and Cambodian—with different ways of life and different languages.

As far as I know, around half of those leaving were from the higher levels of society. After the communists entered South Vietnam many were sent to education camps for as long as nine years—and those from the higher levels were sent for longer than others. Sometimes they escaped from the camps, but they never wanted to explain how.

I have no doubt that some "refugees" were communists, or even infiltrators. But it should be remembered that even the infiltrators have to face the hazards of pirates.

CHAPTER 6

ANTI-PIRACY IN SOUTH-EAST ASIA: US AND INTERNATIONAL EFFORTS AND PROGRAMMES

Harry C Blaney III

Pirate attacks on Vietnamese boat refugees in the Gulf of Thailand have aroused the concern and compassion of people throughout the world. The United States has been in the forefront of nations involved in trying to eliminate this source of so much human suffering. But the problem is international in scope and impact and requires the concerted cooperation of all nations and the entire maritime community.

Statistics of attacks are summarised at Appendices 3 and 4. However, to provide some perspective on the magnitude of the problem, a few further figures might be helpful. In 1986 over 20,000 boat people found first asylum in south-east Asia and Hong Kong. Since the start of 1987 there has been an upward trend in the number of people fleeing Vietnam by boat. Thus the number of targets for pirates have increased.

Most of the boat people land in Malaysia, Thailand, and Hong Kong, with much smaller groups in the Philippines and Indonesia. The recent significant increase in the number of boat people coming out of Vietnam may be due to a number of causes including the deteriorating economic conditions, release of political prisoners and the recent brief suspension of the UN High Commission for Refugees (UNHCR) Orderly Departure Programme (ODP) by which Vietnamese could leave legally. The ODP remains subject to the political atmosphere and changing circumstances.

Those who head towards Thailand and Malaysia are most impacted by piracy. For example, in Thailand some 4,000 boat people landed in 1986 in about 445 boats. Of these arriving boats about 13% were attacked. Each of the attacked boats was hit by pirates some one and a half times with a total of around 111 persons missing and a reported 18 deaths. For both Thailand and Malaysia the attack rate was about 15% with 98 out of a total of 657 refugee boats landing in these two countries being attacked en route. In the first three months of 1987 the attack rate was running about 11%. These statistics if anything underestimate the total since, undoubtedly, many boats are attacked and are never heard from. Details of attacks which were recorded in the first ten months of 1987 will be found at Appendix 7.

Since pirates generally attack refugee boats that arrive in southern and eastern Thailand and in Malaysia, enforcement patrols and particularly land enforcement should concentrate in those areas. Some experts believe figures for piracy against boat people have generally dropped due to more effective efforts at enforcement primarily in Thailand. Much remains to be done, however, in that the decline has not been evenly distributed. Attacks on boats landing in eastern Thailand have declined dramatically from 65% in the early 1980s to about 4-5% in 1986-87. However, attacks on boats landing in southern Thailand have declined only from 64% in 1984 to 44% in 1986. Attacks on boats landing in Malaysia have varied slightly from the 35% attacked in 1981 to about 33% in 1983 and 32% in 1984. Deaths due to acts of piracy increased from 43 in 1983 to 66 in 1984. In 1985 there were 45 deaths, 72 abductees, and 67 women raped in Thai waters.

While the attack figures for 1986 and early 1987 show a general reduction compared with earlier years, the number of people and boats landing in Thai waters increased. Thus, there is much that still must be done to reduce this problem.

Since early 1980 the Department of State has sought to focus international attention on pirate depredations against refugees and to promote action to counter them. In the absence of international involvement, the US developed a bilateral effort with the Royal Thai Government (RTG), and in early 1981 a $2 million programme was inaugurated. In July 1982, the US joined with eleven other donors to fund a second programme to combat piracy in the Gulf of Thailand. The American contribution was $1.2 million of the total $3.67 million programme.

The US contribution to the specific UNHCR/RTG "core programme" in 1983 was $800,000 and has continued each year—in 1986 it was $900,000—plus additional separate funding for specific anti-piracy and rescue at sea projects. There was a total of $5 million allocated to the anti-piracy programme for 1984. The House of Representatives Committee on Foreign Affairs has authorised in 1986 and 1987 $2.5 million for anti-piracy and associated programmes in the Gulf of Thailand. There are also associated programmes of medical help and counselling for piracy victims.

In 1983, under the auspices of the UNHCR, a team of maritime and coast guard experts assessed the situation. They made a number of recommendations to the RTG, the donor governments, and the UNHCR, to enhance the piracy programme by improved air/sea patrol activity and an enhanced role for the Thai police on shore. They also recommended greater efforts to rescue refugees in distress on the high seas. This is referred to on page 90.

A US Interagency Task Force examined the anti-piracy and rescue at sea issues in the winter of 1983-84 and recommended a broader and more comprehensive effort to deal with piracy and rescue of the boat people.

Much of the resulting international effort followed from these two studies.

The Thai government agreed to the renewal and expansion of the UNHCR/RTG Anti-Piracy Programme for the 1984-85 programme year which started in June 1984. This is an extended and more comprehensive programme as a result of the UNHCR Assessment Team and the US Task Force recommendations and now includes funds for law enforcement activities against pirates. The 1985-87 programmes emphasise law enforcement, intelligence operations, better use of patrols, and better coordination between involved RTG agencies.

Since 1984, significant results have been achieved by the Thai authorities with respect to law enforcement and prosecution of pirates, as will be seen from Appendix 5. The Thai naval and provincial police patrols now include the use of rubber boat teams which can board suspected pirate ships and arrest crew members.

A team of international experts in early 1987 reviewed the piracy situation and the UNHCR/RTG Anti-Piracy Program. They recommended continued emphasis on landbased law enforcement with most of the expenditures directed towards training and operations rather than on capital equipment purchases.

In addition to its contribution to this UNHCR/RTG programme, the US has made other contributions to UNHCR, to other organisations, and bilaterally for additional proposals to augment anti-piracy efforts. Among these are rescue at sea measures, assistance to victims of piracy, and development of a "rewards for information" programme, about which some information was provided on Chapter 1.

Important to the rescue at sea efforts are the UNHCR DISERO (Disembarkation Resettlement Offers) and RASRO (Rescue at Sea Resettlement Offers) programmes which are described on page 110.

A total of 871 refugees were resettled between May 1986 and April 1987 under RASRO with the US taking 308. The DISERO programme with eight participating states resulted in 178 refugees being disembarked in its 1986-87 operational year.

Extensive efforts, in particular, have been undertaken in the rescue at sea area through a cooperative programme involving the UNHCR and the International Maritime Organisation (IMO) to promote rescue of refugees at sea by merchant ships. Finally, IMO sent to south-east Asia a regional expert to coordinate and examine anti-piracy and rescue at sea matters among the maritime community. The involvement of the IMO is crucial in view of the indications that some merchant fleets are passing by boat people in distress, contrary to international law and custom.

The US has also made a substantial contribution to an expanded UNHCR reimbursement system to compensate ships for costs associated with rescue of boat people. This scheme is set out in the UNHCR Guidelines at Appendix 8. With the additional funds available for this purpose, it is hoped that ships will not be concerned with any of the added costs of picking up refugees at sea. Early pickups of refugees at sea will prevent them from falling into the hands of pirates or the natural dangers of the sea later in their voyage.

These programmes have, with the support of the Thai government, improved the piracy situation in the Gulf of Thailand. While there may be no proof of a direct correlation between the activities of the programme and the decline in pirates' attacks on refugee boats over the years, nevertheless, it is probable that the programme has had a beneficial effect in this respect.

In examining the particular problem of piracy in south-east Asia and, more specifically, attacks on the boat people, it appears that additional action is required to further reduce this kind of piracy. As has been pointed out by others, no single approach will solve this problem, which is complex and intractable. Direct action by coastal states unilaterally is required both by central authorities and by local officials. Regional cooperation is also essential since this kind of piracy occurs in the waters off more than one state. Further, multilateral cooperation is a key element since piracy and the humanitarian concern for the protection and well-being of refugees is a responsibility of the entire international community. Improvements at all of these levels will be required in order to reduce piracy significantly.

At the national level, several important elements are needed to achieve faster improvements. First, there is a need for greater realisation by officials and the public of the great damage to the international reputation of a country which results from the continuation of piracy off its waters. Second, there is a need for recognition that such acts also harm legitimate commerce and trade in the area and have a real economic cost. They also breed general lawlessness which increases crime and harms a society that is striving for respect for law and order and seeks to protect its citizenry. Also, those crimes have an economic and sociological dimension which needs to be understood and addressed in devising effective and appropriate responses. Also, the individual country can develop more effective means of using existing national assets against piracy. Better coordination between police, navy, local authorities and coastal governments would enhance the effectiveness of these existing programmes.

On the regional level, cooperation among the ASEAN countries can do much to ensure that the problem can be dealt with when it reaches beyond a single state. For example, cooperation between Thailand and Malaysia on how best to police their adjacent and overlapping zones would greatly contribute to ensuring the areas of high attack are fully protected and policed by at least one country's forces and not left open as a "free fire zone". Intelligence about pirate attacks also should be more effectively shared. In addition, those countries can cooperate with one another on a system for rescue at sea of all persons—not just refugees, but other ships in distress. This capability is rather underutilised in the region at present.

On the multilateral level, the existing UNHCR/RTG programme can be enhanced and improved with experience with what individual programme elements work or do not work. Continued support by the international community—especially the donor countries—both via funding and moral concern, is a key element in ensuring that effective action will continue to be taken by the regional countries whose resources are often limited.

The emphasis on the importance of regional diplomatic initiatives to solve this problem in Chapter 8 is correct and important. Also, involvement of other organisations such as the IMO is useful in dealing with particular aspects of the problem. In this case, if merchant ships will pick up refugees *before* the pirates can attack them, they will have effectively denied victims to the pirates. A not unimportant role is played by the voice of world public opinion and the media.

Another important aspect of this problem is its root cause—mainly, the need of so many people to flee from Vietnam. It is vital that the Vietnamese government take actions which will reduce the causes that force people to leave that country—both political and economic. In addition, the UNHCR, in cooperation with the US and others, has established an alternative and safer route for leaving Vietnam in the so-called "Orderly Departure Programme", which is designed to permit Vietnamese to leave that country via a legal and established mechanism and to thereby avoid the dangers and violence of a sea voyage. This programme is mainly focused on Amerasians, political prisoners and those who, in the past, have been associated with US or other western countries or those with close relatives in the West. A major problem has been, however, that this programme has waxed and waned with the political climate in the region.

If we all pursue, with good will, actively and jointly a range of anti-piracy and rescue at sea activities, we can reduce this tragedy to a much rarer occurrence to the benefit of all. While some progress has been made, much more yet needs to be done at every level.

Also the increased cooperation of the majority of law-abiding fisherman will improve significantly the piracy situation—since the minority elements that participate in such crimes are inevitably a threat to all, not just refugees. We should also remember that many Thai fishermen assist the boat people in distress. Law enforcement activities need to be increasingly focused on the relatively small group of pirates who are active and violent—who are essentially outlaws from a peaceful society. Thus, increased investigations and arrests will and have contributed greatly to a decrease in the rate of such crimes. The RTG has made some important improvements in this regard, and we hope this will continue.

On a deeper level, piracy in this region of the Gulf of Thailand and the South China Sea, will not be eliminated in the long run until the existing cultural and social basis for it has been transformed. This requires a long term social, political, economic restructuring of the sub-societies from which most of the pirates and lawbreakers originate. Most of the pirates in Thailand come from specific ports and villages and certain ‘‘clans’’ which harbour a lawless under-class which supports, condones and protects law breakers. Thus significant efforts will need to be made to reform this element and integrate it into a larger law abiding society.

CHAPTER 7

REFUGEES ON THE HIGH SEAS: A DANGEROUS PASSAGE

Joachim Henkel

UNHCR's Mandate and Responsibilities

The office of the UN High Commissioner for Refugees (UNHCR) was established in 1951 to help refugees re-establish lives of dignity and productivity. At that time, in the aftermath of World War II, refugees were principally a European problem, but since then have become virtually a worldwide phenomenon. While UNHCR seeks permanent solutions to the refugees' dilemma, its central responsibility is to provide them with international protection and assistance, representing their interests both on the national and international scene. The classic definition of "refugee" describes an individual who has fled or finds himself outside his native land because of a well founded fear of persecution based on various factors including race, religion, nationality or political opinion. It follows therefore that a basic guiding principle of UNHCR is the doctrine of *non-refoulement*—a refugee must not be returned to his native country against his will. This applies to refugees in the territory of a country of refuge/asylum or at its borders. Thus, in the past UNHCR's programmes have been directed largely towards persons already present in a country of asylum.

Special Problems in south-east Asia

But by the late seventies UNHCR and the international community were faced with a new and unique situation on the south-east Asian littoral. Men, women and children were fleeing Vietnam in large numbers, often in small and unseaworthy craft. The result: many soon found themselves in acute danger from fuel, food and water shortages, foundering, and pirate attacks. These hapless people needed desperately assistance to reach safely a country of first asylum.

The total numbers of "boat people", which are summarised in Appendices 3 and 4, were staggering. By December 31 1984, 552,586 such persons had arrived on first asylum shores (77,768 in Thailand alone). Since then the figures have increased less dramatically—by September 1987 they had reached 613,600 (89,300 in Thailand).

Boat arrivals reached their peak of 202,158 in 1978 and then gradually decreased so that by 1984 the number stood at 24,782. In January 1985 it was 1,074. Annual figures since 1985 have been somewhat under one thousand.

Piracy

The record of pirate attacks on refugee boats at sea has been appalling. Here, for example, is what happened to refugees who reached just one country of first asylum, Thailand, in just one year, 1981. 15,095 persons arrived there in 455 boats. 352 (77 percent) were attacked by pirates. As a result of these attacks an estimated 571 persons lost their lives. 599 women and girls were raped, many multiple times. 243 persons were kidnapped.

These attacks caused inestimable and indeed intolerable suffering. UNHCR—in cooperation with the International Committee of the Red Cross and concerned governments—moved to explore ways and means by which affected coastal states could be assisted to fight piracy in the South China Sea and in the Gulf of Thailand.

These efforts led to an anti-piracy programme, administered by the Royal Thai Government (RTG) and supported by the international community through the UNHCR, which was launched in July 1982. Additional operational detail about this programme can be found in Chapters 4 and 6 above.

The 1984 programme was funded by Australia, Canada, Denmark, France, Federal Republic of Germany, Italy, Japan, Netherlands, Norway, Switzerland, United Kingdom and the United States.

Under the programme the Royal Thai Navy operates patrol ships and aircraft (some donated under the international funding mechanism), as well as leased trawlers for high seas patrolling and general information collection. Among enhancements included in the programme are radar equipment, and landing lights for a local airfield to allow night time patrolling missions.

The provincial and Marine Police Departments receive a smaller slice of the budget to operate patrol boats (12 mile offshore limit), and to strengthen land based information gathering—which is becoming an increasingly critical function—and post-incident investigations. Their budget also includes provision for the supply of rubber patrol boats and for the upgrading of communications equipment to establish more effective links between various headquarters and provincial outposts.

The Harbour Department has been involved in a fishing boat registration project designed to mark prominently the boats with their individual number so that culprit pirate ships may be more easily identified from the sea and air.

The UNHCR functions as the coordinator and the point of review and consultation between the international donors and the RTG. Three UNHCR personnel are assigned to anti-piracy duties and they cover both Bangkok and the coastal coordination centre located at Songkhla, which is also the home base for the patrol planes and craft. They conduct continuing liaison with RTG officials at the capital, provincial and local levels. Examples of the results of this coordination and liaison will be found on page 90. Also assigned to the programme from UNHCR's Branch Office Legal Unit is a legal assistant who, on a full time basis, covers follow-up investigations and piracy prosecutions in the Thai courts.

Lateral coordination between the UNHCR offices in Bangkok and Kuala Lumpur is vital since much of the information which becomes available on pirate attacks on refugee boats and abductions at sea is obtained from refugees arriving on the Malaysian coast.

In 1984 the UNHCR office at Kuala Lumpur introduced the practice of "early warning reports" instituted to quicken the transmission of attack details to Bangkok and to Songkhla. The coordination centre there shares the data with the several operational task forces. Regular and swift communication is crucial in the tracing of suspect boats and abductees.

UNHCR is pleased to be able to report that attack statistics are down, but as long as incidents continue, even at a reduced level, the pressures must not be relaxed. The average of boats arriving in Thailand attacked declined from 77 percent in 1981 to 53 percent in 1983 and again to 14 percent in 1986, and to 7 percent in the first nine months of 1987. In 1985 six individuals in three separate cases were prosecuted in Thai courts. These figures have increased in recent years and fuller details will be found at Appendix 5.

Current data reveal that much work still remains to be done. In 1985, 23 percent of the refugee boats arriving in Thailand were attacked, 72 refugees were abducted and there were 67 rape victims. In the first eight months of 1987 the corresponding figures were 8 percent of boats attacked, four abductions and 43 rapes.

Rescue at Sea

The boat refugees are not only attacked by pirates; in their overloaded, unseaworthy vessels they are threatened, and sometimes defeated, by the elements themselves. The fact is that these refugees often need desperately to be rescued while at sea.

Under international law there is an obligation to rescue any person in distress at sea which, of course, includes asylum seekers (cf Convention of 1910 for the Unification of Certain Rules of Law relating to Assistance and Salvage at Sea; 1958 Convention on the High Seas; 1979 International Convention of Maritime Search and Rescue).

There have been numerous examples of outstanding bravery and selflessness in the rescue of refugees in peril at sea. In 1984, for example, the Nansen Medal was awarded to Captain Lewis M Hiller, master of the US tanker *Rose City* , and two American sailors from his crew who performed notable acts of courage in the rescue from certain death in a heavy storm at night of 85 refugees adrift in the South China Sea on 21

September 1983. The Nansen Medal—named after the distinguished Norwegian explorer and humanitarian, Fridtjof Nansen—is the highest honour UNHCR can bestow for outstanding service in the refugee cause.

But, unfortunately, the general trend line on rescues has been a disturbing one. As can be seen from Appendix 9, the proportion of rescues to arrivals dropped from 21.8 percent in 1980 to 8.8 percent in 1984. A particularly melancholy case in July 1984 involved the odyssey of a boat carrying 84 refugees, of whom 68 perished at sea. The 16 survivors claimed that their distress signals had been ignored by some 40 passing ships.

In an effort to substantially improve the rescue record, in October 1983, the UNHCR and the IMO again issued a joint appeal to seafaring nations and to owners and shipmasters.

In June 1984, the UNHCR promoted the broadcast during a ten day period of a "CQ" radio message to masters of ships in the South China Sea informing them of the problem, outlining rescue procedures to be followed at minimum inconvenience to masters, charterers and owners, and offering UNHCR assistance in meeting the expenses involved.

In November 1984, the IMO Council voted "to give full support in principle to the objective of promoting appropriate humanitarian measures to assist or to rescue persons in distress at sea in accordance with long established maritime tradition".

The two organisations, in addition, have agreed on a project of mutual interest related to anti-piracy efforts and rescue at sea operations. This project envisages the stationing of an expert in the area and the scheduling of a regional familiarisation seminar for government representatives, agents and shipping associations.

New Resettlement Techniques

While there is a clear duty for masters, owners and governments to rescue asylum seekers in distress at sea, international law does not address specifically the question of their disembarkation, and the corpus of relevant law does not impose on the flag state of a rescuing vessel the obligation of according permanent asylum to rescued refugees. UNHCR has developed two programmes to fill these lacunae; the Disembarkation Resettlement Offers (DISERO) Scheme; and, the Rescue at Sea Resettlement Offers (RASRO) Scheme.

DISERO seeks to provide solutions in the instance of ships flying the flags of States who operate an open registry ("flags of convenience") and of countries which for certain reasons are unable to guarantee the permanent admission of refugees. To facilitate the disembarkation of asylum seekers by such ships, it establishes a pool of resettlement guarantees.

In the case of RASRO, which became operational on 1 May 1985, the intent is to lift some of the burden from the rescuing flag States through the creation of a wider international pool of resettlement places.

The intention of this approach is to facilitate further the ready disembarkation of refugees rescued at sea; and thus encourage more rescue endeavours. The US is playing a forward role in this enterprise.

UNHCR has issued recently and distributed worldwide guidelines which explain the procedures to be followed and which recommend actions to be taken by ships' masters. They also explain the arrangements made by UNHCR to help meet some of the financial costs incurred in rescue efforts. These guidelines are reproduced at Appendix 8.

As stated on page 38, the resettlement schemes appear to have had some effect, and the percentage of rescues at sea rose from 8.8 percent in 1984 to 13.0 percent in 1985.

Orderly Departure Programme from Vietnam (ODP)

The truth is, however, that even the sum of all these programmes is not enough to remove completely the threats and dangers which meet these refugees as they set out to sea, poorly equipped and by clandestine means.

In view of this sombre fact, efforts were set in train in 1979 to create a *modus operandi* whereby certain Vietnamese might be allowed to leave their country openly and legally. As a result an agreement was reached between the Vietnamese authorities and UNHCR which would permit such departures in selected instances of family reunification and humanitarian concern.

That year only 1,979 persons departed under the ODP aegis. But, by 1984 it had grown to an annual rate of 29,154, which meant that in that year more persons left via ODP than surreptitiously by boat (24,783). 18,418 people left under ODP in 1986 and a further 7,594 in the first half of 1987. By the middle of 1987 the cumulative total of departures under ODP had reached 125,641.

Conclusion

No report on the refugee situation in south-east Asia, even though it may have a special focus, should fail to stress the enormous problem which remains in terms of the refugees who still reside in camps awaiting a permanent solution to their plight. In 1985 there were 158,521 men, women and children (of which 34,238 were boat people) who have little prospect for any resettlement opportunities in the near term. In 1987 there were around 118,000 occupants of Thai camps and 9,000 occupants of Malaysian camps. Efforts to combat piracy and to encourage rescue at sea of course will continue unabated, but the insistent question continues to loom: how are we going to resettle these refugees who still remain, often after many years in camps? It is a question that only the international community in further acts of compassion and self-interest can answer.

UNHCR could not function in south-east Asia, or indeed anywhere, without the moral and material support of the international community at large, governments, private voluntary agencies and individuals of good will the world over. To all of them UNHCR and refugees everywhere are forever grateful.

This paper, which was updated for the purposes of this book, was first delivered at the Minority Rights Conference on Perceptions, Policies and Practices: Asian and Pacific Americans in the 1980s, at Columbia University in 1985.

CHAPTER 8

THE SITUATION OF REFUGEES IN THE TERRITORIAL WATERS OF THAILAND

HE Bhirabongse Kasemsri

The traditional form of piracy, including acts of violence, terroristic acts and maritime frauds may involve costs, economic and otherwise, but it is not regarded with as much interest as the problem of the so called refugees. The involvement of refugees in piracy adds a highly emotive element to the issue and therefore it has acquired greater public and media attention. But if you look at it from the legal point of view, and here I am speaking of the definition of refugees, there is room for doubt as to whether, strictly speaking or legally speaking, the "Boat People" can be qualified and counted as refugees.

So perhaps the better term that might be used with regard to the victims of such acts of violence on the high seas is "persons or people in distress at sea". That would, I think, include various displaced and uprooted persons who find themselves on an open sea and are subjected to piratical attacks. The problem of piracy in south-east Asia waters is part and parcel of the larger problem of refugees from Indo-China. Since the fall of Saigon in 1975, nearly one million Indo-Chinese have left Vietnam, Laos and Cambodia to seek refuge in my country, Thailand. For example, the Vietnamese crisis and offensive against Kampuchea along the Thai/Kampuchean border in 1984 led to an influx of a quarter million Cambodians into Thailand. As the country of first refuge Thailand has had to bear a very heavy burden in taking care of these refugees and displaced persons on behalf of the international community.

The boat people who first trickled to our shores back in 1975 and came literally in torrents the following year, were part of the streams of refugees from Indo-China. Nearly all the boat people have come from Vietnam, either escaping persecution which would categorise them as political refugees or as economic migrants. The latter would not, strictly speaking, fall within the category of refugees. The Thai government alone has since 1975 offered almost 90,500 of these boat people refuge in

Thailand. At present there are about 10,281 boat people in Phanat Nikhom holding and processing centre which is under the supervision of the Office of the United Nations High Commissioner for Refugees (UNHCR) in Thailand. It has always been the policy and continues to be the policy to provide protection and assistance to these helpless people in ways commensurate with our limited resources and capabilities.

I should also want to emphasise that, since the inception of the problem of the boat people, the ASEAN countries, including Thailand, have been actively involved in various programmes to try to assist. Reception centres and processing centres have been established in various ASEAN countries—in the Philippines, for instance, and in Indonesia as well as in Thailand—to cope with the growing problem. So it is not correct to harbour the impression that the boat people case has been dumped on the international community while the countries of first refuge have done nothing to assist them. I think this would be a travesty and very unfair to the countries of the area.

Since Vietnam, which is the source of the boat people, is situated within a large sea area comprising also part of what we call the Gulf of Thailand, the people seeking to flee from Vietnam (the country of origin) have had to face very long and arduous sea journeys. They must traverse the waters just off the so called Gulf of Thailand which covers an area of approximately 120,000 square miles; but Thailand has, with its limited capacity, the responsibility for an area of only some 18,000 square miles, or 15% of the Gulf's area. This is due partly to the fact that the Gulf comprises high seas as well as exclusive economic zones (EEZs), contiguous zones and territorial waters of other coastal states. Even though it is called the Gulf of Thailand, Thailand does not own the gulf.

We are also faced with the problem that Thailand is quite a substantial pristine water fishing country with a large fleet comprising over 40,000 boats. So on any given day several thousand boats congregate in an area which goes beyond our maritime border, to conduct peaceful fishing operations. As pointed out in a 1983 report on anti-piracy assessment by a team of experts responsible to the UNHCR, there is no method available at the present time to differentiate between the vast majority of fishing vessels going about their legitimate business and the vessels that belong to the occasional pirates. The attacks on the boat people are often initiated in an opportunistic manner, or perhaps some of the fishermen are tempted to prey on helpless boats in the hope of gaining some loot. This would tend to suggest that if there was no loot, then perhaps there would be no piratical acts.

Long before the boat people became an international issue, the Thai authorities provided anti-piracy protection systems with the cooperation of the United Nations. In 1981, the Royal Thai Government began receiving approximately $1 million every year for this anti-piracy programme.

However in June 1982 international donors became actively involved in making allocations to the anti-piracy programme, with the cooperation of the UNHCR. Twelve countries (Australia, Canada, Denmark, Federal Republic of Germany, France, Italy, Japan, Netherlands, Norway, Switzerland, United Kingdom and the United States) donated $3,672,033 through the UNHCR in order to get the first programme started. Further details of the budget will be found in Chapter 6, and of the US Contribution in particular in Chapter 7. This anti-piracy programme, initiated by Thailand together with the UNHCR and the other countries, constitutes the biggest international cooperation against piratical acts anywhere in the world today.

Besides three fast patrol boats, three surveillance aircraft (including spotters) and six or seven "special operation trawlers" have been employed to combat pirate activity. At first some of the trawlers were disguised as fishing boats, but this has been given up because the pirates seemed to recognise them.

The personnel involved specifically in anti-piracy operations number no fewer than 130. The surface unit operates on patrol schedules providing 24 hour patrols every day. Not every boat, of course, can be kept at sea and not every aircraft, which also operate on daily patrol schedules, can cover the area non stop for 24 hours. They take turns. Altogether there is round the clock surveillance in the area that I have mentioned which, unfortunately, covers only part of the gulf.

The aircraft unit continually coordinates with the surface unit to render assistance operationally and to persons in need. This includes spotter aircraft as well as small aircraft borrowed from sources outside of the programme. A team of nine men also manage the small offshore islands located practically in the middle of the area under surveillance. These islands have been in the news because pirates often used them in the past for shore based operations and some of the captives were brought there. The island of Koh Kra is described above on page 85. The government has therefore now stationed a unit comprising military and other agency personnel under a two week rotation arrangement in order to keep the bases from the pirates.

With regard to the police department, the marine and provincial police are responsible within twelve miles from the coast, that is within our territorial waters, where they patrol and investigate all suspected vessels as well as gathering information and coordinating with the Royal Thai Navy. It will be seen that their area of responsibility is somewhat limited by law. Details of the success of law enforcement in bringing prosecutions are stated at Appendix 5.

The Harbour Department takes charge of registering numbers of boats and administers the licensing system which helps to support the Royal Thai Navy and to trace suspected vessels.

Insofar as the effectiveness of all these operations is concerned, the UNHCR sponsored team of experts have assessed the programme and noted a high degree of professionalism and dedication by the people involved in the coordinating arm of the task force. And they also considered the techniques and procedures displayed by the programme to be optimal under the circumstances.

As stated in Chapter 6, the percentage of boats being attacked by pirates has decreased since inception of this programme.

The small (but increasing) number of prosecutions is a good sign that things are improving. However, the problem persists that, as mentioned above, the area in question involves the entire Gulf of Thailand and adjacent waters, which are shared by several little states including Vietnam. Instead of putting the cart before the horse, the problem should be tackled at its source—the country of origin of the refugees—to effect a lasting solution. This could be achieved if conditions in Vietnam were better, or if the Orderly Departure Programme was improved so as to reduce the number of refugees and displaced persons risking escape in leaking boats on the high seas.

This leads to a number of conclusions. First, as stated in Chapter 6, concerted efforts by all the countries in the region are required. Therefore diplomatic means should be pursued and continue to be pursued. It is not a question of adopting a bilateral, regional or international approach—all approaches are essential to alleviate the situation. Further, it would be surprising if we have ever known the true number of deaths as a result of the condition of the boats or other perils at sea. Of course we shall never be sure, but it is believed that the number of so called refugees from Vietnam lost at sea in this way exceeds those killed or injured in piratical incidents. Yet it often happens that the root cause, Vietnam, escapes all blame.

The second point we should bear in mind is that, as stated in Chapter 2, if there was no loot there might be no piracy. In this case the "loot" is persons in distress at sea in leaky boats seeking refuge from Vietnam. If the influx or the flow of these unfortunate people is reduced or even eliminated, then there will be fewer and fewer incidents of piratical attacks against them.

There is another point. There have always been many restrictive economic policies and practices in certain countries, particularly in Indo-China, and these have led to a great deal of smuggling—including smuggling between countries which are outside Indo-China proper. The smuggled goods range from consumer goods to, for example, tin ore for smelting. If we can stop this kind of illicit traffic or smuggling then perhaps the temptation would be reduced and, again, there would be no loot, and fewer and fewer pirates. Of course, there is no record of smugglers being attacked by pirates at sea because, since smuggling is illegal, one cannot expect smugglers to come to a court of law or the police and complain of being attacked by other criminals.

A further point—the unsatisfactory implementation or, if I may say so, the failure, of the rules concerning rescue at sea is partly responsible for the suffering of these boat people. This point has been stressed even by the UNHCR, but often escapes notice. The question could, I think, be resolved through international cooperation, for example by means of

DISERO and RASRO, as defined in Chapter 7. It is too much to expect countries of first refuge to accept without any condition a permanent settlement of people picked up at sea by foreign registered merchant vessels. Some other countries will not wish to add to the refugee burden already facing them; but together I think they could help alleviate the problem and ensure better implementation of the generally accepted rules on rescue at sea.

Another step which could be taken is to explore the possibility of convening an international conference, perhaps under the auspices of the UN Secretary General or the UNHCR, to map out an integrated plan to solve the problem of the boat people in all its aspects. This would include the Orderly Departure Programme, which is a fair option, as well as anti-piracy measures, rescue at sea, and resettlement in third countries. Only if the international community can summon the political will to address the problem in all its aspects will it be finally and completely resolved. This political will could usefully be translated into an anti-piracy centre that would help improve the collation of information, the coordination of monitoring activity and perhaps provide some kind of early warning system.

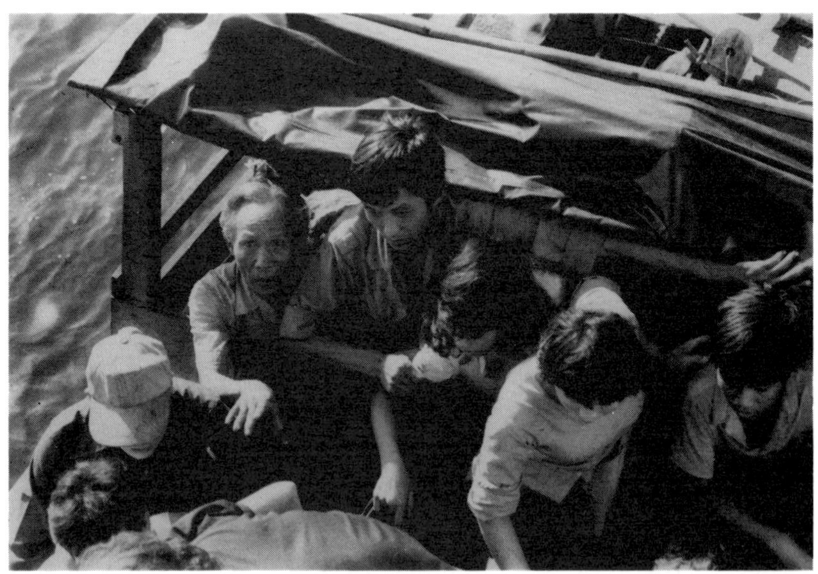

SOUTH CHINA SEA/1986/Boat People/Rescue at Sea
Adrift in the South China Sea: For these Vietnamese refugees it was a happy ending.
Photo: UNHCR/16021/R. Manin

SOUTH CHINA SEA/1986/Boat People/Rescue at Sea
For some refugees, suffering continues after their rescue

THE BOAT PEOPLE

CONFERENCE DISCUSSION

The following discussion between contributing authors took place during the Marine Policy Centre's 1985 update workshop on Piracy at Sea. The workshop was held at the Woods Hole Oceanographic Institute, Massachusetts, USA.

ELLEN: I would like to ask Ambassador Kasemsri how it is that gentle people like the Thais can commit acts of savagery such as abduction and rape and if the boat people problem clears up, will they continue the attacks against other vessels in the area, unless there is some study done into this?

KASEMSRI: I do take exception having the whole people blamed for piratical incidents which sometimes are carried out by people who are not Thai. I don't think one should generalise when one deals with these terrible incidents lest this proves counterproductive and I hope very much that in this scholarly text we will always refrain from making such generalisations. But in answer to the question of savagery, it seemed to me that common criminals sometimes do not have any scruples in acting against their victims. Sometimes these criminal acts, and I am not a criminal lawyer or psychologist, are motivated by exaggerated fear, So being that as it may, it is not easy to delve into the mind of a common criminal. One must never forget when one deals with piratical acts in south-east Asia that there are reports as well as records of refugees being saved by Thai fishermen. This is not big news, so it somehow gets forgotten and not elaborated upon enough in the media. The number of boat people saved and given assistance by the Thai Government and the Thai people far exceeds the number of deaths which might have been caused by Thai fishermen.

BRITTIN: Mr Ambassador, the multilateral activity or cooperation that produced increased activity on the part of Thailand, seems a rather unique situation. I am not aware of other cases in this modern era where countries have cooperated together in trying to decrease violence at sea. I would suspect that the primary reason this cooperation occurred was because it was the humanitarian thing to do. If you could speculate for the future a bit, I suspect that you could get that same kind of cooperation on the basis of humanitarian need if events such as the boat people exodus took place elsewhere in the world. If, in fact, economics was the need, do you see that same kind of cooperation developing in other regions of the world?

KASEMSRI: Well, I certainly hope so. There are several other areas which are of major concern to the international community and certainly each area has its own peculiar conditions and difficulties. Some countries may have differences based on a concern for their own security and which may or may not to help to ensure good cooperation with their neighbours. However I am simply hopeful that, when it comes to humanitarian issues, all countries should endeavour to work together with the support of the international community, either bilaterally or through the UN system. You also have to deal with the historical aspect of it. Obviously countries today are sensitive to any accusing finger, and this may be very counterproductive. Instead of cooperating, they may very well say, "so what?".

With regard to the overall refugee situation, and I am giving my country's case as an example, we often are caught between the devil and the deep blue sea. When Thailand offers refuge to the displaced people who enter our country by land rather than by sea, we risk being accused by the countries of origin of harbouring insurgents aiming to overthrow the government, or of training them and infiltrating them back. On the other hand, if we do not accept these people, then again we risk being blamed by countries which profess humanitarianism. So we have to consider our interests first. If we feel that by ensuring temporary refuge for these people, we are not going to run short of international sympathy and cooperation, then we will do so. If not, then it is difficult to expect a developing country like Thailand to continue bearing the burden indefinitely. So far, I am happy to say that we have been able to continue with our policy, partly because of our own humanitarian convictions and partly because of the support of the international community.

HARLOW: I think that it is very important to note that when you are helping these boat people there are very sensitive political and diplomatic issues that can arise and I think in all fairness the government of Thailand should be commended for diplomatic courage in vigorously participating in an effort to diminish the suffering of the boat people and assuming a degree of political exposure in so doing.

KASEMSRI: Thank you. I would like to add one more point, if I may. The problem of drug trafficking has been mentioned as having some characteristics of a piratical act. It reminds me of the difficulty for the United States with all its resources, in stemming the trafficking of drugs. How can Thailand with its much more limited capacity patrol such vast areas effectively, given that international cooperation has not been longstanding? I would say that the anti-piracy programme, begun in 1981, is still in its infancy.

ELLEN: Mr Blaney, you have a very large investment in prevention, in fact it looks like about $1 million for every person arrested in Thailand at the present time. If the numbers were to drop and refugees were able to navigate safely along the coast of Malaysia, would it not be possible to position a Red Cross ship at a fixed point in the Gulf, with a compass fixing notifying people where she is? This would meet the problem by prevention rather than by trying to take police action.

HENKEL: There actually were ships operating in that fashion in the Gulf of Thailand previously. There were French, German and other ships, but the problem was often one of resettlement after refugees reached the ships. These ships were also perceived as a proof that the Vietnamese wanted to leave. I think these two factors together led, during the last year, to a situation where the ships could not continue to operate.

ELLEN: Well, it seems to me that the governments of the world are bucking the problem. If you are suggesting that there is a resettlement problem, we should try to overcome that problem and position these ships in international waters rather than put all the responsibilities on the Thai government to protect them in the first instance.

BLANEY: What the United States is doing, which I think in the long run will be more effective, is trying to urge the maritime community to pick up the refugees before they go into the pirate zone. If there are hundreds of merchant vessels in the Gulf of Thailand on any given day and they are picking up refugees, chances are this will afford a better chance for avoiding the piracy without putting a "magnet" ship out there. I might add that a ship located out there might be too close to Vietnamese waters and get itself in trouble.

ELLEN: I know that Bermuda opened a registration for ships and the first commitment one of their ships had was to take on board a number of refugees from Vietnam. The government almost dropped the ship's registration rather than to face the problem of taking the people back to Bermuda.

PENTTI: I wonder if I could add something to that from perhaps the merchant shipping viewpoint. Yes, the merchant shipping community has been very responsive in picking up refugees in the past and this has been going on for several years now. Although we must recognise that some forty merchant vessels passed a refugee ship and did not stop, we must also recognise that there is a cost to stopping a merchant vessel. These ships are extremely expensive and the daily running costs are very high. There is a cost in terms of lost time—someone has to pay it. In a sense I am almost surprised that the shipping community has been as responsive as it has over the years. My question is: Is it fair to expect the merchant shipping industry to accept this additional financial burden?

BLANEY: We don't expect the industry to accept that financial burden. The US, through the UNHCR, has provided generous funds for reimbursement schemes, so that any costs of picking up refugees will be fully compensated. The IMO earlier had a programme that reimbursed ships for approximately $5 per day to a limit of $5,000 per ship, and that was during a period of time when they had a smaller budget. They now have a much larger budget, and can compensate a boat for any costs that are reasonable and real in terms of the costs of diverting. There is no longer an economic disincentive.

PENTTI: What are the current limits to the pay off here? We are talking about running costs of $20,000 per day easily on many of these ships.

BLANEY: We provided $600,000 in the fund so I don't think there is a problem.

CYCON: If I may interject here, when I was speaking with IMO officials in London I wasn't made aware of UNHCR reimbursement systems, so I am not sure that the system is as publicised as it should be.

BLANEY: What we have done is to make sure that even the extreme cases are taken care of. The system is now just starting, and it is being disseminated. We are trying to work with the international maritime community in developing it. But an economic problem does not exist under the circumstances. Most ships, through either P & I Clubs or other insurance schemes, absorb the relatively minor cost that it takes to offload the refugees. What they are concerned about are the delays in port. Those delays have been minimised, if not entirely eliminated, by this disembarkation scheme. Still, more needs to be done, and that is why the IMO, for example, will be sending to the region an expert to disseminate more information. I might add that member countries, including the US, have sent CQ messages to their vessels in the area, as has the UNHCR through countries in the region.

ABRAHAMSSON: Although there may not be a financial disincentive to stopping and picking up refugees, I think one has to recognise that the captain's first duty is to his ship, his crew and the cargo. Now whatever backlash he gets from the office at home we really don't know, but I think that it would be a rare captain who would not first sit down and try to figure out what this backlash will be.

BLANEY: Why? If it is not a financial burden, what would be the problem?

ABRAHAMSSON: To set out a boat and pick up people is not the simple thing it seems when we sit and talk about it. It is a major operation out on the open sea. Modern ships do not have boats that are easily launched. Today most ships have life rafts and so on that are for use when the ship is in distress. It is not the way it was fifty years ago when you had a boat that you launched in order to go over to the next ship to have a conversation or lunch or something like that. The captain has to decide who he is going to order to make the rescue, whose life he is going to put in jeopardy. I really would be hard put to find a captain who would say that his responsibility to humanity overrode his responsibility to his crew and ship. I believe that part of the reason that so many ships pass by the refugees is not financial, is not callous, but simply a result of the sheer difficulty and dangers of trying to come to the rescue.

BLANEY: You know in one way I understand that because I have been told by others the same story. But it still makes me wonder who is crewing these ships, who is captaining them and who is giving the orders. We are trying to work at the various levels of a multi-layered problem. One of those levels is the maritime community, including shipping agents, shipping companies, charterers, insurers, port states and maritime authorities; to involve them so that they understand the requirements of international maritime law to pick up people in distress. This is a law and a duty which states have undertaken.

CYCON: How many merchant vessels are we talking about coming though the Gulf of Thailand—the pirate area?

BLANEY: There is no way of knowing the merchant ship traffic. I have been told by people in the area there are in the Gulf of Thailand on any given day hundreds of merchant ships.

PETERSON: How close do you have to be to a refugee boat even to see it, even if you are on the bridge? It is possible not to see refugees on the horizon.

BLANEY: I think that is probably true in some cases. On the other hand, there are cases where they were clearly seen and were waved at and were passed by.

ABRAHAMSSON: This indicates, of course, how rarely ships stop.

BLANEY: It is not so rare. I was in Hong Kong and a German ship had picked up refugees, taken them in. I think a Norwegian ship had done the same thing recently while I was still in Hong Kong. It is not rare but it is declining over the years. This shows a decline in the pick ups and we are trying to put this back up again.

CYCON: Mr Brittin, would you give us clarification on the obligation of the captain.

BRITTIN: It is correct that there is a duty to help those in distress but there is a qualification to that. Let me give you an example. A ship in the Arabian Gulf was hit by a missile and caught fire. The fire became very dangerous and about that time a ship was seen coming from the opposite direction—a supertanker heavily laden with oil. They sent a message by light and radio to the approaching ship. The approaching ship never got closer to them than five miles, and continued to proceed out of the area. It was entered in the log of the supertanker that they were in a combat zone and that the safety of the ship was the primary duty and that therefore, being afraid of being hit by a missile, they proceeded. So there is a basic responsibility towards the ship itself. Fortunately or unfortunately, I spent eleven years at sea on destroyers and I know of many cases, both in and out of combat situations, where all US flag ships have understood full well the responsibility to stop and aid those in distress but the danger to the crew going out in a small boat has simply overridden this responsibility and they have proceeded on.

ELLEN: With the captain's perception of danger to the ship and also with flags of convenience with a foreign crew and no particular loyalty to the flag, it is very often difficult to direct these vessels to pick up refugees. I think you have a very difficult process to educate these people to do their duty. I think we should now be looking at solutions, other than the merchant fleet to pick up the survivors.

BLANEY: It is not *the* solution. It is *a* solution that needs to be worked on. More people were picked up earlier. People were doing it and stopped. I think it may be that ship companies themselves don't know enough about the reimbursement scheme and disembarkation procedures. Perhaps a searchlight needs to be put on those who are behaving badly to enlighten them as to what the costs might be.

WALKATE: I wonder if there could be another reason why ships do not pick up such refugees? It may well be that there have been guidelines to captains to refuse to pick up any refugees because it may pose problems to the flag state in terms of asylum.

CYCON: Let me ask a clarification on that because it was a scenario which I was trying to work out earlier. A merchant ship at sea picks up twenty Vietnamese in a leaky boat, detouring to do it. The Vietnamese request from the captain asylum under the flag of his ship.

BLANEY: They are asking to be saved. Whether the ship is under a flag of convenience or from a country that accepts refugees, they are primarily responsible for them, but under the UNHCR schemes these people can be shared. So it is not correct that the whole group must be granted asylum by that flag state.

CYCON: Okay, now the next step. The ship gets into port. Can you, in a few words, tell us what happens at that port? What is the port captain's obligation? What are the rules under which he deals with disembarking boat people?

HENKEL: What is necessary for the captain is to get the resettlement guarantee. If he has this then the refugees can be disembarked at the first port of call. Under international law the captain has an obligation to rescue persons in distress, but there is no obligation for the first port of call the accept these refugees. So we have to address this issue of resettlement. I think the two UNHCR schemes will help overcome fears that flag states will be overly burdened with resettling refugees. One additional point; if one looks at the figures one will find that in 1980 21% of the persons who arrived were rescued at sea, and in 1981 the figure was still fairly high. At that time there were still the French and German ships out in the South China Sea and they picked up about 5,000 refugees in 1980 and 4,200 in 1981. As soon as the ships ceased to operate in this area the percentage of persons rescued at sea went down drastically. It was very painful to see during the last months of 1981 and in early 1982 how the mercy ships tried to survive and how they tried to approach all the various European countries. They went to the Council of Europe, and France and Germany, notably, were prepared to give some resettlement. We have tried to overcome this problem as much as possible with these two schemes.

CYCON: Is there any reason why, in addition to the UNHCR fund for reimbursement of costs, an insurance clause, which I imagine would have a minimal additional payment requirement, could not be inserted to cover costs incurred in re-routing for refugees?

PENTTI: It certainly strikes me that there would be associated costs in altering operating patterns and procedures to incorporate additional stops and steps which were not understood when the contract with the insurers was made. Maritime insurers are famous for coming up with insurance schemes. There would be a way to do it, but it is, once again, the bottom line.

There are a couple of other observations on our conversation thus far. If indeed the fund is $600,000 and if indeed a day's running costs are somewhere around $20,000, that gives you only thirty stops. It is an expensive business. Basically, as I understand it, international maritime law reflects years and years of tradition, during which a vessel in distress was an occasional encounter. It was not something that was expected to be encountered every fifty miles on a given voyage. I wonder if we are not beginning to divert the original intent of that law in saying that a merchant vessel sailing through a territory like this is now liable for every refugee vessel she comes across.

PETERSON: I think there are a number of things a ship did in the days of sail. The voyage was fairly long anyway and one additional day on the voyage didn't make much difference since the proportional cost to a ship owner of an additional day's diversion was not great, particularly in view of the absence of fuel costs. Further, in many distress incidents ships had been dismasted or had had their sails torn up and needed some assistance or supplies. But you now get into a situation where you are using fuel, you have high running speeds, seamen are being paid decent wages; and one day lost becomes proportionately a much larger cost. The whole equation of rescue at sea has changed.

BLANEY: First of all the figures just given are wrong. The maximum cost of any ship per day in the area is in the realm of $9-12,000, and this usually refers to very large container ships. The reimbursement scheme has access to funds many times in excess of any cost incurred in picking up distressed persons at sea. The ship is not going to come across a refugee boat every fifty miles. They can hardly find them as it is out there. Most ships don't even see a refugee boat. Ships do indeed rescue and they do it effectively all the time, without loss of life. There is no reason why other ships cannot also do so. I understand why a ship that is very large—a huge tanker or a container ship—doesn't see a small boat nearby and I can understand it takes two or three miles to stop a ship and how difficult it is, but there are a lot of other ships out there that don't have that difficulty and which indeed do stop. There are also some container ships, I want to add, mostly American flag or charter, that have done just that. Under the schemes devised there is no reason why any ship should have to worry about offloading their refugees. So both the refugee resettlement issue and the economic questions have been taken care of. There are other issues raised by gentlemen here which are legitimate—safety of ship, conditions of the sea, whether you see them or not. There are a lot of other questions that impact on the decision. And some countries probably give illegal orders to their ships not to pick up refugees—that problem has to be dealt with. Hopefully the problems will be at least partially resolved by the UNHCR schemes.

WALKATE: Someone walking in and hearing us discuss this would be surprised that we were not paying more attention to the actual reasons why the whole thing came about. The Ambassador of Thailand has hinted at this by saying that the problem is at the root—in Vietnam. This is of course a crazy situation. Now here is the international community trying to do something about a phenomenon created by absolutely inhuman and illegal behaviour. So, what actually has to be done is to bring pressure upon Vietnam so that it is going to be isolated in this respect. Public shame has to be mobilised, as has already happened to a certain extent. Now this may not be something for people around this table but this is actually where we have to put the main emphasis and it's a political problem. This has just not been done. We are trying to solve the problem at the margin, as one that will be over in a couple of years when there are no more Vietnamese left with money to leave.

CYCON: Do you feel that this phenomenon is something that is limited to the peculiar circumstances of Vietnam, and now Cambodia, or is it something that can repeat itself in other coastal countries over time? A more permanent scheme might then be required, rather than one designed to address a three or four year phenomenon. I don't know why there can't be a Nicaraguan or a Libyan boat people situation; and I just wonder if there is any reason why it is particular to south-east Asia.

WALKATE: It is inherent to the colonial situation, too, I suppose. Piracy has to be resolved in the long run by enforcement by coastal states and flag stages. That is not, as such, a political problem. Technically it is a criminal problem, although it may sometimes have political roots.

HENKEL: I certainly think it could occur in other situations as well. But here, of course, the main problem of the Vietnamese is that there is hardly any other way out of the country than by boat. Otherwise you would have to go via Kampuchea and that is extremely dangerous and difficult. Whereas in Nicaragua or the Sudan or what have you, you can go to your neighbouring country overland.

SEACARE

P.O. BOX 998, LEE, LONDON SE12 0RH
TEL: (01) 403 2297

Details of the work to be undertaken by this rescue/mission ship will be found in Chapter 5.

Part 3. The Law of Piracy

CHAPTER 9

PIRACY PAST, PRESENT AND FUTURE

P. W. Birnie

As has been observed elsewhere, piracy may well be the world's third oldest profession, medicine being the second oldest.[1] Piracy is an age old offence;[2] references to it were made in Justinian's Digest in 529 AD, in King John's Ordinance of 1201, and in numerous European laws from then on. It was also the subject of Papal Bulls and international treaties from early times. Pope Alexander VI's Bull of 1493 dividing the Atlantic Ocean between Spain and Portugal held each responsible for regulating piracy in its area as did the Treaty of Tordesillas, which confirmed this arrangement the following year. Britain's first Piracy Act came in 1698 and was followed by further Acts in 1721, 1837 and 1850. The Territorial Waters Jurisdiction Act of 1878 finally preserved the offence of piracy *jure gentium* under English law.[3]

Piracy is most familiar to us from the romantic literature of our childhood, in the form it took in the 17th to 19th centuries when pirates operated from distant ports or uninhabited coasts and islands, preying on the commercial explorers of a period when most navies lacked the skills and equipment to dominate the oceans. Madagascar was once for 35 years a pirate republic, for example, calling itself Libertalia and operating its own laws and international language; shipping enterprises dealing in piracy were set up in some US cities.[4] Such pirates were robbers who attacked and plundered other vessels indiscriminately and violently, roaming the oceans for this nefarious purpose and hence being sometimes referred to as 'rovers'. They carried out such activities in all the major sea areas – the Mediterranean, the Atlantic, the Middle and Far East, the Pacific and Indian Oceans. Sometimes states even licensed piratical acts: corsairs were commissioned to commit piratical acts against the enemies of their country.[5] Are we to equate modern terrorists with them? Pirate ships, once captured, could be commissioned as privateers to plunder ships of the same flag as the original attackers, in retaliation. This practice was ended by the Treaty of Paris in 1856,[6] however. Following the growth of certain navies, particularly the Royal Navy, from the 19th century, and Britain's long-lasting control of the world's major oceans and seaways in the period that followed, such forms of piracy virtually disappeared.[7] The growth of colonies in the 19th century also denied to pirates the uninhabited island bases that they had once freely used. By 1925, it was possible to ask 'Is the crime of piracy obsolete?'[8] It is often assumed that in an era of population growth, rapid technological developments in enforcement vessels, telecommunications and comprehensive surveillance of the oceans by aircraft, helicopters and satellites, this remains the situation.

What has happened, however, is that piracy, although it has decreased, has adapted to modern technical, political, economic and social developments and still exists, albeit in new forms which require new means for its suppression. Moreover, the growth period of piracy coincided with the emergence of the jurisdictional basis of the law of the sea, which, from the time of the great doctrinal debates between Grotius, Selden and Welwood in the 17th century,[9] was founded on a simple division of the seas into a narrow belt of territorial sea over which the coastal state exercised sovereignty and, therefore, exclusive jurisdiction, and the high seas, the area beyond, in which the doctrine of the freedom of the seas prevailed. This doctrine was based on the economic necessity of maintaining freedom of navigation to enable the development of trade with the New World and protecting the interests of such fishermen as wished to venture into distant waters. Piracy had to be stamped out on the high seas to preserve these freedoms which were then perceived as being to the advantage of the whole international community. Not only were pirates a threat to the existing global economy they also frequently resorted to such unbridled savagery in the attacking and plundering of vessels, crews and passengers without discrimination that they came to be regarded as *hostes humani generis,*[10] enemies of the whole human race.

It was accepted, therefore, by all states that jurisdiction over piratical acts should be universal, that is to say that the vessels of any state could apprehend them and that any state into whose jurisdiction the pirates were brought or found could try and punish them under its laws, even though the offence had been committed beyond the generally accepted scope of national jurisdiction, namely, at that period, on the high seas.[11] The basis of the international law establishing piracy *jure gentium* was to protect community interests in economic development and humanitarian standards. An understanding of this will help us to ascertain whether, and if so how, the law requires further adaptation today to protect these or other perceived community interests.

Controversy, however, still surrounds the jurisprudential basis of this universal jurisdiction. Some writers and researchers take the view that despite the uniqueness of its designation by international customary law as an offence against the whole human race piracy is not a crime. The compilers of the Harvard Research Draft[12] on the subject commented that it is not a crime against the law of nations but generates a unique solution — a special ground of jurisdiction permitting the exercise of a state's own national laws, the actual exercise of jurisdiction being dependent on the will and national laws of states. Others, such as Johnson,[13] doubt whether it can be regarded as a crime because of the absence of any international criminal court or a treaty to which all states are party; other writers, on the other hand, have no hesitation in referring to it as a crime, because of the heinous nature of the acts performed, and in attributing the basis of universal jurisdiction to this perception.[14]

Controversy also surrounds the precise definition of piracy. This derives from the fact that although there is general agreement on at least a minimum definition, which will be outlined below, some states define, or have in the past defined, the offence more widely in their municipal laws. As the cases come to trial in municipal courts the differences in the scope of international and national definitions have often confused the issue and the underlying reasoning.[15] Attempts to clarify the situation by codifying the international law of piracy in the 1958 Geneva Convention on the High Seas[16] and the 1982 UN Law of the Sea Convention[17] have further confounded matters since the definitions adopted are narrow ones, not consonant with all states' laws, and have been expressed in somewhat ambiguous terms leaving in doubt seizures of vessels by their own crew or passengers and seizure of any vessel for political ends — as occurred in the cases of the *Santa Maria* and *Achille Lauro* — or by states, as in the *Mayaguez* or *Pueblo* incidents. An examination of the present state of the law and its relevance to violent acts performed at sea today has to comprehend analysis of both the international and municipal law perspectives of the offence, as well as a study of the kinds of violence occurring. The definition of piracy will thus be examined first, before the nature and incidence of the acts occurring today, which might be categorized as piracy in its widest sense, are described.

The definition of piracy

The definition has evolved over the years in response to states' needs as evidenced in state practice. It is not proposed to give an elaborate analysis of this process and its ambiguities, as this has been done at length elsewhere,[18] but to point out the main stages of its development and the problems that remain. It must be stressed at the outset that there are preliminary problems deriving from the fact that there are two forms of definition, namely by international law and municipal law, and that the international law definition itself gives rise to two interpretations, one based on that codified in the 1958 Geneva Convention on the High Seas and repeated in the 1982 Law of Sea Convention, appertaining only to the 56 parties to the former, the other open to non-parties to the convention, based on pre-existing customary law. As the UNCLOS is not in force, the position of the 159 states which have signed it and the 32 parties that have ratified is somewhat unclear, except insofar as they include parties to the 1958 Convention. Having established the law under these heads we will finally have to ask whether it is now outmoded in the light of present practices involving violence at sea.

Piracy in municipal law

Every state can (but is not required so to do) promulgate its own laws on piracy, applicable, of course, only to its own nationals or to ships or persons found within its own jurisdiction or vessels registered under its flag. These may (but again are not required so to do) conform to the international definition of the offence or piracy *jure gentium*. Every state is entitled, but not obliged, to assume jurisdiction over pirates *jure gentium* on the high seas. States can prescribe their own penalties; these are not laid down by international law.[19] At one time the death sentence was common but it no longer is so. The municipal law can complement the *jus gentium* even though it cannot *per se* change the nature of piracy *jure gentium* at the international level. The laws of each state thus may vary both in content and area of application. Since the jurisdictional limits of the coastal state have been in state of flux for over 20 years and, in the absence of the entry into force of the new UNCLOS,arguably remain so, both in relation to the precise limits of the territorial sea and the juridical status of the new zones, whether established in the UNCLOS or by state practice, considerable confusion is apparent.

English courts assert jurisdiction over piracy *jure gentium* under common law and thus themselves determine the elements of piracy *jure gentium*. They tend to think of it as a sea term for robbery, which covers any violent dispossession of a master of his ship, including by crew or passengers who subsequently convert the vessel to felonious purposes, although the requirement of personal gain has largely been dropped.[20] The courts' judgments have often been more concerned to find what is *not* piracy than what is, as in the leading case of *In Re Piracy Jure Gentium 1934,*[21] when the court found that frustrated attempts to commit piracy also constituted piracy *jure gentium,* without actual robbery occurring, although in the course of so finding they referred approvingly to Kenny's definition of piracy as any armed violence at sea which is not a lawful act of war.

As recently as 1971 a case that was found to be piracy, which would certainly not be piracy under the current international law, came before the Scottish courts.[22] Five crew members were charged with seizing a British ship, the *Mary Craig,* at sea 'about' three miles off the coast of Aberdeen, taking over command from the captain, whom they put ashore, and navigating the vessel on to the high seas. Amongst the defences made was that the facts alleged did not constitute piracy as internationally recognized and charges that the accused tried to ram another vessel on the high seas about six to eight miles off Aberdeenshire were contended to be irrelevant because committed outside territorial waters. It was also contended that robbery was a necessary ingredient of piracy and that possession of the vessel had to be obtained forcibly for profit. Scottish works defining piracy such as Hume I and Macdonald (5th edition) as well as the case of *In Re Piracy Jure Gentium* were referred to. On the basis of these, Lord Cameron found that robbery of the ship itself was sufficient to constitute piracy. He also approved their Lordships' remark in that case that 'A careful examination of the subject shows a gradual widening of the earlier definition of piracy to bring it from time to time more in consonance with situations either not thought of or not in existence when the older jurisconsults were expressing their opinions'.[23] Lord Cameron also noted their reference to Hall's view (International Law, 8th edn, 1924, p 314) that piratical acts included 'robbery or attempted robbery of a vessel by force or intimidation either by way of attack from without or by way of revolt of the crew and conversion of the vessel and cargo to their own use'.[24] He concluded that there was sufficient authority to find that the circumstances in this case amounted to the crime of piracy *jure gentium,* and equated the requirements to that of robbery on land, finding that a charge of robbery was sufficient to constitute one of piracy even though piracy had not been set out in the indictment. As Merchant Shipping Acts extended jurisdiction of British courts to cover British subjects committing offences on board all British ships on the high seas, Lord Cameron also concluded that the Scottish courts had jurisdiction in this case; the latter conclusion appears to be well founded, unlike the former, but it should be noted that various British statutes also give British courts jurisdiction to try for 'piracy' those engaged in the slave trade or mutiny.[25]

In the USA, however (since there is no common law criminal jurisdiction), the offence of piracy *jure gentium* has been incorporated into the municipal Federal law by a statute of 1909 which provides: 'Whosoever in the high seas commits the crime of piracy, as defined by the law of nations, and is afterwards brought into or found in the United states shall be imprisoned for life'.[26] Even so in the leading US case of *U.S.* v. *Smith* in 1820,[27] a US judge held that *he* could define piracy *jure gentium* and that in his view it was 'robbery upon the sea'. Piracy under US law also covers revolt and mutiny, but no longer the slave trade. In the 1920s, during the Prohibition era, the USA was at first hesitant to regard the hijacking of illicit liquor running 'rumships' off its shores as piracy but in fact to do so would seem to present no difficulty since the acts committed involved both robbery and violence and took place between two ships outside US jurisdiction.[28]

Piracy in customary international law

Writers and draftsmen have experienced great difficulty in defining what constitutes piracy at the international level. From the end of the 17th century, some states began to treat piracy as an international problem that they should eradicate. Certainly it was accepted that robbery, murder, rape, torture and plunder committed from one ship to another constituted piracy. The vessel concerned could be either a private vessel, with or without nationality, or a warship of a state at peace with the flag state of the victims; warships of states at war with states other than the victim's state, not involved in blockade, were also considered to come within the scope of the offence. It was unclear whether piracy was confined to the high seas since in that period the concept of territorial zones was fluid and unfixed.[29]

In the 18th and 19th centuries the definition broadened under the impact of municipal laws but also became controversial. The acceptance of the territorial sea doctrine settled part of the controversy concerning the relation between municipal and international piracy laws; municipal law applied exclusively in the territorial sea to nationals or ships registered in the state concerned and flying its flag. After reviewing the relevant decisions in municipal courts, Johnson concludes that clearly by the 20th century piracy under the *jus gentium* was confined to the high seas.[30] In the territorial sea the concept of the *jus gentium* did not apply, unless specifically enacted (as by the USA), because crimes committed within territorial jurisdiction are perceived as crimes against the state, not the international community.

Continued confusion of municipal and international definitions of piracy

The differences between the two systems were often overlooked and some national courts interpreted piracy *jure gentium* in terms of their own municipal law, as in the *Mary Craig* case outlined earlier. For a period some states thus continued to include mutiny and internal seizure in their municipal definitions of so-called piracy *jure gentium*. Although mutiny was not usually categorized as piracy, because of the similarity of some mutinous acts to piratical ones courts quite often found them to be piratical.[31] Thus a variety of acts have at various times been categorized as piracy.

Internal seizures. Internal seizure of the ship has always presented problems for writers trying to distinguish it from mutiny and remove it from categorization as piracy on the basis either of the status of the individuals undertaking the seizure, the amount of violence involved or the motives for the seizure, which might not be purely private but political, or occasioned by insanity or irrationality.[32] Some courts made no such distinctions and treated all such acts as piracy. This issue in particular still confuses international law.

State acts and belligerent rights. Although, as remarked earlier, for a period it was accepted that states could authorize privateers and corsairs to engage in piratical acts on their behalf to seek revenge or recompense, in certain circumstances this caused controversy and the end of the practice in 1856 was welcomed. Rules developed concerning acts by belligerents, both recognized and unrecognized, but these also gave rise to dissension.[33] By the mid-19th century the maritime forceful actions of recognized belligerents were accepted as legitimate in customary law in response to the numerous revolutions during that period leading to constitutional changes; it was realized that the rebels of today may be the governments of tomorrow and vice versa. Though it was recognized that there was a limit to such actions and that certain acts beyond that limit could be regarded as piratical, the limit was vague and undefined.

It was accepted, however, that actions by unrecognized governments or belligerents could clearly be piratical, as could plundering of ships not party to the hostilities.[34] Although this distinction was helpful, it relied for its success on subjective determination of belligerent status by other states; it was seldom that they concurred given the extent to which national interest dominates such political decisions.

The doctrine of piracy developed in response to particular cases, as it continues to do today, and particularly the growth in its incidence in the 17th and 18th centuries. A few regional treaties were concluded, eg the 1889 Montevideo Convention accepting as a general principle of law that suppression of piracy was the responsibility of mankind, and the 1856 Declaration of Paris already referred to. From the late 19th century onwards it was accepted that a customary international law establishing piracy *jure gentium* had evolved and more states incorporated it into their national laws,[35] but the problems encountered in developing it in municipal law remained embedded in the questions of internal seizure and the distinction between piracy pursued for political and private ends. After reviewing the relevant municipal cases concerning this issue, Johnson found that there were some precedents for the view that piracy could be constituted by both internal seizure and acts for political ends before the conclusion of the 1958 Geneva Convention.[36]

Piracy by analogy. Contentious attempts were made to adapt the doctrine to cover some of the ruthless methods used in submarine warfare during the first world war. *The Washington Declaration* of 1922[37] between the UK, France, Italy, Japan and the USA aimed to punish 'as if for an act of piracy' anyone violating the rules it set out for attacks on merchant shipping by submarines and surface vessels.

The Nyon Agreement of 1937[38] was concluded between Britain, France, Belgium, Egypt, Greece, Romania, Turkey, the USSR and Yugoslavia, following attacks on merchant vessels in the Mediterranean by unidentified aircraft and submarines acting on behalf of Spanish insurgents during the Civil War. Its text referred to acts 'which should justly be treated as acts of piracy' and 'piratical acts' by submarines, but the measures proposed to counteract them differed from the extension of universal jurisdiction.

Both the Washington and Nyon approaches were generally criticized as unjustified, inappropriate and unnecessary attempts to extend the scope of 'piracy' *jure gentium,* similar to 19th century municipal attempts to hold states capable of committing piracy.[39] Thus no attempt was made to accuse of piracy the German Admirals tried at Nuremburg on charges concerning submarine warfare. It seemed then to be accepted that not all unlawful acts or incidents at sea had to be presented as 'piracy', which made its definition easier.

Towards codification – League of Nations' activities

The question of piracy was seen as a topic ripe for codification by the League of Nations. It commissioned a report from a subcommittee of its Committee of Experts for the Progressive Codification of International Law.[40] The report attempted to resolve some of the ambiguities. It restricted piracy to acts on the high seas, but excluded acts of state controlled vessels and acts for political purposes. It disassociated true piracy from the problem of submarine attacks and political actions, which it called 'piracy by analogy' since they were not a danger to the shipping or commerce of all states indiscriminately. It recognized, however, that vessels without flags could commit piracy and that warships, after a mutiny, could be converted to pirate ships and also that unrecognized insurgents could commit piracy. These solutions were not universally accepted, however, and even more contentious was a proposal that foreign vessels could engage in hot pursuit of pirates into the territorial sea of states that were unable themselves to pursue them.

Various other proposals also proved unpopular including one that pirates could be tried by commanders of the warships that captured them.

The few government comments received on the League report did not evidence either interest or enthusiasm for the topic and were disparate. In general it appeared many considered the time was not ripe for codification, perhaps because some thought the crime was virtually extinct. Only Romania saw a positive need for, and submitted a draft of a piracy convention intended to be a forerunner of others establishing crimes against international society and an international criminal court. Nonetheless the League's Assembly decided on the basis of the Report to select piracy as a topic for its Codification Conference. Harvard Law School thereupon undertook to organize research into the international law of piracy and to prepare a draft convention for the International Law Commission. This, with a detailed scholarly commentary, was published in 1932.

The Harvard Research Draft 1932[41]

The draft, the first to formalize the customary law, recognized the individual competence of states over the offence, ie that every state had jurisdiction over piracy (Article 2) which was constituted by any act of violence or depredation (or complicity therein) with intent to rob, rape, wound, enslave, imprison or kill a person or with intent to steal or destroy property (Article 3) as long as the acts were committed in connection with an attack on another ship. Unlike the League draft, it permitted seizure of pirates in the territorial seas of other states in certain circumstances and made it clear by definition that aircraft were now included. Article 16 preserved a state's right to protect its nationals, ships and trade against interference at sea by measures not based on piracy, a provision giving rise to food for thought concerning the development of ship hijacking today. But it clearly excluded from piracy unlawful attacks on persons or property for public purposes whether made on behalf of states, recognized belligerent groups or unrecognized bands of revolutionaries. Jurisdiction over these, it considered, should at present be reserved to the injured state, the states or recognized government for which the actions were carried out, and the state of nationality or domicile of the offender.

The Geneva Convention on the High Seas 1958[42]

The Harvard Draft formed the basis, after the second world war, for the International Law Commission's work on piracy for inclusion in the UN's 1958 Geneva Convention on the High Seas.[43] As Chinese Nationalists were by then allegedly intercepting on the high seas vessels bound for the People's Republic of China, it is not surprising to find that the USSR proposed that acts executed by warships and individuals for political ends could constitute piracy,[44] citing the Nyon Agreements as precedent. A Czech proposal for a general definition that could be interpreted to cover such acts was rejected by the UNCLOS I, which adopted the convention in its present restrictive form. The ICL's draft, aiming to avoid or remove the most contentious aspects of the customary law on piracy, watered down the more detailed Harvard Research Draft and restricted the concept both to acts for 'private ends' only and to the 'high seas' area (Article 15).

As the relevant provisions have been repeated verbatim in the 1982 Convention they will be discussed in detail later in connection with it. It suffices to note here that by adopting a restrictive approach the ICL created two piracy doctrines: one based on the convention; the other, more permissive, on customary practice. In effect the customary law was not fully codified although the High Seas Convention purports in its Preamble to be 'desirous of codifying the customary law', and there was still no global consensus on the definition of piracy.

The UN's Third Conference on the Law of the Sea, required by the UN to produce a single treaty, had to negotiate a political package that would be acceptable to all states overall. It seems to have deemed it wise, therefore, to avoid re-opening old controversies by merely repeating verbatim the relevant articles on piracy from the 1958 Convention.

The United Nations Convention on the Law of the Sea 1982 (UNCLOS)[45]

Although the UNCLOS, like the 1958 Convention, has eight articles (Articles 100-107) specifically devoted to piracy, there are others, particularly those establishing new jurisdictional zones and concepts, that impact upon piracy today. The old weaknesses and ambiguities not only thus remain but are exacerbated by the zonal provisions. The UNCLOS took no account of an International Law Association Report of 1970[46] that simply defined piracy as unlawful seizure or taking control of a vessel by violence, threats thereof, surprise, fraud or other means.

The rapporteur concerned (Professor Johnson) considered that internal seizures and hijackings occurring on the vessel were piracy and should be included in the definition.[47]

Article 100 does not require states to repress piracy but merely to cooperate as fully as possible to do so and then only on the high seas or in places beyond national jurisdiction (generally thought to refer to Antarctica and such uninhabited islands as remain unclaimed, but it should be noted that the Antarctic continent is subject to some territorial claims and that certain of these claimants have asserted territorial sea or 200-mile exclusive economic zones there on the basis of these claims). There is no duty to cooperate in suppressing piracy in the territorial sea, the area in which, as we shall see, it is now most likely to occur.

Piracy is defined in the key article, Article 101, as consisting of:

(a) any *illegal* acts of violence or detention, or any act of depredation, committed for *private ends* by the crew or the passengers of a *private* ship or private aircraft, and directed:

(i) on the high seas, against another ship or aircraft, or against persons or property on board such ship or aircraft;

(ii) against a ship, aircraft, persons or property in a place outside the jurisdiction of any State.

(b) any act of *voluntary participation* in the operation of a ship or of an aircraft with knowledge of facts making it a pirate ship or aircraft;

(c) any act of *inciting* or *intentionally facilitating* an act described in sub-paragraphs (a) or (b).[48]

Piracy is thus clearly confined to private ends; *all* political seizures are ruled out unless 'private' is to be liberally interpreted in certain circumstances.[49] It is not clear that piracy in areas beyond national jurisdiction must involve 'another' ship or aircraft since this is not specified as it is for piracy on the high seas. Nor is it clear what the use of the word 'illegal' signifies.[50] Do the acts concerned have to be tested under national or international law? Surely not the latter unless privateering is to be revived, or authorization of state or rebel groups similarly to become possible?[51]

The remaining articles:

- approve commission of piracy by a warship whose crew has mutinied and converted the ship to that purpose;
- define pirate ship in terms of the interest of those controlling it; and
- allow for retention of the ship's nationality if its flag state so desires and allow every state to seize a pirate ship on the high seas using warships or government vessels.

They do not deal with frustrated attempts although these were widely accepted in the customary definition.

As in the Geneva Convention on the High Seas (Article 15(1) (a)) piracy thus remains circumscribed by geographic limitation, made worse by the fact that the 1982 Convention (Article 3) permits (but does not require) a 12-mile breadth for the territorial sea and the use of a system of straight baselines (Article 7), the increasing use (and sometimes abuse) of which is pushing the outer limit of the territorial sea further from the coasts since bays, offshore islands and coastal indentations can all be included in internal waters. Moreover, each extension of the territorial sea also extends the states's control of the airspace above (Article 2(2)). The UNCLOS accepts, although it also limits, the concept of archipelagic straight baselines connecting the outermost islands of an archipelago and forming the baseline from which the territorial sea of such states is measured (Part IV, Articles 46-54). Such states can regard the waters enclosed and the airspace above them as subject to their sovereignty. Thus vast areas are now removed from the operation of piracy *jure gentium* although some of them, such as the waters off Indonesia and the Philippines, are particularly vulnerable to piracy in its modern forms, as we shall see.

The UNCLOS also provides for an extension of the contiguous zone from the 12 miles permitted in the Geneva Convention on the Territorial Sea to 24 miles, but still does not include piracy within the laws in relation to which a state may exercise in this zone the control necessary to prevent violations. This deficiency incidentally limits the exercise of the right of hot pursuit since it cannot then be exercised for piracy occurring in this zone, which remains piracy on the high seas, however.

Finally, further problems arise from the provisions permitting establishment of a 200-mile exclusive economic zone (Part VI, Articles 55-57) measured from the territorial sea baselines but applicable only to the area beyond that belt, within which the coastal state has exclusive rights to exploit natural resources and over other economic uses, as well as various additional jurisdictional rights. The situation is complicated because the piracy provisions are in Part VI of the UNCLOS relating to the high seas which states (in Article 86) that it applies 'to all parts of the sea that are not included in the exclusive economic zone, in the territorial sea or in the internal waters of a state, or in the archipelagic waters of an archipelagic state'. Although Article 58 states that in the EEZ all states continue to enjoy the freedoms of navigation and overflight and 'other internationally lawful uses of the sea related to them, such as those associated with the operation of ships' and aircraft, it also makes these rights subject to the relevant provisions of the Convention' without making it clear which are the 'relevant provisions' or which take priority. Article 86 adds that the article 'does not entail any abridgement of the freedoms enjoyed by all States' in the EEZ under Article 58, which itself also adds that 'Articles 88 to 115 . . . apply to the exclusive economic zone so far as they are not incompatible with this Part', but coastal states may consider that as the zone's purpose is to secure their exclusive right to its economic uses and as its legal status is arguably left *sui generis* by the wording of the UNCLOS since it is not clearly stated to be part of the high seas, it is their responsibility to protect navigation from piratical assaults; the better view, however, would be that as the zone is by its terms not part of the territorial sea the piracy articles apply in it.[52] States taking the other line might also argue, however, that piracy is an unlawful use outwith the residual rights of other states. The fact that attempts by the UNCLOS Drafting Committee to eliminate this confusion in favour of the better view were rebuffed bodes ill for future interpretation. It may be resolved by resort to the dispute settlement procedures provided by the Convention when it comes into force but it is unlikely that all states will be parties to the Convention and in any case Article 59 concerning attribution of rights and jurisdictions in the EEZ between coastal and other states in the event of conflict is itself ambiguous: it merely provides that such conflicts should be resolved 'on the basis of equity and in the light of all the relevant circumstances, taking into account the respective importance of the interests involved to the parties as well as to the international community as a whole'.

What effect is this opportunity to revise the definition going to have on modern piracy since so much of the area formerly regarded as high seas is, or might be, withdrawn from this categorization? Only 7%-15% of recent incidents of violence at sea would have been classed as piracy had the UNCLOS been fully operational. Although the treaty is not formally in force, much of its zonal provisions is becoming, or is likely to be become, part of customary law through state practice.

Traditional piratical acts against modern vessels using new technology

A recent work based on the proceedings of a workshop on violence at sea[53] provides a wealth of information on this subject, as also do the proceedings of a seminar organized by the Nautical Institute in London last year[54] and the three reports produced by the International Maritime Bureau (IMB) for the IMO[55]. It appears that most attacks against shipping take place in particular geographical areas, in particular off the West Coast of Africa (especially Nigeria, Ghana and Sierra Leone), off Brazil, in the Caribbean and in South-East Asia, particularly in the Straits of Malacca and Singapore and the Phillip Channel, mostly on the Indonesian side where there are many small islands. Some pirates use radar to locate vessels; gather intelligence from radio and from informers in the receiving warehouses (so that even particular containers can be targeted on particular ships) and carry out their attacks with fast motorized boats often armed with sophisticated guns; they use modern boarding gear and have attacked vessels up to 100,000 d.w.t. Most of these pirates are land based and do not roam the seas as of old.

Most of the attacks now occur in ports and harbours or in other parts of internal or coastal waters, not on the high seas, and are thus not piracy *jure gentium,* although some acts do occur as far as 20 miles offshore. There are probably twice as many incidents as are actually reported since owners are loath to attract publicity which could have an adverse effect on unions, insurance premiums and trading partner countries. The states concerned themselves often want to keep the attacks private for commercial and national security reasons. Most attacks off Africa are of the robbery with violence type, but those off Asia often involve also extreme cruelty.

Problems and response

The problem this situation presents, as the offences mostly occur within areas of national jurisdiction (disregarding the existence of an EEZ), outside the scope of the universal jurisdiction accorded under piracy *jure gentium* as presently conceived, is one of ensuring that appropriate national laws exist and that they are enforced. It will be observed that the problem countries are all developing states with large offshore areas. Provision of outside practical or financial aid to improve enforcement would appear to provide the best response in such cases. Although extending the scope of piracy *jure gentium* to encompass at least the territorial sea would also be advantageous, it seems unlikely that coastal states will accept this since they would regard it as an invasion of their sovereignty. States could accept help in enforcement from other states' coastguard or naval vessels by concluding bilateral agreements, as some Caribbean countries have done with the USA.

Other offences fall into the categories of yacht piracy, piracy against boat people, and piracy for political purposes and by belligerents.

Yacht piracy. Accurate statistics on the seizing of yachts also are hard to come by but US authorities believe that in the areas most affected, the Gulf of Mexico and the Caribbean (especially the Bahamas) over 200 people have disappeared.[56] Similar incidents occur in South-East Asian waters, the Gulf of Aden and the Red Sea. A main cause of such seizures is drug smuggling; smugglers steal yachts at sea and either kidnap or dispose of those on board. The yacht is generally disposed of after one trip. The large and growing number of private yachts makes checking and enforcement difficult but in this case the state most affected, the USA, is a highly developed one. The offences, however, generally do not occur in its own territorial sea. The answer seems to be for the USA, as it has done, to enter into agreements with the poorer coastal states concerned to aid them in arresting the offenders.

Piracy against boat people.[57] Available statistics are horrifying and again conceal the true picture. From 1980-85 the UNHCR received reports that overall 1,376 people had been killed, 2,283 women raped and 592 kidnapped by Thai fishermen, only about 100 of whom have been caught.[58] Fuller details appear at Appendices 3 and 4. Most attacks occur in the South China Sea, Gulf of Siam and Straits of Malacca. Some attacks occur on the high seas but most occur within territorial waters, especially those of Thailand and Malaysia; the problem is a regional one with most offences falling to be dealt with under municipal law.

Again the answer for the time being is to try to improve the enforcement capability of the governments concerned by providing international economic assistance. The United Nations High Commissioner for Refugees (UNHCR) has organized appeals for voluntary funds through the International Committee of the Red Cross (ICRC) to purchase more patrol boats, etc for Thailand. The UNHCR is also helping victims of pirate attacks to take legal actions against the pirates. Statistics of prosecutions will be found at Appendix 5.

Piracy for political purposes and by belligerents.[60] These acts have always occurred but have always been rarer than those for robbery; they have now become very rare indeed. Unlike the categories described above they are not confined to any particular region or coastal area and they are more likely to occur on the high seas. The events concerned are isolated, one-off incidents occurring on a single vessel and it is impossible to forecast them. They are thus not so readily dealt with by improving national enforcement capability; the need for fuller international action is more apparent and persuasive but the incidence of such attacks has so far been so small that there had, until after the *Achille Lauro* seizure, been no generalized international law concerning such piracy or hijacking at sea. As developments are now underway in IMO but remain the most contentious issue in further defining and punishing piracy we shall return to them in our conclusions.

There are said to have been about 47 terrorist attacks on ships in the last ten years, with eight hijackings and 11 vessels destroyed. Few of these, however, seriously raised the question of whether they could be regarded as piracy.[61] The most notorious and interesting that did so were incidents involving the *Santa Maria, USS Pueblo, SS Mayaguez* and *Achille Lauro*.

The Santa Maria incident.[62] Although similar incidents have occurred in the past, the modern history of such claims begins with the seizure on the high seas in 1961 of the Portuguese passenger liner, *Santa Maria,* by 71 Portuguese insurgents, led by Colonel Galvao, dedicated to overthrowing President Salazar of Portugal; they came aboard as passengers. In seizing the ship they killed one officer, wounded a crewman and undoubtedly frightened the other passengers, some of whom were not Portuguese nationals. It was far from clear what Galvao's motives were, although it appeared later that Galvao purported to represent the 'Portuguese National Independence Movement', or 'Iberian Liberation Movement', or a General Delgado's Liberal Junta. The Portuguese government designated the insurgents as pirates and asked for US, Dutch and UK assistance in apprehending them, but Galvao threatened to scuttle the ship if warships approached.

The precise events were not so clear at the time as they later became; the UK and the USA at first responded and ordered their warships to search for the *Santa Maria* and arrest her if possible.[63] The UK later withdrew but at first stated that it was acting 'in accordance with international law' in compliance with a request for 'assistance to protect life and property on a ship on the high seas'. The USA stated that its help was in accordance with the well-defined terms of international law relating to piracy and insurrection on board ship 'to protect passengers and crew and return the ship to its rightful owners'; it did not assert any right to aid its 42 nationals on board on the basis of self defence. The *Santa Maria* was spotted by a Danish vessel and the US and Portuguese naval forces moved to intercept the ship and cut off Galvao from escape to Africa. Negotiations took place and Galvao, the passengers and crew finally disembarked in Brazil with so-called exit visas stamped by the 'Independent National Council for Liberation' on whose behalf Galvao purported to be acting. Galvao and his followers were granted asylum in Brazil, which returned the vessel to Portugal.

Since it was clear that the insurgents were unrecognized and that seizure took place on the vessel and was for political purposes, most commentators agreed that it clearly did not constitute piracy under the applicable customary international law. Although the custom had also purportedly been codified in the Geneva Convention, the convention was not in force at the time of this incident and in any case, as Vali points out, it *was* generally considered to be a restatement of existing international law.[64] Most considered that it could not be piracy because there was no evidence of private ends, such as robbery or vengeance. Galvao's act might be punished under Portuguese law as mutiny or piracy, but not under international law which looked to the motive. Although international law does not confer any legitimate status on exiled revolutionary movements unless they are recognized as governments by some state, their activities nonetheless can impact on international law.[65] Van Zwanenberg recognized that there was some doubt about political motive in relation to such a nebulous, unrecognized group as Galvao's. She designated Galvao's group as 'potential insurgents', 'a political elite wishing to begin a civil war' and found even more reason for treating members of such groups as pirates because, there being no factual basis for recognition of any kind of status, international law otherwise had little control over them.[66] Thomas Franck also seems to have had some doubts about limiting piracy to external acts, ie to attacks by one ship against another, and excluding internal acts, since this affects the right to arrest the vessel as a pirate.[67] He advances as arguments in favour of retaining piracy for internal seizure, rather than relying on states giving voluntary assistance to flag states in such cases, the delays involved in notifying incidents, obtaining 'requests' for help and deploying fleets, compared to the speedy response permitted if the ship can be declared an outlaw. Historically, he contends, the narrower distinction may have been valid because of its effect on salvage and prize claims, but not today; he considers the distinction between external and internal acts is a gap which should be closed.

Green suggested,[68] in response to a suggestion by Fenwick,[69] that since Galvao's 'revolution' began *after* he seized the *Santa Maria,* his action could not be regarded as political, that the 'political' nature of an action should be determined not by the character of the offence in furtherance of an organized political movement but by the identity of the individual committing it although the burden of proof falls not on that individual but on the states concerned; he maintains that under this test there would be no doubt that Galvao's actions were political.

The legal character of Galvao's actions is further considered on page 161.

The USS Pueblo incident.[70] This US warship, engaged in electronic eavesdropping off the coast of North Korea, was arrested by a North Korean warship. The North Koreans claimed the vessel was within the North Korean territorial sea at the time. The USA, which claimed only a three-mile territorial limit, denied both that the vessel was in North Korean waters when captured and the charge that it was engaged in illegal activity. The crew were imprisoned, later signed confessions and were eventually released after negotiations which led to the USA endorsing these confessions and also accepting that the vessel was in North Korea's territorial waters, although it later repudiated both admissions. Although this incident is sometimes discussed in connection with piracy there seems to be no ground for doing so, private ends being entirely absent even though violence took place from one vessel against another.

SS Mayaguez.[71] This US merchant ship was seized in 1975 by the Khmer Rouge in the Gulf of Siam on the high seas, and 6.5 miles South of Poulu Wai, a Cambodian island. Cambodia claimed a 12-mile territorial sea; the USA a three-mile one. The USA had not recognized the Khmer Rouge as the government of Cambodia. The USA designated as an act of piracy an illegal seizing of a vessel on the high seas since the *Mayaguez* had not committed any offence and, failing any response from Cambodia, a US warship entered Cambodian waters and released the vessel by force. Even if the *Mayaguez* had been in territorial waters recognized by the USA, it would, of course, still have been entitled to a right of innocent passage but had the *Mayaguez* violated the law concerning such passage it is arguable that a state claiming a 12-mile territorial sea has no right to detain it. The Cambodians claimed to suspect that it was a spy ship and thus a threat to their security, rendering its passage non-innocent. Again the lack of any private motive would seem to prevent this incident being categorized as piracy.[72]

Achille Lauro.[73] On 3 October 1985, an Italian cruise liner, the *Achille Lauro* set sail for Egypt and Israel with 750 passengers of assorted nationalities and a mainly Italian crew of 331; most disembarked in Alexandria for a tour. The rest and the crew, numbering 400 in all, sailed off to Port Said but shortly after leaving Alexandria, outside Egypt's territorial waters, four Palestinian terrorists from the Palestinian Liberation Front (PLF) seized the ship. It seems their intent was retaliation for the 1 October Israeli raid on the headquarters of the Palestinian Liberation Organization in Tunisia. The hijackers demanded the release of 50 Palestinians held in Israel in return for the release of the passengers. They ordered the ship to sail to Syria, which refused them port entry. The hijackers then on 8 October killed Leon Klinghoffer, an elderly American passenger, confined to a wheelchair, and threw the body overboard. The ship was refused entry to Cyprus also and then returned to 15 miles off Port Said where Egyptian and PLO officials, on 9 October, negotiated a safe passage from Egypt for the terrorists in return for the release of the hostages and the ship. The Egyptian authorities disclaimed knowledge of any killing on board and refused to detain, try or extradite the Palestinians. US navy fighter planes intercepted the Egyptian aircraft carrying the hijackers and forced it to land at a US-Italian NATO military base in Sicily, thus bringing the hijackers within the jurisdiction of Italy whose ship they had seized. The Italians thereupon arrested and charged them.

The USA requested that they be held for extradition to the USA and issued an arrest warrant based on three formal charges — hostage taking, piracy on the high seas and conspiracy under relevant US laws.[74] The US Comprehensive Crime Control Act of 1984, s.1203, defines the crime of hostage taking as 'seizing or detaining or threatening to kill, to injure or to continue to detain' another in order to compel a 'third person or government to do (or abstain from) any act as a condition for the release of the detainee'. The piracy charge cited the 1909 Federal Statute, viz 18 USC Sec. 1651, which states, as noted earlier, that whoever on the high seas commits the crime of piracy, as defined by the law of nations, and is afterwards brought into or found in the United States shall be imprisoned for life'. The arrest warrant concerning the piracy charged the hijackers with piracy under the laws of nations, alleging that without legitimate authority they seized control of the *Achille Lauro* by use and threat of violence and had done so for private ends: it also charged them with conspiracy to commit piracy.

The warrant and the US statute thus beg the question as to what is piracy under present international law. The account given in this article, it is submitted, shows clearly that this neither covers acts committed on one vessel (despite some criticism of this aspect) nor acts committed for political ends, which despite the US allegation that they were private, clearly were not so.[75] The facts might ground a charge of piracy under some municipal laws in this case but as the US statute incorporates the international law, US courts are now, the USA being a party to the 1958 High Seas Convention, unlikely to accept that US law covers this case. In any event, even if the contrary view is correct and the case fell within US municipal law, the USA could take no international action; it could not have arrested the *Achille Lauro* on the high seas, only if it was in US jurisdiction or the pirates subsequently came within it.

A different view on this matter is stated in Chapter 13.

The question remains whether the international law needs revision or supplementation to cover such cases. As has been pointed out by Constantinople,[76] the facts of the *Santa Maria* and *Achille Lauro* incidents differ. In the *Santa Maria*'s case the Portuguese ship was seized by Portuguese nationals, ie the ship was under the flag state jurisdiction of the state whose government was opposed by the hijackers; action against the vessel, in the absence of the commission of piracy, was confined to that state. In the case of the *Achille Lauro,* however, so far as the USA was concerned, the ship belonged to a third state (Italy) and the actions were conducted by third parties (PLF). If the law looked more at the nature of the actions and less at the status of the actors, Constantinople suggests such acts as those carried out on the *Achille Lauro* could not be regarded as legitimately conducted for public (political) ends.[77] Thus acts piratical in all other respects (violent and non-humanitarian) if directed at ships, property or nationals of third states neutral to an internal conflict could fall within a definition of piracy adapted to this, whilst actions of the kind executed against the *Santa Maria* would remain outside it.

In support of this approach, it is argued that it is consistent with changes in the rules of war since the second world war, common Article 3 of the four 1949 Geneva Conventions on War making it illegal for parties to them to treat inhumanely individuals taking no part in the conflict, and which forbids, *inter alia,* the taking of hostages.[78] As pointed out in the introduction to this paper even in its earliest form the basis of the universal jurisdiction over piracy was not only protection of freedom of navigation to facilitate trade but also humanitarian consideration generated by the inhumane violence that frequently accompanied the acts constituting piracy. This new approach would, therefore, be in accord with the original purposes of the concession of universal jurisdiction.

Legal Responses to the Changing Nature of Violence at Sea

A wide variety of suggestions has been made by writers on the subject of piracy concerning ways of improving the definition of the offence to include at least some political seizures or single ship seizures and also of enhancing the enforcement of the present law at the national, regional and international levels. A possible doctrine of "reverse hot pursuit" is examined in Chapter 10 and again, on a more restricted basis, in Chapter 11. Other proposals include the following.

Revision of both the Geneva Convention and the UNCLOS

These theoretically could be revised to take account both of the fact that most violence at sea now occurs in territorial or internal waters and that the *Achille Lauro* incident may prompt more internal ship seizures by terrorists; one commentator has recently proposed this.[79] But this would require the convening of conferences of the parties and participants in both conventions either to renegotiate the conventions or add a Protocol to them. There are precedents for the application of international conventions within the territorial sea — the International Whaling Convention[80] and the Common Fisheries Policy laid down by the European Community pursuant to the Treaty of Rome[81] are cases in point — but it seems inconceivable that states would find it acceptable either to revise the 1958 Convention at this date for this sole purpose or to revise the UNCLOS before its entry into force, especially as, for its parties, it will supersede the 1958 Convention.[82] If it were to happen, of course, several other aspects of the definition could also be tied up — the word 'illegal' deleted from Article 110(a) and 'another' inserted in Article 110(a)(ii); the action required of states could be specified as could the penalties they should impose.

However, even the moderate and ingenious suggestion of Constantinople for amendment to include single ship seizures involving third states if executed violently and inhumanely would be difficult to execute in the absence of reconvening the UNCLOS. It is unlikely that all present participants in both conventions would attend any conference convened for this purpose nor would they all accept the amendment; the position in that event would become even further confused. Only a Fourth United Nations Law of the Sea Conference, held in perhaps ten years time, to renegotiate the whole treaty package might achieve the necessary changes.

A new convention dealing separately with modern maritime hijacking offences

This might be a more successful approach and is in fact the one now being pursued in IMO. A new offence of 'maritime hijacking' could be created by separate treaty for single ship hijackings by political groups for political ends on lines similar to the conventions to suppress aircraft hijacking — the Tokyo,[83] Hague[84] and Montreal Conventions,[85] which do not cover maritime hijackings. This could, however, in view of the fact that not all states and probably not even all Geneva Convention and UNCLOS parties would participate, be open to the same objection as revision of the Geneva Convention and UNCLOS, namely that it might exacerbate the existing confusion. At present the incidence of maritime hijackings is so small that it seems highly unlikely that states would act to conclude a separate convention; nonetheless a draft Convention on the Suppression of Unlawful Acts against the Safety of Maritime Navigation is now under consideration in IMO (International Maritime Organization) by an Ad Hoc Preparatory Committee. Its first meeting was from 2-6 March 1987, at IMO Headquarters.[86]

Further bilateral or regional treaties

Brown has suggested the bilateral approach based on extradition and specific measures, which, prima facie, seems more hopeful, particularly as precedents exist, eg US/Cuba Exchange of Notes on Unilateral Hijacking of Aircraft and Vessels.[87] Menefee has suggested a regional approach similar to the Latin American Convention on the Duties and Rights of States in the event of Civil Strife.[88] The IMO draft convention incorporates this approach without need for conclusion of specific bilateral or regional agreements; the new offence would automatically be added to lists of extraditable offences or any extradition treaties concluded by its parties.

The scope of piracy also could be extended, of course, to cover political internal seizures on the basis of mutual recognition in munipipal laws providing for this. Extension of Extradition Treaties to deny asylum, as proposed by Brown, and earlier by the ILA in its 1970 Report, would obviously be beneficial, but these goals are notoriously difficult to achieve in relation to political offences on any scale that is sufficiently widespread to be effective. If any states do not participate, escape is always possible. This difficulty exists as much in relation to conclusion of a new treaty to deny asylum to ship hijackers as proposed by the ILA, as to the establishment of an International Criminal Court as proposed in the 1920s. However, the European Convention on Suppression of Terrorism offers a hopeful model and it is this that the IMO draft convention is following, *inter alia*.[89] Regional treaties could be encouraged in regions where coastal piracy particularly occurs. The problem in these regions is, as we have seen, more one of enforcement capability since the piratical acts occur in near coastal waters not on the high seas. Most states in Africa and South-East Asia, the most affected regions, lack this capability. An increase in outside help is required, perhaps executed through international organizations.

Creation of a new international dispute settlement mechanism

This has been proposed by Dubner,[90] the Harvard Research Draft and in the 1970 International Law Association Report. It is proposed that a court with compulsory jurisdiction to prescribe penalties should be established: again the time certainly does not seem to be ripe for creation of an International Criminal Court, although a spate of hijackings at sea of such violence as to offend basic humanitarian principles might create a more sympathetic climate for this and it has been reported that there was evidence of this at the ILA's meeting in Seoul, Korea in 1986.[91]

Extension of application of related conventions

This approach is favoured by Menefee[92] and is one also adopted in the IMO draft convention. The most relevant would be the 1979 Convention Against the Taking of Hostages,[93] Article 5 of which applies the offences of hostage taking as defined therein to offences *on board a ship* registered in a state party as well as those committed in a territory. The USA also cited this Convention in the *Achille Lauro* case indictment.

Port state jurisdiction

This new concept, as defined in the UNCLOS, Articles 220 and 218, could be extended by separate global or regional agreement (on the lines of the Paris Memorandum on Port State Control 1982)[94] to allow states to take proceedings against the seizers of any hijacked ship entering their ports even if the offence occurred on the high seas or in the EEZs or territorial seas of other states, if the latter so request.

Liberal interpretation of terms in existing treaties

Terms such as 'private ends' as used in the Geneva High Seas Convention 1958 and the UNCLOS 1982 could be given a wider interpretation. International law, as evidenced in Article 31 of the Vienna Convention on Treaties, requires that a treaty, if there is doubt as to its meaning, be interpreted in a way that will make it effective, as long as such interpretation does not conflict with its objects and purposes. The parties can further agree to attribute a 'special meaning' to a term, as provided in the Vienna Convention on Treaties, Article 31(4), if the ordinary meaning in its context does not bear such an interpretation. Since the relevant objects and purposes of the 1958 Convention and the 1982 UNCLOS are the suppression of piracy this approach might be possible if it can be argued that there is doubt concerning the meaning of 'private ends'. It is notable that no works on piracy, so far as the writer has found, apply the specific provisions of the Vienna Convention to the problem of interpretation in this particular context. The objection to such an approach, however, would be the same as to many of the others considered so far, namely that unless there was widespread agreement the situation would be further confused with some states adopting one interpretation and others a different one.

Reliance on general principles of law concerning self defence and self help

In the absence of other effective remedies this approach will increasingly be resorted to as the recent US actions following the *Achille Lauro* seisure evidenced, however attenuated the principle in particular circumstances, in order to respond to terrorist attacks on vessels. A concerted response well founded in international law would surely be more appropriate than unilateral action and would contribute more to the stability of international legal order. If unilateral action is not increasingly to be resorted to, international law must, therefore, make better use of the legitimate means of action available. This would accord with the humanitarian purposes, the economic aims and the objective of ensuring safety of navigation that originally generated the doctrine of international piracy. As the current developments illustrate, through the IMO and other international bodies, the international community is now endeavouring to work out an international response both through new conventions and new guidelines on practical measures.

Current Developments

Protection of boat people and prevention of cargo ship and yacht piracy

Various bodies, as already indicated, are taking measures to improve existing national enforcement of municipal laws, eg the UNCHR and ICRC in relation to the 'boat people'; the ICC's IMB, which has proposed fresh practical measures both for protection of 'boat people' and prevention of piracy against cargo vessels and yachts, is also developing guidelines for improving security against non-political piracy within territorial waters. The guidelines will be useful to owners, operators, masters and crews, port and harbour authorities, coast guards, etc, in taking practical measures to improve security in ways very similar to airport and airline security checks. The public will be subjected to stricter security checks including X-raying of baggage in ports, personal searches, etc. It is suggested that private security firms should be employed for this purpose.

Hijacking and terrorism

There is now political pressure on states to take some further action to prevent increasing precipitate unilateral responses by states. The developments are taking two forms: practical measures and a draft convention.

Practical measures. In December 1985, Egypt and Italy presented a paper to IMO outlining practical measures, similar to the ICC's IMB's ideas, that should be undertaken as a matter of urgency. These were adopted by a Resolution of the IMO Council and passed to IMO's Maritime Safety Committee for action in January 1986. A working group has met to develop guidelines on such practical measures as use of identity cards; scanning devices; ring fences and baggage checks. The guidelines, when issued, will be in the form of IMO recommendations which states can follow or not as appropriate in and to their circumstances. This approach is non-controversial and is supported by both the USA, which is no longer pressing, as it did initially, for immediate political action and is now willing to discuss more appropriate responses, and the USSR. Consultations have taken place with ICAO, which even after 20 years experience of hijacking is still adjusting its guidelines for airports and airlines. States' present attitude seems to be that they should learn to walk before they run and to wait to see if maritime hijacking actually does increase or whether another 24 years will pass before the next incident, as was the case between the *Santa Maria* and *Achille Lauro*. Early discussion in IMO evidenced that most states were reluctant to adopt legally binding measures comparable to the

Aerial Hijacking Conventions of the 1970s, with mandatory requirements for extradition and imposition of specific penalties. This is further discussed in Chapter 17.

Recently, draft guidelines have been published on Detailed Practical Measures to Protect Passengers and Crews from Unlawful Acts against Passenger Ships[95] involved in voyages of more than 24 hours; these thus exclude ferries. 'Passengers' are not defined in the guidelines although some IMO Conventions, such as that on Safety of Life at Sea, do provide a definition. Jurisdictional questions are avoided by omission. The guidelines are adapted to local conditions and are intended to bring about more effective compliance by all involved with security requirements and increased awareness of the vulnerable aspects of operations; port and ship security plans are required to be formulated, including appointment of port and ship security officers.

The IMO draft convention. The text of the draft convention was submitted by the governments of Austria, Egypt and Italy, following the adoption of the UN General Assembly of a resolution[96] adopting Austria's and Italy's proposal that the IMO should study the question of terrorism against ships and make recommendations on measures to combat it. The draft is based on the model of, *inter alia,* the 1970 Hague, and 1971 Montreal Conventions on Safety of Civil Aviation, the UN Conventions on Internationally Protected Persons (1973), Taking of Hostages (1979) and on Torture (1985). It aims 'to provide for a comprehensive suppression of unlawful acts committed against the safety of maritime navigation which endanger innocent human lives, jeopardize the safety of persons and property, seriously affect the operation of maritime services and thus are of grave concern to the international community as a whole'.[97] It thus envisages the absolute and unconditional application of the principle that offenders should be either punished by states entitled to exercise jurisdiction (these are defined as the flag state of the ships against which the offences are perpetrated; states in whose territory, territorial sea or archipelagic waters the offences have been committed; the state of citizenship of an offender, or of habitual residence of a stateless person; the states whose nationals have been seized, threatened, injured or killed during the commission of the offences defined in the draft) or extradited, the offences as defined in the convention being deemed to be included as extraditable offences in any treaty existing between any of the states parties.

It is proposed that five forms of offences be included,[98] viz: those committed by anyone who, unlawfully and intentionally:

(a) by force or threat thereof or by any other form of intimidation seizes a ship in service or exercises control of it; or
(b) performs or threatens to perform an act of violence against a person on board a ship in service if that act or threat is likely to endanger the safety of navigation; or
(c) destroys a ship in service or causes damage to such ship or to its cargo which renders it incapable of operation or which is likely to endanger its safe operation; or
(d) places or causes to be placed on a ship in service by any means whatsoever, a device or substance which is likely to destroy that ship, to cause damage to the ship or its cargo which renders the ship incapable of operation, or to cause damage on it which is likely to endanger its safe operation; or

(e) injures or kills any person during the commission of any of the offences defined in this article (Article 2, Paragraph 1).

It remains to be seen whether, in view of the small number of such offences that occur, the lack of universality achieved by any of the similar conventions relevant to suppression of aircraft hijacking, the previous lack of enthusiasm for conclusion of such a maritime hijacking convention and marked preference for practical measures, any progress will be made by this draft in IMO in the short term or whether, if adopted, it will achieve any ratifications. The longer term remains speculative, related to the occurrence of further incidents. As yet we do not know what form the convention will take. Meanwhile many states still consider that the more urgent and practical solution is to find means of preventing hijackers getting on board ships.

This paper was first published in Marine Policy, Vol. 11, No. 3, July 1987 at page 163-183.

NOTES

1. D. Botting, *The Pirates,* Time Life Books, Amsterdam, 1978, p 22, cited by E. D. Brown, 'Maritime commercial malpractices and piracy under international law', *Maritime Policy and Management,* Vol 8, 1981, pp 99-107.

2. For its early history see T. W. Fulton, *The Sovereignty of the Sea,* William Blackwood and Sons, Edinburgh, 1911, pp 247-272; H. A. Smith, *The Law and Custom of the Sea,* Stevens & Sons Ltd, London, 1950, pp 50-58; C. J. Colombos, *The International Law of the Sea,* Longmans, Green & Co Ltd, London, 1962, pp 402-406; C. Lloyd, *English Corsairs on the Barbary Coast,* Collins, London, 1981; D. M. Johnston, *Marine Policy and the Coastal Community,* Croom Helm, London, 1981; A. P. Rubin, 'The use of piracy in Malayan waters' in C. H. Alexandrowitz, ed, *Grotian Society Papers,* Martinus Nijhoff, The Hague, 1968, pp 111-135.

3. Territorial waters Jurisdiction Act 1878, 41 & 42 Vict., C.90; for earlier acts see D. H. N. Johnson, 'Piracy in modern international law', *Grotius Society Transactions,* Vol 43, 1957, p 63.

4. R. P. Anand, *Origin and Development of the Law of the Sea,* Martinus Nijhoff, The Hague, 1980, pp 113-118.

5. Smith, *op cit,* Ref 2, p 78.

6. Declaration of Paris 1856, 'General Treaty of Peace between France, Great Britain and Russia', *British & Foreign State Papers,* Vol 46, p 26.

7. Colombos, *op cit,* Ref 2, p 53.

8. E. D. Dickinson, 'Is the crime of piracy obsolete?', *Harvard Law Review,* Vol 38, 1924-25, pp 334-360; he emphasized the vitality of the law of piracy and that 'While the occasions for invoking its rules are less frequent now than formerly, it may still be made a potent factor in preventing lawlessness upon the seas'; it belonged to 'the law in reserve rather than to the law in history' and could be invoked to stamp out seizure of rum running ships evading US liquor law.

9. For an outline of these debates see Fulton, *op cit,* Ref 2, Chapter IX, pp 338-377.

10. Colombos, *op cit,* Ref 2, p 402; J. Moore, *Lotus Case,* PCIJ, Ser A, No 10, 1927, p 70.

11. D. P. O'Connell, in Shearer, ed, *The International Law of the Sea,* Clarendon Press, Oxford, 1984, p 966. Universal jurisdiction has at various times remained controversial, however; *ibid,* p 977.

12. Harvard Research in International Law, Draft Convention on Piracy with Comments, *AJIL,* Vol 26, 1932, Supplement, p 749.

13. Johnson, *op cit,* Ref 3, p 69; but see International Law Association, *Fifty-fourth Report,* The Hague, 1970, *Piracy: Sea and Air,* pp 706-771, at pp 709-710.

14. The League of Nations Committee of Experts for the Progressive Codification of International Law so categorized it; League of Nations Document, Vol 5, 1926, p 2, reprinted in AJIL, Vol 20, Special Supplement, 1926, p 223; note also A. D. Wiener, 'Piracy: the current crime', *Lloyds' Marine and Commercial Law Quarterly,* Vol 4, 1979, pp 469-484, pp 469-483.

15. For an analysis of the relevant cases see Johnson, *op cit,* Ref 3 pp 71-78; O'Connell, *op cit,* Ref 11, pp 971-976.

16. Convention on the High Seas, Geneva, 29 April 1958; in force 30 September 1962; UNTS, Vol 450, p 11. Appendix 14.

17. United Nations Convention on the Law of the Sea (hereafter UNCLOS), Montego Bay, 10 December 1982, not in force; *ILM.* Vol XXI, 1982, p 1245. Appendix 15.

18. B. H. Dubner, *The Law of International Sea Piracy,* Martinus Nijhoff, The Hague, 1980; see also Johnson, *op cit,* Ref 3, and O'Connell, *op cit,* Ref 11.

19. O'Connell, *op cit,* Ref 11, and Johnson, *op cit,* Ref 3, refer to piracy under municipal law as 'piracy by analogy', which has no claim to be universally recognized and point out that it must not be confused with true piracy. Nonetheless, it sometimes is—see in particular *H.M. Advocate* v. *Cameron, and Others, Scots Law Times,* 2 July 1971, pp 202-206; *Cameron* v. *H.M. Advocate,* S.C., 1971, p 50.

20. See for example the judgment of Lord Cameron in *H.M. Advocate* v. *Cameron and Others,* p 205.

21. In *re Piracy Jure Gentium,* 1934, A.C. 586.

22. *H.M. Advocate* v. *Cameron, Cameron* v. *H.M. Advocate, op cit,* Ref 19.

23. *H.M. Advocate* v. *Cameron,* p 204.

24. *Ibid.*

25. Johnson, *op cit,* Ref 3, p 68.

26. 18 U.S.C. $ 1651.

27. *U.S.* v. *Smith.* 18 U.S. 153 (1820).

28. E. D. Dickinson, *op cit,* Ref 8.

29. Johnson, *op cit,* Ref 3, pp 71-76.

30. *Ibid,* p. 76.

31. See works cited by O'Connell, *op cit,* Ref 11, p 97, note 250; *U.S.* v. *Brig. Malek Adhel Case,* 43 U.S. 1844 (2 How) p 210.

32. O'Connell, *op cit,* Ref 11, p 973; Johnson, *op cit,* Ref 3; L. Oppenheim, in H. Lauterpacht, ed, *International Law,* 1954, p 609, note 1, cites several authorities for the view that internal seizure can constitute piracy; see also D. Greig, in *International Law,* 1976, pp 331-332.

33. O'Connell, *op cit,* Ref 11, p 173.

34. See *U.S.* v. *Smith,* 5 Wheat. 153 (1820); *The Magellan Pirates* 164 Eng. Rep. 47, 48 (Ecc. & Ad. 1853); *The Huascar,* Br. Parl. Pap., Peri No. 1 (1887) *Crete à Pierrot,* 30 Clunet (1903) 444.

35. O'Connell, *op cit,* Ref 11, p 980; U.N. Legis. Series 1952, Laws and Regulations on the Regime of the High Seas, Vol, II, *passim.*

36. Johnson examined *Republic of Bolivia* v. *Indemnity Mutual Marine Insurance Co.,* 1 K.B. (1909) 785; *The Magellan Pirates*; *The Serhassan Pirates,* 2 W. Rob. 354 (1845); 166 E.R. 788; *The Ambrose Light,* 22 Fel. 408 (1885).

37. Washington Naval Treaty, 6 February 1922, 16 A.J.I.L. (1922) Supplement, p 57.

38. International Agreement for Collective Measures against Piratical Attacks in the Mediterranean by Submarines, 14 September 1937, *UKTS,* No 38, 1937.

39. See, for example, G. A. Finch, 'Editorial comment: piracy in the Mediterranean', *AJIL,* 1937, pp 659-665; R. Genet, 'The charge of piracy in the Spanish Civil War', *AJIL,* pp 253-263; 'The Nyon arrangements, anonymous note', *BYIL,* Vol XIX, 1938, pp 198-208. A Rubin; *op cit,* Ref 2, at p 133 concluded that Britain also manipulated the concept of piracy to suit its political ends in Malayan waters at the beginning of the 18th century to extend its control, creating a different regional international law for South-East Asia. He comments 'once the concept of piracy had become so removed from universal applicability that it threatened to become merely an excuse for political action rather than a definitive legal justification for such action, the concept became more and more elusive as a matter of law'.

40. *Op cit,* Ref 14.

41. *Op cit,* Ref 12.

42. *Op cit,* Ref 16.

43. For an analysis of the ILC draft Articles see Johnson, *op cit,* Ref 3, pp 63-68.

44. *Ibid,* p 64.

45. *Op cit,* Ref 17.

46. *Op cit,* Ref 13, p 710; the draft did not set out a code but the basic principles for a general international convention on Piracy Sea and Air.

47. Principle 3 stated: 'The crime of piracy (sea and air) under general international law is committed by: (1) any person who unlawfully seizes or takes control of a ship or aircraft or who attempts to do so through violence, threat of violence, surprise, fraud or other means'. No reference was made to 'private ends'.

48. Emphasis added.

49. As, for example, proposed by G. P. McGinley, 'The Achille Lauro affair—implications for international law', *Tennessee Law Review,* Vol 52, 1985, pp 691, at pp 700-729.

50. On this point see A. Rubin, 'Is piracy illegal?', AJIL, Vol 70, 1976, pp 92-95. He traced its drafting history and proposed deleting the word 'illegal' and also the word 'another' in clause (b).

51. *Ibid,* at p 93.

52. Brown, however, *op cit,* Ref 1, at pp 102-103, takes the view that there is no incompatibility so far as the piracy provisions (Articles 100-107) are concerned and that the intention that they should apply in the EEZ 'would seem to follow'.

53. E. Ellen, ed, *Violence at Sea, Proceedings of Workshop of the International Chamber of Commerce's (ICC) International Maritime Bureau, San Jose State University, California,* March 1986; ICC Publishing SA, 38 Cours Albert 1er, 75008 Paris, France.

54. *Piracy, Proceedings of a Seminar Organized by the Nautical Institute, 31 October 1985, London,* obtainable from the Nautical Institute, 202 Lambeth Road, London SE1 7LQ; see also A. D. Wiener, *op cit,* Ref 14, at pp 470-473.

55. See p 3.

56. J. Fiksdal, 'Hvor Sjoroverne Herjer', *Na,* No 28, 1985, pp 28-30, Oslo, Norway, at p 30.

57. A. Billard, 'Pirates in the Gulf of Siam', *Refugees Magazine,* May 1983, published by Public Information Section at the Office of the UN High Commissioner for Refugees, pp 24-26; and 'Dossier: the fight against piracy', *ibid,* p 27; see also G. R. Villar, 'Modern day piracy', in *Piracy, op cit,* Ref 54, at pp 3-4.

58. Billard, *op cit,* Ref 57, p 24; Villar, *op cit,* Ref 57, p 4.

59. UNHCR Dossier, *op cit,* Ref 57, p 27.

60. For details of such seizures see J. Simon, 'The implications of the Achille Lauro hijacking for the maritime community', in A. Parritt, ed, *op cit,* Ref 53, pp 17-24, at pp 19-20; T. S. Schiller, 'Maritime terrorism: the threat', *ibid,* pp 87-92; see also Villar, *op cit,* Ref 57, at p 6.

61. B. M. Jenkins, K. Gardela and G. Petty, 'A chronology of terrorist attacks and other criminal actions against maritime targets', in *Violence at Sea, op cit,* Ref 53, pp 63-85, at p 65; a Chronology of Incidents, 1960-1983 is given at pp 69-85.

62. For accounts and comments on the legal problems involved in this incident see A. van Zwanenberg, 'Interference with ships on the high seas', ICLQ, Vol 10, 1961, pp 785-817, at pp 798-801 (for facts) and pp 801-817; she does not think the case was piracy because it occurred on one ship only without the intention of private gain; T. M. Franck, 'To define and punish piracies—the lesson of the Santa Maria: a comment', *NYULR,* Vol 36, 1961, pp 839-844, who concludes that the distinction between *internal* and *external* seizure is no longer valid, at p 844; G. Fenwick, '"Piracy" in the Caribbean', *AJIL,* Vol 55, 1961, pp 426-428, who asks how the offence could be called 'political' when Galvao had held no public office; F. Vali, 'The Santa Maria case', *North-western University Law Review,* Vol 56, 1961, pp 168-175, who considers that as the exile organization on whose behalf Galvao carried out the seizure had no legitimate status in international law, not being a recognized government, it cannot be classed as piracy although evolving international law may take a more liberal view in attributing legal personality to such bodies; L. Green, 'The Santa Maria: rebels or pirates', *BYIL,* Vol 37, 1961, pp 496-499, who categorizes the actions as political. The incident has been reassessed in the articles relating to the *Achille Lauro* seizure referred to in Ref 73 below, viz Constantinople, Menefee.

63. Van Zwanenberg assesses the grounds other than piracy on which the seized vessel might have been stopped and suggests that there would have been no real objection to foreign vessels stopping it to inspect its papers.

64. Vali, *op cit,* Ref 62, at p 171.

65. *Ibid,* p 175.

66. Van Zwanenberg, *op cit,* Ref 62, pp 817-818.

67. Frank, *op cit,* Ref 62, pp 843, 844.

68. Green, *op cit,* Ref 62, at p 505, after reviewing various municipal cases.

69. Fenwick, *op cit,* Ref 62, who considered Galvao's actions plain murder and criminal violence since the law of armed conflict applied only to groups in rebellion and the government against which they rebelled and could not be relied on to protect those attacking civilian lives and property.

70. For a detailed critique see A. Akinsaya, The 'Pueblo affair and international law', *Ind. J.I.L.,* Vol 15, 1975, p 485; S. B. Finch, 'Pueblo and Mayaguez: a legal analysis', *Case Western Reserve J.I.L.,* Vol 9, 1977, p 79.

71. For details and analysis see R. E. Ward, 'The Mayaguez: the right of innocent passage and the legality of reprisal', *SDLR,* Vol 13, 1976, p 765; MacDowell, 'S.S. Mayaguez incident', AJIL, Vol 69, 1975, p 875.

72. C. Crockett, 'Towards a revision of the international law of piracy', *De Paul Law Review,* Vol 26, 1978, pp 78-99, at pp 84-87 regards the 'private ends' test as a 'sledgehammer solution' (p 87) since *inter alia* the USA had not recognized the Khmer Rouge.

73. For a description of and/or a commentary on this incident on which this account is based see S. Menefee, 'Terrorism at sea: the historical development of an international response', in Ellen, *op cit,* Ref 53, pp 191-205; B. Brittin, 'The two faces of piracy', unpublished paper given at 20th Conference of the Law of the Sea Institute, Miami, USA, 1986 (obtainable from Citizens for Ocean Law, 1601 Connecticut Avenue, NW, Suite 202, Washington, DC 20009, USA); G. Constantinople, 'Towards a definition of piracy: the Achille Lauro incident', *Va. J.I.L.,* Vol 26, 1986, pp 725-753.

74. For details of the warrant, etc, see 'Documents concerning the Achille Lauro affair and co-operation in combatting international terrorism', *ILM,* Vol XXIV, 1985, pp 1509-1565.

75. According to the *Shorter Oxford English Dictionary,* Clarendon Press, Oxford, 1978 edition, at pp 1673-1674, 'private' means 'withdrawn from public life, peculiar to oneself; pertaining to a person in a non-official capacity; of pertaining or relating to, affecting a person, or a small group of persons apart from the general community', International law, as evidenced by the 1969 Vienna Convention on the Law of Treaties, 1980 UKTS 58 (Article 31(1) requires that words be accorded their ordinary meaning (unless *all* the parties to a treaty agree to attribute a special meaning (Article 31(4)).

76. Constantinople, *op cit,* Ref 73, at p 748.

77. *Ibid,* p 749, but see Green's opposite view, although arriving at a similar overall conclusion, *op cit,* Ref 62.

78. Constantinople, *op cit,* Ref 73, p 750; relevant conventions cited at p 744, note 103.

79. Britten, *op cit,* Ref 73.

80. International Convention for the Regulation of Whaling 1946, published by the International Whaling Commission, 1964, Article 1(2).

81. For an account of this aspect see P. Birnie, 'Appendix to Fifth Report of the Expenditure Committee of the House of Commons on the Fishing Industry: The History of the EEC Common Fisheries Policy', 1978, H.C. 356.

82. UNCLOS, Article 311(1).

83. Tokyo Convention on Offences and Certain Other Acts Committed on Board Aircraft, 14 September 1963, *ILM,* Vol 2, 1963, p 1042.

84. Hague Convention for the Suppression of Unlawful Seizures of Aircraft, 16 December 1970, ILM, Vol 10, 1971, p 133.

85. Montreal Convention for the Suppression of Unlawful Acts against the Safety of Civil Aviation, 23 September 1971, *ILM,* Vol 10, 1971, p 1151. Brown, *op cit,* Ref 1, pp 103-105, has outlined the relevant features of these three conventions which extend the rights of states not otherwise entitled to exercise jurisdiction over the offences committed to prosecute or extradite the offender is found are required to extend their laws to cover the treaty offences. But see also A. E. Evans, 'Aircraft hijacking: its cause and cure', *AJIL,* Vol 63, 1969, pp 695-710; M. Akehurst, 'Hijacking', *Ind. J.I.L.,* Vol 14, 1974, pp 81-89, both of whom point out that practical measures of airport security are likely to be more effective.

86. IMO Doc, PCUA 1/1, 1 December 1986.

87. Memorandum of Understanding on the Hijacking of Aircraft and Vessels, effected of Exchange of Notes between Cuba and the United States, 15 February 1973; see Brown, *op cit,* Ref 1, p 105.

88. Convention on Duties and Rights of States in the Event of Civil Strife, 20 February 1928, 2749 T.I.A.S., 814.

89. European Convention on the Suppression of Terrorism, concluded by the Council of Europe, 1978 ETS No 97. This specifies in Article 1 that for purposes of extradition between Contracting States, none of six listed offences (eg within the 1970 Hague and 1971 Montreal Conventions) shall be regarded as a political offence or as an offence connected with a political offence or as an offence inspired by political motives. It does not yet cover maritime hijackings but could no doubt be so extended by Protocol should its parties so agree. Article 2, however, states that 'For the purposes of extradition between Contracting States, a Contracting State may decide not to regard as a political offence or as an offence connected with a political offence or as an offence inspired by political motives a serious offence involving an act of violence, other than one covered by Article 1, against the life; physical integrity or liberty of a person'. Offences against property are also covered.

90. B. H. Dubner, 'The law of international sea piracy', *International Law and Politics,* 1979, pp 471-517, at pp 490-491.

91. Statement made in BBC broadcast on terrorism by Professor Paul Wilkinson, University of Aberdeen, 15 September 1986, heard by the writer.

92. Menefee, *op cit,* Ref 73.

93. International Convention against the Taking of Hostages, 18 December 1979, 81 UKTS (1983), Cmnd. 9100; for further examples see J. J. Paust, 'To international terrorism: prevention, punishment and co-operative action', *Georgia Journal of International and Comparative Law,* Vol 3, 1975, pp 431-462.

94. Memorandum on Port State Jurisdiction, done 26 January 1982, Paris; entered into force 1 July 1982; *ILM,* Vol 21, 1982, p 1.

95. Lloyds List, 11 September 1986.

96. UNGAR 40/61, 9 December 1985.

97. IMO Doc., n 86, p II, para 1.

98. *Ibid,* PCUA 1/3 Annex, p 2.

CHAPTER 10

THE LAW OF PIRACY: DOES IT MEET THE PRESENT AND POTENTIAL CHALLENGES?

Burdick H Brittin

Quote from Gentile, *De jure belli.*

> Pirates are common enemies, and they are attacked with impunity by all, because they are without the pale of the law. They are scorners of the law of nations; hence they find no protection in that law. They ought to be crushed by us... and by all men. This is a warfare shared by all nations.

I cite the above quotation because it affirms a strong common ground between Professor Tom Clingan and myself. Using that as a point of departure, Professor Clingan in Chapter 11 most eloquently examines and confirms the existing law. It is certainly the majority view of the world community; for ready reference, it is sometimes referred to as the narrow view. On my part I will raise some issues that are suggestive of desirable changes to the law of piracy that might be beneficial in our quest to meet Gentile's challenge. It is, at this stage, a minority view; within the legal community it is referred to as the broad view.

Piracy is a crime on the high seas that is international in character. Whether it is, in fact, piracy or not is governed by international law; that law is spelled out in Articles 100 through 108 in the 1982 Convention on the Law of Sea which essentially reiterated the piracy provisions set forth in the 1958 Convention on the High Seas ratified by numerous countries including the US (See Appendices 14 and 15).

In posing a challenge to some of these provisions, I will cite some incidents of interest and attempt to weave the facts of the cases into the fabric of the law.

The first case is that of the Portuguese cruise ship, *Santa Maria*, which took place in January-February 1961, and which is also examined at page 147. When the ship sailed from Curacao, Netherlands West Indies, for Miami, some 24 passengers, secretly armed with machine guns and grenades came aboard, along with the other passengers who had boarded at various points on the cruise. 42 vacationing Americans were on the passenger list. Admiral R L Dennison, USN, then Commander in Chief of the US Atlantic Fleet, describes the unfolding incident as follows:

> The initial report was received at Atlantic Fleet Headquarters in Norfolk late on the afternoon of 23 January from the United Kingdom's Senior Naval Officer, West Indies, who was at Santa Lucia where Captain Galvao, who had taken over the ship, had put ashore by board several wounded members of the *Santa Maria's* crew. The report advised that the cruise ship *Santa Maria*, registered under the Portuguese flag, had been forcibly taken over by a group of about seven armed passengers. It appeared that piracy might have occurred. The Senior Naval Officer, West Indies, requested that the US Atlantic Fleet arrange and coordinate a search for the ship in areas to the north of Trinidad and advised he would search to the south and east. Instructions at this time to US ships were to board the vessel to determine if piracy in fact had occurred and, if so, to bring the ship to the nearest United States port, presumably San Juan, using force as necessary.
>
> Expert legal opinions in the United States were unable to support a finding of piracy in international law. Therefore, the need no longer existed to determine piracy by boarding and exercising force. Appropriate modifying orders were dispatched to the naval forces involved. The safeguarding of United States nationals and the humanitarian interest for all other passengers and crew members of the ship still remained as a basis for continuing action.

A second case reports that two Americans stole a cabin cruiser in Florida on 24 April 1960 and had run aground in a desolate area at Elbow key, the Bahamas. A few days later a charter boat, the *Muriel III* with four passengers aboard, hove into sight. The charter boat was signalled and one of the stranded Americans, Billy Sees, swam out and boarded her. With a revolver in hand, Sees attempted to take control of the boat; when the skipper reached for a gun, Sees shot and fatally wounded him. As a result of this both Sees and his companion were hung in Nassau prison in May 1961. The published report labelled Sees and his companion as pirates.

Interrupting the narrative, let us look at Article 101 of the LOS Convention, specifically subparagraph (a)(1):

> Piracy consists of any of the following acts:
>
> (a) any illegal acts of violence or detention, or any act of depredation, committed for private ends by the crew or the passengers of a private ship or a private aircraft, and directed:
>
> (i) on the high seas, against another ship or aircraft, or against persons or property on board such ship or aircraft;

It is clear that in neither case was a second ship involved; yet the subparagraph indicates that the presence of a second ship is an essential ingredient for the act to be considered as piracy. In the *Santa Maria* case, the men involved came aboard peacefully while the ship was moored; that fact prompted the US not to label the act as piracy. In the second case, the perpetrator swam out from the beach without benefit of a pirate ship and while the local Bahamian court called the act piracy (national jurisdictions have and do call many acts piracy) it really didn't qualify as such under the international definition.

The requirement for "another" ship, ostensibly the "pirate" ship, in my judgement, seems too limiting, for it makes a technical point of how the pirates arrived aboard the victim ship. It would appear that just how or where the "pirates" get aboard is of little consequence as long as their purpose was to take control by use or threat of violence. The primary test of piracy is the act itself and not the mechanics of setting the stage for the act. The present requirement presents the arresting ship with the burden of trying to determine just how the boarding took place before acting to stop the violence or theft.

Some respected experts in international law sustain that view:

Oppenheim:

> The crew or passengers who, for the purpose of converting a vessel and her goods to their own use, force the master through intimidation to steer another course, commit piracy as well as those who murder the master and steer the vessel themselves.

Higgins and Columbos:

> Piracy is any armed violence at sea which is not a lawful act of war.

Let us return to the *Santa Maria* incident.

At the time of the takeover by Galvao, a crew member of the *Santa Maria* was killed and another wounded. Although the passengers were guarded with drawn pistols, none were really molested nor was any personal property taken. Galvao, who led the group of "passengers" who took control of the *Santa Maria* claimed that he and his men were part of the "Iberian Liberation Movement", a political movement aimed at overthrowing the existing governments of Portugal and Spain. The group was composed of Portuguese, Spaniards and Latin Americans.

Who was Henrique Galvao? Fenwick, in a short comment on the case noted that, "He (Galvao) said he was an insurgent, that his purpose was to overthrow the tyrant of Portugal, that he was taking the first step in a revolt against the dictator; that the Portuguese colony of Angola was awaiting his arrival." Further reports give us a fuller picture of the man. The *Herald Tribune* characterised him as, "The master *pro tem* of the Portuguese liner *Santa Maria* is a hawk faced revolutionary convicted three times for trying to overthrow Premier Salazar."

Again, let us look at the definition of piracy as in subparagraph (a) of Article 101—the words "for private ends" are pertinent. After Galvao and his helpers killed and wounded members of the crew, and steered the ship on courses of his choice, he was finally persuaded by an international net of warships closing in to enter the port of Recife, Brazil where he surrendered to local authorities. He did not plunder the ship, nor its passengers—although he certainly produced a high degree of anxiety in the crew and passengers. What was his motive—was it "for private ends" or something else? "For private ends" is normally interpreted to mean that the act was for private material gain or hatred or a desire for revenge. If that is the situation in any given case the act can be determined to be piracy.

The need for determining what the motive was for the act causes a major problem for those trying to suppress violence at sea.

In my view, it is most questionable to try to establish motive at the time of a given act of alleged piracy for, in the usual case, the external facts are all that are available. The subjective motivation behind the act can, more frequently, only be determined in retrospect long after the violent act itself. What the perpetrator might say at the time of the act is only a bit of evidence of what was his true purpose and should not be the governing factor in a final determination of whether piracy was committed or not. In essence, it is better in laying down a general principle to be content with the external character of the facts without entering too far into the often delicate question of motives. If such were the standard, reaction time by arresting units would be compressed to the benefit of persons and property. In the *Santa Maria* case, the external facts all pointed to an act of piracy except for the technical matter of how his rag tag group got aboard.

Wheaton is one of a group of authorities who, over the years, have held to the position that "for private ends" is too narrow a test. He said, "Piracy is the offence of deprecating on the high seas without being authorised by any sovereign State, or with commissions from different sovereigns at war with each other." In effect he was proposing that the search for motive should be restructured in large measure.

But central to the *Santa Maria* case was the fact that Galvao proclaimed that he was an insurgent in revolt against the governments of Portugal and Spain. Did his claim of insurgency place Galvao outside the penalties accorded to acts of piracy and give him the specialised status of a belligerent with the rights that flow from that status?

Insurgents are persons who are engaged in a political struggle; classically, they are distinguished from people who are acting "for private ends".

Insurgency necessarily means fighting as in a revolution, but in this case, Galvao had no base of operations nor was there any open fighting in Portugal or Spain to so constitute a revolution. The status of insurgency is not one to be conceded to any and every citizen who believes that the government of his country is tyrannical and should be overthrown. It takes something more than that. A recognition of insurgency by third states or the acknowledged open fighting for control of an area by an organised group against a sovereign state could be the additional factors required.

It should be noted that a country that is being rebelled against can and usually does consider captures made at sea by rebels as acts of piracy. Portugal did in the instant case. It is also true that when such actions involve potential or actual injury to persons or property of their states, such states consider the act to be piratical.

Fenwick takes the thought a step further:

> It matters not that there was no further violence beyond changing the course of the ship and leaving the passengers in suspense as to their fate; it matters not that Galvao's followers were not *hostes humani generis*, as pirates are described; they killed and robbed on the high seas, under circumstances not justified by the law of insurgency.

If the acts of Galvao do not meet the test of insurgency (particularly as regarded by third states) can it be said that he disqualified himself as a pirate because his acts were not "committed for private ends"? It would seem that, if Galvao lacked the status of an insurgent, as generally defined, his act must fall within the purview of "private ends". Yet it is difficult to sustain a private goal in this instance. The act had tremendous propaganda value and certainly served as a possible catalyst for actual revolution. After interception by US units, Galvao was negotiated with and when he landed in Brazil he was granted political asylum. No "pirate" had ever been treated in such a gentlemanly way. In fact, the conclusion that must be drawn is that Galvao's act was for a public end—stillborn, but nonetheless a public venture. Thus an anomaly is present; Galvao was not an insurgent nor did he pursue a "private end," therefore he was not a pirate under Article 101 of the Convention. If neither an insurgent nor a pirate, what was Galvao?

I would submit that not being, technically, a pirate nor an insurgent the only other possible classification for Galvao was something that is almost a daily occurrence in the decade of the 1980s—a terrorist. In today's vocabulary, Galvao was a terrorist. Unquestionably, the great majority of terrorist acts take place on land with few reported cases involving actions at sea, but the threat is present for unprotected ships, oil rigs, and smaller craft at sea which are attractive targets. Pragmatically, it is difficult to distinguish the result of an act of piracy from that of an act of terrorism. At the time of the *Santa Maria* incident, some reporters felt strongly about the US decision, ie, "The minutiae of definitions of piracy are absurdly irrelevant. The gang had behaved as gangsters and pirates and that was how the US Navy, with its long tradition of defence of the freedom of the seas, initially proposed to handle them."

It is submitted that in today's world climate dramatic efforts by terrorists, such as Galvao, will probably be repeated and will have to be dealt with. The better course of action would be to seek amendment to Article 101 of the LOS Convention deleting the requirement of a second or pirate ship and substituting the phrase "without due authority" in place of "for private ends." Lacking that, the anomalous and controversial status as presented in the Galvao case prompts this reporter to suggest that where a like situation arises in the future, the world community should declare the act piracy and react accordingly. Obviously, this writer believes that the *Santa Maria* incident should have been treated as an act of piracy.

On 7 October 1985 armed men seized the Italian cruise ship *Achille Lauro* and held 420 persons hostage. The press labelled the act as piracy (*Washington Post*, 7-10 October 1985). As the facts emerged it became clear that the seizure was carried out by four members of the Palestine Liberation Front, a group that had split off from the Palestine Liberation Organisation (PLO) and then had splintered into several factions and engaged in various acts of terrorism. They had boarded the *Achille Lauro* in Italy as passengers with hidden firearms and false passports; and seized the ship at sea after it departed from Alexandria, Egypt. The terrorists' basic demand was the release of 50 Palestinian prisoners held in Israel. While on board they did not steal or rob; they did use force and intimidation over the passengers and crew and killed an elderly disabled American. They controlled the movements of the ship. In total, their acts were entirely lawless. They surrendered the ship to Egyptian authorities off Port Said after extensive negotiations and eventually ended up in Italian custody at Sicily.

The case of the *Achille Lauro* is remarkably parallel to that of the earlier *Santa Maria*; no second, or pirate, ship was involved nor were their acts "for private ends". Broadening the criteria for piracy would include such acts of terrorism thereby making them an international crime. As such the international effort to contain and meet the challenge of terrorism would be facilitated. A detailed consideration of the legal aspects of the *Achille Lauro* incident will be found in Chapter 13.

I will now turn to some other elements in ocean law that impact on the suppression and control of piracy. Clearly, the suggestions I will make are rather abrupt departures from regimes that have stood the test of time and state practice. Therefore, I do not make the suggestions with the belief that they might receive current international endorsement. Rather, I view them as possibilities for thought should violence at sea continue to increase.

The doctrine of hot pursuit is old and a most valuable tool for coastal states in the pursuit and apprehension of suspected criminals who have violated the law of the coastal state. Historically, it was limited to the pursuit of vessels that had committed illegal activities in territorial waters. In the 1958 Convention of the High Seas, the doctrine was expanded to include particular acts in the contiguous zone. The 1982 LOS Convention expanded it further to include particular illegal acts within the newly recognised 200 miles exclusive economic zone.

In contrast, there is no reverse regime of hot pursuit from the high seas, where an international illegal act such as piracy takes place, into the jurisdictional waters of a coastal state. There follows an examination of what impediments or constraints, if any, exist to hinder hot pursuit into the exclusive economic zone, the contiguous zone, and the territorial sea by a warship foreign to the coastal state.

By definition, while there are particularised jurisdictions of the coastal state in the exclusive economic zone and the contiguous zone, the waters therein are high seas. Accordingly, a pirate ship may be chased into and captured by a foreign warship within these zones. In contrast, the singular characteristic of the territorial sea is that the coastal state exercises sovereignty within those waters and its national law, including policing, applies. Thus, even though the foreign warship is acting for the common good, it may not enter territorial waters in pursuit to seize a pirate ship.

One of the authorities who would permit that pursuit activity within the territorial sea is Lauderpacht: "If a pirate is chased on the open sea and flees into the territorial maritime belt, the pursuers may follow, attack and arrest the pirate there; but they must give him up to the authorities of the littoral state." Should that statement govern, reverse hot pursuit would be a needed reality.

By definition, piracy is a crime on the high seas and is not recognised as such within the territorial sea of a coastal state where domestic law applies. The present worldwide problem of piracy clearly indicates that a great many piratical acts take place within the territorial sea. With the recognised twelve miles breadth of the territorial sea it is pertinent to ask whether the enforcement capabilities of many coastal states can monitor and respond to the growing problem in the large area off their coast. If they can't (and it appears that some can't or won't), what changes in the law would facilitate suppression of piracy in that jurisdictional zone? One thought that emerges is that when the twelve miles limit was negotiated no thought was given to the rights and duties pertaining to the high seas (such as suppression of piracy) in the waters that had been high seas when the three miles limit was in effect.

Collateral to the discussion above, international law, as specific in Article 100 of the LOS Convention, requires that "all states shall cooperate to the fullest possible extent in the repression of piracy on the high seas." For the most part, acts of piracy are concentrated in particular regions of the world such as south-east Asia, the Caribbean and Gulf of Guinea. It is observed that when there is a common regional problem concerning other uses of the seas, international law requires the contiguous states to seek agreement among themselves or through regional organisations to meet the problem. Such is the case for fisheries (Article 63 of the LOS Convention) or protecting an area of the oceans from pollution which includes the development of contingency plans for responding to pollution incidents (Article 199 LOS Convention). Would not the effort to suppress piracy be enhanced if the same kind of specific obligations were made applicable to piracy in the various affected regions?

In summary, perhaps some of the suggestions presented can serve to better equip the world community to meet and contain the modern manifestation of violence on the oceans. There are clear encumbrances in proceeding in that direction at this time. Two such encumbrances are patent.

(1)It is *not* practical or politically desirable at this time to attempt to amend any of the provisions of the 1982 LOS Convention.

(2)Like attempting to define aggression, an agreed upon definition of terrorism is illusive.

Nonetheless it is clear that the present regime is inadequate to contain and control acts of violence at sea; the world community must act to respond to that threat *effectively*. Other possible legal responses were examined in Chapter 9.

My report would be less than complete if I did not take gratifying notice of the work of the International Maritime Organisation in seeking out an international accord to suppress and contain particular acts of violence at sea. While I personally have some reservations concerning the IMO's draft Convention for the Suppression of Unlawful Acts Against the Safety of Maritime Navigation and its protocol concerning fixed platforms (discussed in detail in Chapter 17), in its totality it can serve as a valuable instrument for the international community. It could aid in supplementing the provision of the 1982 LOS Convention, thereby strengthening that body of ocean law.

BIBLIOGRAPHY

Brierly, J L. The Law of Nations—An Introduction to the International Law of Peace. 5th ed Oxford, 1955.

Briggs, H W. The Law of Nations. 2nd ed, New York, 1952.

Brittin, B H. International Law for Seagoing Officers. 5th ed, US Naval Institute, Annapolis, 1983.

Brownlie, Ian. Principles of Public International Law. 3rd ed, Oxford: Clarendon Press, 1979.

Ellen, E. Violence at Sea, ICC Publishing SA. 1986.

Fenwick, C G. International Law. 3rd ed, New York: Appleton-Century-Crofts Inc. 1952.

Freuchen, P. Book of the Seven Seas. New York: Julian Messner, Inc. 1957.

Gould, W L. An Introduction to International Law. New York, 1957.

Hall, W E. International Law. 5th ed, London: The Clarendon Press, 1904.

Higgins & Columbos. The International Law of Sea. 2nd ed, London: Longmans, Green & Co, 1951.

Hyde, C C. International Law, Chiefly as Interpreted and Applied by the US. 2nd ed, Boston, 1945.

Jessup, P C. The Law of Territorial Waters and Maritime Jurisdiction. New York: J A Jennings Co Inc, 1927.

Kelsen, H. Principles of International Law. New York, 1952.

Lauderpacht, H . Insurrection et Piraterie. 46 RGDIP. 1939.

Moore, J B. A Digest of International Law. Vol II, Washington: GPO, 1906.

O'Connell, O P. The International Law of the Sea. Vol II, Oxford: Clarendon Press, 1984.

Oppenheim, L. International Law. Vol 1, 8th ed, London Lauderpacht, 1955.

Poulantzas, N M. The Right of Hot Pursuit in International Law. Leyden: A W Sythoof, 1969.

Reiff, H. The US and the Treaty Law of the Sea. Minneapolis: University of Minnesota Press, 1959.

Scott, J B. Law, The State and the International Community. Vol II, New York: Columbia University Press, 1939.

CHAPTER 11

THE LAW OF PIRACY

Thomas A Clingan Jr

The problem of piracy has existed as long as vessels have plied the seas. Having enjoyed a fairly long period during which recorded acts of piracy were few and far between, we are now thrust into a new era in which, for various reasons, piracy has in fact become rampant in many parts of the globe. It is appropriate, therefore, that we revisit the law of piracy, if only briefly, to review the traditionally understood scope of its definition and application.

We should first attempt to define the term. In examining the meaning of the concept of piracy, we should pay attention to what it is not as well as what it is. Piracy should be contradistinguished from barratry, mutiny, and more esoteric problems such as insurgency. Barratry is generally restricted in meaning to apply to acts of masters with respect to ships and cargo which are outside of his authority, thus constituting a crime in municipal law against the owner of the ship. Mutiny is a crime committed by the crew of a ship against duly appointed authority. Insurgency is a more difficult problem. An insurgent is one who is engaged in acts of rebellion against a country's duly constituted authority. He has not achieved the status, in international law, of a full belligerent, thus the laws of war do not apply. Nonetheless, he may have achieved through the successes of his enterprise a certain special status that is recognised by international law. In the course of his activities, he may have seized one or more vessels of his adversary, and utilised those ships to his own ends. If he has achieved recognition by others as an insurgent, he is not a pirate so far as they are concerned. If he is an unrecognised insurgent, however, he may commit piracy. The line is a very dim one separating the two, and involves delicate political judgements as well as legal ones.

The category of piracy is a special, and a limited one. Its most modern definition is to be found in the 1982 Law of the Sea (LOS) Convention, Article 101 (see Appendix 15):

Piracy consists of any of the following acts:

(a) any illegal acts of violence or detention, or any act of depredation, committed for private ends by the crew or the passengers of a private ship or a private aircraft, and directed:

(i) on the high seas, against another ship or aircraft, or against persons or property on board such ship or aircraft;

(ii) against a ship, aircraft, persons or property in a place outside the jurisdiction of any State;

(b) any act of voluntary participation in the operation of a ship or aircraft with knowledge of facts making it a pirate ship or aircraft;

(c) any act of inciting or of intentionally facilitating an act described in subparagraph (a) or (b).

Furthermore, Article 101 defines a pirate ship as one intended by the persons in dominant control to be used for the purpose of committing one of the acts referred to in Article 101. From this we learn a few important things concerning piracy. First, it is not a crime that may be committed by a warship so long as that warship remains under the control of its flag state. Second, it must be the acts of a private ship (or aircraft), directed against another ship on the high seas or in a place outside the jurisdiction of any state. Third, the crime is not limited, as had once been believed, to acts of plunder. It applies to illegal acts of violence, detention, or acts of depredation.

Several questions arise with respect to the scope and the consequences of the piracy provision. The first question, long debated, is the status of piracy under *international*, as opposed to *municipal* law. Is piracy an international crime? Under municipal law, the crime of piracy is defined by the local authority. States may confine themselves to punishing as piracy fewer acts of violence than those which the law of nations defines as piracy, or they may punish their subjects for a much wider range of acts. We are here considering the international law of piracy which finds its essential elements contained in Article 101. There are two differing points of view with regard to the status of this law. The first, more traditional point of view draws its legitimacy from the traditional concept that only states are the proper subjects of international law, and individuals, *per se*, are not. Under this view, there are no international crimes for which individuals may be punished. Only states possess the legal capacity to enforce their domestic laws against their charges; there is no equivalent international organisation possessing such capabilities. This view is reinforced by Article 105 of the LOS Treaty which places upon states the responsibility for the seizure of pirates, and for determining appropriate penalties, and the disposition of seized vessels. Under this view, the international law of piracy is not an expression of an international crime, but rather an expression by the international community of the appropriateness of individual states extending their jurisdiction to apply municipal law to offenders upon the high seas.

The more modern concept of international law, however, tends in one way or another, directly or indirectly, to recognise the status of individuals. This is particularly so in the case of international human rights. Although this is a comparatively new evolution, it may be that an individual, under international law, bears internationally punishable responsibilities as well as rights. For most purposes, the distinction is not important, but it is a theoretical consideration of some interest.

The "crime" of piracy, under the 1958 Geneva Convention on the High Seas is a crime, the enforcement for which is restricted to the high seas. Although the treaty does not say so, the clear implication is that the usual enforcement cannot take place within the territorial sea of any nation, since that is an area subject to the sovereignty of the coastal state, thus municipal laws apply. Under the 1982 Treaty, the evolution of the legal concept of the exclusive economic zone (EEZ), and its legal status, brought the question of piracy under new scrutiny. Section 100 of the new treaty calls for the cooperation of states in the suppression of piracy outside the jurisdiction of any state. On first blush, this would seem to raise a question about piracy committed within an exclusive economic zone, since Article 56 confers upon a coastal state both sovereign rights and jurisdictions within that zone. There was an attempt by some coastal states to retain special competencies with regard to piracy within these zones. Peru, for example, proposed during the LOS Conference that the piracy articles be amended to require the consent of the coastal state before a third party could seize a pirate within the EEZ. This proposal, however, was resisted, and eventually dropped. While the EEZ is no longer formally considered as high seas, as previously defined, Article 58 makes clear that Articles 88 to 115 (including the piracy articles) apply to the EEZ in so far as they are not incompatible with the rights of coastal states set forth in the treaty. Since enforcement against a pirate, in normal circumstances, could not be viewed as impinging upon any rights reserved to the coastal state, the law of piracy in the EEZ must be viewed as identical to that applying beyond. Of course, any vessel apprehending a pirate in these zones would have to do so in a way that would not interfere with legitimate coastal state exercise of rights, nor may it constitute any threat to the security of the coastal state.

Another interesting, and essentially unresolved, question involves the scope of application of the piracy articles. New uses of the oceans have raised this question. Suppose, for example, the act of depredation is perpetrated not against a vessel or person on board, but against an unmanned, technologically sophisticated data acquisition station (eg a data buoy). Clearly, the policy against preventing acts of depredation against property on the high seas would seem to dictate that the piracy provisions should apply. Arguably, the application of the piracy law to "property in a place outside the jurisdiction of any state" would seem to reinforce this conclusion. There are two reasons, however, why this is probably not the case. First, the history of the 1958 Convention, from which that language was drawn, explains that the reference to property outside of state jurisdiction was intended to apply to uncontrolled territories, and acts therein. Floating stations were simply not comprehended. But the failure to foresee a new situation is not a bar, necessarily, to an expanded definition of old law. We find an analogous situation in the present debate whether, absent a LOS Treaty, deep seabed mining is a "freedom of the high seas" not contemplated by the drafters in 1958. But there is yet another competing policy reason why the law of piracy should not be applied to unmanned stations. As mentioned above, it is the law of the apprehending state that is applied to a pirate, complete with the attendant penalties. In some states, the penalty for piracy is death, a somewhat severe sanction for tinkering with data buoys. Thus, while the potential for theft from unmanned stations is real (it has already occurred in some instances), it would seem to be better to recognise this as a hiatus in international law, and deal with the matter through new international agreement.

The most serious problem in connection with modern day piracy is, of course, enforcement. In the early years of pirating, the offending vessels were largely the private equivalent of men of war, equipped to do battle, at times successfully, with all but the most capital of warships. Today, much of the piracy being committed is on a much smaller scale, in terms of the size of the vessels in use, although of a much larger scale in terms of the frequency of occurrence. Traditional rules, and the treaties, confine enforcement to warships or military ships or other ships ''clearly marked and identifiable as being on government service and authorised to that effect'' (eg coast guard and national police vessels). This limitation imposes an almost impossible burden on would be enforcers. Most nations lack sufficient qualifying enforcement vessels, and supporting air surveillance—in many parts of the world these simply do not exist. Furthermore, disputes over maritime boundaries make accurate delineation of enforcement responsibilities difficult, if not impossible. In addition, enforcement by the vessels of one nation against citizens of another where hostile attitudes exist between the two countries often raises difficult political and diplomatic questions. I am not suggesting that the limitation to authorised vessels be changed. A return to the privateering system in these circumstances would only lead to further conflict and abuse. I am suggesting, however, that the lack of enforcement capabilities in areas of high piracy (whether for financial gain or in conjunction with drug trafficking) is a serious problem that may require international attention. In some areas, regional cooperation may be at least a partial solution. Certainly, at the very least, states should exercise more scrutiny over waters under their own jurisdiction, where pirate vessels may originate.

The law of piracy, whether it be viewed as merely jurisdictional in nature, or in a more substantive way, is adequate on the international level, provided that more is done on the municipal level. Modern day piracy often occurs close to territorial waters that may provide a de facto sanctuary for the pirate. To permit pursuit into such waters, absent the consent of the coastal state, would be an invasion of its sovereignty. Perhaps bilateral or regional arrangements providing for automatic, or almost automatic consent, in carefully limited and prescribed circumstances would be a partial answer to such problems. Such careful arrangements have been explored in connection with drug trafficking with some success. Recently, a combined US/Bahamian force swept the area of the island of Bimini to capture drugs intended for the US resulting in the arrest of a large number of offenders.

Until the critical enforcement problem is solved, the law of piracy, a traditional monument to a policy of the peaceful and protected uses of the seas, will provide little comfort to those that continue, on a local scale, to suffer depredations. If the problem is not solved, however, vessel owners will more frequently resort to self help measures that can only exacerbate the problem.

CHAPTER 12

THE UNCTAD PERSPECTIVE ON PIRACY

Naomichi H Terazaki

Introduction

This paper is intended to outline the activities and concerns of the United Nations Conference on Trade and Development (UNCTAD) in respect of piracy at sea, or rather maritime fraud including piracy.

The Committee on Shipping of UNCTAD, at its tenth session in 1982, adopted Resolution 49(X) whereby it decided to establish an Ad hoc Intergovernmental Group to consider Means of Combating all Aspects of Maritime Fraud, including Piracy. Conference Resolution 144(VI) of the sixth session of UNCTAD in 1983 urged the Ad hoc Intergovernmental Group to expedite its work. The relevant texts of the above mentioned resolutions were adopted in response to the alarming increase in the number of reported instances of maritime fraud and related acts, including piracy. The Committee on Shipping, in the light of the existing international programmes to suppress maritime fraud and piracy, considered that there was a need for a fundamental in depth analysis of possible structural reforms which should be made in an international forum such as UNCTAD, whose primary jurisdiction included maritime matters, in the context of trade and development. Under these circumstances, the first session of the Ad hoc Intergovernmental Group was convened in February 1984. The UNCTAD Secretariat, prior to the meeting of this Group, with a view to facilitating its work, had prepared a comprehensive report on maritime fraud and piracy entitled "Review and Analysis of Possible Measures to Minimise the Occurrence of Maritime Fraud and Piracy".

Although there is no generally accepted definition of the term "maritime fraud", it is usually used to include any dishonest act in connection with maritime affairs (even though such acts may not necessarily involve concealment, deceit or misrepresentation—typically thought to constitute elements of fraud in a legal context). Thus acts of simple theft, piracy and barratry are often included within the term.

The report did not attempt to define the term "piracy"; instead it made reference to the most modern definition under international law, in the 1982 United Nations Convention on the Law of the Sea (UNCLOS)—see Appendix 15. "Piracy" is defined in Article 101 of the

1982 Convention which reiterates Article 15 of the 1958 Geneva Convention on the High Seas (see Appendix 14) which, in turn, codified customary international law. This definition of piracy in international law can be called piracy in a "narrower sense" inasmuch as it is restricted to acts committed on the high seas, or in any other place outside the jurisdiction of any state, and to acts committed against another ship or persons or property on board such ship.

The problem of piracy addressed by the Committee on Shipping and by the Ad hoc Intergovernmental Group is piracy in a "broader sense". In view of the expanded scope of coastal states' jurisdiction with the extension of territorial seas up to twelve miles under 1982 UNCLOS, and of the increasing number of reported thefts, robberies, assaults and even murders perpetrated within port areas or territorial seas, attention in UNCTAD's fora was directed to acts not included in the definition of piracy under international law. The reported incidents against merchant shipping often appear to involve land based gangs. It also appears that the incidents are centred in specific regions where there is a relatively high concentration of shipping traffic, together with insufficient police enforcement by coastal states, arising either from local economic and social conditions or from the existence of extensive coastal areas not fully under central government control. As was noted earlier in this paper, certain acts of piracy and barratry are often included with, or equated to, maritime fraud. Thus the problem of piracy in a "broader sense" was included in the work programme of the Ad hoc Intergovernmental Group.

Current Difficulties

The treatment of piracy in international law has often been considered as an insufficient response to the actual problem in many parts of the world today. Generally the criticisms relate not directly to the powers granted to states, but indirectly through the definition of "piracy", which controls the operation of the extraordinary powers granted to states in UNCLOS Article 105—Seizure of a pirate ship or aircraft:

> On the high seas, or in any other place outside the jurisdiction of any state, every state may seize a pirate ship or aircraft, or a ship or an aircraft taken by piracy and under the control of pirates, and arrest the persons and seize the property on board. The courts of the state which carried out the seizure may decide upon the penalties to be imposed, and may also determine the action to be taken with regard to the ships, aircraft or property, subject to the rights of third parties acting in good faith.

Specifically, the definition has been criticised as being too restrictive in referring only to acts on the high seas, or outside the jurisdiction of a state, and only to acts directed against other ships. The extraordinary state jurisdiction granted in Article 105 therefore does not apply to acts committed within the territorial sea. In view of the expanded scope of the territorial sea to twelve miles and of the fact that the majority of current piratical acts are committed off coastal areas, this restriction in international law removes a large number of acts which otherwise would be considered piratical. However, a piratical act within the territorial sea of a state will result in the application of that state's national laws, since the sovereignty of a coastal state extends to its territorial sea. On the assumption that the attackers remain within the territorial area of the same state, and on the further assumption that instances of insufficient enforcement of national law result, not from the lack of willingness but from lack of practical capability, UNCTAD's attention should be turned to measures which could assist states in enforcing their laws in affected areas.

A reference was made in the UNCTAD report to the eleven nation fund organised by the UN High Commissioner for Refugees to aid the government of Thailand to suppress attacks on the "boat people" in its waters, and which is fully described in Part 2 of this book. This type of international cooperation could be considered for other affected areas, bearing in mind the right of each sovereign state to enforce its national laws in the way it deems appropriate.

The important fact concerning piratical attacks nowadays in many areas of the world is that they occur within territorial seas, and then the attackers flee to the territorial sea of another state. It is suggested that the situation requires regional cooperation arrangements between the affected states, *inter alia* to coordinate their enforcement policies and, perhaps, improve extradition procedures. There still remain cases of acts within territorial seas after which the perpetrators flee to high seas. However, it may be doubted whether there are many such cases that cannot be handled by the right of hot pursuit recognised by international law, and granted to coastal states by UNCLOS Article 111.

The limitation of the definition to acts committed against another ship, or persons or property on board such other ship, excludes acts by the crew or passengers against other persons or property on the same ship. Therefore, acts of barratry and deviation frauds, committed internally on a ship, are excluded from piracy in the "narrow sense". Deviation fraud, in essence, consists of theft of cargo. This is effected by the shipowner deceiving the cargo owner into chartering the vessel to carry the latter's goods to an agreed destination. However, the vessel deviates en route to another destination where the goods are sold for the benefit of the shipowner. Subsequently, the vessel either is intentionally sunk or disappears by changing its name, nominal ownership and country of registration. This type of fraud thrives near areas where, because of war, civil disorders or other factors, there are port areas not under close supervision and control, thereby permitting such illegal sales to occur without great risk of intervention. Not all deviation frauds are premeditated—"accidental" cases arise from charter party disputes where the charterer has not paid the owner his hire, or where the port waiting period is excessive.

There have been some suggestions in international fora that acts of barratry and deviation fraud should be equated in international law with piracy. In practice, due to the restrictive definition of barratry which precludes the involvement of the shipowner, it is a relatively rare event. The suggestions are therefore made more seriously with regard to deviation fraud. However, in the absence of reporting requirements on voyage schedules and an international ship monitoring system, it can only be determined in relatively rare cases that a vessel on the high seas is actually committing a deviation fraud. Even if it can be determined that a vessel is no longer on its intended course, there are numerous practical reasons to justify this. As a matter of practicality until disposal of the cargo has taken place, deviation is at most a violation of the contract of transport, not a crime. Thus only after the fraud has been completed will intervention by ships of other states be feasible. Whether such an expansion of jurisdiction, and the probable negative repercussions of increased interference in international shipping, are warranted by the problem of deviation frauds is a matter to be assessed by states. In making this assessment, account should be taken of the degree to which frauds could be eliminated by the expansion of jurisdiction of all states over ships and perpetrators of fraud found within their territorial jurisdiction, even when the crime has been committed elsewhere.

As a matter of principle, acts which occur internally to a ship, such as deviation frauds against the ship's cargo, are subject to the national law of the flag state. This may be viewed as a crucial distinction from piracy, which merits the intervention of international law. However, it could be argued that it makes little difference whether cargo is stolen in a physical attack from another ship, or whether it is stolen by deceit by the master and crew of one ship alone, agreeing to transport it, but deviating and selling it for their own profit. In both cases the victim and the perpetrator may be of different nationalities. It could be argued that these considerations are irrelevant to the existing general international legal framework, and that they cannot therefore serve as a basis for extraordinary rights to interfere with ships on the high seas. Nevertheless it could be argued that some sort of increased jurisdictional capabilities should be granted to states, in order to combat the problem of deviation fraud for which the current capabilities are clearly not sufficient.

Possible preventive and remedial Measures

The possible establishment of a global ship monitoring capacity, perhaps using satellite communications and shipboard "black boxes", requires careful examination. This has obvious applications for, and is probably financially justifiable only in terms of, safety and traffic control. However, combined with an obligation to report destinations and estimated arrival times, it could also assist in the prevention of deviation fraud and, by extension, of certain types of piracy.

UNCTAD also supports the establishment of systems, including systems operated by the specialised non-governmental or commercial organisations, to facilitate the availability and dissemination of maritime information. This information may be specifically aimed at maritime fraud, but certain parts of it can still be used to combat piratical acts, since they are equated to some types of maritime fraud.

The problem of maritime fraud and piracy is by nature international. The large number of jurisdictions in the world pose particular problems for the administration of justice. In view of the difficulty in obtaining jurisdiction over offenders, or extraditing them to a country prepared to prosecute them, the UNCTAD Secretariat had previously suggested that the feasibility of an international convention to establish greater jurisdictional capabilities for certain countries affected by maritime fraud and piracy should be investigated. Currently, extradition treaties are usually concluded on a bilateral basis. However, given the large number of sovereign states now existing, the bilateral approach may no longer be adequate.

The Ad hoc Intergovernmental Group at its first session in February 1984 adopted Resolution 1(I)[3], in which it requested the UNCTAD Secretariat to prepare in depth studies on the feasibility of improving the administrative and legal procedures for prosecuting authorities and to identify other possible means of international cooperation.

Pursuant to the above request, the UNCTAD Secretariat prepared a report entitled "The feasibility of improving the administrative and legal procedures of prosecuting authorities in cases of maritime fraud". The report revealed that, in view of the international character of maritime criminality, the existing legal principles governing jurisdiction and extradition might certainly be considered as hampering progress in combating it. It suggested the elaboration of an international convention to define maritime offences and to streamline jurisdictional and extraditional procedures for prosecuting fraudsters.

The Ad hoc Intergovernmental Group at its second session in October-November 1985, considered this report. However, the idea of an international convention did not receive the general support of the Group. The Group nevertheless decided in its Resolution 2(II)[4] to request the Committee on Shipping to examine means of increasing cooperation between existing national and international bodies in the investigation and prosecution of maritime crime. In response to this request the UNCTAD Secretariat reviewed the existing systems of investigation and prosecution at the national level, as well as the role of involved intergovernmental bodies.[5] Having reaffirmed that the large number of jurisdictions in the world pose particular problems in the international context, the resulting UNCTAD report pointed out that cooperation at the international level either among states or through intergovernmental organisations was vital. The report suggested that, at the national level, in view of the fragmentation of the present system, the problem might be most efficiently dealt with by a single agency, responsible for the entire system. The report therefore considered the formation of a body to coordinate the various agencies or of a unified body responsible for all the functions of detection, investigation and prosecution of serious maritime crime.

The report also noted that at the heart of the inadequate response by governments and law enforcement agencies to maritime crime is the problem of jurisdiction at the international level. More and more pirates operate in gangs and attack ships moored in ports or waiting to enter ports. It is evident that many piratical attacks occur within a territorial sea of one state, after which the pirates take refuge in a neighbouring state.

In examining means to overcome difficulties deriving from jurisdiction and extradition, the report considered the on going work of intergovernmental organisations concerned with the improvement of cooperation in these areas— such as the Commonwealth Scheme relating to Mutual Assistance in Criminal Matters.

The Ad hoc Intergovernmental Group at its first session decided that all outstanding work from its second session should be transmitted to the Committee on Shipping. The above UNCTAD report was submitted to the Committee on Shipping at its twelfth session in November 1986, together with other UNCTAD reports[6] on other aspects of prevention of maritime crime. The Committee on Shipping, after arduous discussions, adopted Resolution 60(XII).[7]

Matters included in the resolution concerning maritime fraud and thus, by extension, some types of piracy included the following. The UNCTAD Secretariat was asked to monitor work on sea waybills, and on the development of a training programme to combat maritime fraud, currently being carried out by national and international organisations, and to draft non-mandatory minimum standards for shipping agents, who are believed to have great potential in resisting fraud.

NOTES

1. The term "piracy" in this context is used in a liberal sense to refer to a broad range of violent acts at sea which does not necessarily correspond to the term as defined in international law. This is generally referred to as piracy in a "broader" sense.

2. The term "barratry" is defined in many legal systems as a wrongful act wilfully committed by the master or crew to the prejudice of the owner of charterer (when acting as the owner).

3. UNCTAD report TD/B/985, annex 1.

4. UNCTAD report TD/B/C.4/296, annex.

5. UNCTAD report UNCTAD/ST/SHIP/9 entitled "Measures to increase cooperation in the investigation and prosecution of maritime fraud".

6. UNCTAD report UNCTAD/ST/SHIP/7 entitled "Measures to improve the exchange of shipping information". UNCTAD report UNCTAD/ST/SHIP/8 entitled "Prevention of documentary fraud associated with bills of lading. Use of sea waybills"

7. UNCTAD report TD/B/1123, Annex I.

CHAPTER 13

THE *ACHILLE LAURO* AND SIMILAR INCIDENTS AS PIRACY: TWO ARGUMENTS

Samuel P Menefee

Note: For a full discussion of the arguments summarised herein, see S P Menefee, "Piracy, Terrorism, and the Insurgent Passenger: A Historical and Legal Perspective" in N Ronzitti, *The Achille Lauro and International Law* (Martinus Nijhoff, forthcoming).

(See also page 146)

There appears to be some question as to whether passenger ship takeovers such as the *Achille Lauro* are piracy, terrorism, or perhaps both. This is more than academic; if such hijackers were held to be guilty of piracy *jure gentium*, any state would have the right to seize their vessel in a place outside State jurisdiction and to decide on the penalties to be imposed. It seems that there are two possible arguments, minority views, which could lead to this conclusion on at least some occasions. One is textual, the other based on customary international law.

The textual argument arises from the piracy articles of the 1958 Geneva Convention on the High Seas (see Appendix 14). To state this argument in its most succinct form, let us see if there are ways to surmount the two major objections raised to considering the *Achille Lauro* episode as piracy under this Convention: (a) the requirement that *two* boats be involved, and (b) the question of "private ends".

Article 15(1)(a) of the Convention appears to require the presence of two vessels for an action on the high seas to be considered piracy. Only one boat, of course, was involved in the *Achille Lauro* incident. The second division of that paragraph (Art 15(1)(b)), however, speaks only of acts taking place in areas "outside the jurisdiction of any State". No two boat requirement occurs. As Article 19 speaks of "the high seas or ... any *other* place outside the jurisdiction of any State" (emphasis added), it appears that the high seas is such a place. While Art 15(1)(b) is generally acknowledged to have been drafted to apply to Antarctica and certain guano islands and drying reefs, it is plain that its wording also covers high sea piracy which occurs against a ship, aircraft, persons, or property, regardless of the absence of a second ship.

The question of "private ends" is another problem. Article 15 requires this for an act to be considered piracy, but does not say private ends as opposed to what. Public ends? Political ends? Who defines the ends—the judge, the victim, or the perpetrator? Can an end be *both* private *and* political in nature? There is a tremendous amount of ambiguity in the term. In the case of the *Achille Lauro* the hijacking was disowned by the PLO. Further, it was totally against third parties—the vessel involved sailed under the *Italian* flag, and the one fatality was an *American* citizen. To rule such an act "political" or "public" in nature would appear to unduly stretch the definition of those terms at the expense of "private ends". Surely, *any* act has its public or political side; indeed, large numbers of individuals convicted of classic piracy claimed to be privateers. For the Convention's definition to have meaning, some sort of balancing test is necessary. Based on this, the *Achille Lauro* attack might well be deemed piratical.

This situation may be contrasted with the recent attack on the Greek passenger ferry the *City of Poros*. While the private ends argument appears to be even stronger (the Greek government has been generally supportive of Palestinian aspirations and the dead appear to be Greek and French), the ship was *not* "outside the jurisdiction of any state", but rather within Greek territorial waters. A textual argument might therefore founder on the fact that two boats do *not* appear to have been involved.

A second piracy argument, however, deriving from customary international law, is also possible. This might embrace both the *Achille Lauro* and *City of Poros* fact situations by holding that the 1958 definition of piracy, which has been carried over into the 1982 Convention, is *not* exclusive. O'Connell himself, in *The International Law of the Sea*, vol 2, notes (p 970): "Because of its elliptical nature, Article 15 is one of the least successful essays in codification of the Law of the Sea, and the question is open whether it is comprehensive so as to preclude reliance upon customary law, where this may differ or has superseded customary law." Many nineteenth century cases classified passenger takeovers for political purposes as piracy *jure gentium,* and a similar argument can be used for the *Achille Lauro* and *City of Poros* cases.

CHAPTER 14

PIRACY, LAW AND MARINE INSURANCE

Jonathan Ignarski

Introduction

Piracy in its modern public international sense of "any illegal acts of violence, detention or any act of depredation committed for private ends" carried out by one ship and its crew against another on the high seas is merely one of a number of dangers associated, from the classical age onwards, with sea-borne commerce. Since in terms of commercial law most piratical acts amount to simple thefts, robberies and assaults, it is fair to assume that the profession of pirate will always exist as long as societies engage in maritime trade.

It is the very antiquity of piracy and its international dimension rather than the mundane nature of piratical acts which have given rise to definitional difficulties which will necessarily be dealt with here. Whenever crime has an international element the question of jurisdiction is never far away. On the high seas, away from the coastal jurisdiction of States, international politics and national naval strength often in practice determine how difficult life can be made for pirates preying on a given trade route. For the society of States, piracy is above all else a law and order issue, where States must cooperate to shield their citizens and commercial relations from the debilitating effects of parasitic crime.

Piracy and Public International Law

Because the origins of piracy as a crime lie in custom and customary law, it is not surprising that the definition of piracy in international law gave rise to controversy from the middle ages until the twentieth century. A first attempt by the League of Nations to codify the law in draft provisions for the suppression of piracy was dropped in 1927 because of insufficient support. A further pre-war draft piracy convention by the Harvard Research in International Law (*AJIL* Supp. 26: 729 (1932)) served as the basis for the 1958 United Nations High Seas Convention produced by the International Law Commission. This Convention, which is declarative of the customary law, deals with piracy in Articles 14 to 21 (UNIS 450:82). The piracy provisions of the High Seas Convention are repeated verbatim in Articles 100 to 107 in the as yet unratified 1982 United National Convention on the Law of the Sea (see Appendix 15).

The historical progress of attempts to formulate the law of piracy is further dealt with in Chapter 9.

The provisions seem clear enough: for piracy to exist there must be a pirate ship and a victim ship and the piractical act must take place on the high seas. Any piratical act taking place in territorial waters is a matter for the municipal law of the State concerned. In many ways this reduces the law governing piracy into a patchwork of competing municipal laws and indeed there are many who argue that the "international crime" of piracy is no more than the sum of its municipal parts (see A. Rubin: Is Piracy Illegal? *AJIL* vol. 70 (1976), p. 92). The counter argument is that the 1958 and 1982 Conventions confer jurisdiction on States to combat piracy and punish the individuals responsible where they are found on the high seas (for a succinct over-view of the law, see Alfred Rubin, 'Piracy' in R. Bernhadt (Ed.) *Encyclopaedia of Public International Law,* Instalment 11 (in preparation).)

Piracy and Marine Insurance

Since piracy has been a more or less continuing annoyance to international trade, it is not surprising that the owners of ships and cargoes have sought to insure themselves on conditions which also include cover against losses or damage caused by piracy. There are two possible ways in which such cover could be offered. Cover against loss or damage through piracy could either be a feature of the ordinary marine covers available on the world markets, treating the risk as comparable to loss caused by a force of nature or an ordinary maritime misfortune such as a collision or stranding. The other obvious place for the risk would be the war risk policies which the owners of ships and cargoes conclude to cover the many risks excluded under the standard marine covers. There is, unfortunately, no unanimity as to the "correct" market for piracy risks. Until the early 1980s the United Kingdom insurance industry tended to treat piracy as a war risk, ie supplemental to the marine policy. Now the position has been reversed with the drafting of the new Institute of London Underwriters Marine Policy Form, examples of which will follow below. Many national cargo insurance markets which were surveyed at around the time when the new clauses were being agreed followed the Institute's example of the International Union of Marine Insurance Report in (1982) found that Austria, Canada, Denmark, France, the two German States, Greece, Hungary, Ireland, Italy, Norway, Nigeria, Spain and, of course, the UK all treated piracy as a marine peril, whilst Australia, Czechoslovakia, Egypt, Finland, Japan, Netherlands, Portugal, Jordan, Switzerland, Taiwan, the United States of Yugoslavia considered piracy a war risk. Provided the buyer of insurance has bought both kinds of policy for the ship or cargo concerned, the worst that can happen may be a protracted and legalistic dispute as to which of the policies should respond.

The risk of piracy is included by the Institute (Cargo clauses (A) of 1.1.82 (the all risks cover)) by the far from unusual method of an exception to an exclusion.

6. In no case shall this insurance cover loss damage or expense caused by
6.1 War civil war revolution rebellion insurrection, or civil strife arising therefrom, or any hostile act by or against a belligerent power

6.2 Capture seizure arrest restraint or detainment *(piracy excepted),* and the consequences thereof or any attempt thereat

6.3 Derelict mines torpedoes bomb or other derelict weapons of war.

7. In no case shall this insurance cover loss damage or expense

7.1 caused by strikers, locked-out workmen, or persons taking part in labour disturbances, riots or civil commotions

7.2 resulting from strikes, lock-outs, labour disturbances, riots or civil commotions

7.3 caused by any terrorist or any person acting from a political motive.

It should be noted here that the cover excludes terrorist risks and in fact consigns these to the war risk policy.

In the case of hulls, the Institute Hull clauses repeat the exercise bv treating piracy as an ordinary marine peril.

6. Perils

6.1 This insurance covers loss of damage to the subject-matter caused by

6.1.1 perils of the seas rivers lakes or other navigable waters

6.1.2 fire, explosion

6.1.3 violent theft by persons from outside the Vessel

6.1.4 jettison

6.1.5 *piracy* (author's emphasis)

6.1.6 breakdown of or accident to nuclear installations or reactors

6.1.7 contact with aircraft or similar objects, or objects falling therefrom, land conveyance, dock or harbour equipment or installation

6.1.8 earthquake volcanic eruption or lightning.

6.2 This insurance covers loss of or damage to the subject-matter insured caused by

6.2.1 accidents in loading discharging or shifting cargo or fuel

6.2.2 bursting of boilers breakage of shafts or any latent defect in the machinery or hull

6.2.3 negligence of Master Officers Crew or Pilots

6.2.4 negligence of repairers or charterers provided such repairers or charterers are not an Assured hereunder

6.2.5 barratry of Master Officers or Crew provided such loss or damage has not resulted from want to due diligence by the Assured, Owners or Managers.

6.3 Master Officers Crew or Pilots not to be considered Owners within the meaning of this Clause 6 should they hold shares in the Vessel.

Again for hulls the later war, strikes and malicious acts exclusions consign cognate risks arising out of terrorism or malice to the mirror image cover available under war risks and strike clauses:

23 War Exclusion
In no case shall this insurance cover loss damage liability or expense caused by

23.1 war civil war revolution rebellion insurrection, or civil strife arising therefrom, or any hostile act by or against a belligerent power

23.2 capture seizure arrest restraint or detainment (barratry and *piracy* excepted), and the consequences thereof or any attempt thereat

23.3 derelict mines torpedoes bombs or other derelict weapons of war.

24 Strikes Exclusion
In no case shall this insurance cover loss damage liability or expense caused by

24.1 strikers, locked-out workmen, or persons taking part in labour disturbances, riots or civil commotions

24.2 any terrorist or any person acting from a political motive.

25 Malicious Acts Exclusion
In no case shall this insurance cover loss damage liability or expense arising from

25.1 the detonation of an explosive

25.2 any weapon of war
and caused by any person acting maliciously or from a political motive.

Since the redrafting of the Institute Clauses it is now unadventurous to say that loss or damage through piracy are now the proper subjects of marine policies governing hulls and freight (together with cargo all risks) the P & I (''Protection and Indemnity''—shipowner's third party liability) industry necessarily had to draft a wording which would fall into line with this approach. The wording offered by the United Kingdom Mutual Steamship Insurance Association (Bermuda) Limited may be taken as typical:

Exclusion of War Risks

The Association shall not indemnify an Owner against any liabilities, costs or expenses (irrespective of whether a contributory cause of the same being incurred was any neglect on the part of the Owner or on the part of the Owner's servants or agents) when the loss or damage, injury, illness or death or other accident in respect of which such liability arises or cost or expenses is incurred, was caused:

i War, civil war, revolution, rebellion, insurrection or civil strife arising therefrom, or any hostile act by or against a belligerent power;

ii Capture, seizure, arrest, restraint or detainment *(barratry and piracy excepted)* and the consequences thereof or any attempt thereat; (author's emphasis)

iii Mines, torpedoes, bombs, rockets, shells, explosives or other similar weapons of war (save for those liabilities, costs or expenses which arise solely by reason of the transport of any such weapons whether on board the entered ship or not). Provided always that this exclusion shall not apply to the use of such weapons either as a result of government order or with the written agreement of the Directors or the Managers where the reason for such use is the avoidance or mitigation of liabilities, costs or expenses which would otherwise fall within the cover given by the Association.

However, for reasons of uniformity, there has, within the P & I industry, been a general movement towards offering a ''facility'' for war risks liability insurance by means of the so-called ''proviso'':

The Directors may resolve that special cover be provided to the Members against any or all of the risks set out in (this rule) notwithstanding that those liabilities, costs or expenses would otherwise be excluded by this paragraph. . . . and that such special cover should be limited to such sum or sums and be subject to such terms and conditions as the Directors may from time to time determine.

Notwithstanding the above, the philosophy underlying marine covers is straightforward. Piracy is not to be considered a species of war risk: the burden is on the marine underwriter, to show a given loss or damage through "piracy" is, in fact or law, an excluded war risk and thus payable by the war risk underwriters for the claim in question. A considerable settlement sum may yet provide the pretext for further judicial consideration whether a given act of violence at sea may be considered that of a terrorist (a war risk) or a pirate (a marine risk). This possibility has led the drafters of the rules of the United Kingdom Mutual War Risks Association and the Hellenic Mutual War Risks Association (Bermuda) Limited to minimise this prospect, by providing for the possibility of war risks cover for loss or damage through piracy whilst making provision for the possibility of double insurance. Rule 3.1.3 of the Hellenic Club's 1988 rules underlines the nature of most piratical acts as financially relatively small but frequently occurring thefts:

PIRACY AND VIOLENT THEFT—LIMITATION OF AMOUNT RECOVERABLE

3.13.1 The amount recoverable by the Owner of an Entered Ship in respect of a claim arising out of piracy or of violent theft by persons from outside the ship is subject to the limits set out in Rules 3.13.2 to 3.13.5

3.13.2 Any such claim shall be subject to such deductible as the Directors shall have determined before the beginning of the Policy Year during which the claim arises.

3.13.2 If and to the extent that the sum claimed relates to loss of cash held on board by the Master or by a representative of the Owner for the purposes of the Entered Ship's business or trade, then subject to Rule 3.13.4, recovery from the Association in respect of such loss of cash shall be limited to a maximum of US$20,000 each accident or occurrence.

3.13.4 Where the entered ship becomes, or under Rule 3.11.5 is treated as, an actual or constructive total loss as a result of such piracy or violent theft, the liability of the Association in respect of the loss of the ship and the loss of cash referred to in Rule 3.13.3 shall not exceed the aggregate of

(a) the value on which the insurance is based . . . and

(b) the sum (if any) insured in respect of freight and Disbursements.

3.13.5 If and to the extent that the sum claimed relates to loss of cash and personal valuables which are the property of the Crew of the Entered Ship (other than the tools of their trade) for which the Owner is under a legal liability to reimburse the Crew, recovery from the Association shall be limited to a maximum, of US$20,000 each accident or occurrence.

The Hellenic Club's risks covered rule 2A.2 for hull, machinery and freight is also supported by an inclusive clause:

CAUSES OF LOSS

2A.2 The Owner of an Entered Ship is insured as provided in Rule 2A.1 if the loss, damage or expense as the case may be is caused by:

2A.2.1 war, civil war, revolution, rebellion, insurrection, or civil strife arising therefrom, or any hostile act by or against a belligerent power;

2A.2.2 capture, seizure, arrest, restraint or detainment, and the consequences thereof or any attempt thereat;

2A.2.3 Mines, torpedoes, bombs or other weapons of war (whether any of the aforesaid are derelict or otherwise);

2A.2.4 strikers, locked-out workmen, or persons taking part in labour disturbances, riots or civil commotions;

2A.2.5 any terrorist or any person acting maliciously, or from a political motive;

2A.2.6 Piracy and violent theft by persons from outside the ship;

2A.2.6 Piracy and violent theft by persons from outside the ship;

2A.2.7 confiscation or expropriation;

2A.2.8 the risks excluded from the Standard Form of English Marine Policy (Hulls) by Clauses 23 (the War Exclusion Clause), 24 (the Strikes Exclusion Clause) and 25 (the Malicious Acts Exclusion Clause) of the Institute Time clauses—Hulls (edition of 1.10.1983).

It must be said that all the new wordings which have now been adopted by the London market have gone a good way towards setting out the covers provided in a form more readily intelligible than the old system and the central role played by the wording of the historic free of capture and seizure (FC & S) clause.

In some other markets, the buyers of insurance are still subject to the old and complex ways. This may not be of great moment to shipowners who have long experience of the peculiarities of their particular insurances but for, say, the North American yachtsmen sailing in the Caribbean, it may be a far from remote question whether he is covered for loss or damage through piracy. Given the effects of the drugs trade on the Caribbean, yachtsmen would do well to check the extent of their covers.

What all of the wordings cited in this paper refrain from supplying is a definition of the terms used. For guidance, resort must be had to English law and, so far as piracy and marine insurance is concerned, to the *locus classicus* of the *Andreas Lemos* (1978) 2 Lloyds Rep 483. In this case during 1977 the *Andreas Lemos* was boarded at night by individuals intent upon robbery in the port of Chittagong well within Bangladeshi territorial waters. The intruders stole mooring ropes on the ship's forecastle and threw them into a small craft lying off the ship's screw. They were detected whereupon they drew knives but fled at the sight of the ship's master and a Verey pistol fired at them by the second officer. No violence was offered by the robbers before or during the theft itself, though some threat was offered up while the intruders made their escape. The case turned on the definition of piracy or riots for the purposes of the war risks policy. The policy wordings used were based on the old standard form of marine policy and the FC & S clause which then required the question toa be asked whether a particular casualty would have been covered by the standard form of insurance policy and secondly whether it was excluded by the FC & S clause from that policy. If (at that time) the answer to both questions was affirmative, the negative cover of the war risks association would have come into force. An amicable action was brought by the owners of the *Andreas Lemos* and the Hellenic War Risks Association to try to introduce clarity into an issue that was far from clear on the case law then available. As a result of the decision of Mr Justice Staughton, a number of general and perhaps surprising propositions of law emerged.

Firstly, and most unexpectedly, a distinction was drawn between the piracy described by international law (and introduced at the beginning of this paper) and piracy in the context of a policy of marine insurance. Piracy has to take place "at sea" in its ordinary meaning and this was a wider definition than "the high seas"; if an attack upon the ship could be described as "a maritime affair" then for the business purposes of a policy of insurance, the ship was in a place where piracy would be committed. The judge supported this view by reference to rule 8 of the 1st schedule to the Marine Insurance Act 1906 which says the term pirates is to include passengers who mutiny and rioters who attack the ship from the shore. Thus a criminal lawyer's pirate is a different wrongdoer from a marine lawyer's pirate, and a ship is not "at sea" when anchored in port.

The second point established in the case concerned the use of actual force during the commission of the piratical act. The judge also held following earlier authorities that piracy had to have an element of actual force or the threat of force against the persons in charge of the ship:

> The association, by the word "piracy", insured the loss caused to shipowners because their employees are overpowered by force, or terrified into submission. It does not insure the loss caused to shipowners when their night-watchman is asleep (as might occur, although it did not in this case), and thieves steal clandestinely. The very notion of piracy is inconsistent with clandestine theft. . . . It is not necessary that the thieves must raise the pirate flag and fire a shot across the victim's bows before they can be called pirates. But piracy is not committed by stealth.

This has a number of interesting implications depending upon the facts of a given case. A theft becomes a piratical act only when the thieves are confronted during the theft and violence ensues. If the thieves are escaping with the booty (as in the case of *Andreas Lemos*) with the act of appropriation completed and only then offer violence, the act is merely a violent theft (hence the inclusion of this head of cover in the Hellenic Association's Rules).

Two further propositions derived from the case are of interest. Loss from piracy would usually involve theft but it would include damage to the ship, possibly even the accidental destruction of the ship. Finally, piracy was not involved where the persons concerned are acting upon the authority or orders of any State.

Conclusion

So far as marine underwriters are concerned, piracy is a low to medium level criminal nuisance—mugging at sea—exacting an annual toll in lost valuables, ships' cash, cargo and equipment. The human dimension of piracy, the ferocity of piratical attacks as reported by the International Maritime Bureau and other maritime narratives (see Captain Roger Viller, *Piracy Today* (1985)) call out for concerted action at the international level by the Society of States and by private organisations able to play a constructive role. Piracy is and has always been a profession which subsists upon the toil of trading societies. Underwriters must recompense cases of loss but ultimately it is individuals and communities who bear the costs of piracy.

THE LAW OF PIRACY

CONFERENCE DISCUSSION

The following discussion between contributing authors took place during the Marine Policy Centre's 1985 update workshop on Piracy at Sea. The workshop was held at the Woods Hole Oceanographic Institute, Massachusetts, USA.

GARRETTSON: Piracy is an area of universal jurisdiction, isn't it? Anyone could grab pirates and proceed against them under relevant national law in Hong Kong, Singapore or Lagos or wherever the piracy occurred (subject, of course, to the liability in Article 106 which would probably be a great inhibitor). I'd like your comments on that, Mr Brittin, if I may. What would the liability be for proceeding without adequate grounds? Are those the considerations that turned the American and British fleets away from Captain Galvao and sent him to Recife without arrest or investigation; the liability that might result if it proved that there were not adequate grounds for piracy? Could you comment on that and then perhaps comment on the universal jurisdiction aspect, which I don't believe you touched on?

BRITTIN: The question of liability is parallel to the liability occasioned by an illegal visit or right of approach. I think it is a tool which is underused, but there is strict liability if you've made a mistake. It does perhaps serve as a useful constraint if you want to avoid the situation of a country taking advantage of the right of approach or visit and making a further disruption.

Why does piratical jurisdiction differ from other crimes? Quite simply, all agree that piracy is an international, as distinguished from national, crime. The last time that the question of piracy was discussed in any depth was in the UN International Law Commission (ILC) in 1955 and 1956. I had the good fortune to be there as the adviser to the United States Representative. What emerged from the Commission discussions was changed somewhat in the 1958 Law of the Sea (LOS) negotiations. The minority, broader, view of piracy was fairly eloquently expressed in the ILC by Mexico and the Soviet Union but did not gain much support. Perhaps one of the reasons was that the Soviet Union was in favour of it—she did not enjoy much international support in those days. When it came time to get ready for negotiations for the Third LOS Conference in the late 1960s and early 1970s, I think the wide spectrum of difficult ocean problems involved was clear and that the general feeling was that "if it's not broke, don't fix it", ie, the regime for piracy appeared to have stood the test of time. There wasn't much of an international hue and cry for change except from some experts who continued to promote the idea of a broader definition of piracy.

ELLEN: Recognising that these amendments are necessary, shouldn't we be saying to the coastal states that the attacks we are seeing today are clearly piratical attacks under international law, and under most national laws? Shouldn't we give these people confidence to go out and take action against the pirates, knowing that the law will be perfectly adequate for present day purposes?

BRITTIN: If you say that an act is ''piratical'' rather then an ''act of piracy'', then you are broadening the definition. I do not think that the problem is going out affirmatively to try and suppress piracy, or whether a state has a broad view of it or not. What is really the crux of the matter is something that you yourself alluded to—the inability of many countries to mount a meaningful thrust against piracy near their coasts.

ELLEN: I am worried that we are clouding the issue on the problem of modern day piracy. If we start saying that the law is inadequate, it might provide further excuses for nations not to take action.

BRITTIN: I think that would be true.

HARLOW: In the United States, and I think probably in other coastal states, the international law of piracy is incorporated into domestic law; and if an act is piracy, it can be punished as such. The definition, of course, requires an act on the high seas. Most of the acts that we are concerned with have taken place in territorial seas and so, certainly if they occurred in the territorial seas of the United States, there would be a problem in characterising them as piracy. An act might be a crime under other applicable statutes, but not be incorporated as piracy *per se*. It strikes me that if you are talking in terms of actions when the ship is transiting international straits, even though within claimed territorial seas, there remains a vital international interest that somehow should be accommodated and recognised. Mr Brittin, I was wondering if you would comment on a piratical offence occurring, as of course many do, in such an international strait—through which the victim ship had no choice but to pass. In this case shouldn't there be some recognition of the historic balance between the responsibilities of the international community and maritime states on the one hand, and the claim of coastal states to their three mile limits on the other? Could this balance operate to characterise the act as piracy?

BRITTIN: Let me respond this way, Admiral. From the very geography of straits and the fact that there is usually rapid transit passage, if I were the decision maker in a case which appeared to be piracy taking place in a strait, I would lean very heavily on the existence of strait transit passage. I think that trying to suppress piracy in this area would receive more widespread acceptance than in other area of the territorial sea.

HARLOW: So you would treat straits as if they were high seas?

BRITTIN: Precisely.

GARRETTSON: The clarification of the place of the act and the place of the arrest is very much in line because, presumably, the place of arrest might be beyond the strait area itself, as the ship proceeded onward. Do you want to address that issue? When it comes to enforcement, the arrest, you use the hot pursuit analogy which is not built in. You really need to rewrite hot pursuit to allow you, under justifiable means, to arrest within territorial waters if the pursuit is properly begun. I think we should consider separating the two locations—the place of the act and the place of the arrest.

HARLOW: Yes of course. Historically, if the place of the act was in the territorial seas it was not piracy, by definition. At that time, when you were talking about three miles, it made sense—because there remained high seas corridors through key straits. But now perhaps it is a problem—there is a much greater need for the maritime community to act in those territorial seas that comprise straits.

PETERSON: Well there you get into some troubles with your hot pursuit comparison, because hot pursuit assumes that you observe the violation and start chasing, very close to where it occurred. Now since pirates tend to come along at night, by the time the incident is recorded they may well be away, and the ship may be somewhere else. There is less of a direct link between suspecting a crime and going after the criminal in a piracy scenario than there is if you catch somebody fishing in an unauthorised manner in your contiguous zone. In the latter case you see them with the nets, you send your coast guard cutter or helicopter after them. They realise: "Uh oh, they're after us, I'd better get out of here." You can still chase if you have had a fairly continuous chase from the time they were seen engaged in a violation up to the time of arrest.

BRITTIN: You're damn right, it is difficult to convince. It makes sense to a lot of people I have talked to over the years, but the very character of the territorial sea, and the edifice it rests on, makes it difficult to convince countries that they should permit pursuit. As I and Admiral Harlow stated, the character of the waters between three and twelve miles changes from high seas to territorial waters, and it is necessary to consider whether some high seas rights and duties should be kept intact. For example, it is written into the law that where a straight baseline creates "new" internal waters, and if the area had previously been used for innocent passage through territorial waters, then that right of innocent passage remains. That is true today. So there is a precedent for what I am talking about.

BLANEY: Although I am probably one of those people who would side with a definition that opens international jurisdiction as a practical matter, the necessity of the coastal state to assume jurisdiction, to use its forces that are available to it, not only in its own territorial sea, but in the exclusive economic zone (EEZ), is imperative if you are going to solve the piracy problem. As Mr Ellen pointed out, most attacks take place very close to the coast, either in territorial seas or in straits which are monitored by the coastal state. In most cases jurisdiction is assumed by the coastal state. At the same time there is a kind of reluctance—a practical reluctance—on the part of warships of other countries, even of the United States, United Kingdom or France, to take any kind of action other than transiting within areas contiguous to these coastal states. So the practical solution to the piracy problem may be to develop (1) a sense of the legal rights of the coastal state and the concomitant responsibility to act against piracy and (2) an acknowledgement of the need for cooperation with other regional states and the maritime states themselves to enhance enforcement by the coastal state. The problem is a practical one—any state has the right to act in the high seas or in the EEZ—and however the debate ends up it will probably not have much impact on reducing piracy *per se*. To be effective, action is required by the coastal states, and that means national jurisdiction.

BRITTIN: If I understand your position you are suggesting that there is advantage in action to enhance the capability of coastal states to enforce laws against piracy. I fully agree, but to utilise the EEZ jurisdiction as a benchmark is troublesome to me. Incidentally, I never felt that a 200 mile limit is logical for all the jurisdictions that have been acquired by the coastal state—fisheries, continental shelf, pollution and scientific research. But the fact is that we have this single limit. If you wish to add another right for the coastal state—that only it can act to suppress piracy within its EEZ—it takes us that much closer to making the area territorial in character rather than an area of special purpose control.

BLANEY: I was not suggesting exclusive jurisdiction. I was suggesting a practical and policy approach, rather than a legal one. This does not imply that somehow new codification is needed to provide this right to the coastal state, but rather emphasises the need for the coastal state to take action against piracy as the only practical solution. It is irrelevant for most, if not all, acts of piracy to say that a naval vessel has a right to act against pirates anywhere in the world. The fact of the matter is that the only people who can effectively take enforcement action are the relevant coastal state vessels—they must therefore be urged to take action. Even if you were to take the most generous view of the right of any state to act against piracy, which I support from a legal point of view, this is not practical. So even if they were to agree with all you are saying and all the lawyers in the world were to sit down and say: "Yes any country from twelve miles out can do anything they wish", people will not act on that basis. Navies will not act outside their coastal waters against pirate ships of another country.

HARLOW: It would be useful to seek international agreement that, if a coastal state is unwilling or unable to act effectively, and transit rights through straits are prejudiced, then concerned maritime states have the right to take appropriate action.

BLANEY: I guess I agree with you. I think, legally, that is right. I am talking about the practical problems. I don't want to get into a debate about behaviour but while we have affirmed many such rights, very few countries are willing to practise some of them for practical, political reasons. There are questions of relations with other countries, and jurisdictional conflicts which people do not want to bring to the surface.

CYCON: I think Harry Blaney is raising a very important concept here. We have legal regimes, but no matter how well defined they may or may not be, when it comes to practical situations these regimes may not really address what is going on. They may address two per cent of the piracy problem; they may address ten per cent of it. But it seems that the overwhelming majority of the activities that we are concerned with simply don't fit the sort of scenario in which a ship of the US or British Navy, or perhaps of the French Navy (in the South Pacific), happens upon a piratical incident and responds to it. Clearly, we have to be concerned with the realities on the local scene and, as Burt Brittin said, one possibility is regional cooperation. I don't think that it is an all or nothing proposition—that the present legal approach is no good, or that it is the only way to go. However I think we might be able to pull the sides together by considering something like this. A country may or may not have enforcement capacity in a local area. Let's take two neighbouring hypothetical countries and call them A and B. Assume you have piracy incidents which are opportunistic—a lot of the reported incidents involving refugee populations or small cargo ships are opportunistic attacks by fishermen. In one given village or area there is not a lot of law enforcement; this is a typical frontier occurrence in the developing world, in areas where institutions of law don't effectively reach for much of the time. People know when patrols go through, and exactly what their capacities are. Opportunistic attempts at piracy are probably more frequent. The existing legal regime simply doesn't work, and I think that incidents of this type amount to a much greater percentage of piracy attacks than we are giving them credit for. There is the possibility of simple bilateral arrangements between neighbouring states on the right of hot pursuit and concerning incursions into foreign territorial waters. Specific ground rules must be set for those countries which don't have the capacity or willingness to enforce anti-piracy policies. I am afraid that when you open a door like this, countries who are going to intervene can turn around and say: "We'll define what an act of piracy is, and we'll go and exercise our jurisdiction in their territorial waters". This is a problem especially in connection with terrorism—one country's terrorism is another country's recognised public ends. We have to be very careful. When countries don't have the capacity to operate, do we have a right to go in and do something? When there are problem areas on the map I think bilateral arrangements which strictly define the limits of any incursion into territorial waters may be the best way to go. This also takes the teeth out of the concern about whether EEZs are territorial in nature. As long as both parties understand when you can go into these waters and try to prevent piracy attempts, I think we can take this out of the political realm and into the realm of practical enforcement.

KASEMSRI: In response to Mr Cycon's question as to why the Third United Nations Conference on the Law of the Sea (UNCLOS) did not define piracy in the way Mr Brittin would have liked, I think this stems partly from the perception of piracy as a rather peripheral issue at the Conference. There was much more concern with limitation questions—it was more a resource-oriented conference. Attendees were of course concerned with, for example, scientific research and also the right of passage. However, many countries were willing to rely on customary international law. When one realises that the customary international law on piracy was really dictated by the maritime powers, you begin to wonder whether third world countries did the right thing by just going along with their past opinions. When you come to other concerns which are a potential source of international conflict, principally hot pursuit of pirates, there were again no countries wishing to complicate matters. Hot pursuit, as mentioned in Chapter 11, is a two way street. Certainly it gives the coastal state rights, but the coastal state can also as a result fall victim to arbitrary use of force. Acts of hot pursuit can affect a state's security, and its vital and national interests. Therefore many countries at the Conference were very guarded in their approach and their contribution on this matter.

Now, there may be other reasons. For instance, it could be that, especially in the case of aircraft, there was concern that political acts might pass as non-piratical. The question of hijacking is still very much in the limelight and also the need for political asylum, as sought by Mr Galvao—particularly in Latin American countries. This could have distracted attention from the crux of the matter and caused the subject to be dropped. Having said this, the fact that we are meeting indicates that the issue of piracy is far from being forgotten. It is very much alive. The maritime powers have been replaced more or less by flags of convenience, whose ships are increasingly victims of piratical acts. There are refugee boats which have been attacked. Mr Clingan has even brought up the subject of drug trafficking. While there must be multilateral as well as bilateral cooperation, certain matters should be left to the bilateral field. I don't thing it would serve any practical purpose to use the word "piracy" as an umbrella to cover all violent crimes or acts on the high seas or wherever. And we should use bilateral cooperation in trying to end trafficking in illegal products. The mechanism seems quite adequate. Whether or not you can call piracy an international crime is beside the point. We have to guard ourselves against the euphoria of trying to subject individuals to international law. There are certain areas where there is no need at all to call a person an *international* criminal so long as he is recognised as a criminal and so long as some action is taken against him. I wanted to draw a parameter around what we should be discussing. The idea of having drug trafficking coming under the purview of piracy is interesting but I don't think it would be a productive development.

Now we come to the question of attacks on refugees. Here again there is a difference of opinion as to the pragmatic approach—that which would optimise results. It could be unilateral, with coastal states having all the say, or bilateral, so that the country of registry of the ship could take up the matter, or it could be regional, as Dean Cycon has suggested. This last of course comes under some constraints. We would like to alleviate the plight of refugees but you can't just switch off the problem because the country of origin will not sit down and reason with you. Finally you can have a multilateral approach, as exemplified by the text of the Convention. But none of these approaches will work by itself. We will have to find a combination of means in order to improve the situation.

BLANEY: I don't think by changing the legal rules and definitions you are going to change modern day piracy—the problem of enforcement or jurisdiction—in any significant way. The few acts that take place out on the high seas are already taken care of without any changes being necessary. The fact is that no change in definition will change the acts of pirates, for example off the West African coast or in south-east Asia, or alter the practicalities of enforcement.

GARRETTSON: A further view is that the law of piracy is carried into the EEZ. It is the opinion of Professor Hoffsmann and a great many others that those provisions *do* apply to the EEZ, and to the straits, even though the language states "high seas". This is a view we all generally agree upon, I gather.

WALKATE: I must agree with what the Ambassador from Thailand said about the articles as they stand in the Convention. At that time (I am speaking of late 1960s and early 1970s) there was no rise in the number of incidents of this nature. Piracy as defined in Article 101 was not a problem at that moment. As the Ambassador said, everybody was much more concerned with the overriding dominant questions of delimitations and resources.

I have been looking at the proposals put forward by Mr Brittin to change the article—a very academic exercise for at least the coming 100 years. I think in talking about "private ends" and substituting "without due authority", the flag state would keep its jurisdiction and apply its legislation wherever a ship went. "Without due authority", would seem to be a violation of the national laws applicable on the ship. So there is no question of flag state jurisdiction in this respect. I don't think "without due authority" would add very much.

BRITTIN: Just one brief comment. If I have given the impression that I thought amendment to the Convention articles was a cure all, I simply didn't mean that at all. I think it is a step, but it certainly isn't the major problem connected with suppression of piracy. There are a lot of things that can and should be done to strengthen the world community's hand. I think there is potential for looking at the problem from a bilateral or regional basis—a degree of cooperation is possible in various regions. That is really worth exploring. Unquestionably enforcement is a major problem, but in examining that we cannot dilute the relationship between enforcement and law. What would we be enforcing other than the law? Does present international law provide the basis for adequate enforcement?

PINEDA-LUPIAC: I am in the government so I feel in dangerous waters when speaking on the international law of piracy. I would like, however, to try to convey to you our approach to the question of piracy within the intergovernmental framework of UNCTAD and how the Secretariat, as such, is looking at this problem. We are dealing with the question of piracy mainly because it is linked to maritime fraud. It was decided to include this problem, not within the framework of Article 101 of the Convention, but mainly to look at piracy in territorial seas. Regional and bilateral cooperative agreements can be useful. The essential scope of our work is to examine the possibility of negotiating a convention on jurisdiction and extradition to deal with this problem of piracy in territorial seas.

CYCON: Mr Brittin raised a number of questions concerning the "private ends" language that is in Article 101. I guess under the traditional law of piracy if there is a non-private end, ie, political activity, associated with the act, it would fall outside the scope of piracy. But I would like to talk about private ends a little more. How far does the term go? Can terrorist acts be considered private ends? Is state sanction really required for an act to be a public end? In the situation of a self proclaimed liberator—and, I think, in a world of three billion people there are probably one billion self proclaimed liberators—any act can be couched in political terms. It is a matter of argument, for which lawyers are famous. So I am hereby hiring myself out to any pirates who want political coverage. But I think that if we really consider this issue of terrorism, and whether or not piracy can address it, we have to look at this private/public ends dichotomy.

BRITTIN: Historically the cases involving that question have held that private ends are for principal monetary gain, hatred, or vengeance. Those are the normal categories. If there is something beyond that, I am not aware of it. That is what has been the hiatus for a person like Galvao. His goal certainly was public, but he didn't fit the category of being an insurgent.

CYCON So, would you suggest then that terrorists, as a general rule, should be considered under this regime?

BRITTIN: I think they should be. That is one of the reasons that "without due authority" might be the key to the whole thing.

CYCON: Okay, but then you said that without due authority meant without the sponsorship or the approval of a state authority? Any state?

BRITTIN: A flag state.

CYCON: A flag state, okay. Well then we get the problem of the liberation movement and Galvao and his action against his own flag.

BRITTIN: No, you get the problem of whether or not insurgency actually exists.

CYCON: But I think we would be limiting discussion to what happens when people take over their own boat, as in the Galvao case.

BRITTIN: If people who are part of the crew or the captain are the instigators, that is not piracy.

CYCON: In a situation in which there was state sponsored, or state encouraged, harassment or attacks against shipping by pirates, how would your definition of "without due authority" operate?

BRITTIN: I would say that if a state sponsored that kind of activity, then that is an act of war.

HARLOW: I was just going to add that, if you presuppose that the group is private and that it is not acting under the sponsorship or at the behest of any sovereign state, it seems to me that, *ipso facto*, it is working towards some private end. But Burt Brittin is correct that historically the classic definition has been more limited to getting the gold and silver as you characterised. Whether or not the motive is to use the gold and silver, for a political action group to me is a distinction without a difference. The difference really is: is it a truly private group or does it have a status as operating on behalf of a state? If it isn't truly private, whatever its motives might be, *ipso facto*, they have to be private ends.

PETERSON: You have the moment when you are trying to arrest a suspected pirate or trying to free a vessel from the clutches of suspected pirates and then you have the moment, later on, after you have caught them, and have had time to sort of evaluate what their motives are, when you consider whether to apply the full penalties of piracy or accept arguments about political cause in mitigation of the punishment. This is all complicated by the fact that historically, when the customary law of piracy developed, insurgency didn't go on much at sea because it wasn't very effective. If you were going to have a really good insurgency you obviously went after the capital of the country involved. It went on before there was much development in the criminal law on land—which is a nineteenth century phenomenon. The notion of the political offence is that an individual might commit an act that looked like a crime, such as shooting somebody, but that, if he could prove this had been done for political ends, he should be given political asylum, not sent back home to be tried for the offence. The development of ideological warfare, terrorism, and state sponsored depredations of various sorts have all intruded. There are things that the customary law of piracy really didn't have to think about—they weren't around. People's reactions to individuals who claim to be insurgents and take over a vessel to spark a revolution are heavily influenced by these doctrines that have been developing on land but have never much been talked about in the Law of the Sea—political offence, political asylum, terrorism or whatever. This does add complications. The Law of the Sea can't be considered in isolation from what is going on on land, as some of the classical authorities seem to think it could. The two realms are much more tied together.

KASEMSRI: Just one observation on what Dr Peterson has said. I think the customary law of piracy was a matter of convenience for the maritime powers. That is how it came about; it resulted from the mercantile policy of maritime powers. It was just too inconvenient to have ships under the control of private individuals roaming about and robbing at will ships which might be carrying gold back from South America to continental Europe on behalf of a state. In other words, the pirates were as bad as bootleggers. They could not be tolerated. The customary law of piracy provided a convenient way of avoiding issues. When you deal with a criminal you have to cross perhaps three or four stages—(1) you have to claim jurisdiction and resolve any conflict; (2) you have to, as you put it, arrest the culprit or seize him; (3) you have to have legal process to try him and (4) you have to execute your judgement—in other words, enforcement of your law. The customary concept of piracy provided solutions to these four rather complicated problems. Without it there could be problems or difficulties between nations with similar ambitions, interests and intentions. So piracy has taken on the role of an umbrella and I detect today that this trend persists. I must caution against putting everything under this umbrella. I think we should try to devise means to cope with such problems, and to avoid trying to fit everything into a mould which perhaps may be somewhat outmoded because times have changed. I don't know whether what I have said is historically accurate or not but at least one should be on guard against trying to use the concept of piracy as an umbrella simply because it is convenient.

GARRETTSON: Well, umbrella use has been made of the concept because theoreticians in particular have said that piracy is a form of jurisdiction which is universal—it is not territorial, it's not national, it's a universal jurisdiction. I would like to raise one question, because of comments made by the Ambassador. The pollution sections of the

Convention are extensive in their details and are applying important jurisdictional distinctions—flag state jurisdiction, coastal state jurisdiction and court state jurisdiction. Does anyone see that an effort should be made to apply this same approach to piracy?

WALKATE: I think, if it is an act of piracy under international law, then every state has jurisdiction—coastal states, court states and flag states—so there is no problem. The only problem is: do they wish to assert jurisdiction and are they able to enforce the rules? A question: Why would you bring an illegal act which involved only one state under the regulation of an international treaty? That is the case if you refer to an insurgency which takes place on one ship and no other ship or state is involved. The rationale of the articles in the Convention is that more than one jurisdiction is involved and one can say the international community probably ought to act on the matter, in spite of the fact that many Anglo-Saxon lawyers have a problem with the entire concept of "international public order". If there is only one ship involved I think there is no need to make that subject to the rule.

The other point which was raised was whether an act taking place in a strait or in the EEZ would be considered an act of piracy. I would say an act in the EEZ would be considered an act of piracy under the Treaty. In straits, I doubt it, because a right of transit is not one of the freedoms of the high seas which has been mentioned. It is a right to innocent passage, but it is not freedom of navigation because you are not free to navigate as you like. The only thing you are allowed to do is go from point A to point B as quickly as you can without stopping unless that is necessary for any problems you have with the ship. So, I would say that acts in straits would come under the jurisdiction of the coastal state.

GARRETTSON: Both of those points are much discussed in the Conference you are referring to. The EEZ has been turned down by several; and I have heard no one suggest that the law of piracy, as it has been presented, is carried over into the zone.

Part 4. The Control of Piracy

CHAPTER 15

RETHINKING PIRACY CONTROL IN A MODERN MARITIME CONTEXT

Rear Admiral (Ret) Bruce Harlow

It is possible to argue that the way to deal most practically with the problem of piracy control is to use a contemporary definition of piracy, rather than stick to some of the historic applications and broaden them to the point where they could cover what we have characterised as maritime crime. I would resist this for three reasons. Firstly, we talk in terms of piracy being an important and useful international set of rules by means of which we can assert jurisdiction over criminals. The truth of the matter is that the international community has not to my knowledge used this sanction, certainly since the Second World War. So, although in theory it is useful to talk in terms of jurisdictional ability, and indeed methods of arrest, with respect to actual crimes, the world community has not utilised this, and there is no practical set of implementing procedures. I dare say that if we were to pick someone up as pirate there would be many questions asked today as to how to deal with him, even though we all agreed that he should or could be characterised as a pirate. So I am not sure we gain much by using piracy as a handle to solve what might be termed the "maritime problem". Secondly, I think that, certainly if you take the broader perspective of maritime crime, it is difficult to fit all types of it into the classic mould of piracy. Many of these acts could be labelled as acts of violence for private ends and yet there are cases, concerning cargo fraud and situations not involving violence, which a lot of people would have problems characterising as piracy. Thirdly, and no less important, the regimes of the law of the sea are changing. When we used to talk of the high seas being all areas beyond three miles, which left a high seas corridor through international straits, it was possible to define piracy as an act applicable only to the high seas.

This left the all important areas of navigation, and what I call the rivers of navigation—the international straits—within that regime of piracy. Now that most nations claim territorial seas of twelve miles, international straits are overlapped by territorial seas so you have the question as to whether the international definition of piracy is to be utilised within a claimed territorial sea. The impact of an international strait for the maritime community is certainly as compelling today as it was fifty years ago. Territorial seas in general are not that vital for maritime trade but territorial seas comprising straits are. There is also the complicating factor that the exclusive economic zones (EEZs) are no longer explicitly characterised as high seas. This question is developed in Part 3 of this book. I think the definition was changed in the 1958 Convention (see Appendix 14) to take care of this, by talking in terms of piracy being on the high seas or beyond areas of national jurisdiction. I think what was comprehended by this was that the EEZ, as opposed to its resources, is not under the jurisdiction of the coastal state.

I would place maritime crime basically in four categories, the first two only indirectly affecting maritime trade and the last two having a direct and important impact.

The first category, starting form the land and going outward, is *cargo fraud*. This crime may be committed in an office building in Brussels, where documents are forged or the conspiratorial arrangement is first discussed. One could characterise it as a land crime that has an impact on the maritime community. In that connection I would call it a maritime crime in the broader sense—these types of crime can culminate in an illegal act on the high seas. However they do not have the direct impact on the navigability of the oceans which perhaps characterise other acts.

The second type of maritime crime is what I call the *internal waters crime*. That is to say problems resulting from excessive stays in ports, inability to unload cargoes, scheduling problems and lack of port security. Although vessels are in territorial seas or internal waters, they are generally not exercising a maritime right, such as innocent passage. It is therefore most meaningfully characterised as a local law enforcement problem. Certainly it would be reasonable to view those types of crimes as under the exclusive jurisdiction of the coastal state, but with an impact on the maritime community and deserving international discussion and some international coordination in traffic scheduling, port management and training programmes. Having said that, I think it is really up to the coastal state to try and minimise these problems.

When you get into the third category, of *territorial seas*, the impact is more severe. The Malacca Strait, whether by coincidence or for some other reason, has certainly been an area of concern to the maritime community. Nonetheless the incidence of crime statistically is very low, even allowing for the fact that not all crimes are reported. I think this is a problem that should concern the international community, particularly when it concerns international straits, although normally a coastal state problem because of the local jurisdictions and considerations.

The last category, going seaward, is what I call the *high seas* or the *EEZ problem*. In a humanitarian sense, this is an area that everyone would have to agree is of serious magnitude. I am referring to the refugee problem in south-east Asia, and to crimes committed in the course of trafficking drugs on the high seas. The subsets of the high seas or EEZ problem include smuggling and terrorist acts. Terrorist acts have to be thought of in two categories: (1) a private group of people committing violence for some political purpose and (2) a state sponsored act. Either side of the coin, private terrorist act or state sponsored, is complicated in the sense that it is not a pure law enforcement situation. There are political undercurrents involved that make agreement among the international community on how terrorist acts should be handled difficult.

You can quickly leave the arena of law enforcement when you talk about terrorism and issues of national self defence. If I were thinking of a compartment of maritime crime I would exclude anything elevated to a national security problem for any sovereign. This is an area that any imaginative approach coming out of a non-governmental group, or of the IMO, would be well advised to avoid.

It strikes me that these four categories—land crime, internal waters, territorial sea and straits, and high seas—in a jurisdictional sense should be dealt with differently. I think the interests of the maritime community, as opposed to the interests of the coastal state, change with each type of crime. If we are talking about the land crime of cargo fraud I think that international cooperation is certainly appropriate. It would certainly be worthwhile considering a computer programme with a profile of cargo ship availability, size, port location, and whether the ship is on line. If the computer light turns red, it is a warning that there is something amiss. If a voyage passes through all these parameters, then it would at least be an initial indication that the fraud potential was diminished. This could go a long way toward diminishing the cargo fraud problem. As I mentioned earlier, it is something that the coastal state will have to deal with although I would hope that there could be some form of assistance with training and the development of port security and law enforcement measures, perhaps through IMO. Maritime law enforcement is entirely different, the challenges there are entirely different, from land enforcement. There are many complicating factors, and perhaps assistance could be given to the coastal states with these. As far as jurisdiction is concerned, I think it should be viewed as a coastal state problem.

There is greater justification for viewing territorial seas, particularly those comprising straits and therefore having direct impact on the maritime community, as a problem that should be dealt with in coordination between the coastal states concerned and the maritime community. I feel this is also the case with regard to the high seas and the EEZ.

It has been argued that, leaving aside the arena of refugees and drug trafficking, the situation is not of sufficient magnitude to warrant an international conference or an expensive grandiose programme. I do not think the nations would support this. We should look at an interrelated scheme and recognise that, for example, by dealing with drug trafficking, you might also help deal with piracy and, by doing that, you might also deal with smuggling. Perhaps, by putting all maritime crime in one compartment, one might develop a cost effective programme through regional arrangements, or some form of international cooperation. Again, there is a lot to be said for IMO participation, at least as a sponsor, because of the impact of these problems on the maritime community.

I have a number of ideas that could diminish the problem.

The first initiative would be to identify and promulgate protective measures. There is a lot to be done by way of crew training. It would be worthwhile if they were simply alerted as to how to handle a situation, how to avoid getting themselves injured. Ship owners should also be alerted— for example as to what they might do by way of lighting and to the fact that when they slow down they are more vulnerable. Detailed suggestions on these lines appear in Appendices 16-20.

Secondly, there is evidence that we need a more dependable reporting system. Available reports really do not address the situation with precision. It is important to record whether an incident is in a territorial sea or a strait— as well as the circumstances and the items taken. This would permit an intelligent analysis of modus operandi, and indeed the nature of the problem.

There may be a need to consider the establishment of a "comprehensive intelligence centre", a means of gathering the reports and intelligently looking at them and determining what they mean—what are the trends, what are the indications, what are the danger spots that should be viewed as candidates for further national or international action? I call it an "international fusion centre" to which all reports would come, with the understanding, of course, that the information would be available to all the nations of the world involved. I would think IMO might play a role in this, and there is currently an initiative by Interpol.

Consideration might also be given to establishment of an early tracking and warning system. This would be a follow on from the intelligence centre—raw information reported to the centre would be analysed and promulgated by way of notice to mariners or to airmen. There is also the possible use of satellite communication. The potential of this approach is described on pages 176 and 208.

Sooner or later we will probably have to consider the line authority responsibility of flag states versus coastal states. For example, if a vessel is in an EEZ, will actual control measures interfere with her exploitative activity? Many things would have to be addressed in this connection, and this is probably a follow on action, after other actions had been taken and more was known about the nature of the problem.

Certainly there is a need to establish a training programme for people involved in maritime enforcement. Now I am going beyond port responsibilities, I am talking of the intricate and difficult task of effecting arrest on the high seas, or in territorial seas, when a ship is underway. There are problems of approach, boarding and search, which can be extraordinarily difficult if danger to the ship or the crew is to be avoided. The US is very fortunate to have the Department of Transportation, and the Coast Guard designed as a law enforcement agency. They have expertise in this area. I have always been concerned that, when our Navy ships have been involved in anything which could appear to be law enforcement, it may complicate the role of our skippers. It is one thing to talk in terms of "appropriate actions" and national security—that is where we would be if a terrorist act got to the point of being a national security concern. Then you are in a different category of "appropriate action"—you are talking of a military operation. Our Navy is well prepared to do that. However if you are talking in terms of a lower level of law enforcement, of arresting a criminal, then there is a whole different set of responsibilities. Many nations do not have a separate coast guard, they simply have a navy, the primary training of which is to defend national security. It would be very valuable if these navies had some additional training in law enforcement, particularly the right of approach, visit and search. I have a feeling that often those rights that exist are not exercised primarily because of lack of training and understanding of the issues.

If you put all of this together it is appropriate to consider what sort of diplomatic response would make sense in the context of these initiatives. I accept that a multilateral convention simply would not make sense at the present time. On the other hand, I would argue that, through IMO, and perhaps through regional arrangements already effected particularly with regard to the refugee and drug trafficking problems, some initiatives could be broadened to comprehend the broader perspective of maritime crime.

Finally I make the general observation that, although it is easy to think in terms of "let's wait and see until the problem gets more serious", serious consideration, at least, should be given to these issues at the present time. This will avoid the development of a serious impediment to international navigational rights, or the situation where maritime nations or coastal nations felt compelled to take serious action that would exacerbate an already difficult situation. I hope that whatever is done will be done through the cooperative effort, perhaps the germ of which was created here in this book.

CHAPTER 16

THE MARAD VIEW OF MARITIME PIRACY

Frank Pentti

This paper outlines the nature of the interest of the Maritime Administration in the problem of piracy—or, rather, the many problems that are lumped together under the heading ''piracy''. I shall explain how we understand the matter; and give you an idea of what we are doing in this area.

The Maritime Administration, or MARAD, is an agency of the US Department of Transportation. It is the agency of the US Federal Government that is concerned with promotion of the US merchant marine. Overall, MARAD is concerned with the effectiveness and welfare of the US merchant fleet and of the crews that operate the ships.

Our promotional programme is based on the Merchant Marine Act of 1936, as it has been amended over the years, and a few other statutes that affect the operation of merchant ships under the American flag. The 1936 Act provides several mechanisms designed to assist the US merchant marine. Primary among these is the Operating Subsidy Programme. In addition, the Title XI ship financing guarantee programme supports the construction of ships in US yards by providing the operator access to relatively low cost financing. There are also other promotional programmes, that provide indirect assistance to the US industry, such as cargo preference. The US Merchant Marine Academy at King's Point, New York, is also a MARAD activity. We maintain close contact with US maritime labour organisations, with all representatives of the shipping and shipbuilding industries, with US Department of Defense agencies, and with the full range of international organisations with interests in the maritime fields.

As a natural extension of our peacetime activity, we are responsible for planning for the wartime operations of the American merchant fleet and for the US participation in NATO wartime shipping operations. In a future conflict, MARAD plans would create the National Shipping Authority which would be the wartime operating arm of the Maritime Administration.

This structure is relevant because it tends to define MARAD's peacetime role in relation to events that affect merchant ships. It is our defence planning staff that coordinates our response to events that fall in the category termed ''piracy''. Our National Security Plans Division routinely keeps track of the employment of the US merchant fleet and other shipping of interest, and it maintains a general awareness of operating problems encountered by our ships. Since the time that the Iran/Iraq war began to target merchant shipping, we have kept track of damages and ensured that US ship operators were kept informed of hostilities. During the Falklands affair MARAD kept both belligerents informed of the movements of US interest ships in the area.

We are also concerned with other kinds of violence against shipping activities. Over the last years, we have held several meetings to consider piracy, maritime terrorism, and any other violence and criminal activity at sea that would affect shipping operations. These have been attended by, among others, representatives of the Department of State, the Federal Emergency Management Agency, Coast Guard, several elements of the Navy, the Federal Bureau of Investigation, and representatives of the US shipping industry.

The fact that so many different agencies are interested is one indication of the complexity of the subject. The State Department alone has at least five different lines of interest.

The Federal Emergency Management Agency is concerned with incidents on American territory. As a result, its interests are primarily in the prevention of and the response to possible terrorist incidents involving ships in US ports.

The US Coast Guard has general responsibility for port security in the United States in territorial and offshore waters.

The Defense Mapping Agency (DMA), among its other activities, produces notices and special warnings to mariners. The special warnings have been automated and the Automated Notice to Mariners system has been amplified to include warnings of maritime terrorism and piracy incidents. I shall say more about that system in a moment.

The Military Sealift Command has taken the lead among US fleet operators in developing standard procedures for protection against pirate attacks on ships. Other Navy elements deal with intelligence aspects of terrorism and piracy, both domestic and foreign.

The Federal Bureau of Investigation's authority extends to US territory wherever it may be and therefore to US ships at sea.

The US shipping industry is also an active participant. Individuals from companies whose ships have encountered pirates and the American Institute of Merchant Shipping, which represents the industry generally, have attended.

The MARAD meetings on piracy began by surveying the world piracy situation and the actions taken on the problem by US and international agencies.

The meetings have produced some modest but positive results. We have produced a short handbook for ship masters that presents ideas for prudent self protection measures, which are repeated at Appendix 16. The ideas were collected from a notice issued by the Swedish Shipowners

Association (see Appendix 19), from instructions issued by Military Sealift Command, and from other sources. None of the ideas are new, but the pamphlet is a useful reminder to ships' officers and it may serve as a handy checklist. The context of the pamphlet can be summarised as follows:

ANTICIPATE TROUBLE
BE VIGILANT
DON'T BE A HERO

It makes sense because one of the most alarming attacks on a US ship occurred when that ship abandoned its vigilance a little too soon. The theme of the pamphlet is basically "Anticipate trouble". It says "It CAN happen to you." Further, it says if it does and the pirates have the drop on you, take it easy; don't start a fight—because you will probably lose.

The second product of the MARAD meetings is the automated system for recording incidents. Inadequate reporting may be the most serious problem we face in attempting to develop effective response to piracy, terrorism and other crime and violence at sea.

The new record keeping system has been developed by the DMA as an adjunct to the Automated Notice to Mariners system. That system enables a ship equipped with a computer terminal to call up the Notice to Mariners file either by satellite or high frequency radio, and obtain current navigation information. The new system—which is called the Anti-Shipping Alert Message—or ASAM—enables ships, government agencies, and shipping companies to enter reports of incidents of piracy, terrorism, and other violence at sea into the DMA file and to obtain information from the file about such events.

Information can be extracted for a specified area. Geographic areas are identified by two digit numbers which are shown in the back of the weekly Notice to Mariners that is published by DMA. The same numbering system is used for nautical charts; the area numbers are the first two digits of the serial numbers of the charts. The use of a numbering system with which the shipping industry is familiar should make introduction of the system a little easier.

Now we know that people *can* submit reports—but the critical question is *will* they do it? Will they use the ASAM system or make reports by message or letter? Pessimism on that point seems justified.

A procedure for reporting incidents is set out in DMA Publication 117, "Radio Navigation Aids", which all US flag ships carry. The procedure calls for transmission of a simple report, called "Ship Hostile Action Report"—SHAR for short—to the DMA. The procedure has been highlighted on the inside front cover of Pub 117 for many years. By 1985 the DMA had never—and I repeat, NEVER—received a SHAR report.

These are then the two things that we have been able to get under way; a handbook for masters on prudent measures to take to improve shipboard security and a procedure for reporting incidents of violence at sea, the value of which will depend on how much it is used. What else might be done?

The maritime community feels the need to do something about pirates, terrorists and maritime crime in general. This book is clear evidence of that. But it is hard to find a handle for action as we have discussed. One reason is that there is not *a* single problem, but that there is a collection of problems. We see several general categories of maritime crime: Piracy, Robbery in port and at sea, Maritime Terrorism and Maritime Fraud.

We usually think about reported incidents in connection with the places where they occur—primarily the West Coast of Africa and south-east Asia. We tend to slide over the differences among the incidents that are typical of different regions. But different crimes call for different treatments. When we lump all kinds of criminal violence at sea under the rubric "piracy", we make it hard to find workable programmes to deal with the different kinds of violent crime on an individual basis. Let me explain the basis for my view.

"West Coast of Africa" usually means Lagos, but incidents have been reported at other Nigerian ports and Sierra Leone, Dacca, Monrovia and Zaire. Nearly all of the reported incidents follow the same pattern. Let me cite a few reports:

> Visited by approximately 20 pirates who removed personal effects, stores, provisions, etc.
>
> Boarded by armed pirates, crew returned fire. No assistance sent by Nigerian authorities, despite urgent radio appeals.
>
> Three ships boarded by local pirates while lying at anchor off Monrovia.

Generally, the pirates on the West African coast seem to be fairly well organised and not likely to hurt people unless resistance is offered. However, that may not be true everywhere. For example a somewhat enigmatic report of an attack on a trawler in the Bay of Bengal said tersely: "Attacked by 30 pirates on board a merchant vessel. Eight crew stuffed in sacks and tossed overboard. Catch worth about $30,000." Enough!

As stated elsewhere in the book there are several important conditions necessary for an act to be "piracy" in terms international law, including that the act must take place "on the high seas" and "outside the jurisdiction of any state." In the African ports, the so called local pirates are shorebased gangs. Incidents occur in harbours and roadsteads and sometimes at piers. Action to bring this kind of violence under control is basic. Ship operating companies have to complain to governments. Shippers and consignees of cargo have to complain, insurers have to raise rates, governments have to make representations to the governments of the countries where the trouble is occurring. The international community cannot do much to address local crime problems except to appeal to the local governments.

The situation in south-east Asia—the Strait of Malacca, Singapore Strait, Phillip Channel area—is different from the West African situation. In south-east Asia, incidents are of two general kinds: attacks on merchant ships and attacks on small boats.

Straightforward attacks on ships are relatively rare, considering the number of ships in that region. The recent attack on a US ship under charter to the Military Sealift Command was typical of the professionalism of some of the pirates. The ship had maintained a good watch going through the defined danger zone. About twenty minutes after the danger zone was cleared and the watch stood down, the attack was made. A diversionary incident drew the attention of the bridge away from the approach of the attacking boat. The pirates boarded the ship, made their way to the master's cabin, captured him, robbed the safe and left, all without alerting anyone else on the ship.

The objects of attacks on merchant ships at sea so far have been money in the ship's safe and personal property of crew members. So long as the attacks stay at that level, ships probably can protect themselves fairly well by maintaining good watches in danger areas and being prepared with fire hoses and other measures to keep boarders away from the ship. It is at this type of incident that our brochure is directed. And depending on the interpretation of international access to straits and channels, this may be piracy.

Attacks on the boat people in the Gulf of Thailand are a different matter. Targets on merchant ships are money, valuables, or easily disposed of cargo—the "loot" as defined in Chapter 2. When refugees are attacked, however, the targets are the people themselves. They are robbed, they are raped, they are murdered. The moral challenge to the conscience of the world makes these attacks the target for a substantial international effort. The United States, with other nations, has provided funds to improve patrols and other security measures in the region as is explained clearly in Chapters 6 and 7.

Robbery at sea has occurred in regions other than the Singapore Strait and the West Coast of Africa, of course. Ships have been boarded and robbed in Philippine waters. Incidents have been reported in the Caribbean and off the coast of South America. A report dated December 1983 says: "50 to 100 vessels during the past two years" off Santos, Brazil, with no further details except this: "Attacks usually carried out by three to five men with help from the night gang of stevedores." Here again we are dealing with shorebased crime, not with piracy.

Other attacks reported in 1983 and 1984 included, for example, robberies of ships in 1983 and 1984 at Barcelona, Madras, Tampico, Santos, Antwerp and—surprise—Olympia, Washington.

These various kinds of violent maritime crimes have to be dealt with individually, locally, in most cases by local governments. There is some scope for international cooperative action but not very much. Ships can help themselves to some extent. But there is no panacea.

Maritime terrorism is something different from the things we have been calling piracy. Real terrorism at sea has been rare.

Nevertheless, seizure or destruction of ships by terrorists is a credible contingency and it should be planned for. Dealing with terrorists is a problem for governments and international law enforcement agencies and organisations—those outside the intelligence and law enforcement community cannot do much more than emphasise the importance of vigilance and prudent security measures. However, this is useful.

I have been talking about violent maritime crime. But non-violent maritime crime or maritime fraud, can have much greater economic impact. It is said that no one knows the true murder rate because the successful murders are not detected. The same is true of maritime fraud; the successful frauds are never discovered, although the insurers pay for them.

Now that we have come to this far, what does it add up to? Is there a maritime crime problem or just a bunch of violent and non-violent crimes?

We have considered several different types of maritime crimes and I think it is almost self evident that each type calls for its own solution. Sometimes the different incidents are thrown together to make a total that is impressive enough to attract an audience. But we cannot define an overall maritime crime problem in the sense that we can visualise a single overall solution.

How important, then, are the various types of maritime crimes? Fraud is the most important kind of maritime crime in economic terms. But in this book we are concerned mainly with violent maritime crimes, not the non-violent ones whose solutions call for the services of accountants and insurance investigators and, ultimately, lawyers and legislators.

Among the violent crimes, drug related violence is economically important—but in connection with the drug racket, not in itself. Theft of private yachts is not frequent and the costs are borne by a few private individuals and their insurers. The economic impact is unnoticeable.

Attacks on refugee boats affect more people than any other category of violent maritime crime, but again the economic cost is directed against individuals—individuals with less political clout than Caribbean Sea yachtsmen and no economic significance whatever, in international terms.

Finally there is robbery of merchant ships at sea and in or near port, which, for lack of a better word, we may call piracy.

I have been discussing conditions that sound quite alarming to merchant shipping, yet we find that there very little attention devoted to this problem. Why is this? I think it is because the problem is not annoying enough. Let us consider the relative magnitude of the piracy problem as it relates to merchant shipping from two distinct perspectives: ship operations and economic impacts.

For example, there are somewhere around 30,000 transits of the Strait of Malacca in a year. The average annual total of attacks on ships in the area for the seven years covered by the IMB Chronology at Appendix 1 is 32. So we could say that one ship out of every 937, or about one tenth of one percent of the transits, encountered some kind of armed robbery attempt during the year.

From the overall economic viewpoint the perspective is similar. An UNCTAD estimate places the cost of marine fraud and piracy at a billion dollars each year. A figure issued in 1985 by the International Maritime Bureau estimated that maritime fraud alone costs the world shipping industry more than $13 billion a year.

Either of these numbers is large in absolute terms. However, when they are compared to the total value of waterborne world trade, which is roughly estimated to be about one trillion dollars per year, they are considerably less striking. The UNCTAD figure, said to include piracy, is one tenth of one percent of world trade. However important locally, this is clearly not a major economic problem in global terms. Even the much larger IMB figure for fraud alone represents only 1.3 percent of world trade.

The fraud issue continues to be the subject of appropriate IMO attention. The low level of apparent international reaction to the more violent aspects of piracy reflects the relative scarcity of incidents and their economic insignificance. As long as the economic cost remains very low, it is unlikely that the international community will undertake any major concerted action.

This said, violent piracy is nonetheless a very real problem to its immediate victims, both individual and corporate—and in today's uncertain world we have no basis for predicting that it will not grow, as it has in many past periods. It is therefore very important that the nations involved do not lose sight of the problem. Systematic reporting of incidents and the maintenance of a central record will improve our understanding of the problem. The adoption of prudent reactive measures will help ships' masters to cope with the problem and to reduce it. We must also continue and refine national and international measures designed to assist victims and potential victims, particularly refugees.

There is a tendency in some quarters to exaggerate the problem of piracy. I believe that it is best to see it objectively, as it is and to deal with it realistically.

CHAPTER 17

ASPECTS OF INTERNATIONAL ACTION TO COMBAT PIRACY AT SEA

Jaap A Walkate

Introduction

For the purpose of this working paper, as for other papers in this book, the definition of piracy in Article 101 of the 1982 UN Convention on the Law of the Sea (see Appendix 15) appears to be too narrow: "illegal acts of violence or detention ... on the high seas... outside the jurisdiction of any State". Many of the reported incidents of violence and armed robbery at sea are reported to have taken place within the national jurisdiction of the coastal state, either at sea or near the shore.

Moreover, the scope of illegal and/or irregular maritime activities is much wider than piracy or armed robbery. In this respect it is worth recalling the UNCTAD study which divides irregular maritime activities into six major categories: documentary frauds, charter party frauds, marine insurance frauds, deviation frauds, miscellaneous frauds and piracy. In terms of legal intricacies, complexity and sophistication, piracy and armed robbery pose only relatively minor problems to the international community. However, in terms of human suffering, loss of life and injury, piracy ranks first.

Action taken by International Organisations up to 1985

It has been clear from the outset that measures on the international plane are indispensable to deal with acts of piracy and armed robbery at sea wherever they occur and whoever they may concern. Apart from bilateral contacts between governments, multilateral concerted action is absolutely necessary. A fine example of what international action may lead to is the virtual eradication of the worldwide evil of air piracy (hijacking) which reached its pinnacle in the late sixties. Quick and effective action consisted of awakening the consciousness of the international community through the United Nations General Assembly, the adoption of conventions outlawing air piracy through the International Civil Aviation Organisation (ICAO) and technical measures such as security checks and sealing off of airports. Nowadays hijacking of airplanes takes place in the form of isolated incidents only.

Notwithstanding the factual and legal differences between air piracy and sea piracy, the parallel between the two is clear. In this respect it was quite logical that the UN *International Maritime Organisation* (IMO) was seized with the matter upon the initiative of the Swedish government, which in early 1983 proposed consideration of piracy by the Maritime Safety Committee (MSC). This was with a view to formulating an Assembly Resolution requesting governments to provide information on acts of piracy committed against ships flying the flag of member states and urging governments concerned to take all steps necessary to prevent the occurrence of such acts within or outside their waters (Doc MSC/48/23/4). Later Sweden proposed that the Council endorse the view that there is an urgent need for action by IMO (Doc C 50/25).

This initiative resulted in the unanimous adoption of Assembly Resolution A545(13) of 17 November 1983—reproduced at Appendix 21. The Resolution set up a system under which Governments would take, as a matter of highest priority, all measures necessary to prevent and suppress acts of piracy and armed robbery against ships in or adjacent to their waters, and would report to IMO all incidents, indicating location and circumstances of the incident and the action taken by them.

In a follow up report (Doc MSC/19/Add 1) the IMO Secretariat on 15 October 1984 reported that "despite international pressures, progress in stemming the increase in violent attacks at sea has been scant" and "the increasing number of attacks off Central America—estimated by the International Maritime Bureau (IMB) at 100 in 1983, and the continuation of attacks in other regions mentioned (in an IMB report) indicate that Governments are not yet convinced of the need for them to take adequate preventive action". The Central American situation is mentioned in more detail on page 20.

The *Baltic and International Maritime Conference* (BIMCO), a non-political private, international shipping association, proposed that IMO should convene an international conference on the subject of piracy and armed robberies from ships with the purpose of establishing ways and means to prevent and suppress such acts. BIMCO also proposed that non-governmental organisations be consulted and invited to participate as observers and consultants. The International Transport Workers' Federation (ITF) urged IMO to press ahead with the matter, as seafarers were in the meantime under continued exposure to the threat.

During the meeting of the Committee in November 1984 the suggestion of a seminar was discussed. The IMO Secretary General informed the Committee that he was in touch with possible donor Governments, and that according to the funds made available the seminar could be held either on a global or on a regional level. The Committee considered that a seminar on piracy and armed robbery would be most useful and thus, by implication, appeared to prefer it to an international conference (Doc MSC/50/27).

Piracy at sea has drawn the attention of *other* international organisations as well.

The *UN High Commission for Refugees* (UNHCR) in a letter to the UN Secretary General in March 1980 called for concerted international action on the problem of piracy against asylum seekers at sea, particularly in the Gulf of Thailand. This resulted in UN Assembly Resolution 36/125 of 14 December 1981 calling for, *inter alia*, "greater international efforts in the suppression of piracy on the high seas, in accordance with their international obligations, and to take appropriate action to protect asylum seekers from acts of violence at sea". As an indirect result an anti-piracy programme, analysed in detail in Part 2 of this book, was set up. The funding of the programme was prompted by humanitarian considerations rather than by considerations of security at sea. However, the two went nicely hand in hand.

The standing organs of the *UN Conference on Trade and Development* (UNCTAD) took up the issue, considering that the problems of maritime fraud and piracy required analysis and solution, on the basis of the Conference's primary jurisdiction over maritime matters in the context of trade and development. An Ad Hoc Intergovernmental Group was therefore established, and full details of this initiative will be found in Chapter 12.

Action taken in the Framework of the International Maritime Organisation since April 1985

An incident which has influenced much of the work undertaken in international organisations to combat international terrorist acts was the hijacking of the Italian cruise ship *Achille Lauro* on 7 October 1985. The ship was taken over by Palestinians who forced the crew to change course. Three days later, after killing one hostage, they surrendered to the Egyptian authorities.

The agenda of the fortieth session of the *General Assembly of the United Nations* which was taking place in the autumn of 1985 contained an item: "Measures to prevent Terrorism which endangers or takes innocent Lives or jeopardises fundamental Freedoms". Under this item, *inter alia*, the *Achille Lauro* affair was considered. This resulted in a request to the IMO to "study the problem of terrorism aboard or against ships with a view to making recommendations on appropriate measures." (General Assembly Resolution 40/61, paragraph 3, 9 December 1985)

At the same time the *Assembly of the IMO* considered the problem of acts of piracy and armed robbery on ships and small craft at sea on the basis of its Resolution A545(13). In November 1985 the Assembly adopted Resolution A584(14) by which it called upon government authorities, private enterprise and crews to take measures to strengthen port and on board security. It also directed the MSC to develop "practical technical measures" to ensure the security of passengers and crews on board ships.

As a consequence the MSC, early in 1986, drafted on the basis of reports on piracy and armed robbery received from governments (Doc

MSC 52/21) measures to prevent unlawful acts against passengers and crew on board ships (Doc MSC 52/28 Annex 2). It also designed a uniform format for reports on incidents and measures taken to prevent their recurrence. At its 53rd session in September 1986 the MSC gave further consideration to these draft measures and, after having received comments, unanimously approved "Measures to prevent unlawful Acts against Passengers and Crews on board Ships" (Doc MSC 53/24 Annex 14). These measures are intended to assist governments in reviewing and strengthening port and on board security.

The governments of Austria, Egypt and Italy presented in September 1986 to the IMO Council a "Draft Convention for the Suppression of unlawful Acts against the Safety of maritime Navigation" (Doc PCUA 1/3). This was modelled on other international instruments to combat unlawful acts, such as the Hague (1970) and Montreal (1971) Conventions on the safety of civil aviation and the UN Conventions on internationally protected persons (1973), the taking of hostages (1979) and torture (1984). It provided for a legal means to suppress unlawful acts committed against the safety of maritime navigation endangering innocent human lives, jeopardising the safety of persons and property, or seriously affecting the operation of maritime services and thus of grave concern to the international community as a whole.

The draft was based on the absolute and unconditional application of the principle *dedere aut judicare* (to extradite or bring to justice). This means that the perpetrator of an act declared an offence by the Convention will generally be liable to prosecution—either by the state in which he is captured, or by a state requesting his extradition. It is clear that this legal structure will only work if a significant number of states are party to the convention. Further, the obligation can only be to *prosecute* and *not* to punish—punishment is a matter for the courts to decide, and they are—or should be—independent.

With a view to expediting work on the draft Convention, the Council established during its 57th Session in November 1986 an "Ad Hoc Preparatory Committee on the Suppression of unlawful Acts against the Safety of maritime Navigation". This Ad Hoc Committee was declared open to all member states of IMO.

The Ad Hoc Committee had held two sessions by October 1987. At each session it reported to the Council (Docs PCUA 1/4 and 2/5). In the course of its deliberations the Committee has made many drafting changes to the text proposed by the three sponsoring states, but has upheld the main thrust. The text, as it stands in October 1987, is contained in IMO document LEG/ES 13.

Some important characteristics are the following:

The draft applies to ships, meaning vessels of any type whatsoever, not permanently attached to the seabed. This includes dynamically supported craft, submersibles and other floating craft. The original draft included also a reference to "fixed platforms". Although there was no doubt that such installations required protection, it was questioned whether it was appropriate to equate them with ships, in view of possible complications. It was agreed to annex a separate "Draft Protocol for the Suppression of unlawful Acts against the Safety of fixed Platforms on the Continental Shelf" to the Convention, to be adopted at the same time.

The draft Convention declares a number of acts, if unlawfully and intentionally committed, to be criminal offences under national legislation. Examples include:
— The seizing or exercising of control over a ship
— Acts of violence against a person on board a ship, thus endangering safe navigation
— The placing of devices likely to destroy a ship
— Attempting, abetting or threatening the commission of such acts.

Jurisdiction of a state is established over offences affecting its interests—for example where a ship is flying its flag, or the offender is its national, or it is for some reason compelled to act. The draft Convention does not go so far as to declare these unlawful acts "crimes under international law"—like piracy on the high seas. Under general international law a state is entitled to establish jurisdiction over the offence of piracy *wherever* and by *whoever* it is committed, regardless of whether its own interests are affected—this is "universal jurisdiction".

The principle of *dedere aut judicare* is retained, obliging a state party in whose territory an offender is found to submit the case for prosecution to its own authorities, if it chooses not to allow his extradition.

The Ad Hoc Committee has now finished its work and has forwarded the draft Convention to the Legal Committee of IMO, which considered it at its meeting in October 1987. The next, and final, step was the submission of the text to a diplomatic conference, planned to take place in Rome in the first half of 1988.

Epilogue

In combating such international evils as the hijacking of airplanes and acts of violence on board ships the organised international community has availed itself of a number of "instruments" from the "tool box" of the international lawyer. With admirable speed (by the standards of international bureaucracy) the IMO has taken a set of *technical* measures, in the form of *decisions* by its organs, which may assist governments in their approach to the problem. I strongly believe that these kind of measures are the most effective. That is not to say that *legal* action, such as the drafting of a convention or treaty, should not be considered.

However, it should be borne in mind that the drafting, adopting and entry into force of a treaty takes considerable time (and energy). On average it takes around ten years for an important convention to be ratified—this lapse of time is not exactly useful in urgent situations.

Nevertheless, such action of a *repressive* nature ought to be taken in order to match technical, *preventive* action. If preventive measures fail in a particular case, they can be supplemented by a collective effort to bring those committing unlawful acts to justice.

CHAPTER 18

PIRACY CONTROL IN NIGERIA'S TERRITORIAL SEAS

Office of the Defence Attache, Permanent Mission of Nigeria to the United Nations

Introduction

In defining the problem which we face in Nigeria in particular and on the west coast of Africa in general, we cannot accurately represent it as piracy *jure gentium*. Although we have tended to categorise armed robbery in our roadsteads, creeks and at our quaysides as piracy, in the strict sense as defined under international law it cannot be so classified.

In simple terms, "piracy" consists of acts of violence committed on the *high seas* which do not constitute lawful acts of war. As seen above, the definition in the Geneva and United Nations Law of the Sea Conventions (see Appendices 14 and 15) is very restrictive and largely removes protection from piracy occurring in places other than on the high seas or outside the jurisdiction of any state. This has provoked different opinions about the legal status of the concept—that it is a "crime under international law in respect of which all states are allowed jurisdiction"; or that there is no international crime of piracy, but "states are merely authorised by international law to exercise criminal jurisdiction under their municipal law on a universality basis."

Most of the acts of armed violence in West Africa take place in the territorial waters of coastal states. The Nigerian government, while viewing piracy in our own territorial sea as a challenge to world public order, wishes to emphasise that it has always considered it primarily as a threat to national security. Armed violence at sea is only one of a number of security threats which we have, and which we view with serious concern. Our efforts at controlling piracy reflect the degree of importance we attach to other problems in our territorial waters which threaten our security and our economy. These associated problems include illegal fishing; illegal lifting of petroleum products; pilferage at ports; and smuggling. We are aware that armed robbery and its attendant vices made a serious dent in our image within the international maritime community. Our efforts at suppressing these crimes were, amongst other things, meant to reassure the international community that we intended to deploy the necessary resources to increase confidence in our ability to provide adequate security for tankers and oceangoing vessels.

The high incidence of armed robbery in Nigerian waters has been attributed to a number of factors. Prior to the 1970s it was virtually unheard of. After the civil war there were a few reports every now and again of armed attacks against vessels in our internal waters, but it was not until the mid-70s that attacks were reported on ships moored in our ports. Most observers identified a correlation between this increase and the oil boom. The years 1977 to 1979 were the worst in terms of armed attacks on ships in our waters. In 1980 the International Maritime Bureau identified Lagos as the world's number one problem area—in a statement with which we did not necessarily agree.

In particular, the increase in commerce which followed the oil boom, including the notorious "cement armada" is considered largely responsible for the increased number of attacks on vessels waiting in the roadsteads to berth. The shortage of berthing space in the few ports which were operational during this period created long queues and thus made the waiting vessels easy prey for robbers.

Figures from the Nigerian police show that at least three or four oceangoing vessels were attacked daily in the first quarter of 1981. In fact, in March of that year, up to twelve reports of alleged attacks daily were recorded, involving gangs of between 30 and 50 with fast boats. However, most of these alleged attacks could not be independently confirmed. Cargo theft, and related damages, for the first nine months of 1980 cost the Nigerian Ports Authority US$ 183.7 million in claims from importers.

There follow figures of attacks in Nigerian waters, based on the IMB Chronology at Appendix 1.

1981	77
1982	39
1983	26
1984	5
1985	10
1986	11
1987	8

These figures show a marked decline after 1983. There are sceptics and cynics who attribute this to the decrease in the level of commerce and the downswing in the local economy. Our government on the other hand believes that the increased patrolling and surveillance of our territorial waters and waterways, the improved training of our law enforcement officers, and the tightening of our laws and regulations are largely responsible.

Piracy Control Regime

Prior to independence security in Nigerian waters was the responsibility of a few marine policemen "deployed on patrol to prevent incursions from waterfronts into sheds and stocking areas''. After our independence these duties were shared between various law enforcement agencies, each being assigned specific legal responsibilities under various acts of Parliament and bye laws. The Nigerian Ports Authority shared these responsibilities with the Marine Police, and both were short staffed, poorly equipped and generally badly trained. As a result, Military Ports Commandants were employed in the early 1970s to decongest the ports, and restore order and security. In most cases the Commandants were naval officers, and they became a regular feature of the ports.

By 1976 the Nigerian Navy had been assigned the responsibility of coordinating all government agencies concerned with pilferage and robbery in ports and harbour approaches. In 1978 a Ports Police Command took off on a modest scale.

By the end of the 1970s the government had begun to appreciate the enormity of the problem caused by pirates and other criminals operating in our waters. Apart from the threat of increased freight rates and insurance premiums, there was also the danger of an overall boycott of our ports.

In 1979 drastic steps were taken to remedy the deteriorating security situation. A dawn to dusk curfew was imposed on the movement of all ships within Nigerian territorial waters and the Navy was given directives to shoot on sight any persons or ships flouting the order. Conscious of our responsibilities to our citizens, and to the shippers using our waters, the Federal government set up an ''Anti-Piracy Committee'' in March 1981, chaired by the Commissioner of Police. In 1982, a Ministerial Task Force was established to study the piracy problem. The government also decided to set up a mobile para-military body, and to grant the Ports Police Command, mentioned above, much needed autonomy within the Nigerian Police Force.

When the present Federal Military Government came to power at the end of 1983, it was faced with a number of security problems, one of which was the daring manner in which armed attacks were committed in our territorial waters and just outside our twelve mile territorial sea limit but within our exclusive economic zone (EEZ). Of particular concern was the illegal lifting and export by sea, and across land borders, of our major foreign exchange earner, petroleum products. In 1984, a Task Force was set up under the command of the Chief of Staff, Major-General Tunde Idiagbon. Since the establishment of the Force there has been a large drop in crimes in Nigerian waters.

The country's security agencies—including the Navy, the maritime surveillance unit of the Air Force, the Customs and Excise and the Fisheries Department—have instituted both joint and independent 24 hour patrols under the control of the Task Force. The establishment of the Task Force is seen as a step towards the ultimate aim of creating a Nigerian Coast Guard. As a coordinating centre for the activities of all the security services it has functioned very well. We hope to improve our surveillance and intelligence gathering capabilities, so that the activities of pirates can be not only surpassed, but pre-empted. We are fast approaching that goal.

Logging more days at sea requires huge expenditure on patrol craft. By early 1983 the Nigerian Navy had acquired eight offshore patrol vessels (OPVs) and 15 inland patrol craft for the specific duties of combating smuggling and piracy. The government is not taking for granted the huge successes achieved to date. It intends to strengthen the capabilities of our security forces to cope with any future resurgence in armed attacks in our territorial waters, including our EEZ and our contiguous zones, and has approved the purchase of a further 26 OPVs.

Problems of Piracy Control

We acknowledge that effective piracy control can only be guaranteed by increased vigilance on the part of our law enforcement agencies, our citizens, and our ships; and by the willingness of the international community to act effectively. On the other hand, we recognise that large resources have to be diverted from areas of pressing need, particularly in the developing economies of the west coast of Africa, for this purpose. The question therefore is how many countries faced with the problem can afford the cost of effective policing of their territorial sea, not to mention their EEZ and contiguous zone.

In the nineteenth century Great Britain's supreme control of the sea allowed her to use her naval strength and massive wealth to suppress piracy. The preconditions had thereby been set for the effective control of the seas; it could be ensured by unilateral action by naval powers. The problem with this regime was that it did not afford protection to those areas of the world's oceans and shipping routes where particular threats were not posed to the interests of the powerful and developed states with large navies. Although the conventions on the Law of the Sea have since enshrined provisions which afford all states a degree of protection under international law, we believe this is not sufficient. It imposes on coastal states, regardless of their resources, an undue burden for providing security in large stretches of sea.

As we mentioned in our introduction, we are not satisfied with the law as it stands. Our reservations include the general ones shared by most states—the right of pursuit in EEZs, contiguous zones and across boundaries, and the effect on national and international deterrence and enforcement of the 200 mile EEZ itself.

Specific reservations include the absence of uniform sanctions for perpetrators of the crime of "piracy", and also of provisions requiring members of the crew of an attacked vessel to cooperate with law enforcement agencies during the investigative and prosecuting stages. On a number of occasions, when we have succeeded in apprehending suspects, an attacked vessel has sailed out of our waters and we have therefore had no witnesses.

Another area of concern is the fact that allegations are often made of attacks on vessels in our territorial sea, not to the appropriate law enforcement agencies in our country, but instead to relevant maritime authorities of the ship's flag state. We get to hear about some of these attacks by browsing through documents deposited at the International Maritime Organisation. We would like to use this opportunity to appeal to all owners of vessels that sail into our ports, to report promptly all piracy incidents and to cooperate fully with our security officers.

Conclusion

It is obvious that the incidence of piracy in our territorial waters has shown a marked decrease. We however do not believe that this should encourage complacency on our part. We appreciate that most of the states on the west coast of Africa cannot afford the huge expense involved in policing their waters. About 85% of our imports and exports come and go by sea—and the proportion of commerce conducted via the sea by most coastal states in the region does not differ markedly from ours. We have a straight coastline of 420 nautical miles, and it is a tremendous burden to divert resources for the purpose of suppressing piracy. We are willing to bear the burden for as long as is necessary. But the international community must however recognise that states able, like us, to bear this burden are few and far between.

We are pleased with the efforts of a number of UN agencies, such as the High Commission for Refugees, which orchestrated an eleven nation fund to aid the Thai government in its efforts to eradicate the problem in its territorial waters and in the South China Sea. A number of countries in our subregion are in dire need of similar assistance to train law enforcement officers, and to procure patrol vessels.

Finally we would like to commend the International Shipping Federation, the Baltic and International Maritime Conference and the International Maritime Bureau for detailing to their members measures to deter and resist armed robbers. Although we view these measures with appreciation, we see them as short term palliatives which should only complement an international effort directed at specialised training and increased patrols of the world's seaways. We would hope that increased funding will be available for these primary control measures, because the drop in the number of incidents involving armed attacks on the west coast of Africa must not be viewed as a sign that we have finally suppressed piracy in the subregion.

CHAPTER 19

THEFTS AND ROBBERIES ON BOARD SHIPS IN THE SINGAPORE STRAIT

Sharon Tan

Over the last few years there have been a number of reported "piracy" incidents in the Singapore Strait. The term "piracy" has, however, been inappropriately used in this context and requires clarification.

The Singapore Strait is a narrow waterway connecting the Malacca Strait and the South China Sea. The jurisdiction of the Strait is divided among three littoral states bordering it—Singapore, Malaysia and Indonesia. Singapore's territorial waters therefore consist of only a portion of the Strait. There are no international waters or high seas in the Strait. It follows therefore that the reported incidents are simply thefts and armed robberies on board ships, and are not strictly piracy incidents

During the period 1981 to 1984, a total of 179 incidents were reported to the Singapore authorities. The breakdown is as follows:

	1981	*1982*	*1983*	*1984*	*Total*
Cases inside Singapore territorial waters	7	13	8	7	35
Cases outside Singapore territorial waters	28	32	23	25	108
Cases where the positions were not clearly reported	7	9	17	3	36
Total	42	54	48	35	179

Of the 35 cases inside Singapore territorial waters, only seven occurred within Singapore port limits. In spite of some articles in the press, incidents in the Phillip Channel are outside Singapore territorial waters, and the Channel was indeed the location of 46 out of the 108 incidents reported outside Singapore waters.

The annual average for all reports—within and without Singapore territorial waters—is 45. For the years 1985-1987, based on figures in the IMB Chronology at Appendix 1, this average dropped to 27. However, as stated on page 12, the Malacca Straits area is now the most active world "piracy zone", and more than half the reported attacks during 1987 were located there. An examination of the Chronology will reveal that, in more recent years, Singapore authorities are still hampered by jurisdictional problems.

It may be noted that the number of incidents constitutes only a very small fraction of the total amount of shipping movement through the Singapore Strait. For example, a traffic density survey of the Strait conducted throughout October 1984 revealed a total of 5,335 vessel movements.

From reports received a set pattern with the following characteristics is detectable:

(1) No firearms have been used—although they are sometimes carried

(2) The thieves, or robbers, normally attack in groups of three or four, armed with parangs

(3) They normally attack during the hours of darkness while the ships are transiting the Singapore Strait

(4) They normally use small fast boats with outboard motors

(5) They use grappling hooks to climb on board the ship from the stern

(6) They usually avoid confrontation with persons on board

(7) They are normally content with stealing cash and light articles and show no interest in cargoes.

This characterises the incidents as petty thefts, similar to housebreaking on shore. If the incidents occur in Singapore territorial waters, they are classified and investigated on this basis by the Singapore Marine Police. Most of the incidents occur on passing ships, not calling into Singapore port. Therefore, many could not be substantiated with hard evidence. Nevertheless, all cases occurring within the jurisdiction of Singapore are exhaustively investigated.

Various government agencies are concerned. Since the incidents are classified as thefts and armed robberies, they are investigated by the Marine Police, responsible to the Ministry of Home Affairs. Patrols within territorial waters are made by the Republic of Singapore Navy, responsible, of course, to the Ministry of Defence. Safety of shipping is the responsibility, generally, of the Marine Department and, in the port, of the Port Authority. Both these bodies are responsible to the Ministry of Communication. Concerted efforts are made by these authorities to deal with the problem.

Ever since the first report of a theft or robbery on board a ship, the Marine Police and the Republic of Singapore Navy have increased their patrols within territorial waters. Such increased patrols continue, and are intensified during the hours of darkness.

The authorities have had discussions with the shipping community, which is directly affected by the problem. The Port Authority has established a communication channel on VHF, whereby reports of such incidents may be expeditiously made. It has been emphasised to the shipping community that some simple measures may be taken on board. The simplest means is to prevent the robbers from boarding, and this can be achieved by posting additional look outs while ships are transiting the affected area. The passage through the Phillip Channel normally takes less than two hours, and the entire Singapore Strait can be passed in four or five hours. Additional look outs for this brief period can easily be provided by crews. There have been cases where suspicious boats have turned away on discerning the vigilance of a ship's crew.

THE CONTROL OF PIRACY

CONFERENCE DISCUSSION

The following discussion between contributing authors took place during the Marine Policy Centre's 1985 update workshop on Piracy at Sea. The workshop was held at the Woods Hole Oceanographic Institute, Massachusetts, USA.

HARLOW: It probably would be safe to conclude that the real problem is the broader issue of maritime crime. I think we all would support the proposition that there is no simple, singular solution to this problem. I would think most people would agree that some form of international coordination and cooperation would be an essential ingredient to deal with these problems effectively. I think many of us feel that that does not and should not imply a grandiose, international scheme and a UNCLOS IV; but, nonetheless, some form of regional or bilateral discussion would be warranted. Certainly we have had ample evidence that there has been a lot done with regard to the terrible problems of the boat people, and perhaps that experience would be useful in some of these other areas that are creating problems. It is in this spirit that I suggest certain initiatives, certainly not as anything that would be officially sanctioned by this group. Nonetheless, perhaps it would be a basis for focusing discussion areas that we could commend to national decision makers.

WALKATE: To begin, I would like to comment on reporting incidents. I think that is the first thing we need. We must rely on actual and recent information before we can take any action in the international field, either bilaterally or multilaterally, or start drafting rules. There may be a decline in piracy, but that certainly should not lead to less vigilance on the part of flag states because this may lead to a tendency upwards again. There is a close correlation between the two. I would suggest that the answer is to have the International Maritime Bureau continue to collect information from shippers on maritime crime. The IMB has of course released the information as reports and may have more information than has otherwise been collected. My answer would be yes, by all means I do think that there should be additional reports on piracy. Let me comment on Resolution 5 of the IMO (Appendix 21). It is very interesting to see that it almost seems to be intended that the organisation does not request information from non-government organisations, such as the IMB. I hope this is a mistake and I certainly would argue that any information submitted by the IMB to the IMO should be considered and taken up. So in any follow up of IMO action or any other international organisation for that matter, I think there should be an invitation to non-governmental organisations competent in the field to submit directly to the government organisation.

ELLEN: I think it is probably a mistake. The Secretary General of the IMO is on my Board of Directors and he is always calling for information on these matters. We will compile a list and if people want to use it they can. We can get the information from various sources. I think IMO want non-governmental organisations to keep submitting information to them, for they have no means to collect this information.

CYCON: Let me ask a clarifying question also. Eric, are you getting information from the seafaring unions?

ELLEN: Yes.

CYCON: I imagine they wouldn't have that kind of incentive to hide the facts. In fact, they would want to bring it out for the betterment of conditions. But you also state that the quality of information, as reflected in the information you get in, is pretty incomplete, in terms of locations and that sort of thing.

ELLEN: But suggestions made at this conference give a more complete picture, so that a more in depth analysis of the information can be made.

PENTTI: I think a lot of people tend to stay away from the Defense Mapping Agency's computer system, on the basis of its fairly elaborate system. If it were to work, it would be wonderful; because you could sign on to the computer and find out what all the incidents were at a certain given time period in a certain area. But this requires participation and reporting by someone, as opposed to someone like IMB who actually has to go out and pry out the information and put it together in a useful form. Maybe there is some sort of interaction there, it's possible.

CYCON: I had some questions on your system. How complicated is it?

PENTTI: It is fairly easy. You sign on to a computer terminal and dial a telephone number. The problem is that, if you want to plug into the satellite, you are talking about a $50,000 system on a ship. Otherwise, time has to be found on the radio telephone networks. So there is a cost that may well be the reason people don't like to file accident reports.

CYCON: If regional centres, as opposed to individual ships, are supplied with terminals and information that a ship can then pick up by radio transmission as it approaches the strait, for example. Might this be a little more cost effective?

PENTTI: Certainly. There are many ways to approach that question.

CYCON: Any comments on the re-establishment of a comprehensive intelligence centre?

BRITTIN: I think the initiative should be expressed: "Establish a comprehensive international intelligence centre".

PENTTI: I agree. That would be a tremendous advantage. Certainly trying to research my paper, there was no one place to look to find out this information. If there were, it would make everyone's efforts a lot easier, and also would probably focus attention.

CYCON: I might add that there is not even one place to look within a particular agency of a particular government. Is this because piracy is just not something that fits neatly into a category, or because maritime crime does not fit neatly into a category, or because of overlapping jurisdictions within national administrative agencies?

ELLEN: It all stems from the fact that the international agency that should be doing this is Interpol as a police organisation. But Interpol only acts as a great large communications centre, and takes messages from one central bureau in a country and disseminates them to some other country. I asked them in the 1970s to set up what I in fact set up afterwards, the International Maritime Bureau, to focus on this and they just wouldn't do it. They don't have the facilities, they don't have the desire to do this. Therefore, you have no international policing in the merchant commerce sector. Because of that, who else is going to do it? You find in the end that it will probably be done by commerce, only because there is no international organisation prepared to do it.

PENTTI: There are a lot of robberies against merchant ships, but there are certain restricted areas. Overall they have not been that important in the course of world events and therefore no major body has responded. I think, on the other hand, with refugees you have a perfect example of something that reached such outrageous and large proportions that the UN did move and has come up with some very effective programmes. So if the problem is large enough, perhaps then the international body will move. Otherwise it will have to be a commercial operation.

ABRAHAMSSON: So we establish a reporting system, an intelligence system centre, and then a tracking system and even establish lines of authority and so on. What do we use it all for? What is the purpose of it? I don't understand.

WALKATE: Preventive.

ABRAHAMSSON: How do we use it to prevent piracy?

WALKATE: Well, I think to keep states informed about any risks their ships may run in the high seas, and any possible future pirate can see that attacks don't go unnoticed.

HARLOW: A very mundane example would be to communicate the points you made such as raising the gangplank five feet and having a fire hose loaded on the deck. They sound very mundane but they are not obvious to a lot of people; and that can go a long towards helping. The rest has to do with the theory of "forewarned is forearmed". Masters would be more attuned to the level of risk if, for example, they knew what had happened to the ships proceeding through a certain strait, and they should stand a watch for five hours. Hopefully this would raise deterrence to a level at which pirates would no longer view the ships as a lucrative target of opportunity.

BRITTIN: In my view, all of these steps are threshold steps. What is the end result? The end result is a lot more information being developed and spread. It sets the stage for subsequent substantive steps to be taken internationally. So, to me it is difficult to try and go beyond the suggestions here but if these are established then it makes it easier to deal with the problem.

ELLEN: My experience in running a bureau has shown me that you get a lot of information coming in. For example, this ship is going to be sunk next week. I sunk a ship off of Singapore two years ago. I did it for £100,000. It is because they have someone to relate to, they will communicate with a central organisation. I think that unless you have a central organisation you never have proper dissemination of intelligence.

ABRAHAMSSON: I am still puzzled because information can only be useful if you use it and you must know exactly what you are using it for. Just to collect information is meaningless and in that sense I will accept that forewarned is forearmed. I can see that point but I am not quite sure that I can see all the other things. I am afraid that we will collect a lot of information but not have the means of putting it into a meaningful framework. Then we will sit another ten years down the road and will have a new conference where we will say: "Well, we collected a lot of information and didn't know what we wanted it for and therefore what we need is another information centre".

ELLEN: I think the problem can be defeated by law enforcement. The US and other countries have had to deal with similar problems of terrorists. It can be dealt with, but you must start off with a basis of information.

ABRAHAMSSON: Right, basic information for the purpose of having an annual law enforcement seminar. Because your ideas about how to lick this problem came from this workshop not because anyone might have sent you a lot of information. Because the information has been presented in a specific framework.

WALKATE: I would like to say something about international waters vis a vis high seas. I don't think we can accept wording like that and then establish lines of authority.

BRITTIN: As a matter of fact, for purposes of violence at sea, the lines of jurisdiction and authority of states, coastal and otherwise, are already established. They are established in the 1982 Law of the Sea Convention and, except where the EEZ overshadows, it is pretty clear who has authority to do what in the various bodies of water. You start talking about whether it is the flag state or the coastal state and what kind of authority they have in the EEZ and you are raising a red flag.

HARLOW: What I had in mind is the fact that if we are going to develop an intelligent division of responsibility on a regional basis, whether it be for reporting to an intelligence centre or for patrolling, who does what has to be sorted out somewhere. Underlying that though I will admit that lurking in the corner is the potential opening of the wounds of the 1982 discussions as to the nature of the waters. To the extent that the potential exists it is probably best to approach the matter in a more generalised sense.

CYCON: Let me ask you for a little clarification on that. The majority of the incidents seem to be happening in what are clearly territorial waters. But, that question aside, the ability of a nation to respond in such a way that would question these lines of authority seems to be more theoretical than real. I don't know how many times we are going to have to worry about the US Navy going to other states' territorial water, knocking off pirate ships that have been bothering people in the Gulf of Thailand. It may have been real right up to World War II and a few years beyond, but it doesn't seem to be a big issue now. So maybe that is misstating the issue and we should not be as concerned about it. As you rightly say the greater issues are what transpires with the coastal states.

HARLOW: I think I would be less than candid if I didn't express some degree of concern with the potential of impeding or stopping reasonable access to international straits by virtue of crimes at sea. It I think goes without saying that international straits are vital to the maritime community. If the problem of crime at sea goes to the point where it is impractical or impossible to utilise a key, international strait, that has a direct and important impact. A lot of the issues discussed in the Law of the Sea negotiations had to do with how do you balance the interests of the maritime community with those of the coastal states, if you are talking in terms of the potential of twelve miles territorial seas as opposed to three. I think we would not be thinking of the entire story if we didn't have in mind that to talk of crimes that could chill or prevent utilisation of key, important straits is very sensitive. That has a perspective that is entirely different from territorial seas, generally. Now that is an underlying point that is four layers below what we are talking about here but I think it is something we all have to recognise.

WALKATE: I thank Admiral Harlow for his explanation. I think we have been discussing the importance of enforcement. You may have, or you may create rules, but if they are not enforced, they are nothing.

Maybe we should go no further than to "emphasise the responsibility of states to enforce international law in areas under their jurisdiction", without referring to flag or coastal states, nor to special international waters or whatever.

BRITTIN: Admiral, what do you mean by a "common training programme for all people in law enforcement"?

CYCON: Would that mean common to all branches of maritime law enforcement—the navies, coast guards, the harbour police?

BRITTIN: I think the words "establish a common programme", mean training by all countries—this is the commonality we are seeking.

HARLOW: I meant share the wisdom and insights and in that sense there are common things that the people have learned about maritime law enforcement that perhaps would evoke a common denominator. It is like loading the fire hose—there are certain things I think the world community could agree are insights that are important to communicate and train people on.

PETERSON: I would like to comment on the proposal for a common programme of training taking place on a national level. I think what we are really talking about are national programmes which tap into a common fund of knowledge that has been picked up around the world. We are not talking about an international maritime police academy. We are simply talking about when each country is busy training its own coast guards, harbour police, river police, maritime police, etc, that they take benefit of wisdom that has been acquired, usually at a fair amount of cost and energy, in other parts of the world.

BRITTIN: The proposal for an intelligence centre seems to potentially spawn yet another administrative and coordinating agency and it seems that there is a perfect agency in the IMB from which governments can take advice of a pragmatic and immediate nature. I wonder whether that should be emphasised. As I read it, the vehicle for reaching the solution to the problem is to get those countries in the region together that have a problem and have them work it out. So I don't think we are speaking of another large international entity.

PETERSON: The solution may possibly even be an existing regional organisation—there are a lot of regional organisations that have various types of contact with maritime states. ASEAN has its friends in various places. And the African community still exists, most of the members are in Lome in some way or another and that ties them into the EEC. There are ways in which this can all be done.

ELLEN: I think you have to be very careful here about the IMO in any way, because IMO does not deal with maritime fraud, only piracy. UNCTAD deals with maritime crime.

WALKATE: The words "establish a comprehensive international intelligence centre" may be read as referring to a "new" centre. Now what we want, of course, is whatever centre is available, or could be made available—and that could be in a governmental or a non-governmental organisation. Maybe we should say "appoint" or "recognise the need for". "Establish" is too active.

CYCON: Somewhere we might want to add something about encouraging the understanding of rights and responsibilities of ship's masters and crews under different circumstances. We touched at times on the responsibility of refraining from violence, and of picking up refugees.

PENTTI: I wonder if the maritime industry would sort of take that as a slap on the wrist.

CONCLUSION: THE WAY FORWARD

Eric Ellen (Editor)

It was the objective of the Woods Hole Seminars both to examine the question of international piracy in considerable depth and in a way never previously attempted and at the same time to arrive at some form of practical solutions.

The first part of this volume has been the examination of the problem. The Appendices which follow identify the form which some of the solutions should take.

At this point, however, it is proper to take stock and to summarise.

Definition

One of the prime aspects of the problem has been shown to be that of definition. However, this is really only a problem for the legislator and not for those facing the problem. The Conference devoted much time and considerable effort in discussion of the various facets of definition and still more time in discussing whether or not certain acts fitted whatever definition was being considered at any particular moment in time.

But for the security practitioner, it is sufficient to be able to say that a certain act is wrong. Whether it is wrong in that it is piracy according to one definition or another, or is theft, or terrorism, or assault or any other recognisable crime will not necessarily affect his response.

However, the question of definition is essential to the issue because until terminology is standardised, the international co-operation so essential to the containment of the problem cannot begin.

Discussions at Woods Hole and the chapters in this book have emphasised the wide range of criminal acts that can be called piracy. This wide range is of itself a major obstacle to the prevention of piracy as it creates great problems for national legislators who must of necessity work with specific and precise definitions when drafting legislation.

By way of example, the criminal behaviour of gangs attacking ships in the Phillip Channel and other areas cannot be compared in cause, extent, consequence or even potential corrective action with the attacks on the Boat People in the Gulf of Thailand — yet both have been referred to here as "Piracy".

Jurisdiction

Another issue raised by the discussions has been the need for a completely new look at the question of jurisdiction. Until now a national system of jurisdiction has met the need of maritime nations. Jurisdiction over maritime matters has been limited to the areas covered by territorial waters and circumstances covered by provisions of the Law of the Flag. The sole exception to this has been the universal jurisdiction applicable to closely defined acts of Piracy.

However, two factors are now beginning to demonstrate that these definitions of jurisdiction are no longer sufficient for the problems confronting international society.

The first factor is that some crimes occur within the area of jurisdiction of a coastal state and yet do not affect that state in any way at all. In some of these cases there can be an understandable reluctance on the part of the state to become involved in an investigation, particularly if the state lacks the necessary operational capability.

The second factor is that many criminal acts committed on the High Seas, or from land against vessels or cargo on the High Seas, cannot be classified as Piracy and are, therefore, outside the jurisdiction of any government.

There is thus an irresistible logic in arguing that all criminal acts committed in international waters should be within the jurisdiction of any and every State. Whilst such a concept might be logical, it is not yet acceptable to national governments even though there is a precedent for it under the old "Admiralty Jurisdiction" in English Law.

Capability

There is always the risk that an international discussion group examining a particular problem will formulate a solution couched in ideal rather than practical terms.

For example, it is a simple matter to speak of more effective law enforcement and increased resources, but in circumstances where lack of law enforcement and inadequate resources are the cause of the problem these are just empty words.

To give another example, West Africa is often cited as an area in which piracy is a serious problem. It has thus attracted considerable international attention and there is no shortage of advice as to how countries of that particular area should combat the problem. However, those who have a detailed knowledge of the area appreciate the difficulty, amounting to the virtual impossibility, of maintaining any form of surveillance, control or response over the deeply indented tropical coastline typical of the area.

Where this situation occurs against the backdrop of a national economy which has problems financing even basic services for the nation at large, it is difficult for the government of that country to set aside resources to combat a problem which may be considered relatively small.

The Woods Hole group was ever conscious of these basic factors and bore them in mind when drafting its seven initiatives for the future. These initiatives are summarised at Appendix 23, but are expounded here to provide a counterpoint to the problems mentioned above.

1. Identify and promulgate protective measures

Considerable experience by merchant shipping of Piracy worldwide has resulted in an accumulation of expertise which has proved effective in countering the threat.

Every effort should be made to identify this experience and create training useful to crews transiting risk areas. The aim should be to improve their ability to protect themselves until other initiatives tackle the root causes of piracy.

2. Establish a dependable reporting system

As with all types of crime worldwide, intelligence is priceless. However, in the field of piracy, no centralised statistics exist and those figures which are available are not collated into any form of intelligence.

There is a reluctance on the part of some to report attacks but, if only for the reason that governments will not act until the true scale of piracy is proved, a uniform system of reporting incidents is essential.

3. Designate a comprehensive intelligence centre

Raw information is of little practical use until collated and analysed to produce predictions of criminal behaviour. A piracy intelligence centre should be part of a recognised international organisation having an acceptable interface both with the industry and with government departments.

4. Establish an early tracking and warning system

The predictive intelligence created by the intelligence centre would form the basis of both general and specific warnings to the maritime community and national authorities.

Predictive intelligence is a comparatively new concept in the field of law enforcement but it is becoming increasingly apparent that criminal trends can be foreseen and, given the will, nullified by preventive action.

This is no less true in the case of piracy.

5. Enforcement by States of law (national and international) in areas under their jurisdiction

This is obviously essential to the ultimate containment of the problem but has to be a longer term objective.

States with both the problem and the capability to deal with piracy already do so with varying degrees of effectiveness. The main difficulties are in those areas where the problem is not yet properly quantified due to inadequate reporting and where the national response capability is limited both because of limited resources and lack of priority.

Neither of these constraints will disappear in the short term.

6. Pool information to support national training programmes for those responsible for maritime law enforcement

This initiative should develop hand-in-hand with the comprehensive crew training identified in 1. above.

It is obvious that the information which enables self-help techniques to be developed at crew level will also facilitate parallel deveopment of prevention and response techniques amongst those responsible for maritime law enforcement.

7. International co-operation and exchange of information on a regional and, where necessary, worldwide, basis

It is particularly important for neighbouring states to pool resources, information and expertise in order that their responses are co-ordinated.

This is an essential ingredient of all efforts to combat the problem of piracy.

Appendices

THE IMB CHRONOLOGY OF PIRATE ATTACKS ON MERCHANT VESSELS 1981-1987

This Chronology should be used in conjunction with remarks made on page 5.

	Date	Vessel	Flag	Location
	1981			
1.	1 Jan	? 2 containers pilfered	UK	Freetown
2.	2 Jan	**Eastern Harmony** 12 pirates repelled	Liberia	Port Harcourt
3.	4 Jan	**Globe Trader** Pirates boarded from ten boats. Possibly arrested later	Singapore (0100)	Bonny
4.	4 Jan	? (Anchorage) 60-80 pirates stole from deck containers	Japan	Bonny
5.	5 Jan	? Reported boarded by 60-80 pirates	?	Bonny
6.	5 Jan	? Pirates stole foodstuffs, oil, autoparts in numerous attacks	W Germany	Nigeria
7.	6 Jan	**Esmerelda I** (Anchorage) Pirates took considerable cargo	Venezuela	Bonny
8.	7 Jan	**Usambara**	W Germany	Lagos
9.	7 Jan	? 15 pirates stole 2 tonnes of cargo from containers. No assistance rendered from authorities	UK	Port Harcourt
10.	7 Jan	?	UK	Port Harcourt
11.	12 Jan	**Togo Brewer**	W Germany	Lagos/Pt Harcourt
12.	15 Jan	? Unseen thieves stole cartons from container	UK	Takoradi
13.	18 Jan	**Goldvarda**	UK	Bonny
14.	5 Feb	**Britta Oden**	Sweden	Lagos
15.	7 Feb	**Gold Orli**	UK	Lagos
16.	7 Feb	**Lisbet Coast**	Denmark	Lagos
17.	12 Feb	**British Tenacity** (Anchorage) Pirates boarded but jumped overside when confronted by crew	UK (0330)	Lagos
18.	12 Feb	**Remco Remco** Pirates injured crew and stole property	Ghana	Lagos
19.	18 Feb	**Urundi**	W Germany	Lagos
20.	19 Feb	**Opal Bounty** (Anchorage) 30 pirates boarded, injured crew in struggle. Forced and opened containers	Liberia (0715)	Lagos
21.	20 Feb	**Baco Liner**	W Germany	Lagos
22.	24 Feb	**Pep Sea**	Denmark	Lagos
23.	24 Feb	**Chai Varee**	Thailand	Lagos

	Date	Vessel	Flag	Location
24.	? Feb	**Korsten Wesch** (Secured to buoy) Pirates cut mooring ropes, causing ship to hit pier. Stole from containers in confusion	W Germany (Night)	Lagos
25.	4 Mar	**Dosina** (Anchorage)	Dutch Antilles	Singapore
26.	5 Mar	**Gerestros**	Greece	Singapore
27.	17 Mar	**Sabie Star** (Yacht)(Anchorage) 3 armed pirates stole property. Cut yacht adrift. One later arrested.	?	Belem Paraguay
28.	20 Mar	**Mar Negro** (Leaving port) 7 armed pirates boarded from launch—stole hairdryers from container. Crew locked themselves in citadel	Spain (0215)	Buenaventura Colombia
29.	21 Mar	**La Falda**	UK	Apapa
30.	28 Mar	**Seevetal** (Anchorage) Attacked by pirates	W Germany (0225)	Lagos
31.	28 Mar	**Crete Sif**	Denmark	Lagos Crete
32.	29 Mar	**Nedlloyd Manila** Manila Pirates threatened crew- stole 20 bags of rags	Netherlands	Lagos
33.	29 Mar	**Export Champion**	US	Lagos
34.	30 Mar	? Attacked by pirates in two boats No reply from authorities	Yugoslavia	Lagos
35.	31 Mar	**Westwal** Attacked by pirates No reply from authorities	Netherlands (0445)	Lagos
36.	1 Apr	**Riverina** Crew prevented pirates boarding by throwing bags of cement into their boats	UK (0630)	Lagos
37.	10 Apr	**Litiopa** (No details known—event denied by owners)	UK	Singapore
38.	15 Apr	**Tarubi**	Cyprus	Lagos
39.	18 Apr	**Baucis**	?	Lagos
40.	19 Apr	**Anangel Luck**	Greece	Lagos
41.	19 Apr	**Yin Kim**	Panama	Lagos
42.	20 Apr	?	Poland	Lagos
43.	21 Apr	**Northridge**	UK	Lagos
44.	22 Apr	**Mount King**	Panama	Lagos
45.	16 May	**Balticland** (Berthed) 10-15 pirates took 50 tyres from containers and threw them on to quay. One policeman arrived on scene	Sweden (1300)	Abidjan
46.	18 May	**Balticland** (Berthed) 50 pirates with knives threw stones at the crew—stole another 150 tyres	Sweden (0545)	Abidjan
47.	20 May	**Koei**	Liberia	Phillip Channel
48.	22 May	**Balticland**	Sweden	Lagos
49.	22 May	**Nedlloyd Niger** (Anchorage) Pirates threw bottles at crew from boat—crew replied with water hoses—pirates retreated	Netherlands (0400)	Lagos
50.	22 May	**Moolchand** Armed pirates forced containers. Naval boat despatched at 0830—as pirates leaving	Panama (0400)	Lagos

	Date	Vessel	Flag	Location
51.	23 May	?	France	Lagos
52.	23 May	**Nedlloyd Schelde**	Netherlands	Lagos
53.	25 May	**Balticland** (Anchorage)	Sweden (2330)	Lagos
		Crew saw boat alongside and noticed some containers damaged. They then rammed the boat. No reply from authorities		
54.	26 May	?	Japan	Phillip Channel
55.	28 May	?	Panama	Lagos
56.	28 May	?	Japan	Phillip Channel
57.	1 Jun	**Eva**	Greece	Lagos
58.	1 Jun	**Uta-Sabine**	W Germany	Lagos
59.	2 Jun	?(Yacht & Houseboat)	US	Bahamas
		2 boats allegedly harassed by Bahamian speedboats. Scared off with rifles. Attackers apparently later arrested in possession of drugs		
60.	7 Jun	**Chai Varee**	Thailand	Apapa
61.	11 Jun	**Rafeala** (Roads)	Panama	Lagos
		10 pirates with grappling hooks repelled		
62.	13 Jun	?	W Germany	Lagos
63.	14 Jun	**Rafaela**	Panama	Lagos
		40 pirates with knives repelled after 2 hours		
64.	15 Jun	**Rafaela** (10m off shore)	Panama (2230)	Lagos
		A final determined attack—beaten off by crew and by master manoeuvring under power		
65.	15 Jun	**Ocean Eminence**	Liberia	Lagos
66.	16 Jun	**Vallabhbhai Patel**	India	Phillip Channel
		Pirates stole cash and valuables		
67.	16 Jun	**Indian Obo**	?	Phillip Channel
68.	17 Jun	**Vasilikos**	Liberia (0230)	Phillip Channel
		2 pirates stole £420 and clothing		
69.	18 Jun	**Asia Culture**	Liberia	Phillip Channel
70.	18 Jun	**Canis Major**	Panama	Lagos
71.	19 Jun	**Asia Culture**	Liberia	Phillip Channel
72.	19 Jun	**Varenna**	Norway	Off Singapore
73.	19 Jun	**Queen Saphire**	Panama	Phillip Channel
74.	20 Jun	**Stintfang**	W Germany	Lagos
75.	22 Jun	**Unterturkheim**	W Germany	Barranquilla Colombia
76.	25 Jun	**Ocean Eminence**	Liberia	Lagos
77.	5 Jul	**Pia Danielsen** (Roads)	Denmark (0300)	Lagos
		8-10 pirates with crowbars knives and bottles stole cargo of stockfish. Signal station unable to call help due to communication problems		
78.	6 Jul	**Iliana Bay** (Off coast)	?	Mindinao
		Pirates forced vessel to divert and unload cargo of rice. Master killed, passengers wounded, when refusing to help with unloading. Pirates or terrorists?		
79.	11 Jul	**Cheers** (Yacht)	?	Bequia Windward Islds
		Naked pirate with machete stabbed owner in chest and stomach, attempted to rape his wife. Took money		
80.	16 Jul	**Kenyo Maru**	Japan (0200)	Phillip Channel
		Pirates took two bicycles		

	Date	Vessel	Flag	Location
81.	17 Jul	?	Japan (0400)	Makassar Strait
		Pirates took equipment		
82.	17 Jul	**Contender Argent** (20m off shore)	Sweden	Singapore
		Local pirates stole around $30,000		
83.	18 Jul	**Africa Palm**	UK	Lagos
84.	24 Jul	**Mararathe Maersk**	Denmark	Lagos
		Thieves stole jogging shoes from cargo		
85.	25 Jul	**Blue Akeishi**	Japan	Lagos
86.	25 Jul	**Nedlloyd Main**	Netherlands	Phillip Channel
87.	27 Jul	**British Beech**	UK	Phillip Channel
		Local pirates took money		
88.	27 Jul	**Saint Peter** (Yacht)(Berth)	?	Barranquilla Colombia
		Hijacked by drugs traffickers		
89.	28 Jul	**Boringia**	Denmark	Monrovia
90.	29 Jul	?	Greece	Apapa
91.	4 Aug	? (Ferry)	?	Philippines
		50 "guerillas" of Communist New Peoples Army killed 5 passengers, wounded 4		
92.	13 Aug	**Kasuga Maru**	Japan	Phillip Channel
		Pirates with swords took crew's cash and watches		
93.	14 Aug	**Sea Lion**	Japan	Phillip Channel
94.	17 Aug	**Nedlloyd Weser**	Netherlands	Phillip Channel
95.	17 Aug	**Inabukwa**	Indonesia	Phillip Channel
		Money stolen		
96.	17 Aug	**Sinope**	Indonesia	Phillip Channel
		Money stolen		
97.	19 Aug	**Pioneer Maru**	Japan	Phillip Channel
		Pirates with swords took crew's cash/watches		
98.	23 Aug	**Corsicana** (15 knots)	UK (2230)	Phillip Channel
		3 pirates with knives and axes—forced master to take them to cabin, stole £4000 cash		
99.	27 Aug	**Nedlloyd Nile** (Discharging)	Netherlands (0730)	Tema
		Thieves pilfered medicines and razors		
100.	29 Aug	**Melampus**	UK	Lagos
101.	30 Aug	**Nedloyd Nile** (Berthed)	Netherlands	Lome
		Thieves pilfered handbags and tinned food		
102.	30 Aug	**Sloman Merkur**	W Germany	Lagos
103.	31 Aug	**Nuria 767**	Philippines	Philippines
		4 pirates (? 2 crew, 2 stowaways) robbed crew and passengers shot 11 dead - 20 survivors, 24 missing Escaped in 2 fishing boats with $380,000 cash and $126,500 goods		
104.	? Aug	?	?	Port Harcourt
		Pirates prevented by crew from opening containers. Police eventually arrived		
105.	2 Sep	**Mammoth Monarch** (12 knots)	Liberia	Phillip Channel
		$8000 and valuables stolen by pirates		
106.	2 Sep	**Nedlloyd Niger** (Tin Can Island)	Netherlands (0700)	Apapa
		Pirates with knives threatened crew—then fled in canoe after forcing locks on container		

	Date	Vessel	Flag	Location
107.	4 Sep	**Susan Ann II** (Yacht) Unconfirmed report of hijack by drugs traffickers—who were later arrested	?	Cartagena Colombia
108.	8 Sep	**?**	UK	Monrovia
109.	9 Sep	**Nedlloyd Fresco** (Anchorage) 10 pirates tied up crew member. Forced holds. Stole textiles, ropes, electrical equipment	Netherlands (0130)	Tema
110.	17 Sep	**Taifun** Attacked on 3 consecutive days -Master injured	Panama	Apapa
111.	17 Sep	**Fort Coulogne** (Anchorage) Pirates with knives (like hari-kiri swords). Threatened master—stole wallet and cash. Police arrived after pirates left	Bermuda (0400)	Singapore
112.	19 Sep	**Diana** 3 pirates with jungle knives attacked from speedboat	Japan	Phillip Channel
113.	20 Sep	**Hakata Maru** (8 knots) Pirate escaped using rubber hose as ladder when detected - stole nothing	Japan	Phillip Channel
114.	21 Sep	**Nigeria Venture**	Liberia	Phillip Channel
115.	21 Sep	**Elpida**	Greece	Phillip Channel
116.	25 Sep	**Nedlloyd Manila** Containers pilfered in spite of supervision	Netherlands	Abidjan
117.	25 Sep	**Abbey** (Anchorage) Armed pirates stole binoculars and chronometer	UK (0335)	Singapore
118.	25 Sep	**Mount Newman** (Anchorage)	UK	West Jurong
119.	25 Sep	**Kohnan Maru** 5 pirates with knives—ransacked C/O's room—took $520 and belongings	Japan	Phillip Channel
120.	27 Sep	**New Panda** (Roads)	Panama	Lagos
121.	28 Sep	**Nedlloyd Manilla** 7 pirates with speedboat forced container—stole 25 cartons	Netherlands (0715)	Apapa
122.	? Sep	**Rafaella**	Panama	Apapa
123.	? Sep	**Africa Maru**	Japan	Apapa
124.	? Sep	**Pia Danielsen** Pirates took stockfish	Denmark	Apapa
125.	? Sep	**Chai Varee**	Thailand	Apapa
126.	? Sep	**Tendai Maru**	Japan	Apapa
127.	? Sep	**Atlantic Maru** Thieves robbed container	Japan	Apapa
128.	? Sep	**Nedlloyd Fresco** Extensive pilfering—in spite of guards and bow and arrow men	Netherlands	Apapa
129.	? Sep	**Nedlloyd Fresco** Heavy pilferage (impossible to recruit watchmen) Police assistance requested in vain	Netherlands	Lome
130.	? Sep	**Mount Newman** (Anchorage)	UK	West Jurong
131.	? Sep	**Edna Maree** (Yacht) Thailand Pirates from Thai fishing boat stabbed skipper in stomach, partly severed his hand—Raped one woman (others hid below decks) Skipper repelled several before being injured	?	Pulo Lankani

	Date	Vessel	Flag	Location
132.	3 Oct	**Polana**	Greece	Dakar
133.	4 Oct	**Kimanis** (Passenger/cargo ferry) Pirates opened fire from speedboats—ship did not stop	Singapore	Off Borneo
134.	5 Oct	**Nedlloyd Manilla** Unseen thieves broke into container	Netherlands	Lome
135.	7 Oct	**Nedlloyd Manilla** Unseen thieves forced and robbed 4 containers	Netherlands	Tema
136.	7 Oct	**Semporna** 5 armed men holding ship surprised by police—who shot 2 of them	?	Philippines
137.	9 Oct	**Paean** Pirates stole cement	Greece	Lagos
138.	25 Oct	**The Threesome** (Yacht)(20m from coast) Attacked by 2 boatloads of pirates, firing weapons, while fishing. One yachtsman killed—pirates left empty handed	US	Bahamas
139.	28 Oct	**Nedlloyd Marseilles** (Berth) 10-15 pirates threatened crew—forced and robbed 2 containers	Netherlands (0330)	Apapa
140.	28 Oct	**Esk**	UK	Dakar
141.	30 Oct	**Nedlloyd Marseilles** Unseen thieves pilfered from containers	N'lands	Tema
142.	? Oct	**Portoseuta** (Fishing vessel) Boarded by 3 pirates from rubber motorboat 4 fishermen shot —one killed	Portugal (45 miles off coast)	Mauretania
143.	? Oct	**Manchester Fulmar**	UK	Lattakia Syria
144.	? Oct	**Apsaru** (Yacht)(Anchorage) "Officials" and fishermen boarded— tied up crew, stole property Pirates later imprisoned, then escaped	?	Maldives
145.	4 Nov	**Amaranta**	Portugal	Lagos
146.	11 Nov	**Nedlloyd Fresco** Extensive pilferage	Netherlands	Dacca
147.	? Nov	**Banbury**	UK	Santos
148.	? Nov	**British Spey**	UK	Santos
149.	? Nov	**Strut Helgin**	UK	Busan Korea
150.	? Dec	**Kubbar**	S Korea	Buenaventura
151.	? Dec	**?** (Fishing trawler) Pirates with Mig rifles killed all 9 crew	?	?
152.—154.	? Dec	**?**(3 sailing boats) Pirates took cash and supplies	?	Bahamas
155.	? 1981	**Saint Paul** (Roads) 6 pirates with machetes	France	Cotonou
156.	? 1981	**Explorer II** (Shrimp boat) Reported seized by drug smugglers	?	Colombia
157.	? 1981	**Star III** (Fishing boat) Reported attacked by pirates	?	Riohacha Colombia

	Date	Vessel	Flag	Location
	1982			
158.	24 Jan	**Ikan Mas** (Fishing boat) Pirates (actually flying skull and crossbones) stole 40,000 in cash and property	Malaysia	Natunas Islands
159.	28 Jan	**Nedlloyd Marseilles** (Berth) 15 pirates in speedboats beaten off with police assistance (but some pilfering)	Netherlands (0310)	Apapa
160.	28 Jan	**Magnificence Venture**	Liberia	Singapore area
161.	31 Jan	**Alta** (Repairing engines) Fired on by pirates in motorboat— some wearing guerilla uniform. After 30 minutes, during which the vessel tried to ram the pirates, the pirates gave up	Liberia (1100)	Nicaragua
162.	? Jan	? (Anchorage—15m offshore) (0430) 35 pirates in canoes hurles bottles and detonators (one detonator blew hole in defensive hose) Seemed half drunk	?	Bonny
163.	? Jan	**Vegaland** Pirate attack	Sweden	Equit Guinea
164.	? Jan	**Manchester Fulmar**	UK	Naples
165.	2 Feb	**Yuyo Maru**	Japan	Singapore area
166.	5 Feb	**Chief Dragon**	Taiwan	Singapore area
167.	5 Feb	**World Unicorn** (Anchorage) Pirates held officer at knife point—robbed safe	UK (Early hours)	Jakarta
168.	7 Feb	**Apapa Palm**	UK	Freetown
169.	27 Feb	**Crown Atland**	?	Singapore area
170.	9 Mar	**Josephine** Pirates repelled	?	Borneo
171.	13 Mar	**Lei Tsu**	Taiwan	Singapore area
172.	16 Mar	**Asian Hawk**	Panama	Singapore area
173.	18 Mar	**Neptune Turquoise** (8 knots) Master's wife held at knife point—pirates failed to open safe—stole stereo system	Singapore (0330)	Singapore Strait
174.	19 Mar	**Miwon Line**	S Korea	Singapore area
175.	21 Mar	**Frankfurt Express**	Panama	Singapore area
176.	21 Mar	**Piolet Island**	?	Singapore area
177.	23 Mar	**Norman**	?	Singapore area
178.	27 Mar	**Afran Star**	Liberia	Makassco Strait Borneo
179.	29 Mar	? Pirates caused head injury to first officer	Japan	Borneo
180.	6 Apr	**Quellin** (0300) 3 armed pirates attacked chief officer—stole property	Belgium	Abidjan
181.	11 Apr	?	W Germany	Apapa
182.	12 Apr	**Danimar** Attacked by five pirates	Panama	Singapore
183.	12 Apr	**Joseph Lykes** Pirates boarded and took cargo	US	Guayaquil
184.	13 Apr	**James Lykes** Pirates boarded and took cargo	US	Cartagena Columbia

	Date	Vessel	Flag	Location
185.	13 Apr	**Whip Ray** (Yacht)	US	Bahamas
		Yachtsman shot 3 pirates dead after they came on board on the pretext of selling fish. Police were satisfied this was self defence		
186.	27 Apr	**Montauk Gannet**	?	Phillip Channel
187.	25 May	Divine Valley	Panama	Singapore
		5 pirates took $8325 in cash and valuables		
188.	27 May	**Rose Garden Maru**	Japan	Singapore
		4 pirates took $1300		
189.	? May	**Voyager** (Yacht)(At sea)	? (0145)	Manila Bay
		5 armed pirates took £30,000 and much equipment		
190.	5 Jun	**British Kennet** (At jetty)	UK	Santos
		Master attacked when surprised pirates in cabin. Pirates escaped with property—crew gave chase in ship's boat—without success. No help from police		
191.	6 Jun	**Fellow Wealth**	Panama	Singapore area
		3 pirates took cargo worth $200		
192.	17 Jun	**Biscay**	Japan	Phillip Channel
		3 pirates took cash from master's strong box		
193.	18 Jun	**?** (0200)	Japan	Tinta
		Indonesia Pirates kidnapped crew members, took $2300 and property		
194.	26 Jun	**Nordheide**	W Germany	Lagos
195.	26 Jun	**?**	Singapore	Lagos
196.	28 Jun	**?** (Roads)	Greece	Lagos
		10 armed pirates forced and robbed 2 containers		
197.	? Jun	**Costa Andaluza** (at sea)	Spain	Cabo San Lorenzo Colombia
198.	? Jun	**Nordbay**	Singapore	Kingston Jamaica
199.	? Jun	**Mahonia**	Panama	Dar es Salaam
200.	21 Jul	**World Cliff**	Liberia (Early hours)	SW of Singapore
		4 pirates with knives stole personal property—raided safe		
201.	? Jul	**Kirsten Frank**	?	Apapa
		Pirates took fish		
202.	? Jul	**Arlil**	?	Apapa
203.	3 Aug	**African Camellia**	US	Lagos
		4 pirates with pistols and knives robbed master		
204.	5 Aug	**White Star**	Panama	Lagos
205.	6 Aug	**Beauxarts**	Panama	Phillip Channel
		4 pirates took $1500		
206.	8 Aug	**Al Wattyah**	Kuwait	Singapore area
		2-3 pirates took cash and personal property		
207.	11 Aug	**Agrilia**	Panama	Phillip Channel
		8 pirates took a watch, value $89		
208.	12 Aug	**Tulip**	Panama (Daybreak)	Singapore
		4 armed pirates fled with nothing when spotted		
209.	12 Aug	**Port Latta Maru**	Japan	Phillip Channel
		4 pirates took cash from master's cabin		
210.	12 Aug	**Nippo Maru**	Japan	Phillip Channel
		5 pirates took $650		

	Date	Vessel	Flag	Location
211.	12 Aug	**Antares**	?	Lagos
		Pirates damaged accommodation, took property		
212.	13 Aug	**African Hyacinth**	? (Early morning)	Lagos
		Boarded by 4 pirates		
213.	17 Aug	**Seki Rolette**	Japan	Monrovia
214.	19 Aug	**Homeria**	Panama	E of Singapore
		Pirates took $15,650		
215.	19 Aug	**?**	Japan (0500)	Singapore Strait
		Pirates with swords took crew's cash and property		
216.	22 Aug	**Nedlloyd Steenkerk** (5m offshore)	Netherlands	Apapa
		Pirates fired on crew, injuring four Containers forced and robbed. No response to calls for help		
217.	24 Aug	**?**	Greece	Lagos
		7 armed pirates took crew's personal property		
218.	24 Aug	**Seki Rolette**	Japan	Lagos
219.	25 Aug	**Lanka Siri**	Sri Lanka (0515)	Singapore area
		7 pirates with swords and knives fled when spotted in master's cabin		
220.	25 Aug	**Seiwa Maru**	Japan	Phillip Channel
		Pirates repelled		
221.	26 Aug	**Asian Rose**	Japan	Indonesia
		One pirate took $1962		
222.	27 Aug	**Frigo Asia** (Waiting for berth)	Spain (0200)	Lagos
		6 pirates overpowered crew—took $8000 and valuables		
223.	29 Aug	**Bunga Dahlia**	Malaysia (0615)	Phillip Channel
		Pirates took safe and property from master's cabin		
224.	29 Aug	**Pampero**	W Germany	Apapa
225.	? Aug	**Kirsten Frank**	Denmark	Lagos
226.	? Aug	**Arlil**	Denmark	Lagos
227.	? Aug	**Nedlloyd Steenkerk**	Netherlands	Cotonou
		Theft from cargo—in spite of armed guards		
228.	? Aug	**Nedlloyd Steenkerk**	Netherlands	Lome
		Theft from cargo—in spite of armed guards		
229.	? Aug	**Nedlloyd Steenkerk** (Anchor waiting for pilot)	Netherlands	Dakar
		Pirates took cargo		
230.	? Aug	**Nedlloyd Steenkerk**	Netherlands	Gambia
		Pirates threatened crew—took cargo		
231.	? Aug	**Nedlloyd Steenkerk**	Netherlands	Lagos
		Crew injured in pirate attack No reply from authorities		
232.	2 Sep	**Kasugu Maru**	Japan	Phillip Channel
		Pirates repelled		
233-5.	6 Sep	**?(3 ships)**	?	Lagos
236.	9 Sep	**Benvalla**	UK (0615)	Singapore Strait
		Property and cash value $11,000 taken from master's cabin—Pirates, unseen, left rope hanging over the side		
237.	12 Sep	**Nigerian Brewer**	W Germany	Lagos
		8 pirates fired at crew—pilfered containers		
238.	15 Sep	**Palmstar Orchid**	Singapore (0300)	Phillip Channel
		Pirates took safe, $4500 and medicines		

	Date	Vessel	Flag	Location
239.	15 Sep	**Japan Stork** 4 pirates took cash and mooring line	Japan	Phillip Channel
240.	15 Sep	**Iso Kasuma** 5 pirates took $3250	Malaysia	Phillip Channel
241.	16 Sep	**Grand Globe** 4 pirates stole $300	Liberia	Singapore area
242.	16 Sep	**Meiji Maru** Pirates repelled	Japan	Phillip Channel
243.	17 Sep	**San Bruno** Attacked by 5 pirates	Philippines	Phillip Channel
244.	19 Sep	**Neptune Leo** Crewmember chased with machete Ships safe with $17,200 stolen	Singapore	Singapore area
245.	19 Sep	**World Radiance** Pirates took money	Liberia	Singapore area
246.	23 Sep	**Am Carrier** Pirates took medical equipment	Japan	Singapore area
247.	24 Sep	**?** (Roads) 4 armed pirates stole cash	Greece Lagos	
248.	25 Sep	**?** (Anchorage) 5 pirates with swords took crew's property	Japan (0500)	Jurong Singapore
249.	29 Sep	**Golar Kanto** (Taking supplies from launch) Unseen pirates stole master's safe with $30,000	Liberia	Singapore area
250.	12 Oct	**Seki Rokel** Boarded by pirates	Japan	Port Harcourt
251.	16 Oct	**Yick Wing** Boarded by pirates	?	Singapore area
252.	17 Oct	**Hua Hin** Thieves stole television and watch	Malaysia	Singapore area
253.	22 Oct	**Bonvoy** Attacked by 4 pirates	Honduras	Singapore area
254.	22 Oct	**Thai Yung** Pirates injured captain—stole one watch	Taiwan	Phillip Channel
255.	22 Oct	**Plata**	W Germany	Phillip Channel
256.	24 Oct	**Sincere**	?	Off Singapore
257.	26 Oct	**Ratana Bhum** Thieves took radio and cash	India	Off Singapore
258.	27 Oct	**Eiwa Maru** 4 pirates with swords, threatened crew, ransacked vessel, took $2500	Japan	Phillip Channel
259.	29 Oct	**Hand Ming** 4 pirates stole $50,000	Panama	Singapore area
260.	? Oct	**?**	UK	Freetown
261.	? Oct	**?**	?	Port Harcourt
262.	1 Nov	**Kota Suria** 4 pirates stole $3500	?	Off Singapore
263.	2 Nov	**Botany Triumph**	Panama	Lagos
264.	3 Nov	**?** Pirates shot at vessel from fast launch—escaped by making zig zag course	E Germany (0440)	Maldives
265.	8 Nov	**?** (Roads) About 70 pirates in 7 boats decided against an attack when they saw the crew on deck	E Germany (2100)	Madras

	Date	Vessel	Flag	Location
266.	9 Nov	**St Paulia** 4 pirates stole $1550	Panama	Singapore area
267.	10 Nov	**Cys Knight** Attacked by 3 pirates	Liberia	Singapore area
268.	10 Nov	**Seizan Maru** Pirates took cash	Liberia	Singapore area
269.	10 Nov	**Kapitan Trader**	?	Santos
270.	11 Nov	**Orient Coral**	Liberia	Santos
271.	11 Nov	**Sivand**	Iran	Singapore area
272.	11 Nov	**Midas Apollo** (Anchorage) Pirates with machine guns badly beat crew—stole cash and valuables	Liberia	Lagos
273.	12 Nov	**Esso Hafnia** (Petroleum pier) Master stabbed and robbed in cabin when resisted Local guards left shortly after coming on board	Denmark (0200)	Dakar
274.	12 Nov	**Stolt Condor** Pirates stole $13,000 and property	Liberia	Phillip Channel
275.	12 Nov	**Mobil Endurance** Pirates took $100 and property	Norway	Phillip Channel
276.	12 Nov	**Shenandoah** 6 pirates took $5500	Greece (0300)	Singapore area
277.	12 Nov	**Great Fortune**	?	Singapore area
278.	13 Nov	**?** (Roads) Armed pirates repelled by crew	Greece	Lagos
279.	15 Nov	**?**	?	Lagos
280.	15 Nov	**Yuyo Maru**	Japan	Singapore area
281.	22 Nov	**?** (Fishing trawler) 30 pirates from merchant vessel drowned 8 crew by stuffing them in sacks and throwing them in the sea (there were 3 survivors). Pirates took catch value $30,000	?	Bay of Bengal
282.	26 Nov	**Tomoe** Safe stolen	Japan	Phillip Channel
283.	29 Nov	**Eastern Virgo** $4500 cash stolen	?	Phillip Channel
284.	? Nov	**Lucky Penny** (Anchorage) 20 pirates armed with rifles	Cyprus	Lagos
285.	? Nov	**Southwind** (Berth) 20 pirates armed with rifles	Greece	Lagos
286.	? Nov	**Dimitra** 20 pirates armed with rifles	Greece	Lagos
287.	1 Dec	**Baltic** (Anchorage) Pirates with guns forced cook to show them valuables and money whilst rest of crew locked in engine room. Patrol boat arrived killing 1 pirate and causing 4 to drown	Netherlands (0515)	Lagos
288.	15 Dec	**?** (Roads) 15 armed pirates assaulted crew—took property from cabins	Greece	Lagos
289.	24 Dec	**?** Pirates took crew's clothes	Japan (2345)	Singapore Strait

	Date	Vessel	Flag	Location
290.	24 Dec	**Tansondo Express**	?	Lagos
		(Anchorage 12m off shore)(2345)		
		Crew returned pirates' fire—master put vessel (still at anchor) astern under power. Pirates repelled after 45 minutes. No reply from shore to urgent radio appeals		
291.	26 Dec	**Vegaland**	Sweden	Lagos
		(20m off shore)	(2300)	
		Crew locked themselves in accommodation—except one who was forced to assist carrying cargo to pirates' canoes. One crewmember injured (shot in leg)		
292.	28 Dec	**Tarn**	Sweden	Lagos
		(20m off shore)		
		Pirates shot and wounded officer, raped stewardess. Provoked Sweden's submission to IMO		
293.	? Dec	**Snowfrost**	Greece	Cotonou
		(Roads)	(0030)	
		15 pirates in large motor boats with pistols/ knives—Beat crew when he refused to indicate master's cabin—Shot at master and assaulted him. Safe was empty—stole some other property. Pirates were on board for 3 hours		
294.	? 1982	**Nyn** (Early 1982)	?	Port of Spain
		(Yacht)		
		Michael Crocker strangled on board by armed intruder		
295.	? 1982	**Belle Esprit** (Early 1982)	?	Nassau
		(Yacht)		
		Attacked by 5 speedboats—50 bullet holes in hull. Rescued by police spotter plane		
1983				
296.	4 Jan	**Nedlloyd Madras**	Netherlands	Lagos
		(Anchorage)	(Daylight)	
		Pirates forced and robbed two containers		
297.	4 Jan	**Athene**	Sweden	Lagos
298.	5 Jan	**Lucie Delmas**	France	Lagos
299.	7 Jan	**Aegis Athenic**	Greece	Lagos
		(Roads)		
		6 armed pirates forced and robbed containers		
300.	7 Jan	**Nedlloyd Madras**	Netherlands	Lagos
			(Daylight)	
		Pirates forced and robbed containers		
301.	10 Jan	**Diamond Glory**	Panama	Singapore area
		Cash and video camera stolen		
302.	10 Jan	**Sealift Arctic**	US	Singapore area
		7 armed pirates took property—including TV and credit cards from master's cabin		
303.	13 Jan	**Bokuho**	Panama	Singapore area
		2 pirates took $3000		
304.	13 Jan	**Dimitra**	Greece	Lagos
305.	15 Jan	**South Sea**	Liberia	Singapore area
306.	16 Jan	**South Sea**	Liberia	Peak Island
			(0215)	Indonesia
		4 pirates stole cash		
307.	17 Jan	**Export Challenger**	US	Lagos
		12 pirates in fishing canoe stole tinned milk		
308.	17 Jan	**Anne Sif**	Denmark	Lagos
			(0515)	
		30 pirates in 5 boats broke into containers in spite of bow and arrow men on board. Patrol boat arrived too late		

	Date	Vessel	Flag	Location
309.	21 Jan	**Aristee**	France (2200)	Lagos
		8 pirates with revolvers broke into containers and took 150 cases champagne		
310.	23 Jan	**Magnificence Venture**	Liberia (0500)	Singapore area
		6 pirates threatened master with knife. Took $500 cash and property		
311.	25 Jan	? (Anchorage)	W Germany (Morning)	Lagos
		Armed pirates forced and robbed containers		
312.	26 Jan	?	Japan	Aljuna Indonesia
		2 pirates detained crew and took property		
313.	? Jan	**Spartan**	US	Singapore area
		Attack repelled		
314.	? Jan	**Amphion**	Greece	Buenaventura Colombia
315.	? Jan	**Jessica**	?	Lagos
		Pirates took cargo		
316.	? Jan	**Typhoon**	W Germany (0900)	Lagos
		Attacked by armed pirates		
317.	? Jan	**Renica** (Yacht)	?	Antigua
		Attacked and robbed		
318.	2 Feb	**Yuyo Maru**	Japan (0540)	Singapore area
		6 pirates stole cash		
319.	3 Feb	**Golden Wave**	?	Santos
		Money and property stolen from master's cabin		
320.	5 Feb	**Chief Dragon**	Taiwan (0520)	Singapore area
		Pirates took cash and property		
321.	6 Feb	**Bruse Jarl** (Anchorage)	Norway	Lagos
		Armed pirates robbed crew of all their valuables—2 stewardesses raped 27 crew immediately asked to sign off		
322.	7 Feb	**Sea Silk Road**	Japan (0300)	Singapore area
		4 pirates with swords took cash and property		
323.	7 Feb	**Crown Atland** (At sea)	Sweden (0430)	Djakarta area
		4 pirates with knives attacked chief mate in cabin after pirate watch stood down		
324.	11 Feb	**Aminta** (Anchorage)	Italy (0420)	Lagos
		Pirates robbed crew and seriously injured hand of one crew		
325.	17 Feb	**Ouranio-Toxo**	Greece	Lagos
		Pirates stole cargo		
326.	17 Feb	? (Harbour)	? (0400)	Palembang Indonesia
		Pirates threatened master—took cash, property		
327.	21 Feb	**Panama**	Denmark	Lagos
328.	25 Feb	**Lonelil**	Denmark	Benin
329.	? Feb	**USNS Truckee**	US	Naples
		2 pirates discovered by crew—one chased into the water, the other into a waiting boat		

	Date	Vessel	Flag	Location
330.	? Feb	**Del Monte** (Anchorage) Thieves pilfered foodstuffs	US	Takoradi
331.	? Feb	? 12-16 pirates boarded, shot at, threatened crew—spent 3 hours searching for valuables	? (0130)	Apapa
332.	? Feb	**Juncta Maru** Cash and valuables stolen—Some arrests made	Japan	Musi River Indonesia
333.	8 Mar	? 7 pirates with knives and cudgels took mooring line—Left when confronted by master—after inflicting facial cut on him	E Germany (2100)	Singapore Strait
334.	9 Mar	? 3 pirates took cash	Japan	Singapore Strait
335.	12 Mar	**Amelia Topic** Thieves took safe while master ashore	Liberia	Santos
336.	13 Mar	**Lai Tsu** 2 pirates with long knives took $350	Taiwan (0300)	Singapore area
337.	13 Mar	**Archilles**	Singapore	Singapore area
338.	15 Mar	**Orco Trader** Pirates with knives abandoned attempt after confronting master—Stole wristwatch	Liberia (2330)	Singapore area
339.	16 Mar	**Asian Hawk** Pirates stole $4182	Panama (0100-0500)	Singapore area
340.	18 Mar	**Avra Bravery** Cassette player and radio stolen	Liberia (0230)	Singapore area
341.	18 Mar	**Neptune Turquoise** Pirates took hi fi system	Singapore (0400)	Singapore area
342.	18 Mar	? (Anchorage) 20 pirates took property worth DKr 200,000	Denmark	Lagos
343.	19 Mar	**Miwon Line** Pirates took property	S Korea	Singapore area
344.	19 Mar	? (Roads) Armed pirates punched, wounded one crew, and shot another in fibula Naval vessel turned up too late	W Germany (Night)	Lagos
345.	20 Mar	? Pirates took cash	Japan	Singapore Strait
346.	21 Mar	**Frankfurt Express** (At sea) Some property stolen	Panama (0110)	Singapore area
347.	21 Mar	**Piolet Island** Pirates stole cash and long sword	? (0540)	Singapore area
348.	21 Mar	**Strider Crystal** (At berth) Safe removed, master's property stolen	Bermuda	Santos
349.	23 Mar	**Norman** Pirates took $1600	Panama	Singapore area
350.	23 Mar	**Stolt Crown**	Liberia	Phillip Channel

	Date	Vessel	Flag	Location
351.	24 Mar	**African Express**	Netherlands (0815)	Malacca Strait
		Pirates stole around £76,000		
352.	25 Mar	**Narnian Sea** (14 knots)	UK (0330)	Malacca Strait
		7 pirates in speedboat with knives- succeeded in stealing rope before frightened off by crew		
353.	5 Apr	**Pegasus Pride**	S Korea (2308)	Malacca Strait
354.	7 Apr	**Pacific Exporter**	Liberia (0315)	Phillip Channel
		Pirates took $3000 and property		
355.	7 Apr	**Strathconan**	Singapore (0430)	Malacca Strait
		Thieves stole property and cash		
356.	7 Apr	**Setco Mammoth**	? (2220)	Singapore area
		Thieves stole $1100 cash and property		
357.	10 Apr	**Sidharta** (Yacht)	?	Spratly Islands
		Shelled, set on fire—one crew killed May have been Vietnamese soldiers		
358.	13 Apr	**Sun Grace** Singapore	Japan (2330)	Pulau Kutup
		Unknown items taken		
359.	14 Apr	**To Yo Fujimaku**	Japan (0100)	Phillip Channel
		Pirates fled empty handed when discovered by crew		
360.	14 Apr	**Bunga Mas** (At sea off Channel)	Malaysia (0250)	Phillip Channel
		Pirates stole $4000 cash		
361.	14 Apr	**Skoun Ambassador**	?	Malacca Strait
		Cash and property stolen		
362.	15 Apr	? (Harbour)	Japan (0400)	Java
		2 pirates with swords took cash and property		
363.	18 Apr	**Van Er Stel**	? (0400-0600)	Singapore Strait
		Cash and equipment stolen		
364.	20 Apr	**Lips**	Greece	Santos
		Safe removed, property stolen from master		
365.	22 Apr	**Yumiko** (At sea)	Panama (0200)	Indonesia area
		Cash and watch stolen		
366.	22 Apr	?	Japan	Tinta Indonesia
		4 pirates took cash 1 pirate captured by crew—handed to police		
367.	? Apr	**Quedlingburg** (At sea)	E Germany	Phillipines area
		Pirates repelled		
368.	4 May	**Palm Star Cherry**	Singapore (0500)	Phillip Channel
		9 armed pirates took $400 from master's cabin		
369.	4 May	**Montauk Garnet**	Panama	Phillip Channel
		2 armed pirates put knife to master's throat—stole safe containing $1700		
370.	8 May	?	E Germany (0245)	Lagos
		Pirates robbed containers		

	Date	Vessel	Flag	Location
371.	8 May	?	Japan (0100)	Singapore Strait
		Pirates with swords took cash and property		
372.	8 May	**Aurora Glory**	? (0300-0430)	Phillip Channel
		Safebox containing $1500 stolen		
373.	12 May	**Southern Cruiser**	? (2200-2300)	Phillip Channel
		Property stolen from master's cabin		
374.	13 May	**Estherlu**	Panama (0300)	Singapore area
		Empty safe stolen from master's cabin		
375.	19 May	**Benvalla** (13 knots)	UK (0300)	Singapore Strait
		8 pirates stole watch from cabin—fled when alarm sounded		
376.	19 May	?	E Germany	Malacca Strait
		Pirates stole property		
377.	19 May	?	Greece	Singapore Strait
		7 armed pirates repelled by crew		
378.	19 May	**An Ping**	?	Singapore area
379.	1 Jun	?	Norway	Sierre Leone
		Armed pirates repelled		
380.	2 Jun	**Benvalla**	UK	Singapore Strait
381.	3 Jun	**Benvorlich** (Discharging)	UK (0200)	Santos
		Armed pirates attacked and bound master, struck radio officer on head—took £2300		
382.	14 Jun	?	Japan (0500)	Olympia USA
		Pirates attacked crew and took cash		
383.	16 Jun	?	Japan (2100)	Singapore Strait
		Pirates repelled		
384.	16 Jun	?	Japan (0100)	Singapore Strait
		Pirates boarded from speedboat—took equipment		
385.	20 Jun	**Yaguari**	?	Santos
		Pirates caught pilfering containers fled to waiting boat		
386.	24 Jun	**Lanka Siri**	Sri Lanka	Singapore area
387.	25 Jun	**Takachiho Maru**	Japan	Santos
		6 pirates attacked master, forced him to open safe—Master injured on forehead		
388.	? Jun	**Lucy of Wessex** (Yacht)	? (Anchor)	Antigua
		Pirates took property		
389.	2 Jul	**Chie Maru** (13 knots)	Japan (0030)	Malacca Straits
		5 pirates with machetes attacked master—Robbed crew of £1800 cash		
390.	7 Jul	**Stena Oceania** (13 knots)	Sweden (2230)	Phillip Channel
		Pirates took safe, attacked radio officer—left without being discovered by rest of crew		
391.	7 Jul	? (Roads)	W Germany (Night)	Dakar
		Pirates repelled		
392.	8 Jul	**Neptune C** (Berth)	Greece	Santos
		Safe forced open while master ashore		

	Date	Vessel	Flag	Location
393.	9 Jul	**Mega Taurus**	Japan (Early hours)	Malacca Strait
		5 pirates with machetes robbed Master of 80,000 yen		
394.	21 Jul	**Asia Honesty**	Liberia	Santos
		Thieves stole property from cabin		
395.	23 Jul	? (Inner Roads)	E Germany (0400)	Penang Malaysia
		5 pirates repelled		
396.	26 Jul	?	W Germany (Morning)	Lagos
		15 armed pirates forced and robbed containers Disappeared on arrival of police		
397.	27 Jul	**La Minera**	Bahamas	Conakry
		Up to 100 pirates attacked vessel in daylight for two days—without interference from authorities. Took hydraulic jacks, forced, robbed containers. Attacked two crew		
398.	2 Aug	**Margas**	UK	Santos
399.	5 Aug	?	Indonesia	Phillip Channel
		Armed pirates forced safe—took $15,000 5 members of gang later arrested by Indonesian police at base on Batam Island, property seized		
400.	19 Aug	**Great Universe**	Taiwan	Santos
		Armed pirates forced master's cabin—stole property		
401.	24 Aug	?	Japan (0300)	Lagos
		20 pirates injured crew—forced and robbed containers		
402.	31 Aug	**Seven**	Italy	Monrovia
403.	31 Aug	**Lloyd Genova**	Brazil	Monrovia
404.	31 Aug	**Export Challenger**	US	Monrovia
405.	9 Sept	**Angelic Protector** (At berth)	Greece (2030)	Santos
		Armed pirates with stocking masks kidnapped chief officer, ransacked master's cabin and took safe. Police arrived after pirates had left		
406.	9 Sep	?	Greece	Santos
		5 armed pirates stole cash from master's box		
407.	13 Sep	?	Greece	Santos
		Armed pirates attacked two crew—robbed cabins		
408.	13 Sep	**Kapetanissa**	Greece	Santos
		Pirates seriously wounded several crew Took $3000 cash		
409.	21 Sep	**Fengtien**	UK	Lagos
410.	? Sep	**Almaloz**	?	Santos
411.	? Sep	**Yaguan**	?	Santos
412.	4 Oct	**Amazona**	Panama	Benin
413.	4 Oct	**Amazona**	Panama (0430)	Bonny
		Ship's laundry raided by women pirates		
414.	8 Oct	**Durian**	Singapore (Early hours)	Santos
		Pirates took safe with $2,700 and valuables from master's cabin		
415.	13 Oct	?	W Germany (Successive nights)	Matadi Zaire
		Containers forced and robbed—General alarm sounded but no help available at night		
416.	15 Oct	? (Inner roads)	W Germany (Night)	Abidjan
		20 pirates bound crewman on watch—forced and robbed containers Authorities did not respond to calls for help		

	Date	Vessel	Flag	Location
417.	17 Oct	?	?	Sabah
		(Fishing vessel)	(44 km from coast)	
		5 fishermen reported missing after being shot at from 2 speedboats		
418.	23 Oct	**Sara Hashim**	S Arabia	Spratly Island
419.	23 Oct	?	W Germany	Matadi Zaire
		Armed pirates—injured crew Authorities took no action		
420.	25 Oct	?	W Germany	Matadi Zaire
			(Night)	
		10 armed pirates—forced and robbed 8 containers Held crew at gun-point		
421.	27 Oct	?	E Germany	Chittagong
		(Roads)	(0030)	
		4 mooring lines stolen—undetected by crew patrols		
422.	6 Nov	?	W Germany	Lagos
		(Loading)	(Morning/Noon)	
		20 pirates made two attacks—One crewman injured in head and shoulder Harbour police appeared but pirates escaped		
423.	10 Nov	?	E Germany	Chalna
			(1030)	(Bangladesh)
		20 pirates with knives and crowbars retreated when alarm sounded		
424.	12 Dec	?	Netherlands	Guayaquil
			(1930)	Ecuador
		10 pirates with knives stole equipment—fled when crew resisted		
425.	20 Dec	?	Denmark	Lagos
		(Roads)	(0145)	
		20 armed pirates hit crewman with iron pipe and stole property		
426.	25 Dec	**Lago Izabal**	Guatemala	Tampico Mexico
427.	28 Dec	**Maaskant**	Belgium	Madras
		(At anchor)	(2030)	
		Crew pursued pirates escaping with mooring rope in small boat—but failed to catch them		
428.	? 1983	**Tarn**	Sweden	Equit Guinea
429.	? 1983	**Agrilia**	Panama	Off Singapore
430.	? 1982/3	?(Yacht)(Nov 1981-May 1983)		Tobago
		(At anchor)		
		Yachtsman strangled		
431.	? 1982/3	?(Yacht)(Nov 1981-May 1983)		Grenada
		Shots exchanged between Swedish yacht crew and local policeman—one Grenadian member of yacht crew killed Crew held for a few days, then released		
432.	? 1982/3	?(Yacht)(Nov 1981-May 1983)		St Lucia
		(At anchor)		
		American couple robbed at gunpoint, woman raped		

1984

	Date	Vessel	Flag	Location
433.	? Jan	**Pocahontas**	Belgium	Santos
		Pirates trying to open safe fled when surprised by master		
434.	10 Feb	**Scilla**	W Germany	Port Harcourt
		(Loading)	(Evening)	
		2 attacks by 20 pirates with knives, boathooks, bottles. Fought off with signal rockets, but crew injured by thrown bottles Authorities did not respond to calls for help		
435.	12 Feb	**Warri Flyer**	Belgium	Lagos
436.	17 Feb	?(Fishing vessel)	?	Savah
		One fisherman killed, 2 wounded by gunfire		
437.	18 Feb	?	Greece	Warri Nigeria
		Armed pirates stole ropes		

	Date	Vessel	Flag	Location
438.	19 Feb	**Chevron Pacific** (Roads)	Liberia (1000)	Madras
		5 pirates in sailing boat took hoses and equipment Merged into nearby fleet of fishing vessels		
439.	22 Feb	**Chevron Pacific** (Approach to Roads)(14 knots)	Liberia (Night)	Visakhapatnam
		Pirates repelled with water jets No police action taken in response to complaint		
440.	? Feb	**Inverlock**	Liberia	Barcelona
441.	? Feb	**Severance** (Yacht)(At Anchor)	? (Night)	Antigua
		2 black pirates—under influence drink and drugs Took yacht out to sea—Bound crew—Raped woman twice One pirate detained by crew—other arrested later		
442.	19 Mar	?	UK (0300)	Phillip Channel
		8 pirates stole crewman's watch and mooring lines		
443.	25 Mar	?	UK (0330)	Phillip Channel
		Armed pirates withdrew when challenged by armed patrol on ship		
444.	28 Mar	**Ho Ming No 7**	Panama	Puerto Sardin
		Attacked from submersible craft		
445.	3 Apr	?	Greece	Singapore Strait
		2 pirates assaulted, bound crew Took unspecified goods		
446.	19 Apr	**Akindynos C**	Greece (0330)	Freetown S Leone
		Armed pirates stole equipment worth $50,000		
447.	3 Jun	?	Greece (0330)	Singapore Strait
		5 armed pirates punched, bound crew—took property		
448.	25 Jun	?	?	Singapore area
449.	29 Jun	?	? (0100)	Singapore Strait
450.	25 Jul	?	? (0255)	Phillip Channel
451.	3 Aug	?	? (0005)	Singapore Strait
452.	4 Aug	?	? (0300)	Singapore Strait
453.	6 Aug	?	? (0030)	Singapore Strait
454.	11 Aug	? (Motor launch)	?	Samporna
		Philippines Pirates with sub machine guns killed 33 out of 51 passengers—abducted 3 girls		
455.	29 Aug	? (On roads)	Netherlands (0145)	Santos
		4 pirates with 2-way radio—one shot fired Crew retreated to accommodation—Forced container, took radio equipment		
456.	3 Sep	?	Netherlands (0430)	Monrovia
		Pirates with pistol threatened officer on watch—lowered equipment from foc'sle into small boat alongside		
457.	10 Sep	? (Roads)	E Germany (2050)	Chittagong
		Pirates stole mooring lines—undetected by ship's patrols		

	Date	Vessel	Flag	Location
458.	12 Sep	? (Roads)	W Germany (0625)	Freetown
		Armed pirates forced and robbed 3 containers—stole crew's property. Naval vessel arrived too late		
459.	21 Sep	**Gianina/Samual Antonio**		Nauta Peru
		Pirates attacked convoy carrying gasoline—shot 8 passengers and crew dead. One survived by jumping into river. Pirates transhipped gasoline—tug and barge later found moored downriver		
460.	22 Sep	?	W Germany (0600)	Abidjan
		20 armed pirates forced and robbed containers		
461.	? Sep	**Santo Trader** (At quay)	Liberia (Evening)	Cilacap Java
		Pirates with machetes threatened master, took cash from safe		
462.	3 Oct	?	Japan (0100)	Singapore Strait
		Unseen pirates stole master's property		
463.	6 Oct	?	W Germany	Monrovia
		Pirates held crew at gunpoint. Forced and robbed containers		
464.	9 Oct	?	W Germany (0520)	Abidjan
		Armed pirates seriously attacked crew—stole some property		
465.	12 Oct	?	W Germany	Freetown, S Leone
		Armed pirates forced and robbed containers		
466.	28 Oct	?	Greece (1000)	Conakry
		Armed pirates forced and robbed crew cabins and transit stores—Stole sacks of cargo		
467.	6 Nov	?	W Germany (0320)	Abidjan
		30 armed pirates forced and robbed 7 containers		
468.	7 Nov	? (At quay)	Japan	Santos
		Intruder stole property		
469.	12 Nov	? (Roads)	Netherlands (2330)	Georgetown Guyana
		8 armed pirates stole equipment		
470.	22 Nov	?	Japan	Singapore Strait
		Pirates stole $6000 from master		
471.	25 Nov	? (Roads)	W Germany (0400)	Kingston Jamaica
		Pirates forced containers—stole equipment. Spent 1.5 hours on vessel		
472.	1 Dec	?	Greece (2000)	Singapore Strait
		4 armed pirates punched master, robbed crew cabins		
473.	8 Dec	?	Greece	Singapore Strait
		Pirates using grapnels repelled		
474.	9 Dec	?	Denmark (0520)	Lagos
		Pirates with knives stole 100 metres of rope Patrol boat arrived too late		
475.	12 Dec	?	W Germany (0200)	Matadi Zaire
		Armed pirates forced and robbed containers		
476.	14 Dec	?	W Germany	Douala
		20 armed pirates damaged containers and emergency equipment		
477.	14 Dec	?	W Germany	Dakar
		Pirates wounded stevedore—forced and robbed container		

	Date	Vessel	Flag	Location
478.	16 Dec		W Germany	Freetown S Leone
		Pirates forced and robbed containers		
479.	20 Dec	?	W Germany	Abidjan
		Containers forced and robbed		
480.	23 Dec	?	W Germany (0410)	Lagos
		Pirates forced and robbed container		
481.	28 Dec	**Nedlloyd Westerhamm** (Discharging)	W Germany (1520)	Freetown S Leone
		Armed pirates stole textiles and 40 cases of cigarettes—in spite of armed guards on board Collusion suspected		
482.	29 Dec	?	W Germany	Abidjan
		Armed pirates stole and damaged emergency equipment		
483.	? Dec	?	?	Georgetown Guyana
		Pirates boarded from 2 canoes—jumped into water when confronted by crew. (Compulsory) watchman suspected of collusion		
484.	? 1984	? (Yacht)	?	Exumas Islands
		William and Pat Kemerara murdered when they apparently came across a drugs transfer		
485.	? 1984	**Polymer III** (Yacht)	?	Florida Strait
		Walter Falconer and his yacht disappeared		
486.	? 1984	**Snowbound**	?	Bahamas
		Yachtsmen shot at, but escaped		
487.	? 1984	? (Yacht)	?	Colombia
		All on board killed		
488.	? 1984	? (Yacht)	?	Borneo
		Pirates with knives took everything—including the engine		
489.	? 1984	? (Yacht)	?	West Africa
		Yachtsman woken when 2 pirates tripped over—shot both of them dead. Left without telling authorities		
490.	? 1984	**Sea Wind** (Yacht)	?	Palmyra Island
		Yacht found abandoned on atoll—wife's skull found later. Attackers later convicted		
	1985			
491.	1 Jan	?	W Germany (0200)	Monrovia
		Armed pirates held crew at gunpoint, but were repelled		
492.	2 Jan	**Neptune Pegasus**	Australia (0100)	Singapore
		Thieves forced cabin—took $11,000 and property		
493.	7 Jan	?	W Germany	Conakry
		Armed pirates took lifesaving equipment before being repelled		
494.	12 Jan	?	W Germany (2300)	Freetown S Leone
		5 armed pirates forced open container and took contents (medical equipment)		
495.	15 Jan	?	?	Cartagena Spain
496.	20 Jan	**Fat Choy**	Liberia (0430)	Singapore Strait
		6 pirates bound crew member, took property value $12,000—no one else saw them come or leave		

	Date	Vessel	Flag	Location
497.	20 Jan	**Ocean Premier**	Singapore (0530)	Phillip Channel
		Unknown thieves took $63000 and property from master's cabin		
498.	22 Jan	**Kriti Emerald**	Greece (0300)	Malacca Strait
		Pirates forced captain's door and took property		
499.	23 Jan	**British Fidelity**	UK (0015)	Singapore Strait
		5 pirates with knives tied up Chief Officer and took property. No one else saw them arrive or leave		
500.	23 Jan	**Million II**	Malaysia (0215)	Singapore Strait
		5 pirates with knives attacked and bound master—Stole cash and property		
501.	25 Jan	?	W Germany	Freetown S Leone
		Gang stole electrical equipment from truck		
502.	28 Jan	?	W Germany	Abidjan
		Gang forced and robbed 12 containers		
503.	29 Jan	**Falcon Countess** (Chartered to US Navy)	US (2310)	Malacca Strait
		6 pirates with knives boarded using bamboo poles and hooks—Held crew at knifepoint—tied up Master—Took $19,500 and made off in speedboat		
504.	30 Jan	**Gas Al Minagish**	Kuwait	Phillip Channel
505.	30 Jan	**Tomoe 305**	Panama (0215)	Singapore area
		7 pirates with daggers—bound master—stole cash. No one else saw them arrive or leave		
506.	31 Jan	? (14 knots)	Kuwait	Phillip Channel
		Overtaken by pirates in boat travelling 20 knots Repelled them with fire hoses and alarm whistles		
507.	? Jan	**Hilaire Maurel** (At berth)	France (Daytime)	Conakry
		100 pirates stole "everything" from vessel—no official intervention		
508.	? Jan	? (At berth)	Panama (Daytime)	Conakry
		100 pirates again took an entire cargo—Police, customs, soldiers in quay ignored alarm signals		
509.	? Jan	**Coral Princess** (Entering port)(Passenger vsl)	?	Cebu Phillipines
		4 pirates scrambling up the side from canoes—Retreated when Coast Guard fired at them		
510.	1 Feb	?	?	Antwerp
511.	2 Feb	?	?	Cartagena
512.	12 Feb	**Warri Flyer**	Belgium (0300)	Lagos
		15 armed pirates threatened crew, took equipment After 30 mins, driven away by police		
513.	15 Feb	?	W Germany (0500)	Abidjan
		Pirates forced and robbed 7 containers		
514.	16 Feb	**Ratu Konsortium**	Malaysia (2215)	Phillip Channel
		5 pirates with parangs threatened crew—took Sing$3000 cash and property		
515.	20 Feb	**Pegasus Pride**	S Korea (0315)	Singapore Strait
		Armed pirates took $5000 cash and property		

	Date	Vessel	Flag	Location
516.	21 Feb	?	W Germany	Dar es Salaam
		Gang stole paint worth DM 12,000		
517.	21 Feb	**Ikan Dari**	Singapore (0500)	Singapore Strait
		Pirates with long swords tied up master Stole cash and property		
518.	21 Feb	**Rina** (10 knots)	Malaysia (0330)	Singapore Strait
		10 pirates with long swords—threatened crew, Stole some valuables		
519.	21 Feb	**Asia Star**	Panama (0520)	Singapore Strait
		3 armed pirates threatened crew—then fled when alarm sounded		
520.	24 Feb	**Sungari**	Liberia (0430)	Phillip Channel
		Entire safe and contents stolen by unseen pirates		
521.	27 Feb	**Stolt Venture** (Full speed)	Liberia (2245)	Malacca Strait
		4 pirates with knives tied up master Took cash bag with $12,000 from safe		
522.	4 Mar	**Maersk Rando**	Denmark (0150)	Malacca Strait
		5 pirates with knives and axes stole cash and goods		
523.	5 Mar	? (Roads)	Liberia (0600)	Port Esquivel Jamaica
		3 armed pirates held engine room crew at gunpoint. Stole goods		
524.	6 Mar	**Bunga Seroja**	Malaysia (0550)	Phillip Channel
		5 armed pirates threatened crew—then retreated to their boat without taking anything		
525.	8 Mar	**Ogden Brimstone**	Panama (0230)	Phillip Channel
		2 pirates seen leaving in boat, ropes seen hanging over stern- $8000 missing from cabin		
526.	15 Mar	?	W Germany	Abidjan
		Thieves cut mooring line		
527.	16 Mar	?	Denmark (2345)	Yanbu China
		4 pirates tied chief officer up—robbed him and master		
528.	16 Mar	**Dirch Maersk**	Denmark	Malacca Strait
529.	16 Mar	**Gandabrawira**	Liberia (2400)	Singapore Strait
		Unseen thieves stole master's cash		
530.	26 Mar	?	W Germany (0300)	Dar es Salaam
		1500 litres paint stolen		
531.	29 Mar	?	?	Port Harcourt
532.	3 Apr	?	Greece (0300)	Singapore Strait
		Armed pirates hit master—Took property (and video recorder) and cash		
533.	21 Apr	**Taifun** (Entering harbour)	Panama (0715)	Freetown S Leone
		20 armed pirates took equipment before being fought off by crew with signal rockets. Chief Officer attacked but escaped unhurt		
534.	22 Apr	**Jalagouri**	India (0030)	Dawe's Island Nigeria
		25 pirates with knives and iron bars threatened lookouts and took equipment from foc'sle store. No response to radio call for assistance		
535.	30 Apr	?	Greece	Singapore Strait
		Pirates punched Captain. Took video and goods and $750		

	Date	Vessel	Flag	Location
536.	3 May	**Stolt Heron** (Anchor)	Liberia (0600)	Jamaica
		Armed pirates stole portable tools. Crew called to bridge by master—and stayed there		
537.	5 May	**Vanelius** (Leaving port)	W Germany (1600)	Freetown S Leone
		20 pirates fired on and threw stones at vessel from boat. 2 Sierra Leone troops ran out of ammunition, allowing pirates to board and take household appliances and frozen chickens from containers. Value DM 120,000		
538.	12 May	?	?	Lagos
539.	19 May	?	Greece (0400)	Rouen
		2 armed pirates forced crew cabin—attacked and robbed him		
540.	24 May	**Kii-Maru**	Japan (0400)	Malacca Strait
		3 pirates frightened off by Master		
541.	29 May	**Kaga Maru**	Japan (0400)	Malacca Strait
		3 pirates with knives tied up Chief Officer. Took $30 and jewellery		
542.	29 May	**Kempas**	Malaysia (0520)	Malacca Strait
		6 armed pirates took cash and property		
543.	30 May	**Hoegh Drake**	Norway (0520)	Malacca Strait
		4 pirates climbed over stern rail, went to master's cabin, tied him up and stole some possessions and cash		
544.	10 Jun	**Yunus II**	Turkey	Monrovia
545.	11 Jun	**Nordstrand**	W Germany (0300)	Port Harcourt
		Boarded and robbed by 20 armed pirates with stones and bottles—Police arrived after 1.5 hours—when pirates had just left and chased them		
546.	12 Jun	**World Sanpo**	Panama (0335)	Malacca Strait
		Cash and property stolen from master's cabin by thieves leaving a trail of footprints		
547.	12 Jun	**Bunga Kiambang**	Malaysia (0500)	Malacca Strait
		4 armed pirates threatened crew—Took cash and property		
548.	13 Jun	**Mandalay**	Burma (0045)	Malacca Strait
		5 pirates took safe containing cash		
549.	14 Jun	**Carla A Hills**	Liberia (0600)	Malacca Strait
		6 pirates with knives in fast launch stole master's safe and contents		
550.	? Jun	?	?	Santos
551.	4 Jul	? (Fishing vessel)	?	Malaysia
		30 pirates with sub machine guns attacked 5 fishermen—stayed on board for 2 hours. Took possessions and the catch of fish—then made off in their own boats for international waters		
552.	29 Jul	?	?	Genoa
553.	8 Sep	? (Roads)	Greece (0430)	Dakar
		Armed pirates repelled		
554.	12 Sep	?	Greece	Santos
		Armed pirates forced cabin, attacked Chief Officer. Took $2000 in cash and goods		

	Date	Vessel	Flag	Location
555.	18 Sep	?	Greece (0300)	San Sebastiao Brazil
		Armed pirates repelled		
556.	23 Sep			
		Attack by "pirates" on village of Lahad Datu, Sabah, Malaysia—10 dead 11 injured Took $82,000 from bank and airline office and escaped to sea. Was this "piracy" or a "political" act (Moro Liberation Front?) aimed at destabilisation? Police gave chase in gunboats and returned with five bodies—but were they the pirates or the victims of a "reprisal attack" on a MLF base?		
557.	24 Sep	?	Greece	Bonny
		4 armed pirates repelled		
558.	1 Oct	?	?	Santos
559.	4 Oct	?	Greece	San Sebastiao
		Armed pirates repelled		
560.	7 Oct	**Achille Lauro**	Italy	Off Egypt
		Hijacked by Front for Liberation of Palestine 1 US disabled passenger killed		
561.	14 Oct	**Marianna**	Greece	Singapore area
		Escaped from pirates with fast boat and machine gun by increasing speed		
562.	15 Oct	?	Japan	Dumai Indonesia
		Pirates stole paints		
563.	17 Oct	?	Switzerland (0200)	Matadi Zaire
		Thieves forced hold padlock—took frozen fish Disappeared on discovery by watchmen		
564.	18 Oct	?	Switzerland (0200)	Matadi Zaire
		Pirates threatened crew with crowbars. Took electrical and rescue equipment		
565.	25 Oct	?	?	Singapore Strait
566.	? Oct	?	?	Chalna
		6 pirates took minor items		
567.	? Oct	?	?	Kingston Jamaica
568.	10 Nov	?	Japan	Dumai Indonesia
		Pirates damaged paint store, stole nothing		
569.	22 Nov	**Kongsaa**	Denmark	Conakry
		Several piratical attacks Some damage caused to ship's equipment		
570.	27 Nov	**Makedonia** (Loading)	? (0100)	Santos
		Armed attack by 10 pirates repelled by alertness of Master—Master convinced by this experience that if he returned to Santos he would carry at least a hunting gun to protect his crew		
571.	5 Dec	**Grey Fighter**	UK (2210)	Bonny
		Pirates stole two mooring ropes. Master radioed to authorities—got no response		
572.	? 1985	?	?	Agbowa
		Several passengers drowned trying to escape from attack—Six Nigerian pirates later executed		
573-582.	? 1985	?(10 ships)	W Germany	Sierra Leone
583-589.	? 1985	?(7 ships)	W Germany	Ivory Coast
590-592.	? 1985	?(3 ships)	W Germany	Nigeria

	Date	Vessel	Flag	Location
593-594.	? 1985	?(2 ships)	W Germany	Cameroon
	1986			
595.	12 Jan	? (In port) 5-6 pirates in canoes broke into containers. Stole 60 cartons of medicine	Denmark (1845)	Apapa
596.	27 Jan	**Hanlim Mariner** (Under way) Armed Sri Lankan pirates intercepted in vessel motor boat—assaulted crew. Stole cargo worth $000's. Local fishermen taken in for questioning	S Korea	Colombo
597.	28 Jan	**Hanlim Mariner** (Waiting for anchorage) Thieves pilfered items—caused minor damage	S Korea	Colombo
598.	28 Jan	**Kriti Garnet** (Waiting for anchorage) Attacked with Hanlim Mariner —minor damage and pilferage	Greece	Colombo
599.	? Jan	**Maritime Triumph**	Panama	Thailand
600.	? Jan	**Mae Nam Bridge**	?	Thai Coast
601.	3 Feb	? Pirates damaged safe, took Sing $272 in goods Singapore authorities unable to investigate due to lack of precise location	Malaysia (0650)	Singapore Strait
602.	12 Feb	**World Prologue** (Waiting to discharge) Pirates tried to board vessel from fast launch—Beaten back by crew using clubs and chains. Nigerian coastguard did not answer call for help	Greece	Port Harcourt
603.	12 Feb	**Monte Ruby** (Waiting to discharge) Armed pirates stole electrical, china and other goods worth $000s from 18 containers. Police did not respond to calls—but person later arrested	Panama (0345)	Thai coast
604.	13 Feb	**Antigioni** Pirates threatened crew with guns and knives. Stole 200m mooring rope	Cyprus	Abidjan
605.	16 Feb	**Kapetan Yannis** (Port) 3 armed pirates repelled. One crew slightly wounded	Greece (0150)	Santos
606.	18 Feb	**Hammurbai** (At anchor) Pirates with daggers and swords threatened crew. Took radio and metal drums	?	Colombo
607.	? Feb	**Deburgo** 6 pirate with speedboats threatened crew with knives. Forced store and stole paint	Cyprus (0500)	Guayaquil
608.	15 Mar	? 3 pirates with knives stoke $5000 and personal property	Japan (0130)	Malacca Strait
609.	18 Mar	? (Anchorage) 20 pirates stayed 2 hours—took property and cash	Panama	Lagos
610.	21 Mar	? Pirates stole cash and goods from Master's cabin	Japan	Singapore Strait
611.	21 Mar	**Ikan Duri** 6 pirates with swords—caused minimal damage	Singapore	Singapore Strait
612.	22 Mar	**Anangel Diligence** Armed pirates punched crew, bound master—took unspecified property	Greece (0410)	Singapore Strait

	Date	Vessel	Flag	Location
613.	29 Mar	**Fionia**	Denmark (0410)	Abidjan
		6 armed pirates observed whilst vessel in port—Left when alarm raised 3 men later arrested, then released		
614.	3 Apr	**Stavros GL** (Roads)	Greece (0200)	Dakar
		2 pirates repelled		
615.	4 Apr	**Odyssee** (Luxury yacht)(Coastal waters)	France	Mindinao
		12 pirates in fast launches stole $71,000 in cash and valuables—Crew set adrift in rubber raft. Intense search by Indonesian Navy amongst islands		
616.	10 Apr	?	?	Madras
617.	17 Apr	?	India	Singapore
		Pirates with knives stole Master's watch and cash. 1 crew with knife wound		
618.	29 Apr	?	?	Rangoon
619.	? Apr	**Fulmarus**	?	Sierra Leone
		Personal effects stolen		
620.	? Apr	**Jade Kim**	Panama	Sierra Leone
		Personal effects stolen		
621.	? Apr	**Benvalla**	UK	Sierra Leone
		Pirates repulsed by pressure hoses		
622.	5 May	**Fionia**	Denmark	Sierra Leone
		9 pirates boarded but stole nothing		
623.	7 May	**Maersk Bella**	Denmark	Freetown
624.	10 May	**Pahlawan/Feng Nan**	?	Colombo
		Mv Pahlawan was towed into Galle, Sri Lanka by Feng Nan. Crew had contradictory stories of pirate attack—claiming 6 crew had been killed. Suspicion of involvement in textile smuggling. Everyone detained by police for questioning		
625.	17 May	? (After leaving port)	(2300)	Singapore area
		Pirates with knives left one crew with knife wound. Master lost watch and Sing $1200		
626.	17 May	**Ravenscraig** (Leaving port)	UK (2300)	Singapore
		Pirates stole £1,200 and master's property		
627.	24 May	**Omissis** (Roads)	? (2015)	Bonny
		Pirates in speedboats, no lights, climbed grapnels/anchor chain—stole 8 mooring ropes. Master chased pirates as far as shallow water		
628.	26 May	?	Denmark (2205)	Chittagong
		30 armed pirates stole stores and property—1 crew wounded. No response from authorities		
629.	27 May	?	Japan (2400)	Phillip Channel
		Pirates cut and stole hawser		
630.	31 May	?	?	Mangalore
631.	16 Jun	**Anro Australia** (9 knots)	Australia (0430)	Singapore Strait
		4 pirates with knives stole $3000 from master Singapore authorities unable to investigate without precise location		
632.	19 Jun	?	Switzerland (Early hours)	Belawan Indonesia
		Pirates forced bosun's store—stole firemans suit. Suspect arrested and charged by police		

	Date	Vessel	Flag	Location
633.	24 Jun	?	?	Singapore
		Pirates took personal effects value $4000		
634.	1 Jul	**Chie Maru**	Japan	Malacca Strait
		5 pirates in speedboat took cash and property		
635.	9 Jul	**Mega Taurus**	?	Malacca Strait
		5 pirates with machettes took cash and property		
636.	19 Jul		Philippines	
		Hans Junzli, Swiss businessman/tourist and female companion kidnapped by pirates from beach. Pirates mistreated them and demanded $100,000 ransom. Released, without ransom, after intervention by local Moslem official		
637.	24 Jul	**Thai Wong**	Thailand	Thailand
		20 masked pirates with M16 rifles and pistols, using a speedboat resembling an official boat boarded vessel, handcuffed crew, forced master to navigate south for 20 hours and transferred cargo worth $751,000 and equipment worth $10,000 to a second vessel. There is doubt whether this was really piracy—or deviation by master and crew		
638.	7 Aug	**Jolly Marone** (At berth)	Italy (Night)	Abidjan
		Pirates with knives stole cargo from containers on 2 occasions during the night		
639.	14 Aug	?	W German	Lagos
		Pirates took property from container		
640.	25 Aug	?	? (0100)	Singapore
		Pirates took property worth Sing $4000		
641.	28 Sep	?	?	Bangkok
642.	29 Sep	?	? (0430)	Singapore
		3 pirates with knives beat master to try to force him to give safe key. Stole $350 and captain's coat and equipment		
643.	25 Oct	**Crane Phoenix**	Panama	Malacca Strait
		Pirates with guns and sickles assaulted, stripped and tied up master—stole $4,400		
644.	8 Oct	**Bogo**	Panama	Malacca Strait
		4 armed pirates boarded with grapple hooks—Stole $7000. An unusual attack in Malaysian waters		
645.	9 Oct	?	?	Chittagong
646.	15 Oct	?	? (2215)	Esmereldas Ecuador
		12 pirates with guns and speedboats boarded by high stairs—took $3000 in cash and equipment		
647.	29 Oct	**Mendoza** (Entrance to Harbour)(0230)	Argentina	Singapore
		5 armed pirates bound master, forced him to open safe—Took US$1600 and firearms		
648.	23 Oct	**Benvalla** (Anchorage)	UK (1945)	Chittagong
		80-100 pirates in 5 boats boarded with poles and long hooks—took 3 mooring ropes. Repelled with pressure hoses		
649.	? Oct	?	?	Dakar
650.	13 Nov	**Kriti Art** (Roads)	Greece (2200)	Madras
		Attack by many pirates repelled		
651.	? Nov	?	?	Thailand
652.	4 Dec	**Stolt Luisa Pando**	Spain (2330)	Malacca Strait
		Ships safe stolen with medicine and cash/property. Marine police took no action—outside jurisdiction		

	Date	Vessel	Flag	Location
653.	28 Dec	?	?	Bonny
654.	29 Dec	**Pasadena**	Greece	Bonny
		(Roads)	(2000)	
		Armed pirates stole five ropes		
655.	31 Dec	?	?	Abidjan
		7 armed pirates stole 7 bags cocoa		
656-667.	? 1986	?(12 ships)	W Germany	Sierra Leone
668-671.	? 1986	?(4 ships)	W Germany	Ivory Coast
672-675.	? 1986	?(4 ships)	W Germany	Nigeria
676.	? 1986	?	W Germany	Cameroon
677.	? 1986	?	W Germany	Brazil
	1987			
678.	7 Jan	**Seapearl**	?	Singapore
		2 pirates with knives fled in speedboats when observed		
679.	17 Feb	**Kritonas**	?	Monrovia
			(0415)	
		Pirates with knives boarded from canoe. Stole hatch canvas		
680.	19 Feb	**Transberlin**	?	Monrovia
		Pirates stole mooring ropes		
681.	21 Feb	?	?	Singapore
		Pirates stowed away when vessel in port Stole personal property value $1,500		
682.	25 Feb	**Forum Pioneer**	?	Phillip Channel
683.	27 Feb	**Madonna**	?	Monrovia
		(Outside harbour)	(0100)	
		Pirates cut up and stole tarpaulin		
684.	? Feb	**Slutsk**	USSR	Singapore
		3 pirates with knives repelled by crewmember (who was wounded)—escaped into boat		
685.	8 Mar	**Torbay**	UK	Singapore
		Master woken by 4 pirates with machettes. Took cash from safe, left by stern leaving footprints and a cut mooring rope		
686.	16 Mar	?	?	Bonny
		Oil tanker boarded by pirates		
687.	17 Mar	?	?	Colombo
		Local pirates stole paint and equipment. Left when discovered and ship's whistle blown		
688.	25 Mar	**Polymnia**	Greece	Bonny
			(0130)	
		Pirates repelled		
689.	26 Mar	?	?	Jahore Strait
		(Anchorage)		
		4 pirates with knives tied up master—Took $13,000 from safe and personal property		
690.	5 Apr	**Erodna**	?	Madras
		(At anchor)	(Daytime)	
		Unknown persons stole fire equipment		
691.	8 Apr	**Evangelos L**	Greece	Malacca Strait
			(0110)	
		6 armed pirates stole money and valuables		
692.	8 Apr	**Mercator**	Belgium	Singapore
			(0535)	
		Master bound—cash/property value $2500 taken		

	Date	Vessel	Flag	Location
693.	9 Apr	**Polymnia**	Greece (0215)	Bonny
		6 pirates repelled		
694.	23 Apr	**Igloo Moss**	Norway (2330)	Singapore Strait
		5 pirates with knives and small fast boat boarded vessel unseen by 3 crew on watch—tied up crewman, stole goods worth $2500. Escaped in fast boat "It's incredible no one saw them"		
695.	24 Apr	**Evelyn Maersk** (Full speed)	Denmark (0045)	Phillip Channel
		5 pirates with knives boarded by ladders. Went to Master's cabin, woke and threatened him. Stole property and safe contents		
696.	24 Apr	?	UK	Phillip Channel
		Alleged to have suffered attack similar to Evelyn Maersk		
697.	26 Apr	**Zoom** (Yacht)	US	Antigua
		Pirates stole $2000, seriously stabbed crew when disturbed		
698.	? Apr	?	Singapore	Iju Kekil Indonesia
		3 pirates with knives tried to open safe—then made off with valuables		
699.	1 May	**Durmitor**	Yugoslav	Singapore area
		Attacked by pirates with knives		
700.	1 May	**Krk**	Yugoslav	Singapore area
		7 pirates with knives and machetes took cash and property		
701.	1 May	**Product Endeavour**	Hong Kong (Night)	Singapore Strait
		Pirates boarded twice during night—bound master—took cash and property		
702.	3 May	**Bream** (13 knots)	Greece (2330)	Singapore
		5 pirates with guns and cutlasses threatened crew Stole safe and £100		
703.	3 May	**Lydia V**	UK (0215)	Malacca Strait
		Fast expert pirates boarded from boat. Took complete steel safe and contents Left hurriedly when seen		
704.	3 May	**Kavo Peiratis**	Greece (0130)	Singapore
		5 pirates took money and valuables		
705.	7 May	?	?	Port Harcourt
706.	7 May	**Maersk Bella**	Denmark	Freetown
		Container ship attacked		
707.	8 May	**Beaver**	? (Night)	Phillip Channel
		Captain's safe (containing cash and medicine) lowered from poop into boat		
708.	22 May	?	?	Callao Peru
709.	29 May	**Molly Laura**	Panama (Pre-dawn)	Phillip Channel
		6 pirates, with knives and pistol, took First Officer hostage—and took $16,000 in cash and valuables. Left in waiting boat		
710.	29 May	**Nafkratis**	Greece (0215)	Singapore
		4 armed pirates tied up crew and stole property		
711.	8 Jun	**Siri Bhum**	Thailand (0430)	Phillip Channel
		5 pirates with knives tied 2nd Officer up Took property and clothing worth Sing $3190		

	Date	Vessel	Flag	Location
712.	12 Jun	**Sea Heron** (On tow)	Panama	Sri Lanka
		Approached by pirates in four boats. Crew radioed authorities—21 pirates caught after high speed boat chase		
713.	? June	?	?	Nigeria
		Pirates stole hawsers and equipment		
714.	1 Jul	**Fina America** (Anchorage)	Belgium (0745)	Bonny
		4 pirates stole ropes—repelled by water jets		
715.	1 Jul	?	?	Singapore
		Property stolen from cabins after vessel called at Singapore for bunkers Pirates assumed to have stowed away		
716.	2 Jul	?	?	Rio
717.	2 Jul	**Peter Maersk**	Denmark (0200)	Singapore Strait
		6 pirates bound crewmember, took property		
718.	2 Jul	**Iver Chaser**	UK (2250)	Singapore Strait
		Pirates bound master forced safe and took cash		
719.	3 Jul	**Peter Maersk**	Denmark	Singapore Strait
		3 pirates bound master—took cash and property		
720.	6 Jul	**Nafkratis**	Greece	Singapore area
721.	6 Jul	?	?	Rouen
		2 armed pirates forced Chief Engineer's cabin and assaulted him		
722.	6 Jul	**Nordheim** (Roads)	W Germany (0345)	Georgetown Guyana
		10 pirates stole 50 drums of paint—then repelled		
723.	26 Jul	**Petrobulk Lion**	Belgium	Singapore Strait
		4 pirates with knives stole wristwatch		
724.	? Jul	?	?	Singapore Strait
		Secretly boarded by 5 pirates with large knives. Woke Chief Officer, bound him when he refused to reveal location of safe, but left without finding it		
725.	17 Aug	**Maersk Rando** (0610)	UK (Indonesia)	Belawan
		6 pirates stole life raft		
726.	18 Aug	**Orion Trader**	Panama	Malacca Strait
		4 armed pirates bound steward, stole property		
727.	? Aug	?	?	Singapore area
		Pirates with guns and knives took $7000 cash and goods		
728.	29 Sep	**Vida I** (Anchorage)	France (0130)	Bonny
		Pirates stole ropes from store—injured crew member		
729.	29 Sep	? (Coastal waters)	Netherlands (0415)	Malaysia
		4 armed pirates threatened master, stole property		
730.	2 Oct	**Makran** (Coastal waters)	Pakistan (2300)	Malaysia
		4 pirates forced crew to hand over cash and watches		
731.	27 Oct	**Mobil Petroleum** (Coastal waters)	Liberia (0200)	Malaysia
		Armed pirates threatened master—took $11,000 from safe		
732.	3 Nov	**Vic Bilh** (Anchorage)	? (0215)	Bonny
		Pirates took mooring ropes Vessel unable to contact authorities		
733.	17 Dec	**Cresta I** (Harbour)	Philippines	Manila
		Reportedly sea-jacked by armed men. Investigations are continuing		

ANALYSIS OF THE IMB CHRONOLOGY

The Threat

The following charts indicate the total number of piracy attacks included in the Chronology, in each of the three regions defined in Chapter 1 — West Africa, Malacca Straits Area and the Rest of the World. As stated on page 5 a number of attacks are included about which either few details are known, or the perpetrators of which are unobserved by their "victims" — for example "sneak thieves". In order to make it easier to identify confirmed, or "real", piratical attacks, which have a recognised element of potential violence or confrontation, the two categories are distinguished in the charts.

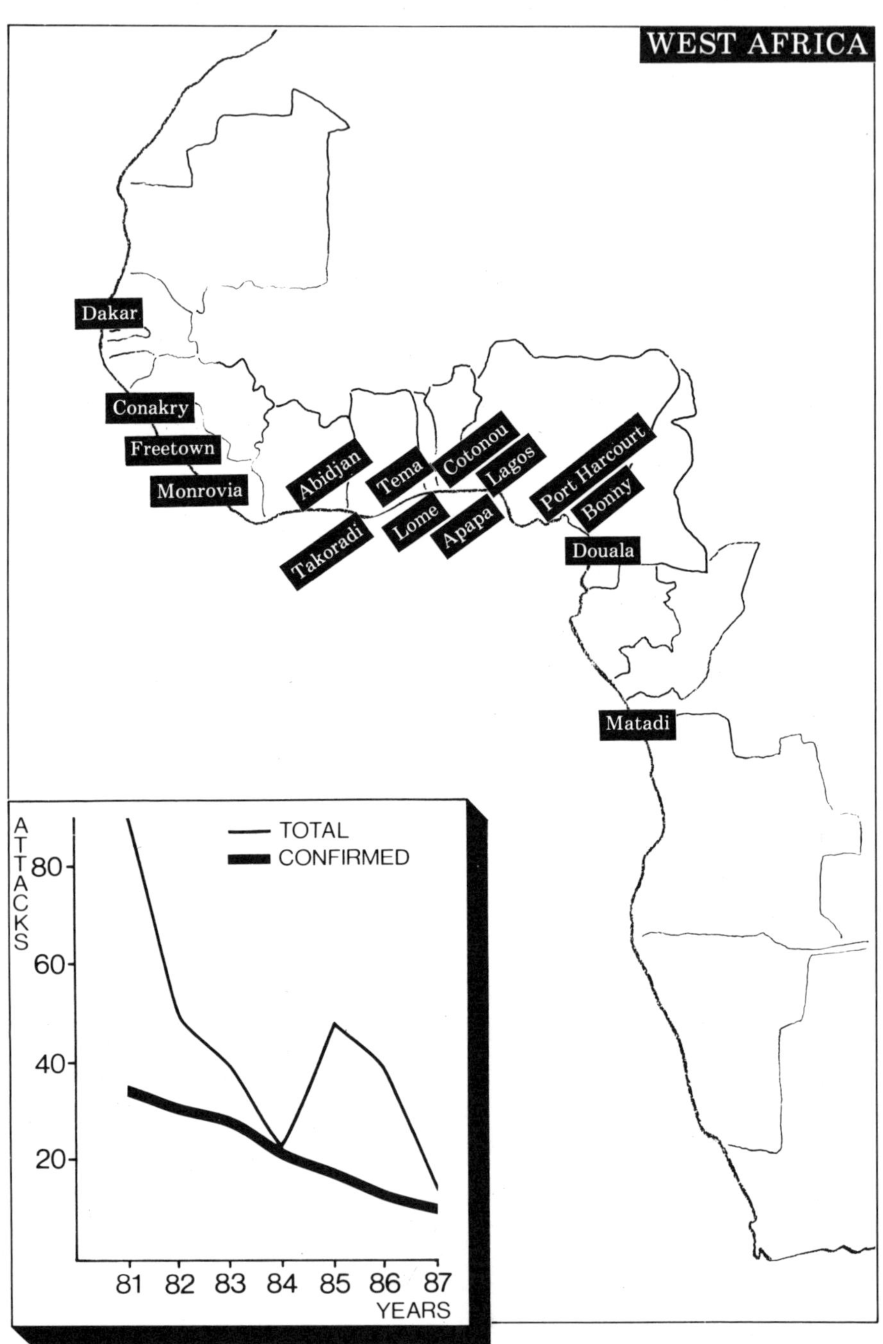

WEST AFRICA
Dakar
Conakry
Freetown
Monrovia
Abidjan
Takoradi
Tema
Lome
Cotonou
Apapa
Lagos
Port Harcourt
Bonny
Douala
Matadi
ATTACKS
80
60
40
20
TOTAL
CONFIRMED
81
82
83
84
85
86
87
YEARS

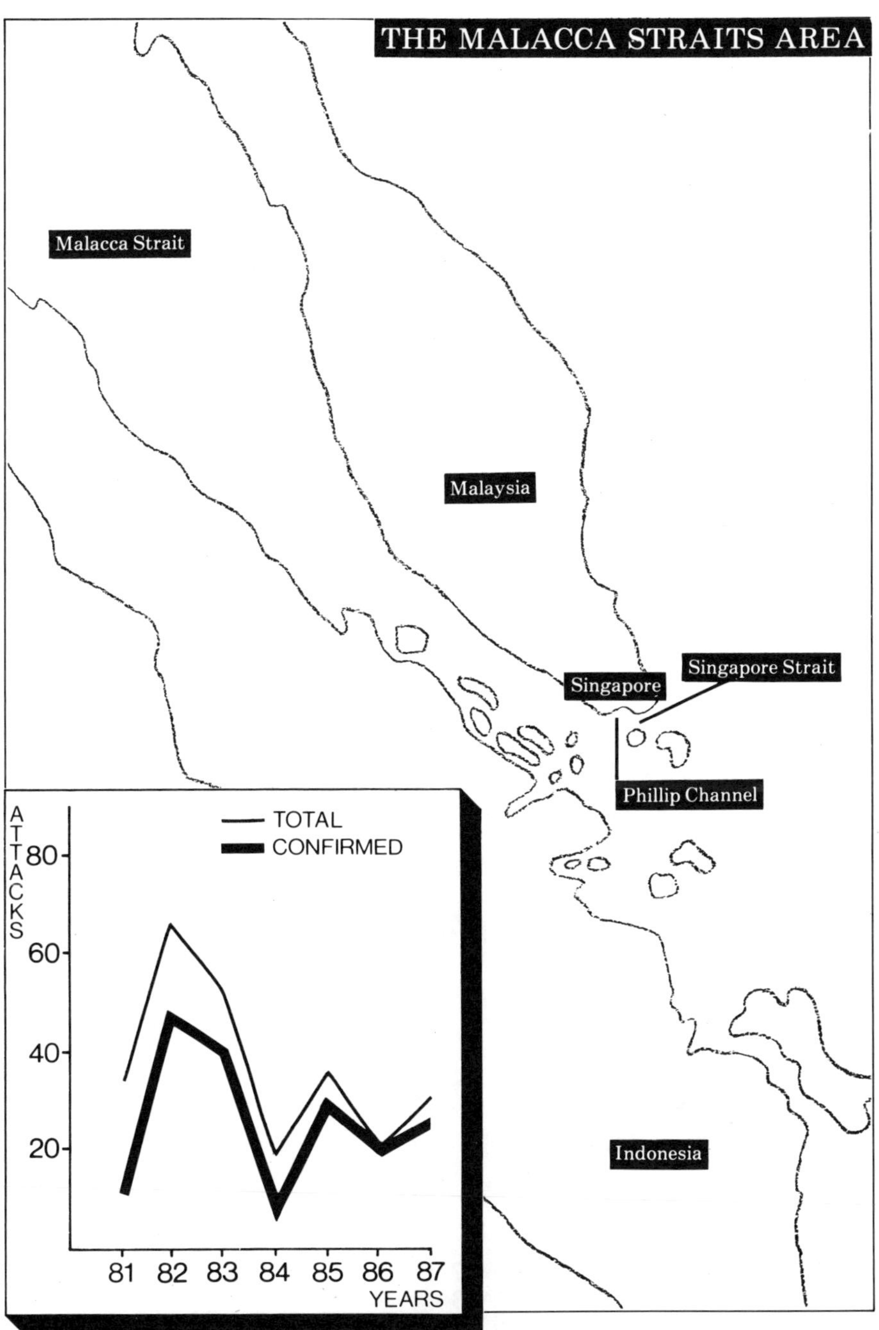
THE MALACCA STRAITS AREA
Malacca Strait
Malaysia
Singapore
Singapore Strait
Phillip Channel
Indonesia
ATTACKS
80
60
40
20
TOTAL
CONFIRMED
81
82
83
84
85
86
87
YEARS

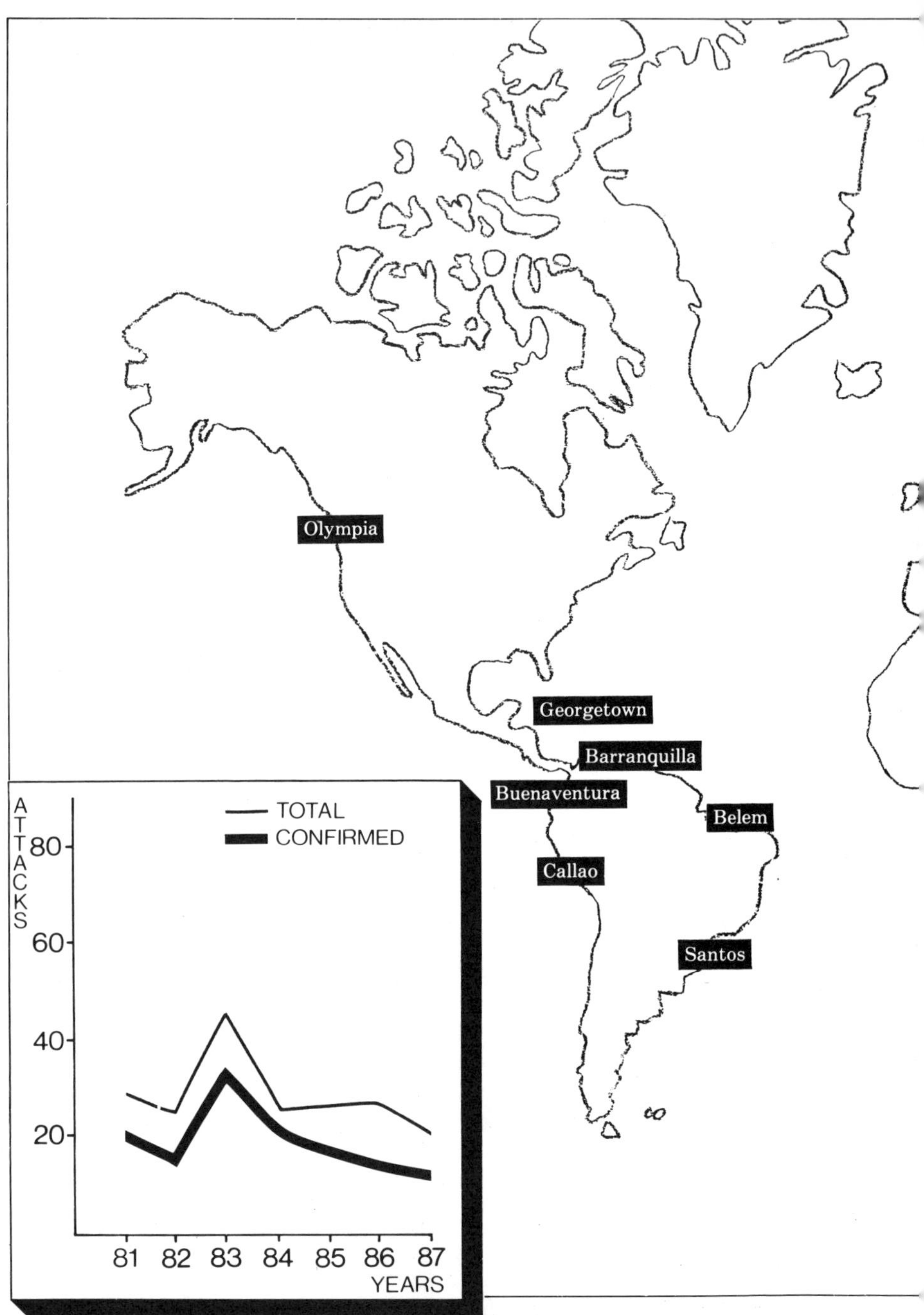
Olympia
Georgetown
Barranquilla
Buenaventura
Belem
Callao
Santos
ATTACKS
80
60
40
20
TOTAL
CONFIRMED
81
82
83
84
85
86
87
YEARS

THE REST OF THE WORLD

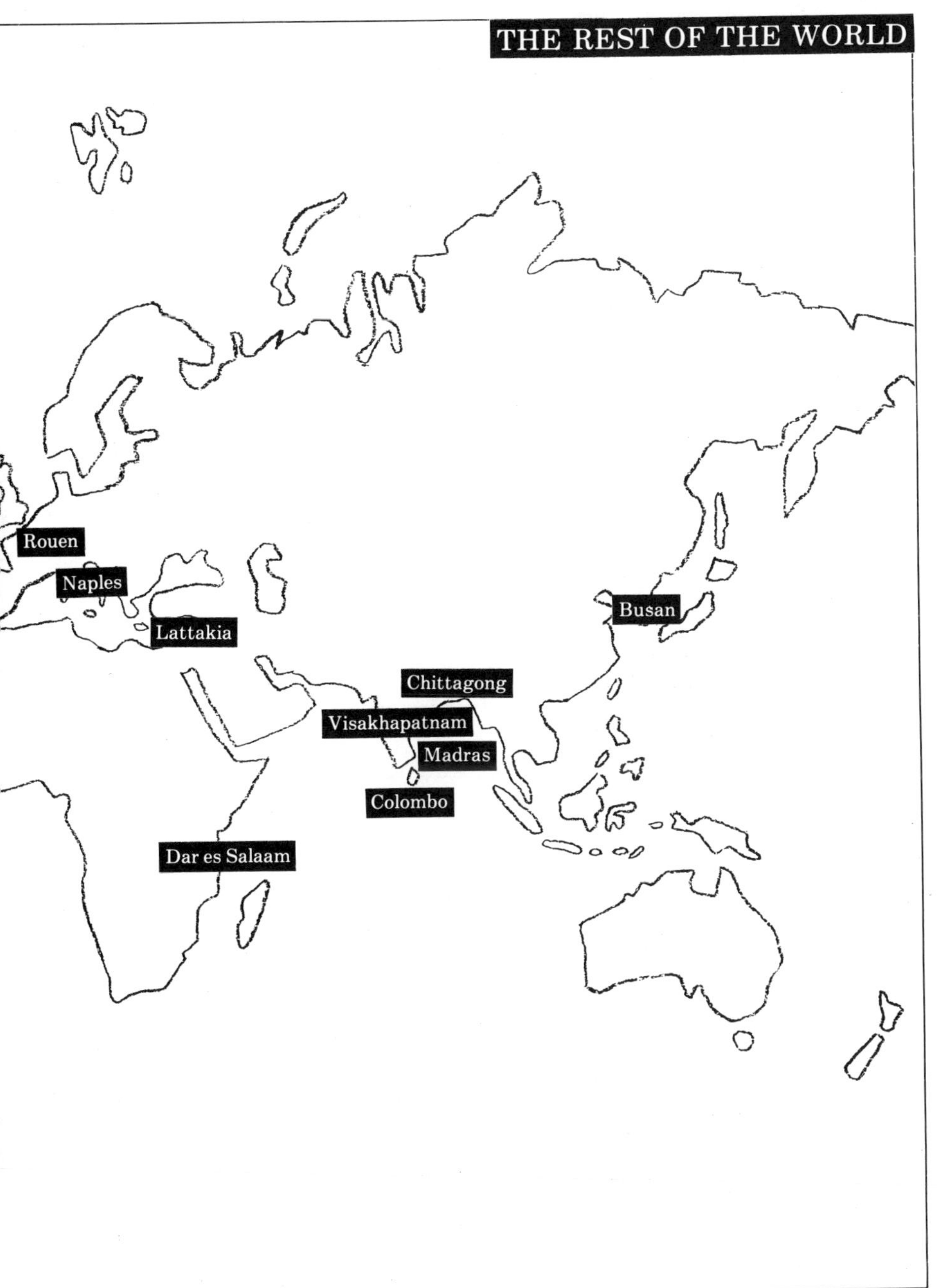

Intimidation

The following chart is intended to isolate the most potentially violent or otherwise dangerous piracy attacks in the Chronology. This is done from two points of view: by identifying, firstly, attacks during which someone was killed or injured (whether "victim" or pirate) and, secondly, attacks by pirates in gangs (of over 20) or carrying firearms. Two statistical points require to be made. One, some attacks may clearly be counted twice (or more often) — for example, a crew-member could have been injured in the course of an attack by an armed gang of 30 pirates. Two, the figures for "Injuries" and "Fatalities" refer to the number of incidents in the course of which an injury or a fatality occurred — not to the actual number of injuries and fatalities.

		FATALITY	INJURY	FIREARMS	LARGE GANG
1981	WEST AFRICA	1	3	1	6
	THE MALACCA STRAITS AREA	0	0	1	0
	THE REST OF THE WORLD	6	4	7	1
1982	WEST AFRICA	1	6	14	4
	THE MALACCA STRAITS AREA	0	1	1	0
	THE REST OF THE WORLD	3	1	4	1
1983	WEST AFRICA	0	6	11	7
	THE MALACCA STRAITS AREA	0	2	5	0
	THE REST OF THE WORLD	5	5	10	1
1984	WEST AFRICA	1	3	15	4
	THE MALACCA STRAITS AREA	0	2	3	0
	THE REST OF THE WORLD	6	2	6	0

		FATALITY	INJURY	FIREARMS	LARGE GANG
1985	WEST AFRICA	1	0	9	6
	THE MALACCA STRAITS AREA	0	1	6	0
	THE REST OF THE WORLD	2	3	10	2
1986	WEST AFRICA	0	0	4	1
	THE MALACCA STRAITS AREA	0	5	3	0
	THE REST OF THE WORLD	1	2	6	3
1987	WEST AFRICA	0	1	0	0
	THE MALACCA STRAITS AREA	0	1	5	0
	THE REST OF THE WORLD	0	2	4	0

Spoils

The following chart is intended to give an impression of the motives, and success, of pirates around the world. This is done, firstly by indicating attacks on containers, successful or otherwise, which account for most piratical attacks on cargoes. Secondly, thefts of cash in excess of US$2000 are highlighted. Thirdly, attention is drawn to "other thefts" — cases where the pirates have got away with any property — this may be smaller sums of cash (belonging to the crew, or from the ship's safe), personal property of the crew, ship's equipment (ropes are popular because they are accessible and have a reasonable re-sale value), or non-containerised cargo. The information, like everything else in the Chronology, is of course incomplete — the point is made on page 5 that not all attacks are reported, and not everything is known about the ones which are.

		ATTACKS ON CONTAINERS	CASH THEFT OVER $2000	OTHER THEFT
1981	**WEST AFRICA**	18	0	14
	THE MALACCA STRAITS AREA	0	3	12
	THE REST OF THE WORLD	2	0	8
1982	**WEST AFRICA**	3	1	15
	THE MALACCA STRAITS AREA	0	8	24
	THE REST OF THE WORLD	0	1	6
1983	**WEST AFRICA**	13	0	8
	THE MALACCA STRAITS AREA	0	9	34
	THE REST OF THE WORLD	1	3	22
1984	**WEST AFRICA**	13	0	7
	THE MALACCA STRAITS AREA	0	1	6
	THE REST OF THE WORLD	1	0	7

		ATTACKS ON CONTAINERS	CASH THEFT OVER $2000	OTHER THEFT
1985	**WEST AFRICA**	5	0	11
	THE MALACCA STRAITS AREA	0	6	18
	THE REST OF THE WORLD	0	1	9
1986	**WEST AFRICA**	3	0	7
	THE MALACCA STRAITS AREA	0	4	14
	THE REST OF THE WORLD	1	2	10
1987	**WEST AFRICA**	0	0	7
	THE MALACCA STRAITS AREA	0	2	21
	THE REST OF THE WORLD	0	3	7

APPENDIX 3

THAILAND
PIRACY STATISTICS (BASED ON REFUGEE REPORTS)

	1981	1982	1983	1984	1985	1986	1987	1987 1ST 10 MOS	1988 JAN	FEB	MAR	APR	MAY	JUN	JUL	AUG	SEP	OCT	NOV/ DEC	1988 TOTAL
Total Persons Arrived	15479	5813	3384	3077	3343	4392	12842	8474	2467	799	153	434	124	308	83	55	178	139		4740
Women Raped	571	176	95	68	67	58	67	61	0	7	13	6	0	1	0	0	0	0		27
Abducted	228	157	93	72	72	33	4	4	2	15	5	0	4	0	0	0	0	0		26
Recovered (of above)	85	92	39	35	39	11	1	1	0	6	4	0	0	0	0	0	0	0		10
% Recovered	37%	59%	42%	49%	54%	33%	25%	25%	0%	40%	80%	0%	0%	0%	0%	0%	0%	0%		38%
Deaths due to Piracy	454	155	42	59	45	18	0	0	8	11	0	0	1	0	0	0	0	0		20
% of All Refugees	2.8%	2.5%	1.2%	1.8%	1.2%	0.4%	O.1%	0.1%	0.3%	1.3%	0.0%	0.0%	0.8%	0.0%	0.0%	0.0%	0.0%	0.0%		0.4%
Total Missing*	427	266	211	86	219	111	36	19	7	34	1	0	4	0	0	0	0	0		46
% of All Refugees	2.6%	4.3%	5.8%	2.7%	6.1%	2.5%	0.3%	0.2%	0.3%	4.0%	0.6%	0.0%	3.1%	0.0%	0.0%	0.0%	0.0%	0.0%		1.1%
Boats Arrived	452	220	155	186	269	448	1112	788	161	45	11	22	15	16	9	10	8	10		307
Boats Attacked	349	141	82	66	63	58	91	66	14	10	5	1	1	1	1	1	0	0		34
% of Boats Attacked	77%	64%	53%	35%	23%	13%	8%	8%	9%	22%	45%	5%	7%	6%	11%	10%	0%	0%		11%
No of Attacks	1122	373	181	117	101	87	117	81	15	19	12	1	1	1	1	1	0	0		51
Attacks per Attacked Boat	3.2	2.6	2.2	1.8	1.6	1.5	1.3	1.2	1.1	1.9	2.4	1.0	1.0	1.0	1.0	1.0	0.0	0.0		1.5
Average No. of Persons per Boat	34	26	22	17	12	10	12	11	15	18	15	20	8	19	9	6	22	14		15

*MISSING INCLUDES PERSONS ABDUCTED BUT NOT RECOVERED

APPENDIX 4

REGIONAL OVERVIEW
PIRACY STATISTICS (BASED ON REFUGEE REPORTS)

	1985	1986	1987	1987 1ST 9 MOS	1988 JAN	FEB	MAR	APR	MAY	JUN	JUL	AUG	SEP	OCT	NOV/ DEC	1988 TOTAL
Thailand																
Persons arrived	3337	4386	12841	8474	2467	799	153	434	124	308	83	55	178	139		4740
Boats arrived	265	442	1110	788	161	45	11	22	15	16	9	10	8	10		307
Boats attacked	63	58	91	66	14	10	5	1	1	1	1	1	0	0		34
% Boats attacked	24%	13%	8%	8%	7%	22%	50%	5%	7%	6%	11%	11%	0%	0%		11%
Deaths	45	18	0	0	8	11	0	0	1	0	0	0	0	0		20
Missing	185	111	36	35	7	34	1	0	4	0	0	0	0	0		46
Rapes	67	57	67	61	0	7	13	6	0	1	0	0	0	0		27
Abductions (Recovered)	72(38)	33(11)	4(1)	4(1)	2(0)	15(6)	5(4)	0(0)	4(0)	0(0)	0(0)	0(0)	0(0)	0(0)		26(10)
Malaysia																
Persons arrived	7383	7400	8013	6224	759	432	1726	1904	2433	982	612	427	427	1008		10710
Boats arrived	194	215	215	174	18	13	39	51	65	21	12	11	9	27		266
Boats attacked	52	40	27	24	0	3	12	9	11	1	2	2	1	6		47
% Boats attacked	27%	19%	13%	14%	0%	23%	26%	18%	17%	5%	17%	18%	11%	22%		18%
Deaths	28	0	2	2	0	0	0	0	5	0	0	0	0	0		5
Missing	47	29	56	54	0	0	0	40	19	0	75	72	81	6		293
Rapes	46	84	13	11	0	0	4	2	11	0	0	1	0	1		19
Abductions (Recovered)	39(9)	31(6)	11(5)	7(2)	0(0)	0(0)	8(8)	12(9)	6(1)	0(0)	5(5)	5(0)	16(4)	6(0)		58(27)
Indonesia																
Persons arrived	6278	2558	1758	1540	21	0	68	36	444	211	101	252	165	108		1406
Boats arrived	147	54	27	25	2	0	3	2	8	6	3	5	5	4		38
Boats attacked	3	3	4	4	1	0	0	0	0	0	0	2	1	0		4
% Boats attacked	2%	6%	15%	16%	0%	0%	0%	0%	0%	0%	0%	40%	20%	0%		12%
Deaths	116	0	0	0	0	0	0	0	0	0	0	0	0	0		0
Missing	0	0	0	0	44	0	0	0	0	0	0	9	4	0		57
Rapes	0	0	0	0	0	0	0	0	0	0	0	6	0	0		6
Abductions (Recovered)	0(0)	0(0)	0(0)	0(0)	8(0)	0(0)	0(0)	0(0)	0(0)	0(0)	0(0)	9(0)	5(1)	0(0)		22(1)

REGIONAL OVERVIEW
(continued from previous page)

	1985	1986	1987	1987 1ST 9 MOS	1988 JAN	FEB	MAR	APR	MAY	JUN	JUL	AUG	SEP	OCT	NOV/ DEC	1988 TOTAL
Philippines																
Persons arrived	2651	2049	2685	2638	5	9	128	276	508	877	594	604	700	123		3824
Boats arrived	66	66	68	67	1	1	2	6	13	22	16	13	19	2		95
Boats attacked	0	0	2	2	0	0	0	0	0	0	0	0	0	0		8
% Boats attacked	0%	0%	3%	3%	0%	0%	0%	0%	0%	0%	0%	0%	0%	0%		0%
Deaths	0	0	0	0	0	0	0	0	0	0	0	0	0	0		0
Missing	0	0	0	0	0	0	0	0	0	0	0	0	0	0		0
Rapes	0	0	0	0	0	0	0	0	0	0	0	0	0	0		0
Abductions (Recovered)	0(0)	0(0)	0(0)	0(0)	0(0)	0(0)	0(0)	0(0)	0(0)	0(0)	0(0)	0(0)	0(0)	0(0)		0(0)
Hong Kong																
Persons arrived	1112	2169	3437	3044	358	91	349	1381	2973	4045	5593	2375	368	155		17708
Boats arrived	52	111	171	156	8	4	13	44	128	131	170	67	11	7		583
Boats attacked	0	0	1	1	0	0	0	0	0	0	0	0	0	0		0
% Boats attacked	0%	0%	6%	1%	0%	0%0	0%	0%	0%	0%	0%	0%	0%	0%		0%
Deaths	0	0	0	0	0	0	0	0	0	0	0	0	0	0		0
Missing	0	0	1	1	0	0	0	0	0	0	0	0	0	0		0
Rapes	0	0	1	0	0	0	0	0	0	0	0	0	0	0		0
Abductions (Recovered)	0(0)	0(0)	0(0)	0(0)	0(0)	0(0)	0(0)	0(0)	0(0)	0(0)	0(0)	0(0)	0(0)	0(0)		0(0)
Singapore																
Persons arrived	891	729	831	805	21	0	0	0	96	119	143	0	218	76		673
Boats arrived	30	18	22	21	1	0	0	0	3	3	4	0	4	1		16
Boats attacked	2	0	1	1	1	0	0	0	0	0	0	0	1	0		2
% Boats attacked	7%	0%	5%	5%	100%	0%	0%	0%	0%	0%	0%	0%	25%	0%		13%
Deaths	0	0	0	0	0	0	0	0	0	0	0	0	0	0		0
Missing	0	0	0	0	0	0	0	0	0	0	0	0	0	0		0
Rapes	3	0	0	0	1	0	0	0	0	0	0	0	0	0		1
Abductions (Recovered)	0(0)	0(0)	0(0)	0(0)	0(0)	0(0)	0(0)	0(0)	0(0)	0(0)	0(0)	0(0)	0(0)	0(0)		0(0)

	1985	1986	1987	1987 1ST 9 MOS	1988 JAN	FEB	MAR	APR	MAY	JUN	JUL	AUG	SEP	OCT	NOV/ DEC	1988 TOTAL
Japan																
Persons arrived	425	321	104	80	0	0	0	17	59	3	0	0	69	72		220
Boats arrived	17	12	5	4	0	0	0	1	3	1	0	0	2	2		9
Boats attacked	0	0	0	0	0	0	0	0	0	0	0	0	0	0		0
% Boats attacked	0%	0%	0%	0%	0%	0%	0%	0%	0%	0%	0%	0%	0%	0%		0%
Deaths	0	0	0	0	0	0	0	0	0	0	0	0	0	0		0
Missing	0	0	0	0	0	0	0	0	0	0	0	0	0	0		0
Rapes	0	0	0	0	0	0	0	0	0	0	0	0	0	0		0
Abductions (Recovered)	0(0)	0(0)	0(0)	0(0)	0(0)	0(0)	0(0)	0(0)	0(0)	0(0)	0(0)	0(0)	0(0)	0(0)		0(0)
Others																
Persons arrived	199	496	24	24	0	0	0	1	52	38	5	0	0	0		96
Boats arrived	-	-	3	3	0	0	0	1	1	1	1	0	0	0		4
Boats attacked	0	0	0	0	0	0	0	0	0	0	0	0	0	0		0
% Boats attacked	0%	0%	0%	0%	0%	0%	0%	0%	0%	0%	0%	0%	0%	0%		0%
Deaths	0	0	0	0	0	0	0	0	0	0	0	0	0	0		0
Missing	0	0	0	0	0	0	0	0	0	0	0	0	0	0		0
Rapes	0	0	0	0	0	0	0	0	0	0	0	0	0	0		0
Abductions (Recovered)	0(0)	0(0)	0(0)	0(0)	0(0)	0(0)	0(0)	0(0)	0(0)	0(0)	0(0)	0(0)	0(0)	0(0)		0(0)
TOTAL																
Persons arrived	22276	20108	29693	22829	3631	1331	2424	4049	6689	6583	7131	3713	2125	1681		39357
Boats arrived	711	918	1621	1238	191	63	68	127	236	201	215	106	58	53		1308
Boats attacked	120	101	126	98	16	13	17	10	12	2	3	5	3	6		87
% Boats attacked	16%	11%	8%	8%	8%	21%	25%	8%	5%	1%	1%	5%	5%	11%		7%
Deaths	189	18	2	2	8	11	0	0	6	0	0	0	0	0		25
Missing	232	140	93	90	51	34	1	40	23	0	75	81	85	6		396
Rapes	116	141	80	72	1	7	17	8	11	1	0	7	0	0		52
Abductions (Recovered)	111(47)	64(17)	15(6)	11(3)	10(0)	15(6)	13(12)	12(9)	10(1)	0(0)	5(5)	14(0)	21(5)	6(0)		106(38)

APPENDIX 5

SUMMARY OF ARRESTS, PROSECUTIONS, CONVICTIONS AND SENTENCES IN THAILAND FOR PIRATICAL OFFENCES AGAINST BOAT PEOPLE 1982-1987

APP Unit Responsible for Arrests	January 1982-December 1985		January 1986-October 1987		Total	
	No. of suspects arrested	No. of piracy cases	No. of suspects arrested	No. of piracy cases	No. of suspects arrested	No. of piracy cases
Arrested by Songkhla Marine Police	16	5	57*	19	73*	24
Arrested by Sri Racha Marine Police	—	—	2	1	2	1
Arrested by Laem Njob Dist. Police, Trad Province	—	—	7**	2	7**	2
Arrested by Songkhla Naval Station Piracy Patrol Boat	2	1	—	—	2	1
Arrested by Muang District Police, Rayong Province	12***	1	—	—	12***	1
Total	30	7	66	22	96	29

Footnotes:

* includes 4 suspects released for lack of evidence

** includes 1 suspect released for lack of evidence

*** includes 10 suspects released for lack of evidence

SUMMARY OF SENTENCES OF THAI AND MALAYSIAN FISHERMEN (1 JANUARY 1982-31 AUGUST 1987)

Date of Verdict	No.	Verdict at Court Trial	Sentence Handed Down	Amended Sentence*
Jan 1982	1	Guilty of rape and deprivation of liberty	Total of (3 + 1) 4 yrs imprisonment	2 yrs imprisonment
Jul 1982	2	Guilty of attempted armed gang robbery	10 yrs imprisonment	no change
	3	Guilty of attempted armed gang robbery	10 yrs imprisonment	no change
	4	Guilty of attempted armed gang robbery	10 yrs imprisonment	no change
	5	Guilty of attempted armed gang robbery	10 yrs imprisonment	no change
Mar 1984	6	Guilty of rape, attempted robbery and deprivation of liberty	Total of (6 + 10 + 2) 18 yrs imprisonment	9 yrs imprisonment
Mar 1984	7	Ditto	Ditto	9 yrs imprisonment
	8	Ditto	Ditto	9 yrs imprisonment
	9	Ditto	Ditto	9 yrs imprisonment
Sep 1984	10	Guilty of rape	6 yrs imprisonment	3 yrs imprisonment
Jul 1985	11	Guilty of gang robbery	22 yrs 6 mths imprisonment	no change
	12	Guilty of gang robbery	22 yrs 6 mths imprisonment	11 yrs 3 mths—imprisonment**
	13	Guilty of murder, gang robbery and rape	Total of (20 + 30 + 10) 60 yrs — imprisonment	50 yrs imprisonment***
Sep 1985	14	Guilty of gang robbery and rape	Total of (30 + 14) 44 yrs — imprisonment	no change
	15	Guilty of gang robbery	30 yrs imprisonment	no change
Apr 1986	16	Guilty of rape	40 yrs imprisonment	no change
	17	Guilty of rape	15 yrs imprisonment	no change
May 1986	18	Guilty of Indecent assault of a minor, rape, deprivation of liberty & abduction	Total of (6 + 9 + 1 + 2) 18 yrs — imprisonment	9 yrs imprisonment
May 1986	19	Guilty of rape	6 yrs imprisonment	3 yrs imprisonment
	20	Guilty of rape	6 yrs imprisonment	3 yrs imprisonment

APPENDIX 5

SUMMARY OF SENTENCES OF THAI AND MALAYSIAN FISHERMEN
(continued from previous page)

Date of Verdict	No.	Verdict at Court Trial	Sentence Handed Down	Amended Sentence*
Jul 1986	21	Guilty of indecent assault of a minor, rape, deprivation of liberty & abduction	Total of (6+9+1+2) 18 yrs — imprisonment	9 yrs imprisonment
Nov 1986	22	Guilty of gang rape, deprivation of liberty	Total of (28x16+1) 449 yrs — imprisonment	50 yrs imprisonment
		Guilty of gang rape, rape, deprivation of liberty, and operating an unlicensed fishing boat	Total of (28x16+4+1+1 mth) 453 yrs one mth imprisonment	50 yrs imprisonment
Dec 1986	24	Guilty of gang robbery	15 yrs imprisonment	no change
	25	Guilty of gang robbery	15 yrs imprisonment	11 yrs 3 mths
Dec 1986	26	Guilty of gang robbery and gang rape	Total of (20+24) 44 yrs	22 yrs imprisonment
	27	Guilty of gang robbery and gang rape	Total of (20+24) 44 yrs	29 yrs 4 mths — imprisonment
	28	Guilty of gang robbery and gang rape	Total of (20+24) 44 yrs	no change
	29	Guilty of gang robbery and gang rape	Total of (20+24) 44 yrs	29 yrs 4 mths — imprisonment
Dec 1986	30	Guilty of gang robbery and murder	Total of 22 yrs 6 mths — imprisonment and death	Death
	31	Guilty of gang robbery	22 yrs 6 mths imprisonment	15 yrs imprisonment
	32	Guilty of gang robbery	22 yrs 6 mths imprisonment	11 yrs 3 mths — imprisonment
	33	Guilty of gang robbery	22 yrs 6 mths imprisonment	no change
Dec 1986	34	Guilty of gang robbery, attempted murder, and attempted rape	Total of (22 yrs 6 mths+10+6) 38 yrs 6 mths imprisonment	no change
	35	Guilty of gang robbery	22 yrs 6 mths imprisonment	11 yrs 3 mths — imprisonment
Dec 1986	36	Guilty of rape and deprivation of liberty	Total of (8+2) 10 yrs imprisonment	no change
Sep 1986	37	Guilty of robbery and rape	Total of (2+7) 9 yrs imprisonment	no change
	38	Guilty of robbery	2 yrs imprisonment	no change
	39	Guilty of robbery	2 yrs imprisonment	no change

	40	Guilty of gang robbery	24 yrs imprisonment	no change
May 1987	41	Guilty of gang robbery	24 yrs imprisonment	no change
	42	Guilty of gang robbery	24 yrs imprisonment	no change
	43	Guilty of rape and deprivation of liberty	Total of (6+2) 8 yrs imprisonment	5 yrs imprisonment
Jul 1987	44	Guilty of rape and deprivation of liberty	Total of (6+2) 8 yrs imprisonment	6 yrs imprisonment
	45	Guilty of rape and deprivation of liberty and robbery	Total (6+2+12) 20 yrs imprisonment	15 yrs imprisonment
Aug 1987	46	Guilty of robbery	5 yrs imprisonment	no change
	47	Guilty of gang robbery and operating an unlicensed fishing boat	15 yrs + 2 mths imprisonment	no change
Oct 1987	48	Guilty of gang robbery	15 yrs imprisonment	no change
	49	Guilty of gang robbery	15 yrs imprisonment	no change
	50	Guilty of gang robbery, rape and deprivation of liberty	Total of (15+20+2) 37 yrs imprisonment	

Footnotes:
*Sentences of imprisonment are sometimes halved in cases where defendant enters guilty plea
**Sentence halved on account of defendant's being a minor at the time the offence was committed
***Under Thai Penal Code, maximum permitted for accumulated sentences of imprisonment is 50 years imprisonment

APPENDIX 6

GULF OF THAILAND: ANTI-PIRACY ACTIVITIES AND SELECTED MARITIME CLAIMS

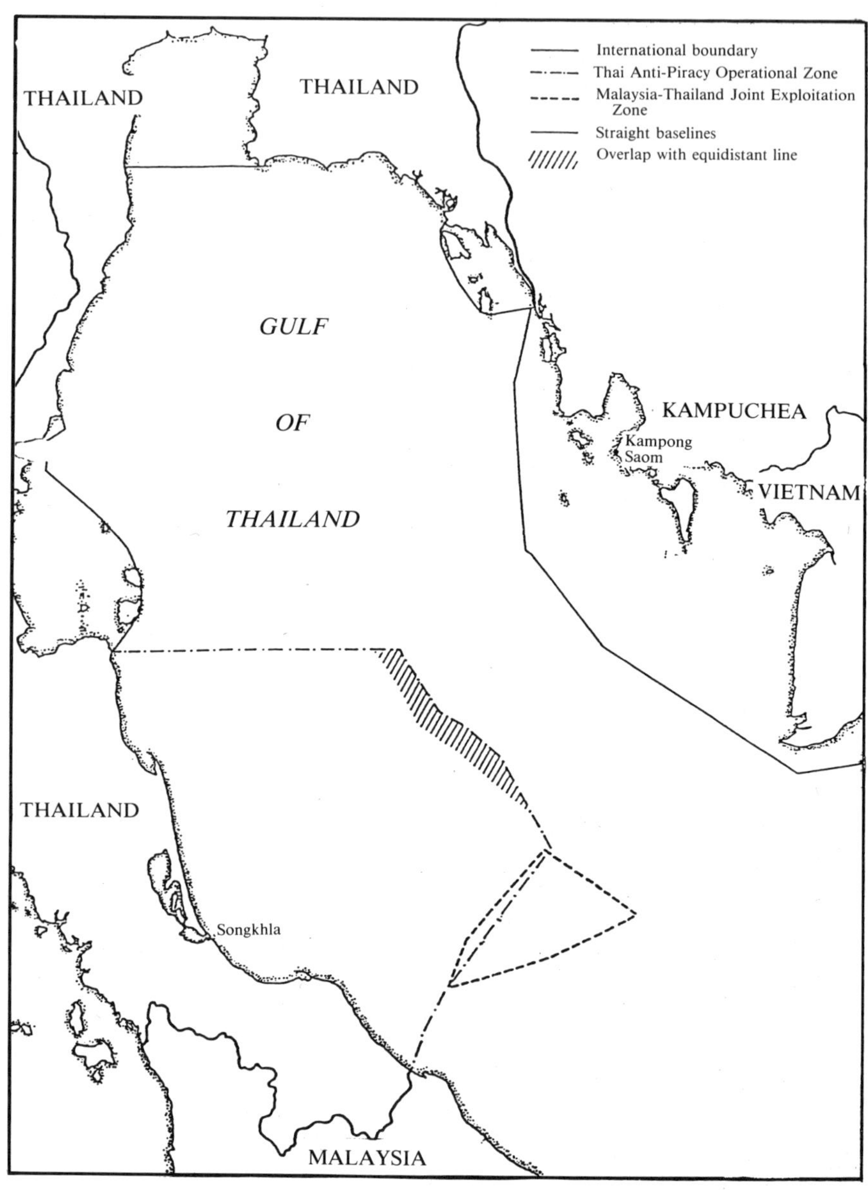

CHRONOLOGY OF PIRACY INCIDENTS AFFECTING VIETNAMESE REFUGEES—JANUARY-OCTOBER 1987

1. Group of 3 refugees left Cong Ngiep, Minh Hai on 7 January at 1300. On 8 January at 0900 the two crewmen of a fishing vessel, one of whom was armed with a pistol, boarded their boat and robbed the refugees of their valuables. On 9 January at 1000 they were again attacked by the crew of a fishing vessel, two of whom were armed with rifles, but no valuables were found during the boat and body search. The group arrived in Songkhla on 10 January.
2. Group of 20 refugees left Rach Gia, Kien Giang on 15 January at 1900. On 19 January at 1200 they were attacked and robbed by the crew of a fishing vessel. The same day they were rescued by a merchant vessel and arrived in Singapore on 23 January.
3. Group of 16 refugees left Camau, Minh Hai on 19 January at 2230. On 20 January at 1000 they were attacked by the crew of a fishing vessel, armed with an M-16 rifle and a pistol, who conducted a boat and body search, after which five women were raped on board the fishing vessel and returned to the refugee boat the next morning. The group arrived at Koh Samui on 24 January.
4. Group of 82 refugees left Hoc Nang, Minh Hai on 21 January at 2400. On 23 January at 1200 they were attacked by two fishing vessels, the crew of which conducted robbery, assault and raped five woman. They were released the next morning and landed in Perhantian Besar, Malaysia on 21 January.
5. Group of 6 refugees left Camau, Minh Hai on 10 January at 1000. On 14 January at 0800 they were attacked by one crew of a fishing vessel, who did a boat and body search. The group arrived at Koh Pangan on 27 January.
6. Group of 92 refugees left Rach Gia, Kien Giang on 3 February at 1400. On 4 February at 1000 they were robbed by the crew of a fishing vessel. At 1130 they were again attacked by the crew of another fishing vessel. During the same day a third attack occurred by the crew of a fishing vessel, during which they were robbed and 10 women were raped. On 5 February at 0500 the crew of another fishing vessel did a boat and body search, after which they provided assistance. The group arrived at the oil rigs on 14 February and were transferred to Songkhla on 24 March.
7. Group of 16 refugees left Rach Soi, Kien Giang on 12 February at 2000. On 14 February at 0900 they were attacked by the crew of a fishing vessel, who conducted boat and body search, damaged the engine, and robbed some valuables. The group landed at an unknown location on 15 February, where they spent two nights after which they continued their journey to land in Tumpat, Malaysia on 17 February.
8. Group of 19 refugees left Rach Gia, Kien Giang, on 12 February at 0500. On 13 February at 1400 they were attacked by the crew of a fishing vessel, who conducted a boat and body search. The same day at 1800 they were again attacked by another fishing vessel, the crew of which took away more valuables. They arrived at 2200 at Klong Yai.
9. Group of 8 refugees left Camau, Minh Hai on 12 February at 0100. The same day at 1100 they were attacked by the crew of a fishing vessel, who armed with two rifles and one pistol conducted a boat and body search, after which they took three women and one child to the fishing vessel, where the women were repeatedly gang raped and released the next morning back to their boat. A few hours later later at 0800 the group was again attacked by two other fishing vessels. The three women and one child were abducted, after which the refugee boat was rammed and sunk, after four men had fallen overboard. After half an hour the four men were picked up by the crew of the second vessel, their hands were tied and they were thrown back into the sea. They were again picked up, their hands re-tied and put into the fish hold of the second vessel. One of the four abductees of the first vessel was thrown into the sea, with her hands tied, on 18 February after having been beaten and kicked. She managed to untie her hands and was rescued that evening by the crew of a fishing vessel, who treated her well. They prepared a bamboo-float on which she was released that night. The next day she was rescued again. After having switched boats on 21 February she arrived in Pattani on 23 February. There is no information on any other survivors.
10. Group of 45 refugees left Rach Gia, Kien Giang on 17 February at 2000. On 19 February at 1100 they were attacked by the crew of a fishing vessel, who did the boat and body search, assaulted many of the refugees, and forced the women and

children to board the fishing vessel, where they stayed until the next morning, during which time one woman was raped. The other eight women resisted being raped by the crew and were subsequently beaten. The group landed in Thepa on 20 February.

11. Group of 31 refugees left Badong, Cuulong on 17 February at 2300. On 22 February at 0600 they were attacked by the crew of a fishing vessel, who did a boat and body search taking away some valuables. Thereafter this fishing vessel towed the refugee boat until they landed in Sathing Pra on 1 March.

12. Group of 12 refugees left Hatien, Kien Giang, on 18 February at 0400. On 28 February at 1200 they were attacked by the crew of three fishing vessels, who conducted a boat and body search after which assistance was provided. They landed in Prachuab on 3 March.

13. Group of 7 refugees left Rach Gia, Kien Giang on 19 February at 2200. On 24 February at 1000 they met a fishing vessel, the crew of which did a boat and body search and also attempted unsuccessfully to abduct one woman. The group landed at Sichon on 25 February.

14. Group of 4 refugees left Rach Gia, Kien Giang, on 19 February at 1600. On 24 February at 1130 they met a fishing vessel. The sole crew provided assistance until around 1900 when another vessel arrived, the crew of which did a boat and body search taking away some valuables, after which the group continued their journey to land in Pak Nam, Chumporn on 25 February.

15. Group of 4 refugees left Rach Gia, Kien Giang, on 26 February at 0100. On 2 March at 0100 they were attacked by the crew of a fishing vessel, who conducted a search taking away some valuables. The group landed at Klong Yai on 2 March at 0900.

16. Group of 5 refugees left Koh Kong, on 2 March at 0400. The same day at 0800 they were robbed by the crew of a fishing boat, after which they landed in Klong Yai at 0830.

17. Group of 46 refugees left Can Tho, Hau Giang, on 5 March at 2200. On 7 March at 1800 they were attacked by the crew of a fishing boat, who did a boat and body search taking away some valuables. After providing assistance they left the refugee boat. The group landed in Pulau Bidong, Malaysia on 9 March.

18. Group of 29 refugees left Koh Kong, on 8 March at 0400. On 9 March at 0730 they were attacked by the armed crew of a fishing vessel, who conducted robbery. Two hours later the crew of two small fishing vessels searched the refugees, but did not find any valuables. The group landed at Klong Yai on 9 March at 1000.

19. Group of 18 refugees left Koh Kong, on 12 March at 0600. On the same day at 0900, the crew of three fishing vessels conducted a boat and body search, after which the group landed in Klong Yai at 1500.

20. Group of 8 refugees left Long Phu, Hau Giang, on 12 March at 1530. On 18 March at 1400 they met a fishing vessel, the sole crew of which was asked for assistance. But when three refugees boarded his vessel, he told one refugee, a boy, to navigate, whilst he raped the two women. The boy started screaming and was beaten and thrown overboard. At 1800 another fishing vessel, also with one crew, joined the attack and one woman was passed to this vessel. The next morning the women were released and all continued their journey until 21 March they met another fishing vessel, the crew of which did a boat and body search, taking away one engine. On 25 March at 1100 they landed at an unknown location, where they were provided with food, fuel and water, after which they were told to leave. The group arrived the same day in Petchburi.

21. Group of 9 refugees left Camau, Minh Hai, on 24 February at 2300. On 26 February at 0800 they were met by a fishing vessel. the crew of which towed the boat to Tho Chu island, where they robbed the refugees, also taking their boat. At 1700 the refugees found a damaged boat which they repaired. On 8 March at 0700 they left. On 13 March at 0800 they were attacked by the crew of a fishing vessel, who did a boat and body search. At 0900 three small boats met the refugee boat. The armed crew boarded the boat and did a boat and body search, after which the refugees landed in Koh Pangan at 1200.

22. Group of 2 refugees left Koh Kong, on 13 March at 1500. On 14 March at 0100 they were attacked by the armed crew of a small fishing vessel, who robbed them of some valuables, They landed in Klong Yai the same day at 2200.

23. Group of 17 refugees left Rach Gia, Kien Giang on 19 March at 0330. On 22 March at 1200 they were attacked by the crew of a fishing vessel, who attempted to take two women, but this was successfully prevented. The group arrived in Sattahip the same day at 1700.

24. Group of 3 refugees left Koh Kong, on 30 March at 0300. At 0700 they were attacked by the crew of a fishing vessel, who took away some valuables. At 0830 the group landed in Klong Yai.

25. Group of 4 refugees left Rach Gia, Kien Giang on 27 March at 2300. On 31 March at 0630 the crew of a fishing vessel robbed them, after which at 1900 they arrived in Klong Yai.

26. Group of 16 refugees left Koh Kong on 31 March at 0300. On the same day at 1000 they were attacked by six fishing vessels, the crew of which took away some valuables. They landed in Laem Glut/Trad at 1600.

27. Group of 32 refugees left Kien Giang on 30 March at 0900. On 2 April at 1900 they were attacked by a fishing vessel, which towed their boat to Koh Man Nai, where the crew conducted a boat and body search, following which five women were raped. Thereafter the group was returned to their boat and landed in Laem Ngob on 3 April.

28. Group of 6 refugees left Kampongsom on 2 April at 1900. On 3 April at 1100, they were attacked by the crew of a fishing vessel, who conducted boat and body search. The group landed in Laem Ngob on 4 April.

29. 1 refugee left Koh Salad on 2 April at 1700. On 3 April he was robbed by the crew of a fishing vessel and landed thereafter in Klongyai.

30. Group of 10 refugees left Kampongsom on 3 April at 1100. On 4 April at 0700, the crew of a fishing vessel robbed the refugees of some valuables. The group landed in Klongyai the same day.

31. Group of 14 refugees left Ong Doc, Minh Hai, on 8 April at 2200. On 11 April at 1000; 12 April at 1300; 13 April at 2400; and 14 April at 1200 they were attacked by the crew of fishing vessels, who each time conducted the boat and body search. During the last attack one woman was raped. On 16 April they landed at an unknown location and were generously assisted. On 21 April they were provided with a new boat and landed in Kuala Besar, Malaysia the same day.

32. Group of 10 refugees left Cai Doi, Minh Hai, on 9 April at 2400. On 10 April at 1500 they were attacked by the crew of a fishing vessel, who did a boat and body search and raped two women. The group landed in Pulau Bidong on 14 April.

33. Group of 4 refugees left Go Cong Ong Trang, Minh Hai, on 11 April at 1700. On 14 April at 1800 they were attacked by the crew of a fishing vessel, who did a boat and body search, taking away some valuables. The group landed in Kuala Besar, Malaysia, on 15 April.

34. Group of 19 refugees left Camau, Minh Hai, on 6 April at 0800. On 15 April they arrived at an uninhabited island, from where they left again on 16 April at 1400. At 1500 they were attacked by the crew of a small fishing vessel, who conducted a boat and body search. Thereafter they were joined by three more fishing vessels, the group was brought ashore, more items were robbed and three women were raped. The group was released and continued their journey until 17 April at 0700 when they arrived in Pathiew, Chumporn.

35. Group of 29 refugees left Camau, Minh Hai, on 13 April at 1900. On 16 April at 1000 they were attacked by the crew of a fishing vessel, who conducted a boat and body search. They arrived in Ranode, Songkhla on 18 April.

36. Group of 21 refugees left Co Gong, Minh Hai, on 22 April at 1900. On 26 April at 1300 they met four fishing vessels, one of which attacked their boat, and robbed them of some valuables. The group continued their journey and landed at Songkhla on 27 April.

37. Group of 28 refugees left Ho Chi Minh City on 22 April at 1900. On 25 April at 1730 they were attacked by the crew of a fishing vessel and robbed of some valuables. The group continued their journey and landed at Galang, Indonesia on 5 May.

38. Group of 13 refugees left Camau, Minh Hai on 26 April at 2330. On 30 April at 1900 they approached a fishing vessel in order to request assistance, which was generously provided. Thereafter the crew searched the refugee boat during which some refugees gave some valuables. The group continued the journey and landed at Pak Panang on 1 May.

39. Group of 27 refugees left Cong Nghiep, Minh Hai, on 28 April at 0330. On 1 May at 1800 they were attacked by the crew of a fishing vessel, who conducted robbery, assault, rape of two women after which they abducted one woman. On 3 May at 1400 the remaining refugees were again attacked and suffered robbery. They landed at Pulau Bidong, Malaysia, on 5 May. Abductee was recovered in Thailand on 13 May.

40. Group of 55 refugees left Lien Thoi Thuang, Hua Giang on 4 May at 1930. On 6 May at 1900 they were robbed by the crew of a fishing vessel, who also attempted to abduct and rape, but failed. The group landed at Galang, Indonesia on 8 May.

41. Group of 23 refugees left Ganh Hao, Minh Hai on 5 May at 2030. On 7 May at 1300 they were attacked by the crew of a fishing vessel, who conducted boat and body search taking away some valuables. The group landed at Pulau Bidong, Malaysia, on 8 May.

42. Group of 18 refugees left Rach Gia, Kien Giang on 8 May at 0430. On 9 May at 0600 they met a fishing vessel, the crew of which did a boat and body search, taking away some valuables. Thereafter the group continued the journey and landed at Pulau Bidong, Malaysia on 11 May.

43. Group of 11 refugees left Kampongsom on 14 May at 1900. On 15 May at 0100 they were attacked by the crew of a fishing vessel, who conducted a boat and body search taking away many valuables. The group landed in Klong Yai on 16 May.

44. Group of 43 refugees left Rach Gia, Kien Giang on 13 May at 2100. On 16 May at 1100 they were attacked by the crew of two fishing vessels, who robbed them of some valuables. The group arrived at the oil rigs on 17 May and were transferred to Songkhla on 26 June.

45. Group of 40 refugees left Rach Gia, Kien Giang on 22 May at 1800. On 24 May at 1500 they approached two fishing vessels for assistance, but instead the crew of a fishing vessel came aboard their boat and robbed some valuables. Thereafter generous assistance was provided. The group landed at Koh Kra on 26 May.

46. Group of 35 refugees left Rach Gia, Kien Giang on 25 May at 0400. On 26 May at 0800 they were attacked by the crew of a fishing vessel, who took away some valuables. The group landed at Pulau Bidong, Malaysia on 28 May.

47. Group of 14 refugees left Camau, Minh Hai on 25 May at 0300. On 26 May at 1500 they were attacked by the crew of a fishing vessel, who conducted armed robbery and raped four women. The group arrived at the oil rigs on 31 May and were transferred to Songkhla on 26 June.

48. Group of 103 refugees left Can Tho on 26 May at 1830. On 29 May at 1700 they were attacked by the crew of a fishing vessel, who robbed them of their valuables, after which they provided assistance. The group landed in Palawan, Philippines on 6 June.

49. Group of 21 refugees left Vinh Hai, Hau Giang on 6 June at 0500. On 9 June at 1500 they were ordered by the crew of a fishing vessel to board their boat. During their stay on board until 1200 of 10 June they were robbed of their valuables and two women were raped. On 12 June at 1500 they were again attacked by the crew of another fishing vessel, resulting in one robbery victim. The group landed in Sichon the same day at 1700.

50. Group of 25 refugees left Camau, Minh Hai on 4 June at 1600. On 15 June at 1600 they were assisted by the crew of a fishing vessel, following which the crew conducted a body search, resulting in two robbery victims. The group landed at Koh Kra on 17 June.

51. Group of 5 refugees left Kampongsom on 4 June at 0500. On 5 June at 0900 they were attacked by the crew of two fishing vessels, who conducted a boat and body search, taking away some valuables. The group landed at Koh Kut the same day.

52. Group of 5 refugees left Koh Kong on 21 June at 2400. On 22 June at 0100 they were attacked by the crew of a small fishing vessel, who robbed them of some valuables and a boat engine. The group landed in Klong Yai the same day.

53. Group of 11 refugees left Phu Quoc on 21 June at 1930. On 23 June at 1400 they were approached by a fishing vessel, the crew of which told the women and children to board their vessel. During their stay on board four women were raped. They were released on 24 June at 0400. The group landed in Rayong on 27 June.

54. Group of 122 refugees left Dinh An, Hau Giang, on 24 June at 2200. On 28 June at 1400 they were attacked by the crew of a fishing vessel, two of whom were armed with an axe and a knife. They requested valuables, searched the boat and assaulted three refugees. The group landed at Yaring, Budi on 3 July.

55. Group of 17 refugees left Kampongsom on 24 July at 2200. On 26 July at 0700 they were attacked by the crew of a fishing vessel, who conducted robbery. On 27 July at 0900 they were robbed of their remaining valuables. The group arrived in Koh Kut that same day.

56. Group of 13 refugees left Kampongsom on 6 August at 2400. On 7 August at 1800 they met a fishing vessel with a crew of three, who ordered them to give valuables, which they did not have. The refugee boat tried to flee but was caught up again. After making some remarks, the crew of the fishing vessel left at high speed causing waves which sank the refugee boat. The sole survivor swam to shore and landed in Klong Yai the same day.

57. Group of 16 refugees left Hatien, Kien Giang on 20 August at 2000. On 23 August at 1100 they were attacked by two crew of a small fishing vessel who robbed them of some valuables. The group landed in Klong Yai on 25 August.

58. Group of 211 refugees left Go Cong, Tien Giang on 3 September at 2300. On 6 September at 0700 they were met by the crew of a fishing vessel, who provided assistance and towed their boat until 1500. Then, all armed, the crew boarded the refugee boat and conducted body search. Three women were repeatedly raped, and one woman sexually assaulted. The attack lasted for three hours after which they released the boat. On 13 September the refugees were rescued by a merchant vessel and arrived in Bangkok on 16 September.

59. Group of 9 refugees left Kampongsom on 27 September at 1900. On 28 September at 1100 they were threatened and robbed by the crew of a fishing vessel, who took away valuables. Thereafter this vessel was joined by another. All refugees were forced to board the first vessel, they were body searched and more valuables were taken. The group arrived in Koh Kut the same day.

APPENDIX 8

GUIDELINES FOR THE DISEMBARKATION OF REFUGEES

United Nations High Commissioner for Refugees

What are the Procedures?

1. When a vessel picks up refugees at sea, it should normally proceed to the first *scheduled* port of call, informing the ship's agent by radio of the number of refugees the vessel has on board and the circumstances of their rescue.

2. The ship's agent should in turn inform the port and immigration authorities of the presence of refugees on board, requesting permission for the ship to enter the harbour. The ship's agent should also inform the local UNHCR office and the diplomatic representative of the country whose flag the ship is flying.

3. Should the vessel be flying the flag of a country in a position to resettle refugees, the diplomatic representative of that country will inform the local authorities of his government's willingness to accept the refugees for resettlement, normally within 90 days of their disembarkation.

4. If the vessel flies a flag of open registry, or a flag of a country which cannot reasonably be expected to accept refugees for resettlement, UNHCR will contact countries which have contributed to a special pool of resettlement places known as Disembarkation Resettlement Offers (DISERO) to provide disembarkation guarantees and share responsibility for subsequent resettlement.

5. Once the guarantee has been conveyed by the relevant diplomatic mission to the local authorities, immigration and UNHCR officials will board the vessel to interview the refugees. Upon completion of the interviews, the refugees will be allowed to disembark. It should be noted that once refugees are disembarked, they are no longer of concern to the vessel or the company which owns, charters or manages the vessel.

6. Upon disembarkation, each refugee will be examined by local health authorities and given medical assistance as necessary. UNHCR covers all care and maintenance expenses.

Checklist on Action to be Taken

A. by the ship's master

The following information is generally required by all ports before permission for the disembarkation of refugees can be granted and should be radioed or cabled to the next scheduled port of call as soon as possible:

- Name of the rescuing ship.
- Flag and port of registry of the rescuing ship.
- Name and address of the owner of the ship.
- Owner's agent at the next port.
- Estimated date and time of arrival at the next port.
- Estimated date and time of departure from the next port and destination.
- Exact number of refugees on board.
- Date, time, latitude and longitude position at time of rescue.
- State of health of refugees on board and whether any are in need of emergency medical treatment upon arrival.

It will hasten disembarkation if a list of refugees' full names, by family groups, showing date of birth, nationality and sex, is typed out and handed to the port immigration authorities on arrival or, if possible, is transmitted to the ship's agent prior to arrival.

B. by the ship's agent

All information supplied by the ship's master should be conveyed to the ship's owner, or diplomatic representative of the ship's flag state and the UNHCR office in the country of disembarkation.

What Costs are Reimbursable

On request, UNHCR will reimburse shipowners for the subsistence of refugees on board ship, which will normally be calculated at US$ 10 per refugee per day. In addition, other expenditure arising as a direct result of rescue can be claimed.

Claims should be directed to the appropriate P & I Club which will examine and forward them to UNHCR. Shipowners not belonging to a P & I Club should submit claims directly to UNHCR Headquarters. All documentary evidence, including original receipts where appropriate, should be submitted with the claim.

The maximum amount reimbursed under any single claim should not normally exceed US$ 30,000. On an exceptional basis claims in excess of US$ 30,000 will be considered.

Special Guidelines

General Location

Generally, refugee boats are found in the South China Sea area within the latitudes 0° 23° north and longitudes 102° to 120° east. When ships are in that area, the radar observer and lookouts, watch officer and quartermaster on the bridge, should be cautioned to be vigilant and alert at all times as the refugee boats are usually small and difficult to sight. Lookouts in particular should be instructed to scan not only forward, but abeam and astern.

Gulf of Thailand

For masters of those merchant ships which trade in the Gulf of Thailand, we ask that you also be guided by the suggestions outlined in this pamphlet as there are numerous refugee boats crossing the southern half of the Gulf.

Embarkation Precautions

When the refugee boat comes alongside, precautions should be taken by the ship's crew to prevent the boat from striking the hull of the rescuing vessel as the refugee boats are quite fragile. This can best be done, particularly in inclement weather, by launching one of the ship's lifeboats with two or three crew members, to instruct the refugees on how to approach the larger vessel. These crew members should also instruct the refugees to remain calm during embarkation procedures and not to surge to one side of their boat as this could cause capsizing.

Before actual embarkation begins, if possible, a cargo net should be spread beneath the accommodation ladder in the event someone falls.

Small children, the elderly and the infirm should be assisted as much as possible during embarkation procedures.

Medical Attention

Many of the refugees may have been at sea for weeks and will be suffering from exposure, hunger, dehydration and extreme fatigue. During their first days aboard they should be given liquids and food in small portions, but very frequently, say, every two hours. For any specialized medical problems, advice should be sought by ship's radio through the vessel's agent.

Life or death – You could be the difference!

The following are representative summaries of recent reports provided by surviving refugees in Singapore, Hong Kong and Malaysia. While in all three cases merchant ships eventually performed rescues, in two of the cases lives were lost, because the refugees were not rescued in time.

– One describes a journey made by an average size refugee boat with 24 refugees on board... After five days at sea the engine broke down. Ships flying various flags passed by, one refused requested assistance. After seven days the refugees ran out of food and water. Many more ships passed by. After 20 days, two men tried to swim towards a light at sea, but disappeared. After 21 days, two more refugees attempted to reach a light and were not seen again. On the 23rd day, a ten year old boy and a 23 year old man died of starvation. On the 24th day one young man fell overboard and was drowned. On the 26th day the boat reached land and the survivors were hospitalized.

– Another stated... At 12:00, at approximately the same location where their ultimate rescue took place, a ship passed within 150 metres, heading for Singapore. It was a container ship and the refugees clearly saw the crew on deck looking at them. The ship also slowed down as it passed.

– From a third report... The refugee boat departed with 30 refugees on board. They had engine trouble and drifted for 20 days during which they encountered at least 20 merchant vessels but none stopped to rescue. Some ships actually altered course to avoid passing close to the refugee boat. Five children and four adults died of exhaustion while one adult died after being rescued.

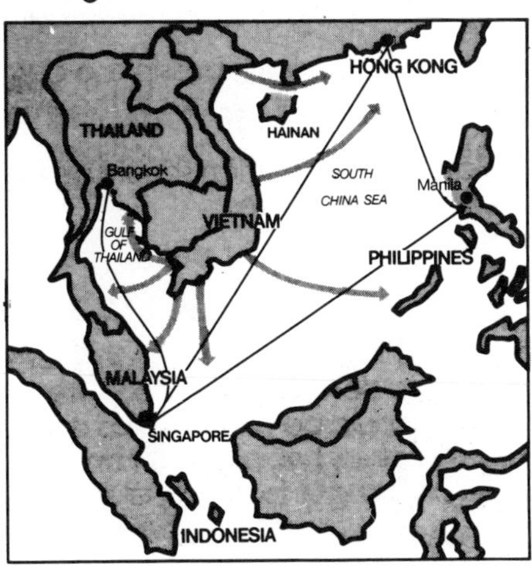

Cable Addresses, Telex and Teleph

UNHCR Headquarters
P.O. Box 2500
CH-1211 Geneva 2 Dépôt
Switzerland

ASIA AND OCEANIA

UNHCR Regional Office for Australia, New Zealand and the South Pacific
Tel: (062) 57 20 55
Telex: 61741 HCRAUL
Cable: HICOMREF Canberra (Australia)

Office of the UNHCR Chargé de Mission in China
Tel: 532 37 31-35
532 16 47
Telex: 22 314 DPBJG CN
Cable: HICOMREF Beijing (China)

Office of the UNHCR Chargé de Mission in Hong Kong
Tel: 3-780 9271-4
Telex: 34 980 UNHCR HX
Cable: HICOMREF Hong Kong

Office of the UNHCR Chargé de Mission in India
Tel: 69 93 02
69 72 79
Telex: 3162885 HCR IN
Cable: HICOMREF New Dehli (India)

UNHCR Branch Office in Indonesia
Tel: 33 32 47
Telex: 61842 HICREF
Cable: HICOMREF Jakarta (Indonesia)

UNHCR Branch Office in Japan
Tel: 475 1615/16
Telex: 34 181 HCRTKY
Cable: HICOMREF Tokyo (Japan)

UNDP Office in the Republic of Korea*
Tel: 633 9451-54
679 9455
Telex: K 27 366
Cable: UNDEVPRO Seoul (Korea)

* UNHCR is represented by UNDP in Korea.

UNHCR Branch Office in Malaysia
Tel: 03-241 13 22
Telex: 30 061 UNHCR MA
Cable: HICOMREF Kuala Lumpur (Malaysia)

UNHCR Sub-Office in Karachi, Pakistan
Tel: 54 48 47
54 46 45
Telex: 23050 UNHCR PK
Cable: HICOMREF Karachi (Pakistan)

UNHCR Branch Office in the Philippines
Tel: 818 5121/22
818 18 23
Telex: 66 908 UNHCR
Cable: HICOMREF Manila (Philippines)

UNHCR Branch Office in Singapore
Tel: 222 1393
Telex: 33 684 HCRSIN
Cable: HICOMREF Singapore

UNHCR Branch Office in Thailand
Tel: 281 1671
Telex: 84 327 UNHCR-TH
Cable: HICOMREF Bangkok (Thailand)

e Numbers of UNHCR Offices

Tel: 39 81 11
Telex: 27 492 UNHCR CH
Cable: HICOMREF Geneva (Switzerland)

EUROPE AND NORTH AMERICA

UNHCR Branch Office in Austria
Tel: 26314047/48
Telex: 115 951 UNHCR A
Cable: HICOMREF Wien (Austria)

UNHCR Branch Office for Belgium and Luxemburg
Tel: 6 490 151/153
6 498 117/119
Telex: 64 352 HICOM B
Cable: HICOMREF Bruxelles (Belgium)

UNHCR Branch Office in Canada
Tel: 232 86 91
232 09 09
Telex: 534 853 HCR OTT
Cable: HICOMREF Ottawa (Canada)

UNHCR Branch Office in the Federal Republic of Germany
Tel: 36 40 11-13
Telex: 885 529 UNHCR D
Cable: HICOMREF Bonn 2 (Federal Republic of Germany)

UNHCR Branch Office in France
Tel: 47 45 74 00
Telex: 613 480 F UNHCR
Cable: UNHCR-F. Neuilly (France)

UNHCR Branch Office in Greece
Tel: 3 633 607
3 610 295
Telex: 222 650 HCR GR
Cable: HICOMREF Athens (Greece)

UNHCR Branch Office in Italy
Tel: 87 81 55
87 71 19
Telex: 622 430 UNHCR I
Cable: HICOMREF Rome (Italy)

UNHCR Branch Office in the Netherlands
Tel: 46 88 10
Telex: 34 418 UNHCR NL
Cable: HICOMREF Den Haag (Netherlands)

UNHCR Branch Office in Portugal
Tel: 57 98 62
57 98 12
Telex: 42 812 UNHCR
Cable: HICOMREF Lisbon (Portugal)

UNHCR Branch Office in Spain
Tel: 456 3649
456 3503
Telex: 23 255 ACNUR
Cable: HICOMREF Madrid (Spain)

UNHCR Office for the Nordic Countries
Tel: 08-72 30 560
Telex: 8 106 198 UNHCR
Cable: HICOMREF Stockholm (Sweden)

UNHCR Branch Office for the United Kingdom and the Republic of Ireland
Tel: 222 3065/6
Telex: 8 951 252 HCRLDN G
Cable: HICOMREF London (UK)

UNHCR Liaison Office in the United States of America
Tel: 387 8546-49
Telex: 64 406 HICOMREF
Cable: HICOMREF Washington D.C. (USA)

DIRECT ARRIVALS AND RESCUE

Further information about rescues at sea from 1984 to 1987 will be found on page 37.

	1980			1981		
direct arrivals	71451			74749		
of whom rescued at sea	15563 (21.8%)			14869 (19.9%)		
Flag country	**ships**	**persons**	**%**	**ships**	**persons**	**%**
ALGERIA	1	12	0.08	1	36	0.24
ARGENTINA	—	—	—	3	139	0.93
AUSTRALIA	2	99	0.64	1	99	0.67
BANGLADESH	—	—	—	1	26	0.17
BELGIUM	—	—	—	3	113	0.76
BERMUDA	1	24	0.15	1	85	0.57
BRAZIL	—	—	—	1	115	0.77
CANADA	2	5	0.03	—	—	—
CYPRUS	2	16	0.10	2	4	0.03
DENMARK	8	374	2.40	10	561	3.78
FRANCE	3	257	1.66	8	598	4.02
GERMANY Fed. Rep.	20	4986	32.03	18	4253	28.60
GREECE	12	524	3.37	4	202	1.36
HONG KONG	2	74	0.48	2	27	0.18
INDIA	1	1	0.01	1	28	0.19
INDONESIA	—	—	—	2	57	0.38
IRAN	—	—	—	—	—	—
IRAQ	—	—	—	1	38	0.26
ITALY	3	141	0.91	1	63	0.42
JAPAN	13	333	2.14	13	339	2.28
KOREA	—	—	—	1	16	0.11
KUWAIT	5	173	1.11	—	—	—
LIBERIA	9	343	2.20	11	578	3.89
MALAYSIA	1	61	0.38	—	—	—
NETHERLANDS	28	1806	11.60	19	1285	8.64
NORWAY	21	1375	8.84	16	1079	7.26
PAKISTAN	—	—	—	5	146	0.99
PANAMA	17	729	4.68	10	320	2.15
PHILIPPINES	1	39	0.25	1	2	0.01
POLAND	1	3	0.02	3	7	0.05
QATAR	—	—	—	—	—	—
SINGAPORE	6	214	1.38	4	21	0.14
SOUTH AFRICA	—	—	—	1	62	0.42
SWEDEN	—	—	—	1	12	0.08
SWITZERLAND	—	—	—	—	—	—
THAILAND	2	121	0.78	1	1	0.01
TUNISIA	—	—	—	—	—	—
UNITED KINGDOM	15	980	6.30	14	610	4.10
U.S.A.	41	2872	18.45	58	3945	26.53
VIETNAM	1	1	0.01	—	—	—
UNKNOWN	—	—	—	2	2	0.01
TOTAL	218	15563	100%	220	14869	100%

AT SEA FROM 1980 TO 1984

1982 43811 6590 (15.0%)			1983 28055 3416 (12.2%)			1984 24783 2172 (8.8%)		
ships	**persons**	**%**	**ships**	**persons**	**%**	**ships**	**persons**	**%**
—	—	—	—	—	—	—	—	—
1	79	1.20	—	—	—	—	—	—
—	—	—	—	—	—	—	—	—
—	—	—	—	—	—	—	—	—
3	91	1.38	1	88	2.58	1	12	0.55
—	—	—	—	—	—	—	—	—
—	—	—	—	—	—	—	—	—
—	—	—	—	—	—	—	—	—
—	—	—	—	—	—	—	—	—
11	468	7.10	8	271	7.94	3	162	7.46
18	1720	26.10	8	392	11.48	4	200	9.21
3	628	9.53	—	—	—	1	42	1.93
1	2	0.03	—	—	—	2	97	4.47
—	—	—	—	—	—	1	16	0.74
—	—	—	—	—	—	—	—	—
—	—	—	—	—	—	—	—	—
—	—	—	1	30	0.88	—	—	—
—	—	—	—	—	—	—	—	—
1	25	0.38	—	—	—	—	—	—
5	194	2.94	6	372	10.89	4	201	9.25
—	—	—	2	20	0.59	—	—	—
1	17	0.26	1	99	2.90	—	—	—
4	347	5.27	4	142	4.15	4	289	13.31
—	—	—	—	—	—	—	—	—
2	105	1.59	3	112	3.28	1	66	3.04
15	730	11.08	7	215	6.29	6	229	10.54
—	—	—	—	—	—	—	—	—
5	135	2.05	5	191	5.59	5	192	8.84
—	—	—	—	—	—	—	—	—
—	—	—	—	—	—	—	—	—
—	—	—	1	20	0.58	1	45	2.07
2	31	0.47	1	118	3.45	3	105	4.83
—	—	—	—	—	—	—	—	—
—	—	—	—	—	—	—	—	—
1	52	0.79	—	—	—	—	—	—
1	27	0.41	—	—	—	—	—	—
1	113	1.71	—	—	—	—	—	—
2	40	0.61	10	327	9.57	5	203	9.35
38	1785	27.09	15	1019	29.83	13	313	14.41
—	—	—	—	—	—	—	—	—
1	1	0.01	—	—	—	—	—	—
116	6590	100%	73	3416	100%	54	2172	100%

APPENDIX 10

THE ORDERLY DEPARTURE PROGRAMME 1979-1988

Resettlement Countries	1979 Jun-Dec	1980	1981	1982	1983	1984	1985	1986	1987	1988 Jan	Cumulative TOTAL
AUSTRALIA*	112	41	63	184	904	2776	2087	2856	1427	166	10616
AUSTRIA	—	9	100	50	100	70	44	23	11	2	409
BELGIUM	280	226	643	359	448	333	137	77	40	1	2544
CANADA*	58	341	1601	1946	3253	1623	5837	2373	1318	111	24461
DENMARK	2	1	47	22	74	54	32	37	110	45	424
FINLAND	—	—	19	12	15	5	10	9	18	4	92
FRANCE	591	1806	2231	2150	2229	1618	1394	801	405	91	13316
GERMANY FR	392	333	1180	629	1678	1733	1148	564	271	21	7949
GREECE	—	—	—	1	13	7	14	4	13	—	52
HONG KONG	7	77	22	11	18	11	7	—	2	—	155
ICELAND	—	—	—	—	12	4	1	—	—	—	17
IRELAND	—	—	—	4	9	3	6	4	3	—	29
ITALY	23	61	70	72	164	93	50	32	27	7	599
IVORY COAST	5	67	26	19	39	60	5	12	13	—	246
JAPAN	—	25	35	23	32	21	16	46	36	30	264
LUXEMBOURG	—	13	24	13	12	3	1	4	8	—	78
NETHERLANDS	141	28	130	78	177	208	133	52	42	15	1004
NEW CALEDONIA	6	23	21	39	36	15	19	11	9	—	179
NEW ZEALAND	—	21	28	24	115	78	44	53	57	7	427
NORWAY	—	1	122	23	197	236	158	101	138	36	1012
PHILIPPINES	—	3	—	2	—	—	6	—	—	—	11
SENEGAL	—	—	—	7	—	10	2	—	—	—	19
SINGAPORE	—	3	5	1	—	—	—	—	—	—	9
SWEDEN	6	9	509	212	225	168	83	98	149	10	1469
SWITZERLAND	44	80	212	82	117	86	29	42	21	—	713
UNITED KINGDOM	20	77	394	200	844	609	314	213	164	26	2861
UNITED STATES	289	1397	2297	3871	8242	13304	13322	10988	8667	904	63181
OTHER COUNTRIES	3	64	36	23	25	26	41	18	12	1	249
TOTAL	1979	4706	9815	10057	18978	29154	24940	18418	12961	1377	132385

* Family reunification programme (bilateral)

INDOCHINESE IN CAMPS

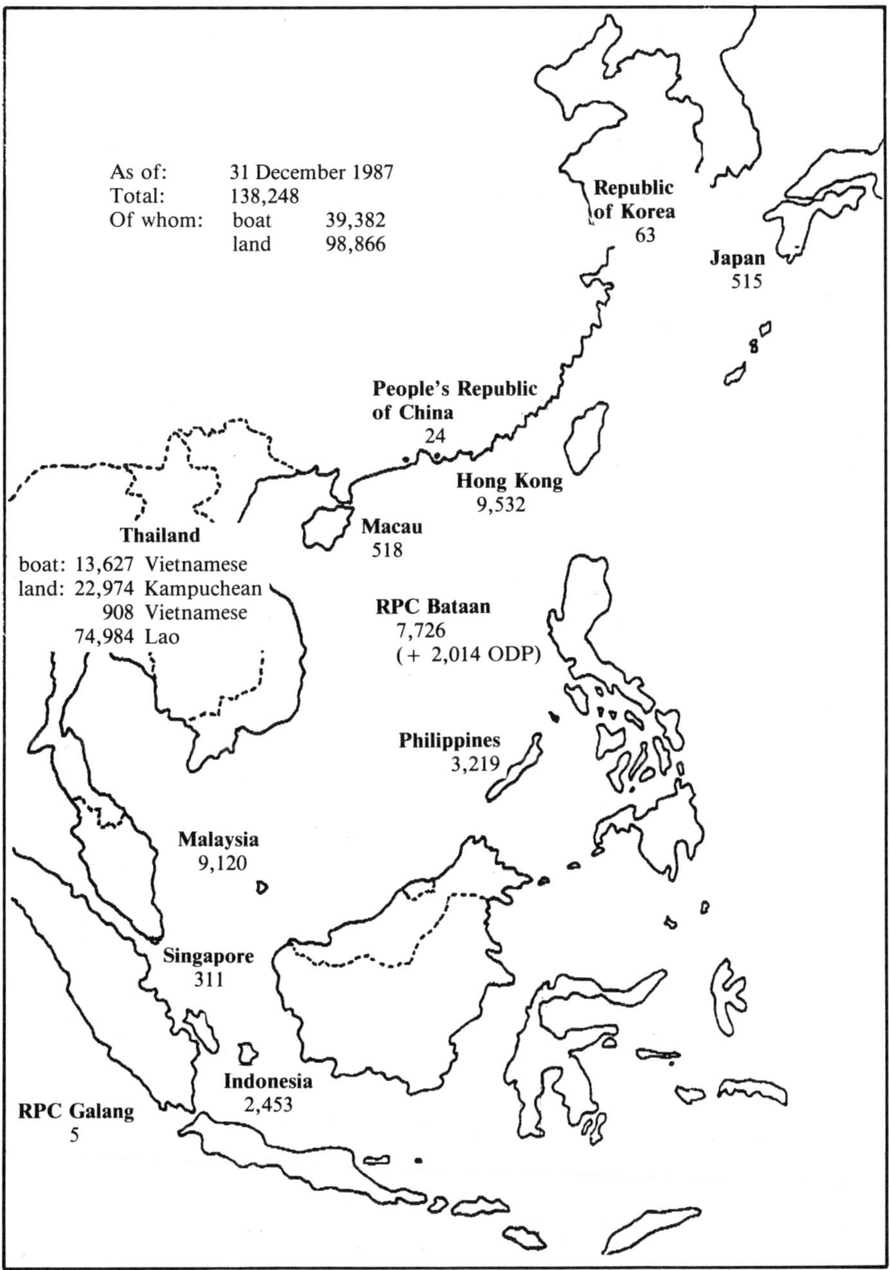

SOME INSTANCES OF POSSIBLE YACHT PIRACY INVOLVING UNITED STATES VESSELS AND NATIONALS

1969	
?	**Kacky Jean** Disappeared from Apalachicola, Florida under mysterious circumstances 1971
1971	
June	**Nina** Hijacked by crew—one of whom suffered a heart attack. Full details on page 66
6 August	**Kamalii** Hijackers intended to go Thailand to collect drugs. Full details on page 66
? August	**Esprit** This yacht, which was in the same race as the **Kamalii,** was hijacked from Honolulu, Hawaii, by three men and disappeared. (1974 Hearings at 160)
1972	
16 July	**Whirlaway** Hijackers intended to go to live on a desert island—violently resisted arrest. Full details on page 66
?	**Ta'aroa** Captain and female crewmember murdered by ex-Nazi. Full details on page 66
1973	
May	**Imamou** Suspected that 2 crew, with known drug involvement, murdered the other 2. Full details on page 67
26 Oct	**Hedonist** Resident of a boat (not an experienced seaman) forced to sail from Los Angeles, murdered at sea. Full details on page 67
1974	
March	**Saba Bank** This yacht, carrying band leader Cy Zenter, disappeared while on a trip from Nassau to Miami. Drug Enforcement officials report that prior to departure potential and known drug suspects were "hanging around" the yacht. The disappearance is considered a drug hijacking by some, but not by the Coast Guard. (1974 Hearings at 158, 160; 1977 Hearings at 131)
? July	**Spook** A charter sports fishing vessel from Key West, Florida, the **Spook** was hijacked by Clifford Thomas and his wife, Patricia Ann McRary (along with their two children) near the Dry Tortugas, Bahamas. Both adults produced weapons and forced the **Spook's** captain, Earl Werner Widner, and crew member, Molly Christine de Witt, to take the boat to Havana, Cuba. There, authorities seized the hijackers and released Widner and de Witt (Mueller and Adler at 135 (Coast Guard Case 5); 1974 Hearings at 170; United States v McRary, 665 F 2d 674 (5th Cir 1982); M Leigh 76 AM J Int'l L 619 (1982))
July	**Ardel** Two New Jersey girls and two young Miami brothers who may have witnessed a smuggling operation using this stolen cabin cruiser were found shot in the head. A fifth casualty, a man known to be involved with narcotics, was found shot in the head and chest and wrapped in a canvas sheet and chains about fifty yards offshore (1974 Hearings at 159)
pre-Aug	**Kat Mai** This new, well equipped trawler disappeared after leaving a Caribbean port with a pick-up crew. A drug connection is suspected. (1974 Hearings at160, 213)

pre-Aug	**Tecumseh** Similar circumstances to **Kat Mai** above. Full details on page 67
pre-Aug	**Lupita** Crew suspected of murdering lessors for one-time drug run. Full details on page 67
pre-Aug	**Perregrine** Disappeared en route to Grand Cayman. Drugs suspected. Full details on page 67
pre-Aug	**Puerto Limon** Suspected drugs hijacking en route to Costa Rica. Full details on page 67
pre-Aug	**Como No** Suspected drugs hijacking. Full details on page 67
? Aug	**Seawind** Owners murdered ("made to walk the plank") by drug traffickers. Full details on page 68
pre-Oct	An Irwin 37 owned by Dr Smith was stolen from Hilton Head Island, S Carolina, and recovered by him in the Caribbean (1974 Hearings at 206) 1976
1976	
18 July	**Feisty** 2 crew killed by pirates off Colombia—the other 2 escaped. Full details on page 68
26 Oct	**Flying Dutchman** Disappeared off Florida coast—authenticated note about "Cubans". Full details on page 68
1977	
27 Jan	**The Pirate's Lady** This vessel with two crewmen vanished on a trip between Apalachicola, Florida and Clearwater, Florida. A Coast Guard search failed to turn up any sign of the ship and the owner stated that he believed it had been hijacked. On 7 March the Drug Enforcement Agency furnished information that the ship had been physically altered and had possibly departed Rio Hache, Colombia on 3 March, bound for the United States. No firm information has been developed that a hijacking occurred (1977 Hearings at 15-16 et passim Los Angeles Times 5 December 1980)
pre-Feb	**Mar** Captain shot attackers (escaped murderers). Full details on page 69
1978	
August	**Sunchaser** Attackers repelled when owner fired over their heads. Full details on page 69
1979	
26 May	**Nooderkroon** Pirates put occupants adrift in rubber raft. Full details on page 69
June	**Divorsea** This boat, with Kathleen Kelly and three friends, vanished off Venezuela en route to Aruba. Her brother suspects an attack by drug runners (Los Angeles Times 5 December 1980)
August	Roy Attaway and Manuel Gracia, while sailing a Blue water 53 in the Yucatan Channel, were twice approached and chased by strange boats (Motor Boating & Sailing January 1980 at 110; *id* May 1980 at 76)
?	**Rig-n-Tom** Received a fake SOS asking for its *own* position. Full details on page 69
? April	**Polymer/Pollymere III** This boat, along with two Americans, owner Lester Conrad (68)

and William Falconer (60) disappeared in light seas while on a trip between Great Harbour Cay, Bahamas and West Palm Beach. Conrad had made this 7 hour trip at least 40 times previously. The vessel was equipped with an automatically inflatable lifeboat and an SOS radio beacon which would have switched on had the boat sunk. A 6 day Coast Guard search turned up no traces. Conrad's family suspected piracy, hiring private investigators and posting a $25,000 reward for information (Time 22 September 1980; Chicago Tribune 5 July 1981; Villar at 149)

June — **Snowbound**
Attackers (in Bahamas) demanded drugs Full details on page 69

25-31 July — **Kalia III**
Mr and Mrs Kamerer murdered off Bahamas. Full details on page 69

Oct/Nov
Unidentified sailboat (US) boarded by bandits from high powered boats in the Bahamas. Boaters were robbed and threatened with guns. No injuries (Chicago Tribune 5 July 1981; Villar at 148)

? Dec — **Eidolon**
While cruising between Key West, Florida and Fort Meyers Beach, Florida, the vessel was followed at night by an unidentified boat without running lights. The Coast Guard stated later that this was probably one of their cutters (A C Ettinger, Hijack Prevention: What you can learn from one Man's terrifying Experience: Motor Boating & Sailing April 1981 at 52)

December — **Bell-Esprit/Belle Esprit**
Chased and shot at by men claiming to be Customs. Full details on page 70

1981

2 June
Unidentified US sailboat and houseboat—allegedly harassed by drug dealers in Bahamas. Full details on page 70

25 Oct — **The Threesome**
Pirates murdered 1 out of 3 people fishing on boat off Bahamas. Full details on page 70

1982

13 Apr — **Whip Ray**
Yacht owner shot 3 pirates—after wife diverted their attention—off Bahamas. Full details on page 70

1987

Apr-May — **Zoom**
2 crew severely injured when surprised pirates stealing travellers cheques off Antigua. Full details on page 71

PROPOSED YACHTJACKING COUNTERMEASURES

From a Document prepared by the Senior Duty Officer, Coast Guard Headquarters Operations Center

(Report of Congressman John M Murphy on the Hijacking of US Pleasure Yachts and Cruisers, House Merchant Marine and Fisheries Committee, 27 August 1974, reprinted in *Coast Guard Miscellaneous—Part 2: Boating Safety. Hearings Before the Subcommittee on Coast Guard and Navigation of the House Merchant Marine and Fisheries Committee* at 157-58 (1975) (1974 Hearings.))

What can the cruising yachtsman do to protect his vessel and its party? The following measures are some that might be considered:

(1) Know your crew! Particularly, hired crewmen, but do not overlook that charming tagalong guest you met around the marina or the docks who was agreeable to making the voyage just for the fun of it! Before setting out on any cruise, regardless of its planned length, insist on positive identification of anyone not an established friend or otherwise well known to you. If the individual is a United States citizen sight his Social Security card and any secondary ID which has a picture or a physical description of the person. If the person is not a citizen, sight his passport and entry visa or alien registration. Record the person's name, date and place of birth and the official numbers of any of the documentation previously discussed. Before departing, deliver personally or mail the complete crew and passenger list to a trusted friend or relative along with the voyage plan and instructions to notify the Coast Guard if you fail to arrive at your destination after a reasonable time. Let all hands know that you have taken this precaution. Do not fail to keep the voyage plan and crew list updated as you progress along your cruise track by frequent contact with the person holding these documents for you.

(2) Before leaving the dock or mooring, check the boat for stowaways!

(3) When going to the assistance of anyone found in apparent distress during your voyage, as any good sailor is of course expected to do, make every effort to contact the nearest Coast Guard radio facility or any coastal radio station and describe the situation along with your intentions. In responding to the situation, apply the first aid principle of taking those fundamental measures necessary for the saving of life while being alert for anything unusual or suspicious which just doesn't seem to fit the situation. This is particularly true when the apparently distressed party insists on boarding your vessel.

(4) When departing on a foreign cruise from a US port, consider clearing with the local Customs Agent. This is not a requirement for non-commercial craft, but the time taken may be well worth the effort. Provide the agent with a complete crew list as mentioned above. List on a Customs Form 4455 all firearms, high value personal and portable boat equipment, particularly foreign made cameras, optical and navigation equipment, and the like, and wherever possible, list the serial numbers of such equipment. This step not only provides a record which may be valuable in case of loss for whatever cause, but may save you considerable trouble in entering and clearing foreign ports and in returning to the United States and clearing Customs if you retain a copy certified by the Customs Officer.

APPENDIX 14

CONVENTION ON THE HIGH SEAS, DONE AT GENEVA ON 29 APRIL 1958

ARTICLES 14 - 23

Article 14

All States shall cooperate to the fullest possible extent in the repression of piracy on the high seas or in any other place outside the jurisdiction of any State.

Article 15

Piracy consists of any of the following acts:

(1) Any illegal acts of violence, detention or any act of depredation, committed for private ends by the crew or the passengers of a private ship or a private aircraft, and directed:

(a) On the high seas, against another ship or aircraft, or against persons or property on board such ship or aircraft;

(b) Against a ship, aircraft, persons or property in a place outside the jurisdiction of any State;

(2)Any act of voluntary participation in the operation of a ship or of an aircraft with knowledge of facts making it a pirate ship or aircraft;

(3) Any act of inciting or of intentionally facilitating an act described in sub-paragraph 1 or sub-paragraph 2 of this article.

Article 16

The acts of piracy, as defined in article 15, committed by a warship, government ship or government aircraft whose crew has mutinied and taken control of the ship or aircraft are assimilated to acts committed by a private ship.

Article 17

A ship or aircraft is considered a pirate ship or aircraft if it is intended by the persons in dominant control to be used for the purpose of committing one of the acts referred to in article 15. The same applies if the ship or aircraft has been used to commit any such act, so long as it remains under the control of the persons guilty of that act.

Article 18

A ship or aircraft may retain its nationality although it has become a pirate ship or aircraft. The retention or loss of nationality is determined by the law of the State from which such nationality was derived.

Article 19

On the high seas, or in any other place outside the jurisdiction of any State, every State may seize a pirate ship or aircraft, or a ship taken by piracy and under the control of pirates, and arrest the persons and seize the property on board. The courts of the State which carried out the seizure may decide upon the penalties to be imposed, and may also determine the action to be taken with regard to the ships, aircraft or property, subject to the rights of third parties acting in good faith.

Article 20

Where the seizure of a ship or aircraft on suspicion of piracy has been effected without adequate grounds, the State making the seizure shall be liable to the State the nationality of which is possessed by the ship or aircraft, for any loss or damage caused by the seizure.

Article 21

A seizure on account of piracy may only be carried out by warships or military aircraft, or other ships or aircraft on government service authorised to that effect.

Article 22

1. Except where acts of interference derive from powers conferred by treaty, a warship which encounters a foreign merchant ship on the high seas is not justified in boarding her unless there is reasonable ground for suspecting:

(a) That the ship is engaged in piracy; or

(b) That the ship is engaged in the slave trade; or

(c) That though flying a foreign flag or refusing to show its flag, the ship is, in reality, of the same nationality as the warship.

2. In the cases provided for in sub-paragraphs (a), (b) and (c) above, the warship may proceed to verify the ship's right to fly its flag. To this end, it may send a boat under the command of an officer to the suspected ship. If suspicion remains after the documents have been checked, it may proceed to a further examination on board the ship, which must be carried out with all possible consideration.

3. If the suspicions prove to be unfounded, and provided that the ship boarded has not committed any act justifying them, it shall be compensated for any loss or damage that may have been sustained.

Article 23

1. The hot pursuit of a foreign ship may be undertaken when the competent authorities of the coastal State have good reason to believe that the ship has violated the laws and regulations of that State. Such pursuit must be commenced when the foreign ship or one of its boats is within the internal waters or the territorial sea or the contiguous zone of the pursuing State, and may only be continued outside the territorial sea or the contiguous zone if the pursuit has not been interrupted. It is not necessary that, at the time when the foreign ship within the territorial sea or the contiguous zone receives the order to stop, the ship giving the order should likewise be within the territorial sea or the contiguous zone. If the foreign ship is within a contiguous zone, as defined in article 24 of the Convention on the Territorial Sea and the Contiguous Zone, the pursuit may only be undertaken if there has been a violation of the right for the protection of which the zone was established.

2. The right of hot pursuit ceases as soon as the ship pursued enters the territorial sea of its own country or of a third State.

3. Hot pursuit is not deemed to have begun unless the pursuing ship has satisfied itself by such practicable means as may be available that the ship pursued or one of its boats or other craft working as a team and using the ship pursued as a mother ship are within the limits of the territorial sea, or as the case may be within the contiguous zone. The pursuit may only be commenced after a visual or auditory signal to stop has been given at a distance which enables it to be seen or heard by the foreign ship.

4. The right of hot pursuit may be exercised only by warships or military aircraft, or other ships or aircraft on government service specially authorised to that effect.

5. Where hot pursuit is effected by an aircraft:

(a) The provisions of paragraph 1 to 3 of this article shall apply *mutatis mutandis*;
(b) The aircraft giving the order to stop must itself actively pursue the ship until a ship or aircraft of the coastal State, summoned by the aircraft, arrives to take over the pursuit, unless the aircraft is itself able to arrest the ship. It does not suffice to justify an arrest on the high seas that the ship was merely sighted by the aircraft as an offender or suspected offender, if it was not both ordered to stop and pursued by the aircraft itself or other aircraft or ships which continue the pursuit without interruption.

6. The release of a ship arrested within the jurisdiction of a State and escorted to a port of that State for the purpose of an enquiry before the competent authorities may not be claimed solely on the ground that the ship, in the course of its voyage, was escorted across a portion of the high seas, if the circumstances rendered this necessary.

7. Where a ship has been stopped or arrested on the high seas in circumstances which do not justify the exercise of the right of hot pursuit, it shall be compensated for any loss or damage that may have been thereby sustained.

UN CONVENTION ON THE LAW OF THE SEA 1982

(ARTICLES 100 - 107 AND 110 - 111)

Article 100
Duty to cooperate in the repression of piracy

All States shall cooperate to the fullest possible extent in the repression of piracy on the high seas or in any other place outside the jurisdiction of any State.

Article 101
Definition of Piracy

Piracy consists of any of the following acts:

(a) any illegal acts of violence or detention, or any act of depredation committed for private ends by the crew or the passengers of a private ship or a private aircraft, and directed:

(i) on the high seas, against another ship or aircraft, or against persons or property on board such ship or aircraft.

(ii) against a ship, aircraft, persons or property in a place outside the jurisdiction of any State;

(b) any act of voluntary participation in the operation of a ship or of an aircraft with knowledge of facts making it a pirate ship or aircraft;

(c) any act of inciting or of intentionally facilitating an act described in subparagraph (a) or (b).

Article 102
Piracy by a warship, government ship or government aircraft whose crew has mutinied

The acts of piracy, as defined in article 101, committed by a warship, government ship or government aircraft whose crew has mutinied and taken control of the ship or aircraft are assimilated to acts committed by a private ship or aircraft.

Article 103
Definition of a pirate ship or aircraft

A ship or aircraft is considered a pirate ship or aircraft if it is intended by the persons in dominant control to be used for the purpose of committing one of the acts referred to in article 101. The same applies if the ship or aircraft has been used to commit any such act, so long as it remains under the control of the persons guilty of that act.

Article 104
Retention or loss of the nationality of a pirate ship or aircraft

A ship or aircraft may retain its nationality although it has become a pirate ship or aircraft. The retention or loss of nationality is determined by the law of the State from which such nationality was derived.

Article 105
Seizure of a pirate ship or aircraft

On the high seas, or in any other place outside the jurisdiction of any State, every State may seize a pirate ship or aircraft, or a ship or aircraft taken by piracy and under the control of pirates, and arrest the persons and seize the property on board. The courts of the State which carried out the seizure may decide upon the penalties to be imposed, and may also determine the action to be taken with regard to the ships, aircraft or property, subject to the rights of third parties acting in good faith.

Article 106
Liability for seizure without adequate grounds

Where the seizure of a ship or aircraft on suspicion of piracy has been effected without adequate grounds, the State making the seizure shall be liable to the State the nationality of which is possessed by the ship or aircraft for any loss or damage caused by the seizure.

Article 107
Ships and aircraft which are entitled to seize on account of piracy

A seizure on account of piracy may be carried out only by warships or military aircraft, or other ships or aircraft clearly marked and identifiable as being on government service and authorised to that effect.

Article 110
Right of visit

1. Except where acts of interference derive from powers conferred by treaty, a warship which encounters on the high seas a foreign ship, other than a ship entitled to complete immunity in accordance with article 95 and 96, is not justified in boarding it unless there is reasonable ground for suspecting that:

(a) the ship is engaged in piracy;

(b) the ship is engaged in the slave trade;

(c) the ship is engaged in unauthorised broadcasting and the flag State of the warship has jurisdiction under article 109;

(d) the ship is without nationality; or

(e) though flying a foreign flag or refusing to show its flag, the ship is, in reality, of the same nationality as the warship.

2. In the cases provided for in paragraph 1, the warship may proceed to verify the ship's right to fly its flag. To this end, it may send a boat under the command of an officer to the suspected ship. If suspicion remains after the documents have been checked, it may proceed to a further examination on board the ship, which must be carried out with all possible consideration.

3. If the suspicions prove to be unfounded, and provided that the ship boarded has not committed any act justifying them, it shall be compensated for any loss or damage that may have been sustained.

4. These provisions apply *mutatis mutandis* to military aircraft.

5. These provisions also apply to any other duly authorised ships or aircraft clearly marked and identifiable as being on government service.

Article 111
Right of hot pursuit

1. The hot pursuit of a foreign ship may be undertaken when the competent authorities of the coastal State have good reason to believe that the ship has violated the laws and regulations of that State. Such pursuit must be commenced when the foreign ship or one of its boats is within the internal waters, the archipelagic waters, the territorial sea or the contiguous zone of the pursuing State, and may only be continued outside the territorial sea or the contiguous zone if the pursuit has not been interrupted. It is not necessary that, at the time when the foreign ship within the territorial sea or the contiguous zone receives the order to stop, the ship giving the order should likewise be within the territorial sea or the contiguous zone. If the foreign ship is within a contiguous zone, as defined in article 33, the pursuit may only be undertaken if there has been a violation of the rights for the protection of which the zone was established.

2. The right of hot pursuit shall apply *mutatis mutandis* to violations in the exclusive economic zone or on the continental shelf, including safety zones around continental shelf installations, of the laws and regulations of the coastal State applicable in accordance with this Convention to the exclusive economic zone or the continental shelf, including such safety zones.

3. The right of hot pursuit ceases as soon as the ship pursued enters the territorial sea of its own State or of a third State.

4. Hot pursuit is not deemed to have begun unless the pursuing ship has satisfied itself by such practicable means as may be available that the ship pursued or one of its boats or other craft working as a team and using the ship pursued as a mother ship is within the limits of the territorial sea, or, as the case may be, within the contiguous zone or the exclusive economic zone or above the continental shelf. The pursuit may only be commenced after a visual or auditory signal to stop has been given at a distance which enables it to be seen or heard by the foreign ship.

5. The right of hot pursuit may be exercised only by warships or military aircraft, or other ships or aircraft clearly marked and identifiable as being on government service and authorised to that effect.

6. Where hot pursuit is effected by an aircraft:

(a) the provisions of paragraphs 1 to 4 shall apply *mutatis mutandis*;

(b) the aircraft giving the order to stop must itself actively pursue the ship until a ship or another aircraft of the coastal State, summoned by the aircraft, arrives to take over the pursuit, unless the aircraft is itself able to arrest the ship. It does not suffice to justify an arrest outside the territorial sea that the ship was merely sighted by the aircraft as an offender or suspected offender, it it was not both ordered to stop and pursued by the aircraft itself or other aircraft or ships which continue the pursuit without interruption.

7. The release of a ship arrested within the jurisdiction of a State and escorted to a port of that State for the purposes of an inquiry before the competent authorities may not be claimed solely on the ground that the ship, in the course of its voyage, was escorted across a portion of the exclusive economic zone or the high seas, if the circumstances rendered this necessary.

8. Where a ship has been stopped or arrested outside the territorial sea in circumstances which do not justify the exercise of the right of hot pursuit, it shall be compensated for any loss or damage that may have been thereby sustained.

RECOMMENDATIONS FOR SECURITY: US MARITIME ADMINISTRATION (MARAD)

GENERAL PRECAUTIONS

1. BE VIGILANT. ANTICIPATE TROUBLE.
2. Provide a general alarm system, to alert all crew members.
3. Have water hoses under pressure nozzles ready at likely boarding places when at sea and in port.
4. Illuminate sides, bows and quarters while running in threat areas and in dangerous ports.

IN PORT

5. Ensure gangway watch can contact shipboard support if needed.
6. Ensure gangway watch can contact local security forces for assistance, if available.
7. Maintain roving patrol on deck in port and at anchor, and ensure that the patrol and the gangway watch are in contact.
8. Use ratguards on all mooring lines, and illuminate the lines.
9. At anchor, use anchor chain collar and messenger line on chain to determine if anything has been attached.
10. Use covers on chain hawse and keep hoses running.
11. Keep bumboats away, and vendors off the ship.

UNDER WAY

12. Keep good radar and visual lookout— including lookout aft.
13. Have searchlights available to illuminate suspected boarding parties.
14. Have signalling equipment, including emergency rocket pistols and guns, available for immediate use.

WHEN SUSPECTED BOARDERS ARE DETECTED

15. Sound the general alarm.
16. Establish VHF contact with shore stations and other ships in the vicinity.
17. Increase speed if practicable.
18. Fire warning rockets.
19. Switch on outside lighting.
20. Use searchlights to illuminate and dazzle suspects.
21. CONTINUE TO MAINTAIN GOOD ALL ROUND WATCH.

AFTER PIRATES HAVE BOARDED

22. Barricade bridge and engine room, if practicable.
23. Barricade the crew in secure areas, if practicable.
24. Report the situation by radio and call for help, if available.
25. DON'T BE HEROIC, if the boarders are armed.

RECOMMENDATIONS FOR SECURITY: BALTIC AND INTERNATIONAL MARITIME COUNCIL (BIMCO)

1. Cargo lights overside.

2. A minimum of two watchmen must be used to patrol decks continuously in addition to the duty officer. On approach of pirate boats, sound the whistle in a series of rapid blasts. Safety helmets should be provided and heavy clothing worn to lessen the impact of broken glass and explosive blast. A good supply of missiles should be ready on board. These can be effectively made from empty beer bottles filled with sand. Empty beer bottles are not recommended since many of them do not break and can merely be thrown back. Hoses should be rigged on both sides of the vessel, at least three on each side. The fire pump should be started and water pressure on deck should be maintained throughout the hours of darkness with the hoses running. The hoses can be loosely lashed to the bulwarks.

3. If the vessel is fitted with a searchlight this should be used to scan the surrounding waters. The aldis lamp can be used to the same effect.

4. Walkie talkies or vessel's loud hailer system should be in operation for direct communication between the watchmen and duty officer.

5. Anchor hawse pipes should be closed with plates provided.

6. For additional protection, weld main storeroom doors using a short length of pipe. This pipe can be tack welded on the bulwark and door edge. This has proved to be far more effective than padlocks.

Emergency Drill in Case of Pirates Boarding

1. If it proves impossible to stop pirates boarding then all crew members should come inside the accommodation.

2. There should only be one entrance remaining open, all others to be securely battened down. This entrance must then be secured.

3. The continuous ringing of the general alarm bell is the signal for everyone to go down into the engine room as quickly as possible. Again only one entrance to remain open.

4. One man to be detailed to check that everybody is inside and to then secure the last remaining door. This means that everyone is enclosed in the steel engine compartment. Generators could be stopped in order to black out the vessel depending on the circumstances, and bearing in mind that there would be no ventilation in the engine room itself.

5. Off West Africa and, generally, elsewhere vessels should steam out to sea during the evening and lie fifteen miles off the general anchor position (form this distance VHF contact is still possible at Lagos and Port Harcourt).

Use of Stronger Deterrents

1. Guns—here one must remember that the prime object is to repel and frighten off boarders, not to kill them. In cases where pirates are unarmed, a shotgun fired in the air form the main deck would be an extremely effective deterrent. In cases where pirates are armed, there is no other choice but to retreat to the most safe place on board, for instance, the engine room.

2. Gas bombs— tear gas would be extremely effective against pirate boats. Even in strong winds, the short duration of concentrated gas would cause chaos and provide a useful deterrent against boarders.

RECOMMENDATIONS FOR SECURITY: INTERNATIONAL SHIPPING FEDERATION

1. Rather than remain in anchorages where ships are most vulnerable to attack either (a) steam at between 20 and 40 miles offshore at night, and only return within VHF range at regular intervals for orders/news from agents or (b) drift (with engines on standby) out of sight of the coast (40-50 miles offshore) at night.

2. When it is necessary to anchor inshore, choose an anchorage away from the fairway, extinguish all lights and do not report exact position by radio to the signal station.

3. Strengthen night watches, with continuous patrols and forecastle head policing and radio contact between watchkeepers and the bridge.

4. Maintain constant short range radar watch, broadcasting on VHF the presence of suspicious craft, seen either visually or on radar; sound general alarm by ship's whistle to alert the crew or other vessels.

5. Seal off all possible means of access to the ship, eg by fitting hawse pipe plates, locking doors and hatch covers, removing all ladders/gangways, maintain constant supply of water to hawse pipes.

6. Fully light the deck, sides and bow and have searchlights and aldis light ready for use. Equip bridge wings with searchlights.

7. Securely seal off access to the accommodation.

8. Rig fire and deck wash hoses with water pressure on.

9. Remove all portable equipment from the deck.

10. Stow containers loaded with valuables door to door or in tiers.

11. Cruise while awaiting pilot.

12. Issue minimum number of cargo manifests, with only a general description of the cargo if possible.

13. Increase speed to seaward when approached by small boats or boarded by pirates to prevent canoes following and to impede the transfer of stolen goods into craft alongside.

RECOMMENDATIONS FOR SECURITY: SWEDISH SHIPOWNERS ASSOCIATION

A. General Precautions

1. Stores etc to be locked and portable equipment on deck and possibly also in lifeboats to be locked away.

2. No ladders or loose ends on the outside.

3. Water hose under pressure with jet pipes ready at possible boarding places.

4. Signalling equipment including emergency rockets, rocket pistols and guns ready for immediate use.

5. Continuous radar and visual lookout to be kept. The lookoutman to watch his eyes darkness adoption and have a good binocular at hand. Furthermore he should be trained to use the search lights vessels are recommended to carry when employed in dangerous areas.

6. The possibility to discover boarding attempts will increase if the ship's sides, bows and quarters are lighted.

7. At anchor the hawse pipes should be covered by steel hatches with the water jets in operation. Otherwise actions as stated above.

8. The barricade locality shall accommodate the entire crew. Doors should be rigid and arranged for safe closing/self-locking, able to be opened only by a key from the outside. It is recommended that the same closing/locking devices are arranged for engine room, bridge and crew's/passengers' accommodation. This locality should be equipped with VHF radio, day signalling lamp and emergency rockets. It is an advantage if there is a compass and arrangements for emergency stop of the engine.

B. Detection of suspect Vessel, Canoe etc before Boarding

1. Trigger off alarm— crew in state of alert.

2. VHF connection to be established with signal station in port, coastal radio station and other ships in the vicinity.

3. Increase speed.

4. Water on deck— hoses to be pressurised.

5. Execute escape manoeuvre.

6. Fire warning rockets with the signal equipment.

7. Utilise the search lights for target detection and following (dazzling).

8. Switch on outside lighting.

C. Action after Pirates have boarded

Should be concentrated on barricading the entire crew in the prepared locality, which should be defendable and possibly have free visibility, at least forward and windows, within reach from outside, should be bullet proof.

D. Policy

The Swedish Shipowners' Association has initiated development project for an electronic

indication, detection and alert system, active at a distance from the vessel.
Furthermore an intensive work is in progress through diplomatic channels to induce the local authorities to increase measures for the protection of merchant vessels. Work is also in progress to try to eliminate undue waiting on the roads after dark.
Regardless if an incident results in boarding or not the master shall notify the local port authorities, the police, his agent and his nearest diplomatic/consular representative.

RECOMMENDATIONS FOR SECURITY: ICC INTERNATIONAL MARITIME BUREAU (IMB)

1. General Preventive Action

1. Local agents should be selected with great care.

2. Cargo and containers should be so stowed as to (a) Keep any theft prone cargo below deck, and (b) Have containers with theft prone cargo, if stowed on deck at all, stowed door to door or stacked in tiers.

3. Lock and bolt all outer doors of deckhouses and the forecastle or, where appropriate, weld them shut (caution: Fire escape routes must be kept unobstructed).

4. Prearrange a retreat (wheelhouse or engine room) for the entire crew and provide it with radio equipment.

5. Provide additional signalling equipment on board.

6. Develop safety plans; instruct all crew members; carry out safety drills and exercises and sound test alerts.

2. Preventive Action when in Areas in which acts of Piracy or armed Robbery may occur

1. Keep in the vicinity of other ships.

2. Establish radio contact and agreed emergency signals with:
—ships in the vicinity
—local authorities (coastguards, harbour policy, harbour master)
—the flag state embassy.

3. Keep the area close around the ship under continuous visual and radar surveillance.

4. Strengthen night watches.

5. Arrange for difficult to control deck areas to be patrolled by extra watchmen carrying walkie talkies.

6. At night, fit additional lighting around the ships to illuminate the area and keep it switched on when in port or in the roads; alternatively, ships should proceed to a position out of sight of the coast and not report positions by radio.

7. Re-check the crew's retreat or retreats that are to be used on board and remind crew members of the instructions.

8. Make the following appliances ready for immediate use:
—fire pumps and hoses
—all available signalling guns complete with signalling ammunition
—objects of any appropriate kinds for throwing, including bags filled with paint
—searchlights.

9. When at anchor seal all openings including hawse pipes.

10. Lock up all portables away from deck, and lock and bolt all doors with the exception of one door leading to the crew's retreat.

11. On sighting any suspicious craft, sound the general alert and report the sighting to the authorities listed at paragraph 2 above, and especially to all ships in the vicinity.

3. Action to be taken when Pirates are boarding

1. Sound the general alert.

2. Report the boarding to the authorities listed above, and especially to all ships in the vicinity.

3. Get the ship underway and start making way.

4. Make appropriate use of signalling equipment, fire pumps and hoses, and objects for throwing, in particular bags filled with paint so that both pirates and craft are marked.

5. Switch on lighting and use searchlights to dazzle pirates.

4. Action to be taken when Pirates are on Board

1. Crew to retreat to pre-arranged retreat.

2. Report the situation to the authorities listed above, and especially to all ships in the vicinity.

INTERNATIONAL MARITIME ORGANIZATION

RESOLUTION A545(13)

Adopted on 17 November 1983

MEASURES TO PREVENT ACTS OF PIRACY AND ARMED ROBBERY AGAINST SHIPS

THE ASSEMBLY,

RECALLING Article 16(j) of the Convention on the International Maritime Organization concerning the functions of the Assembly in relation to regulations concerning maritime safety.

NOTING with great concern the increasing number of incidents involving piracy and armed robbery against ships including small craft at anchor and under way.

RECOGNIZING the grave danger to life and the grave navigational and environmental risks to which such incidents can give rise.

DESIRING that Governments take all necessary action to prevent and suppress acts of piracy and armed robbery against ships including small craft.

HAVING CONSIDERED the advice of the Council at its fiftieth session and of the Maritime Safety Committee at its forty-eighth session.

1. URGES Governments concerned to take, as a matter of the highest priority, all measures necessary to prevent and suppress acts of piracy and armed robbery against ships in or adjacent to their waters, including strengthening of security measures.

2. INVITES Governments concerned and interested organizations to advise shipowners, ship operators, shipmasters and crews on measures to be taken to prevent acts of piracy and armed robbery and minimize the effects of such acts.

3. FURTHER INVITES Governments and organizations concerned to inform the Organization of action taken to implement the aims of the present resolution.

4. REQUESTS Governments concerned to inform the Organization of any act of piracy or armed robbery committed against a ship flying the flag of their country, indicating the location and circumstances of the incident and the action taken by the coastal State.

5. REQUESTS ALSO the Secretary General to circulate to Governments and organizations concerned the information referred to in paragraphs 3 and 4 above.

6. FURTHER REQUESTS the Council to keep this matter under review and take such further action as it may consider necessary in the light of developments.

APPENDIX 22

A "PIRACY AND MARITIME VIOLENCE INCIDENT REPORT" EXPLANATION OF FORM

Purpose

The purpose of the Piracy and Maritime Violence Incident Form, a prototype of which follows, was indicated at page 4. It is intended to provide a standardised method for recording information concerning maritime problems. It covers piracy and robbery at sea, armed conflicts or single actions taken by a state involving the use of force, similar action by state proxies, attacks by insurgents or terrorists, violence related to smuggling or protests of a political or environmental nature and other shipboard activities involving violence or the use of force. Armed robberies in port, arrests of fishing vessels, incursions into restricted zones, or near collisions between ships of rival navies might all fall under the purview of reporting system.

Use

Information and leads provided by these forms will permit an increasingly representative compilation of ocean related problems. This will be of use to governments, international organisations, shippers, shipowners, unions, police forces, port authorities, scholars, and concerned individuals in isolating and assessing problems and risks, and devising new strategies successfully to avoid or deal with such incidents.

Who Should Submit

Anyone who is aware of a possible incident involving piracy or maritime violence.

Important

When in doubt, submit. Don't feel obligated to fill in all information when this is not readily available. Partial knowledge beats ignorance any day.

Other

Date
If the incident carried on for more than one day include them all.
Use the time *at the place of incident*
Use 24 hour clock (2345 hours, not 11.45 pm)

Place:
Latitude and Longitude: Degree, minutes and seconds if available.
Body of water: As full a description as possible.
Nearest countries: Nearest district and town as well as if known.
Next Scheduled Port of Call: This may differ from the next port actually visited.

Vessel(s) Involved:
Repeat for *each* vessel involved (aggressor as well as victim). Full information will normally not be available, but every bit helps.

Details of Incident:
As full a description as possible. If sources differ about important facts, please so indicate.

Details of Victims
Fill out for as many individuals as possible. Other information such as passport number or identity card is invaluable.

Sources of Information:
Printed—append all relevant printed accounts (giving name, date, and page of publication) whenever possible.
Oral—Identify source as fully as possible.

General:
If information is uncertain, so indicate. If information cannot be generally released, please indicate this fact in the relevant blank.

PIRACY AND MARITIME VIOLENCE INCIDENT REPORT

DATE	Year:	Day:
	Month:	Time (Local):
PLACE	Longitude & Latitude:	
	Body of Water:	
	Nearest Countries:	
	Next Scheduled Port of Call:	

VESSEL(S) INVOLVED			
Name:		Flag State:	
Date Built:		Gross Tonnage:	
Vessel Type:			
Operator:			
Further Information:			

DETAILS OF INCIDENT:

VICTIMS:

Originating from:	
Address:	
Telex:	Fax:
Date:	

APPENDIX 23

SEVEN INITIATIVES FOR THE FUTURE

These initiatives are defined on page 4, and developed throughout the conference discussion on the Control of Piracy, and in the Editor's Conclusion on page 234.

1. Identify and promulgate protective measures

Ship security (communications, procedures, etc)
Crew training

2. Establish a dependable reporting system

Nature of crime, photos, other evidence
Location (territorial sea, high seas etc)
Property stolen

3. Designate a comprehensive intelligence centre

International exchange of information
International "Fusion Centre"
Possible use of appropriate international organisations

4. Establish an early tracking and warning system

Threat analysis
Communications network

5. Enforcement by States of law (national and international) in areas under their jurisdiction

6. Pool information to support national training programmes for those responsible for maritime law enforcement

7. International cooperation and exchange of information on a regional and, where necessary, worldwide, basis

Regional negotiations— perhaps under co-sponsorship of key coastal state in region and an appropriate maritime state

NOTES ON CONTRIBUTORS

Bernhard ABRAHAMSSON is Professor and Head of the Department of Marine Transport at the US Merchant Marine Academy, Kings Point, New York.

P W BIRNIE is with the Department of Law at the London School of Economics and Political Science.

Harry C BLANEY is Research Associate at the Institute for the Study of Diplomacy at Georgetown University and former Director of the Office of Asian Refugee Assistance in the US Department of State.

Pascal BOULANGER is an officer in the Belgian Merchant Marine.

Burdick H BRITTIN is Chairman of the Executive Committee of the Council on Ocean Law in Washington and formerly Co-Ordinator of Ocean Affairs at the US Department of State.

James M BROADUS is Director of the Marine Policy Center, Woods Hole.

Thomas A CLINGAN Jr is Professor of Law in the University of Miami.

Dean E CYCON is a practising lawyer in Providence, Rhode Island.

Eric ELLEN is Director of the ICC International Maritime Bureau.

Albert GARRETTSON is Professor of Law at the New York University School of Law.

Rear Admiral (Ret) Bruce HARLOW is on the staff of the Office of the Judge Advocate General, Department of the Navy, Washington.

Joachim HENKEL is Senior Protection Officer of the UN High Commission for Refugees in Washington.

Ian HYSLOP is Information Officer with the ICC International Maritime Bureau.

Jonathan IGNARSKI is an Underwriter with Through Transport Mutual Services, London.

The Honourable M L Birabhongse KASEMSRI is Ambassador and Permanent Representative of the Government of Thailand to the United Nations.

Samuel P MENEFEE is Senior Fellow at the Center for Ocean Law and Policy and Senior Associate at the Center for Law and National Security in the University of Virginia. He is also Counsel to the law firm of Barham and Churchill in New Orleans.

Frank W PENTTI is Director, Office of Policy and Plans, US Department of Transportation Maritime Administration.

M J PETERSON is Assistant Professor at the University of Massachusetts at Amherst.

Napoleon PINEDA-LUPIAC is Deputy Chief, UN Council on Trade and Development, New York.

Sharon TAN is a member of the Singapore Diplomatic Service.

Naomichi H TERAZAKI is a member of the Maritime Legislation Section, Shipping Division UN Council on Trade and Development.

Maurice VITTY is a former British Merchant Navy officer who now works full time for Vietnamese related charities, and in particular for "Seacare", P.O. Box 998, Lee, London SE12 0RH.

Jaap A WALKATE is Head of the Legal and Social Affairs Division, International Organizations Department, Ministry of Foreign Affairs of the Netherlands.

Francis WIYONO is a Claims Executive with PT Assuransi Ramayana, Jakarta.